New York University School of Social Work

Advanced Seminar in Professional Practice
Third Edition

SIMON & SCHUSTER CUSTOM PUBLISHING

Printed in the United States of America

10 9 8 7 6 5 4 3 2 1

This publication has been printed using selections as they appeared in their original format. Layout and appearance will vary accordingly.

ISBN 0-536-00778-0
BA 97542

SIMON & SCHUSTER CUSTOM PUBLISHING
160 Gould Street/Needham Heights, MA 02194
Simon & Schuster Education Group

Copyright Acknowledgments

Contents

PREPARING FOR PRACTICE: MOTIVATIONS, EXPECTATIONS AND ASPIRATIONS OF THE M.S.W. CLASS OF 1990

NEIL ABELL, JAMES R. MCDONNELL

Graduate students' commitment to serve poor and disadvantaged populations is a recurrent concern among social work educators. In the context of increasing federal abandonment of public service, faculty fear a trend is developing among MSW students toward careers in private practice, jeopardizing the profession's capacity to fulfill its traditional roles. Based on a national survey of full-time graduate students in public and private programs, this paper examines the characteristics and practice orientations of the Class of 1990. Comparison of 1990 graduates with earlier cohorts suggests that while students' personal characteristics have shifted dramatically, their motivations and goals are largely compatible with traditional social work functions.

The degree to which graduate social work students demonstrate a commitment to serve poor and disadvantaged populations is a recurrent concern among social work educators. Despite efforts to challenge students to a greater sense of public responsibility, faculty increasingly express reservations about students' willingness to abandon agency-based social work in favor of private practice.

For Land (1987), the concern is that "altruism and political commitment may be devolving into secondary motivations, taking a backseat to psychotherapy for profit" (p. 75). Despite expectations among some faculty that social work programs should emphasize the alleviation of poverty and its effects (Roff, Adams, Jr., & Klemmack, 1984), it has been observed that students appear concerned primarily with benefits to self, not others

(O'Conner, Dalgleish, & Khan, 1984). Falck's "loud and shrill protest" (1984, p. 3) contended that the desire of entering social work students to practice psychotherapy amounted to an illegitimate expectation for their future practice. More recently, Aviram and Katan (1988) decried the potential shortage of interested students to fill traditional social work roles.

As the debate regarding appropriate roles for social workers continues, observations on the desirability of private practice are surfacing in both the professional and popular literature. West, Gaffney, Allen, and Barboza (1988) attributed the recent rise in graduate social work enrollment in part to opportunities for training in such potentially lucrative specializations as occupational social work and psychotherapy. Jayaratne, Siefert, and Chess found in a national survey that social workers in private practice enjoyed a higher income and greater job satisfaction than their agency-based counterparts did, prompting the assessment that "from an outsider's perspective . . . it makes good sense to go into private practice" (1988, p. 331).

Attempts to survey social work students' opinions, values, and career plans have taken a variety of forms, producing occasionally inconsistent results. Lusk and Miller (1985), citing work conducted between 1958 and 1970, concluded that most students began their graduate education with values compatible with the goals of the profession. Golden, Pins, and Jones (1972) conducted one of the earliest comprehensive surveys of first-year graduate students in accredited programs in the United States and Canada in 1966. They found that students entered graduate training largely because they believed that social work made an important contribution to individuals and society and because they enjoyed "working with people" (1972, p. 61). When Rubin and Johnson (1984) surveyed a convenience sample of students in 1982, however, the results were considerably different. The authors reported that

> the majority of entering direct-practice students are pursuing MSW degrees not because they want to perform distinctive social work functions, . . . work with clients whom social work is uniquely suited to serve, and not because they esteem social work's dual focus on the person-in-environment interface, but because they think that an MSW education will help them practice some form of family or individual counseling or psychotherapy, preferably in a private practice setting (p. 11).

Whereas nearly 71% of students in the original sample reported a desire to enter private practice within five years of graduation, this figure had declined to 42.3% when the authors conducted a follow-up survey on a reduced sample at the point of students' graduation (Rubin, Johnson, & DeWeaver, 1986).

Given these findings, the present study attempts to answer recent calls for a large-scale, national examination of graduate student values, expectations, and practice preferences (Aviram & Katan, 1988; Valentine, Gandy, & Weinbach, 1986). Major questions addressed include the characteristics of current graduate students, their motivations for choosing social work over other professional opportunities, their expectations for graduate training, and their professional aspirations immediately and five years after graduation. The authors propose that any effort to motivate students to practice in the public, nonprofit arena must be made with a clear understanding of students' views on these issues.

METHOD

A voluntary, anonymous survey was conducted at 11 graduate schools of social work (7 public and 4 private) during the Fall 1988 semester. Programs were selected through a national, stratified random sample, proportionally representing both public and private institutions accredited by the Council on Social Work Education. Contact persons were identified at each participating program to monitor the administration of survey instruments.

At each site, incoming full-time graduate students were asked to complete questionnaires at or near the time of orientation. The questionnaires included a brief introductory statement explaining the purpose of the research and soliciting participation, and a series of items addressing demographic characteristics, motivations, expectations, and aspirations. Students were asked to rate the relative importance of factors influencing their general decision to enter graduate school, their decision to enter a particular institution, and their reasons for selecting the master's in social work over other professional degrees. In addition, they were asked to project their postgraduation career plans.

Results of a companion survey, conducted on graduate faculty at the same sites, are reported elsewhere.

FINDINGS

Student characteristics

A total of 687 students (53.9% public; 46.1% private) responded to the survey, representing an overall response rate of 72.4 percent. Of those responding, the mean age was 32 (S.D. = 8.7), with a range from 21 to 61 years. 80.2% were female, while 19.8% were male. The sample was dominated by Caucasians (79.1%), with the remainder consisting of Blacks (9.1%), Hispanics (7%), Asians (2.8%), and "other" (2%). Minority males, as a group, constituted slightly less than 5% of the sample; Black males accounted for only 1.3%. Sample statistics on gender and ethnicity closely approximate those reported by the Council on Social Work Education for full-time social work students enrolled as of November 1988 (Spaulding, 1989). CSWE statistics report a national class comprised of 81.7% females and 18.3% males, with ethnic representation as follows: Caucasians (81.8%), Blacks (8.8%), Hispanics (3.6%), Asians (1.8%), and "other" (.6%).

One-half of the sample were single (49.7%), 35% were married, and 13.1% were separated or divorced; 63% of the sample had no children. Of those who did have children, the mean number was 2.1 (S.D. = 1.0). On the average, students completed their undergraduate study in 1981. Nearly ⅓ of the sample (32.7%), however, earned the bachelor's degree within the last two years. Approximately 15% of the students held the BSW.

Whereas students had an average of 3.2 years of postbachelor's social work or human service employment (S.D. = 4.3), 34.7% reported no experience. 69.7% of students intended to work during their graduate studies, planning an average of 17.8 hours per week (S.D. = 15.87). More than one-third of students (36.6%) plan to work over 20 hours per week.

Only 13.3% of the students were current members of NASW; however, 54.4% rated active involvement in the organization as important or very important.

Motivations

Over one-half of the students (54.1%) reported considering another field of graduate study before selecting social work. Fields most commonly indicated were psychology (19.2%), law (6.8%), counseling (6.2%), and education (5.6%).

Students were asked to rate (on a scale of 1 = very unimportant to 5 = very important) the significance of factors influencing their overall decision to enter graduate school. In descending order of importance, mean ratings for the factors were: A) Increasing the range of available job options (4.6); B) increasing autonomy and influence (4.1); C) increasing potential for promotion (3.8); D) earning more money (3.5) and increasing status (3.5); and E) fulfilling one's family's career expectations (2.4).

Table 1 reports the mean importance ratings of factors influencing students' decisions to pursue the MSW as opposed to some other advanced degree. As indicated, the versatility of the MSW was of primary importance. The desire to enhance skills and potential for serving disadvantaged populations followed closely, as did an appreciation of the profession's commitment to the disadvantaged. These fac-

TABLE 1
Importance of Factors Influencing Students' Decision to Pursue MSW

Scale Item	Mean Response*	Standard Deviation
The occupational/professional versatility of a social work degree.	4.6	.76
A desire to enhance my skills as a social worker.	4.3	.95
A desire to enhance my potential for serving disadvantaged populations.	4.3	.90
Social work's traditional commitment to disadvantaged populations.	4.1	.96
A desire to prepare myself for private practice.	3.6	1.26
Social work is the most direct route to private practice.	3.2	1.26
The MSW is a logical extension of my BSW.	2.6	1.30

*Ratings scaled from 1–5 where 5 = highest degree of importance.

tors were ranked as more important than private practice concerns, which fell slightly above the neutral point on the continuum of perceived importance.

Bivariate analyses were conducted to determine the influence of race, gender, age, and years of postbachelor's experience on students' motivations to pursue the MSW. Analysis of variance (ANOVA) revealed that minorities placed significantly higher value on social work's traditional commitment to disadvantaged populations ($F = 8.2$, $df = 1$, $p < .01$) than whites did, although the practical significance of the relationship was trivial (eta^2 = .01). Race was also a significant factor in judging the importance of extending the bachelor's degree, with minorities being less likely to devalue this factor ($F = 33.98$, $df = 1$, $p < .001$; eta^2 = .05). Gender, race, years of postbachelor's work experience, and student's age were all insignificant in predicting the importance of private practice preparation.

Expectations

When asked about the intended focus of their education, 60.1% of students indicated direct/clinical practice, 15.7% indicated planning/administration, 8.3% indicated "generalist" practice, and 16% were undecided.

Asked to rate (again on a scale of 1 = very unimportant to 5 = very important) the significance of factors influencing their decision to enter a particular graduate school, students ranked as most important the program's local reputation, its convenient location, and an attractive curriculum (mean ratings = 4.1). Mean ratings for other factors of secondary importance included the program's national reputation (3.8), perceived clinical skills of the faculty (3.6), and the extent to which the faculty are well-known (3.2). Offering the best financial aid package or a joint degree opportunity were relatively unimportant (mean ratings = 2.6), while being actively recruited by the program was least influential (mean rating = 2.3).

Bivariate analyses were conducted to determine whether public vs. private status influenced students' reasons for selecting a specific graduate school. Analysis of variance (ANOVA) revealed that students attending private institutions placed a higher value on the national reputation of the program (mean rating = 4.0) than their public counterparts did (mean rating = 3.7) (F = 12.35, df = 1, p < .001).

As indicated in Table 2, students gave high importance ratings to a number of factors related to their educational expectations. While students seem to value challenging, skill-focused training in the classroom and the field, they are relatively neutral regarding the significance of private practice field opportunities.

Aspirations

Students were asked to indicate the field of practice they planned to concentrate in immediately after graduation. As shown in Table 3, when asked to select only one of the options provided, the greatest percentage indicated family & children's services, followed by mental health. Fields categorized in Table 3 as "other," provided as written responses to the request to "specify," included social welfare policy, school social work, women's issues, gay/lesbian issues, corrections, and advocacy. The large number of missing cases may reflect a substantially larger percentage of undecided students or a failure to capture the range of curricular concentrations offered.

In addition, students were asked about

TABLE 2
Importance of Students' Expectations for Graduate Education

Scale Item	Mean Response	Standard Deviation
Practical training in clinical, planning, or management skills.	4.5	.75
A high degree of intellectual stimulation and challenge.	4.4	.79
Training in a broad range of interventions and/or modalities.	4.4	.79
A broad range of field placement opportunities.	4.3	.90
Availability of faculty for individual contact/consultation.	4.3	.82
Preparation for licensure.	4.2	1.00
An opportunity to select my own field placement.	4.1	1.01
Training with a focus on specific interventions and/or modalities.	4.0	.96
An opportunity for private practice field work.	3.6	1.22

* Ratings scaled from 1–5 where 5 = highest degree of importance.

TABLE 3
Students' Preferences for Fields of Practice Immediately Following Graduation

Field	N*	Percentage
Family and children's services	263	38.3
Mental health	118	17.2
Medical social work	55	8.0
Alchohol/substance abuse	43	6.3
Gerontological social work	40	5.8
Industrial social work	22	3.2
Undecided	20	2.9
"Other"	47	6.9
Missing	79	11.5
Total	687	100.0

* Students indicated only their primary preference.

the settings in which they planned to practice both immediately and five years after graduation. As shown in Table 4, the percentage of students planning an agency-based career declines by 14.5% over the projected five-year period. The percentage planning to combine agency and private practice involvement also declines, by 11.9%. However, the percentage planning to concentrate solely on private practice increases by 17.6%.

Gender, race, age, and years of post-bachelor's experience were examined for themselves to these roles and what they involve, they concentrate on learning to handle certain difficult aspects of role content.

Although the process of adaptation to the supervisory role is never really complete, one who has worked through these three phases has done the major work or role transition and should be out of crisis and able to turn energy outward to the work at hand.

Role Identification

The problem for new supervisors in this phase of transition is to identify their roles, to learn the norms, values, and behaviors of their new peer group, and to begin to move into the group, usually with very little help or support. In fact, there may be many factors working against the achievement of this transition. A public welfare supervisor complained that: "After I became a supervisor, I still felt closer to my caseworker friends. I just didn't see any cohesive group of supervisors to relate to. I got no support from them; they didn't even support each other. We have supervisory meetings, but these are very formal. There is no way to initiate a relationship."

Inability of the new supervisor to initiate relationships with new peers is due, in part, to use of supervisory time, most of which is spent with supervisees rather than with other supervisors. Relationships develop through shared tasks and shared emotions, but there is little time for sharing among supervisors. It is no wonder that new supervisors may continue to feel closer to caseworker staff. Another problem is finding a physical place in which interaction with other supervisors may take place. Some agencies have no lounge in which supervisors might meet informally over coffee, and supervisory meetings, as the above supervisor explained, may be very formal and not lend themselves to relationship building.

At times, new supervisors themselves are reluctant to move into relationships with other supervisors. Particularly in large organizations in which power struggles, shake-ups, and infighting are frequent occurrences, new supervisors may hesitate to align themselves with any one person or faction for fear that alliances made too early may be regretted later. They may prefer loneliness to involvement in turmoil that could leave long-lasting scars. A second reason for the reluctance to move into a new peer group is the feeling of betrayal of friendship.[2] For one who has worked previously in an agency as caseworker and has returned to the same agency as supervisors, the promotion may be felt by the supervisor as undemocratic. He or she may try to convince old peers that nothing has changed, that things are "just like old times." This cannot ring true, though, and the supervisor will quickly realize that something has changed; he or she has a new position, new duties, and responsibilities, new status, new authority, and a new peer group. For a time, the supervisor may feel uncomfortable with his or her old peer group and the new.

Reactions of Others

Because one cannot correctly locate oneself in a new role without the help of a supporting cast of characters, new supervisors need to be aware of the reactions of others in the environment as they struggle to adapt. Unfortunately, other supervisors, workers, and administrators may not be uniformly supportive of, and are, in fact, apt to be ambivalent toward, a new supervisor. They will have expectations, fears, and some stereotypes based on previous experiences and will need to test a new supervisor in light of these. Other supervisors may look toward a new supervisor as someone to bring new ideas and new life into the organization, but at the same time they may be afraid that they will be measured against him or her. They may fear that their knowledge has lapsed since they were in school, wonder if the new supervisor will be successful where they had failed, or fear the workers will prefer the newcomer over them.

Though other supervisors may sincerely want the new supervisor to succeed, they may not want this success to pale theirs. In a large agency in which personal contact among supervisors is infrequent, it may be a long time before they can overcome their fears and be unambiguously helpful to the new supervisor.

Supervisees are also ambivalent toward a new supervisor. They may be excited about the possibility of new experiences and new learning, but at the same time they may be unsure and fearful of what might be demanded of them. They have expectations and know that a new supervisor must have expectations of them. Supervisees wonder how a new supervisor will operate. Will long coffee breaks be allowed, or will the new supervisor be a stickler for time? Will weekly conferences be required or will problems be handled on an emergency basis? Will the workers be asked to change? One new supervisor reported that her worst problems were with her experienced workers. They had been handling their work in the same adequate but uninspired manner for years, with much support and praise from their old supervisor, who was untrained. Any suggestions the new supervisor made were seen as attacks, not only on the experienced workers, but also on their old supervisor.

Another supervisor, who returned to her public welfare department after educational leave, said she found it impossible to meet the demands of her workers. They wanted her to have changed, to have new knowledge and ability to share with them, yet any indication of her having changed was viewed with suspicion. Moreover, some of the workers, perhaps those who had aspired unsuccessfully for supervisory positions themselves, tended to downgrade the M.S.W. One supervisor reported hearing such comments as, "You might have the M.S.W., but I have the experience," and "I took a course in social work once and didn't learn a thing!" This made the new supervisor feel very unsure of herself in her new role.

Reactions of Agency Administrators

Agency administrators may also be ambivalent toward new supervisors. Although they may look to the supervisors to bring fresh points of view to the agency, they may also fear these fresh points of view as threats to the established order; they do not want too much change too soon. Agency administrators who are themselves M.S.W.s know that students are taught how to examine policy critically and how to bring about change, but they are not sure they want this know-how applied to their agencies. They may anticipate confrontations with overenthusiastic and idealistic supervisors.

In short, new supervisors may be seen as a problem to the administrator rather than a help, in that the administrator may have to cope with new ideas and a new personality. Some agency administrators forthrightly state that they do not want to hire an M.S.W., such as the administrator who told an applicant for a supervisory position that he was supposed to hire an M.S.W. but always tried to get around the rules, because he would rather hire an experienced worker.

In spite of the lack of opportunity for new supervisors to form relationships with their new peer group and factors within and outside themselves that make identification with the new group difficult, new supervisors usually do, over time and not without pain, begin to identify their new role and its requirements and to move into it.

Divesting and Investing

The problem for the new supervisor during the second phase of adaptation is to give up the old in favor of the new, to let go of what was pleasurable, comfortable, and satisfying in the old role and to begin to invest emotions, intellect, and energy in the new role. For the new M.S.W. supervisor this might involve two exchanges: giving up the student role in favor of the agency employee role, and giving up the caseworker role in favor of the supervisor role. One of the purposes of field experience in social work education is to introduce the student to the context of service—the social agency.[3] True acculturation to the agency, however, usually does not occur during the field experience, because of the special nature of the student role. A new supervisor explained this problem in the following way. "It's hard to switch from student to agency employee; you have to start dealing with reality. In school you get so much respect. Everyone wants to listen to your ideas. You discuss everything. In a job you just have to get the work done. People are really depending upon you."

Relinquishing the Student Role

The student role emphasizes generation of new ideas, critical analysis of existing policies, procedures, and organizational structure, and evaluation of these in terms of professional standards. The student does not have the power to make many decisions based on his or her ideas, and this lack of decision-making power plus the authority of the supervisor protect him or her from possible consequences. The agency employee role, however, emphasizes criticism and evaluation of ideas not only against professional standards, but also against agency standards of efficiency.

Moreover, the agency employee must take responsibility for his or her ideas, because they may result in policy decisions affecting the lives of many. New supervisors must, therefore, be ready to give up the comfort of the protected position as students and take on the responsibility of realistically evaluating ideas against agency as well as professional standards and of making important decisions based on these evaluations. They must be willing to use their energy and intelligence in getting the work of the agency accomplished. It should be emphasized, however, that the supervisor must not completely give up professional standards in favor of agency standards, but must creatively face the struggle of blending the two.

Relinquishing the Caseworker Role

Some supervisors find giving up direct practice particularly difficult. Much time, emotion, and effort have been invested in learning direct practice, and new supervisors have fresh memories of poignant experiences and meaningful relationships with clients. M.S.W.s leave school full of knowledge, skills, and excitement and ready to invest energy in work with new clients in a new agency; then they realize that they have no clients. They long for the comforts and satisfactions of their old helping relationships.[4]

Many supervisors are unable to resolve this problem successfully, but rather try to work it out in ways that are inappropriate and often harmful. New supervisors may be tempted to cast their supervisees in client roles, to focus on worker personality problems rather than learning problems and on worker adjustment rather than on effective and efficient worker performance of duties, thereby putting workers in the untenable position of feeling compelled, by real or imagined supervisory power, to open up to the supervisors personal aspects that they would rather keep private. They may become dependent on the supervisor while resenting the invasion of their privacy. Roles become confused. Such a relationship cannot exist for long without having devastating effects on supervisor, supervisee, and the entire supervisory unit.

Another way new supervisors may compensate for their loss of clients is by continuing to do direct practice vicariously through their supervisees. Rather than facilitating supervisees' handling of cases, they direct the case handling from behind their own desks. This leads to worker dependence, lack of learning, stifling of creativity, and, again, resentment toward the supervisor.

Ambivalence about Accepting a Supervisory Role

A factor bearing on the problem of new supervisors' investing themselves in a new role is that although professional advancement almost always requires one to accept a supervisory position, not everyone who goes into the field of social work wants to supervise. It is not enough to say that one should not accept a supervisory position if one would rather be in direct practice; to "stay behind" would create as many problems for the social worker as to accept a position one does not completely want. Salary increases would be severely limited, status and recognition would not be available, and the worker might be considered by others to be unmotivated.

As long as agencies equate higher education and longer experience with supervisory and administrative positions, this will remain a problem. Some social workers may find direct service positions as advanced practitioners, but these positions are usually limited to professional agencies and are less often found in large public agencies. If one feels he or she must accept a supervisory position, yet is ambivalent about giving up direct practice, the only realistic way to respond is to learn to find satisfactions in the supervisory role that may equal or exceed the old satisfactions found in direct practice. Such satisfactions are certainly there to be found as one gains knowledge and skills in supervision and begins to see oneself making a difference to supervisees, service delivery, and, ultimately, clients.

A supervisor who successfully accomplished divesting and investing said: "If I had been offered a promotion as caseworker, I would have taken it. I enjoyed casework and found it unpleasant to think of giving it up. It took me a while to adjust, but now I find satisfactions in being a supervisor. I like to see services being delivered. I still see myself as a helping person. I feel good when I can help my workers with their job problems."

Completing the Transition

When new supervisors have reached the third phase of adaptation, they have already intellectually and emotionally extricated themselves from the student and direct practitioner roles, think of themselves as supervisors, feel some "we-ness" with other supervisors, and have gained some acceptance and credibility as supervisors. There remains the problem of adapting to certain aspects of the supervisory role that are felt as particularly difficult. As one moves into any new role, acceptance of and adaptation to requirements of the role are apt to occur unevenly, because some aspects of the role will be more comfortable than others. For instance, the newly married man may enjoy being provider, protector, and lover, but find it difficult to be responsible to another person; the new elementary teacher may find great satisfaction in planning lessons, teaching, or mothering her students, but find handling discipline quite stressful. Complete adaptation to a new role requires identifying aspects of the role that one finds particularly uncomfortable and learning attitudes and behaviors that allow one to accept those aspects with minimal stress. There are two aspects of the supervisor role that have particularly high potential for creating stress for new supervisors. These are handling authority and being middle-management personnel in the agency hierarchy.

Formal and Functional Authority

It is necessary to distinguish between

formal authority and functional authority, because they may be felt as separate, though related, problems. Formal authority is the right, conferred by the agency, to direct and control the actions of others. Formal authority is inherent in the supervisory role and is not dependent on personal qualities or how the role is played. Functional authority, on the other hand, is granted by others in relation to how they perceive the qualities and performance of the one carrying the role. The amount of functional authority one is granted aids or impedes his or her use of formal authority.[5]

How new supervisors adapt to the formal authority inherent in the supervisory role will vary depending largely upon individual personality. The more authoritarian person probably will not feel uncomfortable initially about his or her authority, but may experience problems later if others do not want to accept this authority or do not perceive it in the same way that he or she perceives it. If supervisor and supervisee do not see eye to eye on the authoritarian aspects of the supervisory role, either because duties and responsibilities have not been made clear, or because of different perceptions of what the role should be, conflict is apt to develop.

Also, if the authoritarian supervisor is not seen by his or her supervisees as possessing adequate knowledge and skills for the position—in other words, if he or she does not have functional authority—the discrepancy between functional and formal authority will interfere with the supervisor's role performance. One supervisor who considers herself to be fairly authoritarian reported the following problem: "In a highly structured agency, if you try to be too democratic you get into trouble. It's not fair to your workers to pretend to give them freedoms they really don't have. But I do remember my first experience at using my authority. A worker received a call from state personnel about her paycheck, and she went to the program supervisor about her problem rather than to me, her direct supervisor. I reprimanded her, telling her she was to come to me with such problems. I felt as though she was testing my authority, and it was very uncomfortable for me. I felt I had to prove myself."

Many new supervisors feel uneasy about carrying authority, preferring to see themselves as one among equals. Such a supervisor may have had problems regarding authority in the past and may try to cope with it by denial rather than adaptation, but the position will not allow one to deny his or her authority. One supervisor reported that she was determined not to be like other supervisors, not to be an authority figure. She was dismayed to find, however that from her first day at the agency she was seen by her workers as part of the establishment, an authority, a "they," regardless of how she played her role. A whole set of attitudes and behaviors—suspicion, fear, antagonism, deference—were expressed toward her, unrelated to anything she did or did not do. Each worker reacted in his or her own unique way to the supervisor's formal authority. The supervisor quickly learned that she could not run away from her problem but had to start working on her own attitudes toward and ideas about authority.

Unlike formal authority, which is automatic, functional authority is granted or withheld by others in relation to how they perceive one. When supervisors are competent, they may expect functional authority gradually to come to them, as they demonstrate their usefulness to workers. New supervisors, though, may be uncertain about their knowledge and skills, and this uncertainty, added to the strong desire to be helpful and to find satisfactions as a supervisor, can be a source of anxiety. They may doubt that they can achieve functional authority. Realistically, most new supervisors do have the knowledge and skills needed to be helpful to their workers.

One cannot deny that some M.S.W.s are less well prepared than others, but even the poorer students learned something in school that can be used. The new supervisor's feelings of inadequacy are more likely to be a result of problems in translating what has been learned into something perceivable as useful by his or her workers than to lack of knowledge. It takes some practice for supervisors to discover what parts of their knowledge can be useful to workers and relevant to their most pressing problems. They may not immediately see that what they have learned about working with resistant clients in therapy also has meaning for the overworked public welfare worker who cannot understand why her clients do not keep important appointments, do not bring in verifications for eligibility, and lie to the worker. Learning to translate principles from direct practice to supervision, thereby enhancing functional authority, is part of the new supervisors' adaptation to their roles.

Adaptation to a Middle-Management Role

The new supervisor often has difficulty adapting to being a middle manager within the agency structure. No amount of intellectual preparation regarding the role of the middle management can adequately prepare one for the experience of being in the middle of a complex network of communications and loyalties or for the accompanying feeling of being, as one supervisor described it, "drawn and quartered." New supervisors know that they are an important link in agency communications and that information flows through them upward to administration and downward to their workers. They soon also learn that this process does not always go smoothly. Handling this communications responsibility effectively involves collecting information accurately, filtering it to decide what part of it should be communicated, and deciding how, when, and to whom the information should be communicated. At each step in this process there is potential for error that could result in misrepresentation, misunderstanding, and conflict.[6]

Until new supervisors have had considerable experience as middle managers, they may expect to commit errors—to wear out their welcome with administration by communicating too many worker dissatisfactions, to reveal administrative decisions orally prior to arrival of a formal memo, or to share with workers information, such as a particular decision-making process, that the administration had not intended to be made public. The new supervisors' communications problems are complicated by their ambivalence in terms of loyalties. Often they want to speak out as an advocate for workers but, at the same time, don't want to threaten newly formed identifications as part of management. They feel demands for loyalty in both directions, toward workers and toward administration, and this can create considerable tension. Their adaptive task here is, as security and confidence increase, to learn to see loyalty as belonging primarily to clients and to focus on efficient delivery of high-quality services.

Conclusion

This article has presented a framework for looking at the problems of newly trained M.S.W. supervisors in terms of adaptation to a new role. Adaptation was seen as involving three phases: (1) identifying the new role and beginning transition; (2) divesting oneself of the old role and investing intelligence, emotions, and energy in the new role; and (3) completing the transition by identifying requirements of the role that are particularly difficult and working out ways of coping and of handling the role requirements comfor-

tably. It is believed that new supervisors, by examining their situation within this framework, will gain a better understanding of the adaptation process and thus be helped to see their problems as normal, shared by others, and time-limited.

Agency administration, on the other hand, by understanding the sources of stress for new supervisors, may begin to look at ways of being more supportive during the three phases of adaptation. For instance, to ease the stresses of phase one, administration may provide a place for supervisors to socialize, provide some time during regular staff meetings for informal interactions, or assign an experienced peer to work with the new supervisor in a supportive way. Phase two stresses may be lessened by the provision of special opportunities for the new supervisor to feel some early accomplishment and by interpreting the supervisor's role as important.

Phase three stresses can also be lessened by administrative action. For instance, new supervisors can be helped to adapt to the authoritarian aspect of their role by the provision of clear guides regarding duties and responsibilities, so extent and limits of the supervisory authority will be understood by both supervisor and workers. It is hoped that agencies will be stimulated to expand this list of suggestions of aids as they examine their own policies, procedures, and structures.

1. Hilda Arndt. "Effective Supervision in a Public Welfare Setting." *Public Welfare* 31 (Summer 1973): 50–54; Alfred Kadushin. *Supervision in Social Work* (New York: Columbia University Press, 1976); Carlton E. Munson. "Professional Autonomy and Social Work Supervision." *Journal of Education for Social Work* 12 (Fall 1976): 95-102; Fred Berl. "An Attempt to Construct a Conceptual Framework for Supervision," *Social Casework* 41 (July 1960): 339-46, and "The Content and Method of Supervisory Teachings," *Social Casework* 44 (November 1963): 516-22; and Irving Miller. "Supervision in Social Work." *Encyclopedia of Social Work* (Washington, D.C.: National Association of Social Workers, 1977), pp. 1544-50.

2. Dorothy Pettes. *Supervision in Social Work* (London: George Allen and Unwin, 1967).

3. M. Lyons, "The Administrator," in *Supervision in Social Work: A New Zealand Perspective*, ed. Education and Training Committee, New Zealand Association of Social Workers, Inc. (Christchurch: Bookstall, 1972), pp. 29-36.

4. Frank M. Loewenberg. *Fundamentals of Social Intervention: Core Concepts and Skills for Social Work Practice* (New York: Columbia University Press, 1977).

5. John M. Pfiffner and Marshal Fels, *The Supervision of Personnel* (Englewood Cliffs, N.J.: Prentice-Hall, 1964).

6. Lucille N. Austin. "Supervision in Social Work." *Social Work Yearbook* (New York: National Association of Social Workers, 1960), pp. 579-86.

KEEPING SECRETS: SOCIAL WORKERS AND AIDS

MARCIA ABRAMSON

THE CURRENT EPIDEMIC of human immunodeficiency virus (HIV) infection and acquired immune deficiency syndrome (AIDS) poses major ethical questions for society (Pellegrino, 1987). Urgent questions have been raised about fundamental ethical problems concerning prevention, including changes in sexual behavior, mandatory screening, and isolation of those thought to be infected (Brandt, 1987). Equally difficult questions cluster around the care of people with AIDS. These questions concern unequal access to health care, discouraging results, fears of contagion, needs of other patients, determination of valid consent when competence is declining because of dementia, and the morality of rational suicide (Volderding & Abrams, 1985). To deal with these increasingly perplexing questions, every profession will need to design a coherent professional ethic governing work with people with AIDS in the years ahead (Walters, 1988).

Social work is a core profession in the provision of services for people with AIDS, from counseling about testing to bereavement work with families and loved ones of people who have died from the disease. Social work roles in working with people with AIDS, their families, and their communities are expanding. Although social work clearly is establishing a body of literature on the psychosocial issues surrounding AIDS, much less attention has been paid to the particular moral problems that social work practitioners face in their day-to-day practices with people with AIDS. For every psychosocial problem that social workers must attend to for their clients, there are concomitant moral issues that create dilemmas, distress, and uncertainty for the practitioners.

Barnard's (1988) articulation of dis-comfort about moral problems occurring on several levels at once is useful here. According to Barnard, the ethical level is concerned with principles and processes. Ethical discomfort calls for clarification of concepts and articulation of values and norms as well as systematic analysis of issues and justification of conclusions. However, even when there is agreement about what is the morally correct thing to do, there can be disagreement about whether the situation in question fits the moral category about which there is agreement. The technical level addresses whether a case fits a particular moral category as well as the prediction of the consequences of alternative interventions. The behavioral level is concerned with action and the communication skills necessary to operate in a complex bureaucratic environment. Finally, the existential level of moral problems, which is the most neglected and least understood, focuses on the subjective experiences, vulnerability, and shared personhood of both the person with AIDS and the caregiver (Barnard, 1988).

Identifying Problems

To begin to identify the most relevant and salient moral problems for hospital social workers who have people with AIDS in their caseloads, in-depth semi-structured interviews were conducted with 16 social workers between June 1988 and February 1989. The social workers came from four hospitals in two states where the incidence of AIDS is very high. They spent from 20 percent to 100 percent of their time working with people with AIDS from the high-risk groups: gay and bisexual men, intravenous drug users and their sexual partners and children, and hemophiliacs.

The interviews, which lasted from 1 to 1-1/2 hours, were taped and then transcribed. They focused on the following questions:

• What, if anything, is different about working with this population than with others with whom you have worked?

• What is particularly difficult about your work with this population?

• What do you find most satisfying about your work with this group?

• What difference does it make to you or to the other health care providers how the person contracted the disease?

• Are there things about your work with this population that cause value conflicts for you? What are they?

• How do your family and friends react to your working with people who have AIDS?

• Are there things that we ought to be teaching social work students about work with this group?

The author analyzed the interviews for emerging themes and topics. This review and categorization helped in formulating additional questions during the interview process (Glaser & Strauss, 1967). Themes that emerged from the data included the difficulty in establishing personal and professional boundaries and the uncertainty of the trajectory of the illness. However, no other theme emerged as frequently, nor did any other issue call forth as much moral pain, as the issue of secrecy. Although the sample is small and not necessarily representative of the entire social work population working with people with AIDS, the strength and frequency with which the major theme emerged certainly suggests its importance in social work practice with people with AIDS, and it serves as an excellent source of hypotheses for further research.

Therefore, this article focuses on the

dominant theme that emerged from the research: secrecy. The theme is analyzed below according to the dimensions articulated by Barnard (1988), and implications for practice are suggested.

Secrecy

Bok (1982) has written the seminal work on the subject of secrets and has captured some of the profound difficulties that people have with keeping secrets:

> Secrecy both protects and thwarts moral perception, reasoning. and choice. Secret practices protect the liberty of some while impairing that of others. . . . In situations of moral conflict, secrecy often collides with a crucial requirement for justifying a choice; that the moral principles supporting it be capable of open statement and defense. (p. xvi)

The following statements, which were made by the respondents in response to questions about differences, difficulties, and value conflicts in working with people with AIDS, reflect the discomfort with which the respondents considered the issue of secrecy. Three areas of secrecy were reported by the respondents: (1) from the people with AIDS, (2) from others who might be endangered by not knowing of a person's HIV seropositivity, and (3) from the world at large.

• Keeping secrets from people with AIDS—

> The hardest thing is going into a room where you know a person has AIDS and you don't know whether they know. The doctors change so often that you don't know who feels comfortable telling a patient that he has AIDS or whether anyone has done it.

> I feel like I'm shirking my responsibility because I don't want to be the one to tell that they tested positive.

• Keeping secrets from others who might be at risk—

> I'm not sure who should be the one to notify a partner if the person doesn't want to tell.

> I really feel guilty when I know that someone is HIV positive and that person is living with a woman of childbearing age who doesn't know and I can't tell her that she might have a child who could develop AIDS.

• Keeping secrets from the rest of the world—

> Their problems are just compounded if the wrong person finds out.

> Keeping it a secret just means that the family has to use so much energy when their efforts really should go in the direction of getting the support they need from others.

> I think we really need to take the risk of telling, because if we keep protecting them, they will face even greater isolation. Somebody is going to have to take some risks before society will be ready to handle it. The illness is not going to go away, and it needs to be normalized.

Finally, as one respondent said, keeping secrets was pervasive. For this respondent and others, it did not seem to matter from whom the secret was kept:

> Does the patient know? Does the family know? Who needs to tell the patient and who needs to know this or that? Is it your place? What if you open up the Pandora's box and start things that weren't supposed to be stirred up?

Thus, these social workers found themselves designated the keepers of secrets. The secrets were kept from many others, including the people with AIDS themselves, particularly children, adolescents, and elderly people who were not told they were HIV positive or the name of the disease; family members who were not told about the status or illness of an adult child, a parent, a spouse, or a sibling; and agencies and schools that were not given full information about the HIV status of people who were referred to them.

Ethical Dimension

"Confidentiality" is the name given to the boundaries surrounding shared secrets and to the process of guarding those boundaries (Bok, 1982). For the professional, the principle of confidentiality postulates a duty to protect confidences against third parties under most circumstances. Although few professionals regard the principle as absolute, most see the burden of proof as resting on anyone who claims a reason for overriding the confidentiality (Bok, 1982).

According to the National Association of Social Workers' *Code of Ethics* (1980), "The social worker should respect the privacy of clients and hold in confidence all information obtained in the course of professional service." This guideline is qualified by the statement that "the social worker should share with others confidences revealed by clients, without their consent, only for compelling professional reasons." In general, this phrase is meant to protect the client from having confidences revealed to third parties. However, at times it has been applied to family members who did not want their infected adolescents or elderly parents to know that they were seropositive. The decision to protect or share confidences also raises the question of who the client is.

Is the fear that a person with AIDS will infect another person through unprotected sex or through shared needles a "compelling professional reason"? Some social workers consider the duty to warn someone of danger a compelling justification for overriding the principle of confidentiality, whereas others are concerned that disclosure will prevent those infected from seeking early treatment and erode the trust between the health care community and people with AIDS. Ethical discomfort arises from the need to balance the competing principles and to systematically analyze the justifications for choosing one principle over another.

Technical Dimension

Given the principles and processes of importance, how does one both individualize the case situation and ascertain whether it fits the category that suggests concealment or disclosure? Keith-Lucas (1977, p. 352) referred to what Barnard (1988) called the technical dimension as

> the tension between the scientific process (that is, essentially, the reduction of a plethora of data to simple generalizations) and the humanistic process (that is, the appreciation of a situation in its unique configuration).

The social workers interviewed struggled with the principle of respect for individual differences in the need for concealment or disclosure while trying to treat like situations alike. This conflict demonstrated that even if there is agreement that secrets ought to be kept in certain situations, one still has to determine whether the particular case fits one of those situations.

The second aspect of the technical dimension concerns the prediction of consequences following a particular action. As indicated by the comments made, for some social workers the stigma and discrimination that could result from revealing the diagnosis was much more powerful and dangerous than keeping secrets. For others, the drain of energy, the inner turmoil, and the isolation that resulted from keeping secrets was seen as being much more detrimental to the individuals and families involved.

Behavioral Dimension

The behavioral dimension includes the social context in which secrecy exists, as well as the communication skills necessary to deal with the issue in that context. An important factor cited by many of the respondents that added considerably to the tension around the secrecy was that information about AIDS is generally so public. AIDS has forced into public scrutiny issues, such as sexuality, that have recently become quite private, because the disease has burdened these private acts with social consequences (Bayer, 1989). Thus, while patients and families are keeping secrets from each other and from those who surround them, the media are exposing the secrets, implying that anyone who tests positive or who is sick has yet another secret in his or her life: homosexuality, bisexuality, promiscuity, or intravenous drug use.

An even more practical reason that secrecy is problematic for health professionals is that the laws and regulations concerning confidentiality about AIDS vary from state to state and are constantly being reviewed for change. Most states have medical confidentiality laws, usually as parts of their laws on communicable disease, medical records, licensure, or public health. In recent years, however, more than two-thirds of the states have enacted or are considering laws dealing directly or indirectly with the issue of disclosure and confidentiality in a way that is different for HIV infection than for other diseases (Hafferty, 1988). The variations in law, the question of change through legislation, and the difference between the laws governing AIDS and those applicable to other diseases all add to the uncertainty and complexity of bureaucratic procedures and the communication process (Presidential Commission on the Human Immunodeficiency Virus Epidemic, 1988).

The complexity of the law, as well as different emphasis on the importance of either concealment or disclosure, leads also to disagreements about disclosure to other agencies by the various disciplines involved in the care of people with AIDS. These disagreements can, in turn, impede referrals and prevent access to needed services.

Secrets also interfere with another aspect of the behavioral dimension of social work: the communication between client and worker. Secrets can interfere with the ability of the social worker to engage, explore, establish a contract, complete a thorough assessment, and plan possible interventions when a client, a family member, a significant other, or agency personnel lack access to needed information. As one respondent said of his work with an adolescent who had tested positive for HIV and was losing weight but whose parents did not want him told about his HIV status:

It was extremely difficult for me to establish a relationship with him, because he didn't know what was going on and I couldn't ask any questions about it. I have to talk to the adolescents about high-risk behavior and sexual activity. I don't know how to answer what is the purpose of my asking all those questions. I try to focus it as part of the developmental stages, but my agenda is different. How can I help him cope with what is happening when he doesn't know what is going on?

Existential Dimension

The focus of the existential dimension is the subjective experience and the issues of care, meaning, and awareness of death for both the client and the social worker (Barnard, 1988). Sontag's (1989) analysis is valuable here. According to Sontag, AIDS evokes the most basic human fears and inhibitions through its association with sex, blood, drugs, and death. It is seen as being not only repulsive and retributive but also collectively invasive and is becoming a metaphor for contamination and mutation:

The way viruses are animistically characterized— as a menace in waiting, as mutable, as furtive, as biologically innovative—reinforces the sense that a disease can be something ingenious, unpredictable, novel. (Sontag, 1989, p. 70)

This status of AIDS as an unexpected event and an entirely new judgment adds to the dread with which it is viewed.

Another powerful image of AIDS is that it is morally as well as physically contagious. This image is compounded by the stigma attached to the behaviors most prominently associated with the infection and the disease, homosexual intercourse and intravenous drug use. Thus, most people with AIDS already have what Goffman (1963) referred to as a "spoiled identity." They are already discredited because of "blemishes of individual character," that is, their homosexuality or intravenous drug use, or "tribal stigma" resulting from the fact that they are poor black or Hispanic women and children. Add to this the "abominations of the body" that accompany the full-blown disease of AIDS, and it is easy to understand the "leakage" of stigma to people who contracted the disease through contaminated blood or perinatal transmission.

Given the power of these images and metaphors, it is not difficult to understand why one of the respondents spoke of his fear of opening up a Pandora's box by his disclosure. As one of the most powerful tales of calamities befalling those who uncover what is concealed and thereby release dangerous forces that should have been left in darkness and silence, the Pandora's box metaphor speaks to the dread and loathsomeness with which AIDS is regarded and the fear that with its disclosure may come unspeakable horrors (Bok, 1982).

Keeping secrets from patients, especially dying patients, long has been a part of health care practice. Glaser and Strauss (1965) have articulated the various forms that secrets take around dying persons. Although there has been a tremendous change in attitudes about the truthful disclosure to cancer patients documented from 1961 to 1979 (Barnard, 1988), which essentially has mirrored the changes in metaphors about cancer (Sontag, 1989), there is still a great deal of concern among health care professionals that frank exchange about bad news might unleash uncontainable emotions that will prove destructive to those involved. These anxieties underlie the intellectual arguments concerning patients' abilities to handle the truth when it is considered to be too painful (Barnard, 1988).

Implications for Practice

The premises supporting confidentiality are strong, but they cannot support practices of secrecy—whether by individual clients, institutions or professionals themselves—that undermine and contradict the very respect for persons and for human bonds that confidentiality was meant to protect. (Bok, 1982, p. 135)

Bok was warning professionals against using secrets to protect themselves to cover up poor care, mistakes, or questionable or dangerous practices. However, even when keeping secrets is being used to protect not the health care professional but the interests of the client, it can undermine and contradict respect for people and the human bonds upon which it is predicated. Jung (1933), for example, suggested that the keeping of secrets can act as a psychic poison that alienates the possessors of secrets from the community. Although keeping secrets may be beneficial in small doses, concealment has an overall potential for causing harm. It is for this reason that most therapists attempt to help clients share their secrets within the therapeutic relationship. For people with AIDS, keeping secrets can add to double-taboo-induced isolation, coming from within the person as well as from without.

How can social workers help clarify and justify keeping secrets concerning AIDS? Bok raised a series of questions about lying (1978) and secrets (1982) that might be useful here:

• Is there a crisis that requires secrecy?
• Are there alternatives to the secret?
• What are the moral justifications for and against the secret?
• What effect will the secret have on those who keep it?
• What effect will the secret have on these excluded?
• What effect will the secret have on general trust?
• What harm will the secret cause?
• What would a reasonable person think?
• What effect does prolonged secrecy have on people?
• How do these effects differ from those of concealment of shorter duration?

• What difference does it make that the secret may be something that others may need to know?
• How are these factors affected by whether the experience is voluntary or the result of coercion?
• How are these factors affected by what might happen if the secret were revealed?

These are questions that ought to be raised generally about keeping secrets concerning AIDS as well as on a case-by-case basis when the question of keeping secrets arises.

Conclusion

The Presidential Commission on the Human Immunodeficiency Virus Epidemic (1988) found that aside from the illness itself, discrimination was most feared by those infected by HIV. The commission recommended confidentiality as the most effective barrier against that fear.

Confidentiality may be a protection for the individual against fear of discrimination, but it also may be an obstacle to active social change toward overcoming discrimination. On a metaphorical level, as Sontag (1989) suggested, the process whereby diseases acquire meanings that stand for society's deepest fears and thereby inflict terrible shame and stigma is always worth challenging. "But the metaphors cannot be distanced just by abstaining from them. They have to be exposed, criticized, belabored, used up" (Sontag, 1989, p. 94). The disease, its metaphors, and the identities of those whom its metaphors afflict cannot be kept secret. Shame, guilt, and dread and the resulting discrimination cannot be detached from the illness if it is kept secret and not talked about; revelation and disclosure are required to contend with the power of the images.

On a practical level, secrets can impede understanding, foster isolation, prevent access to services, increase stigma, and interfere with a sense of community, keeping society separated into "us" and "them." More important, the energies that should be invested in finding a cure, changing behaviors, and fighting discrimination are drained by the demands of secrecy by patients, families, and health providers.

It is not possible or even necessarily beneficial at this time to try to create

an all-embracing moral framework to settle these issues. AIDS and society's understanding of and reactions to it are too new, and much more dialogue and debate about the important moral issues are needed. Bok (1982) suggested that one of the most important aspects of the ethics of secrecy is that it mirrors the larger field of ethics, bringing the complexity of the moral issues into clearer focus and forcing those who deal with them to become much more aware of themselves in relation to others. Social workers can take advantage of the importance of secrecy, as described by Bok and articulated by the respondents in this study, to begin designing a coherent professional ethic for social work with AIDS in the years to come.

References

Barnard, D. (1988). Love and death: Existential dimensions of physicians' difficulties with moral problems. *Journal of Medicine and Philosophy, 13*, 393–409.

Bayer, R. (1989). *Private acts, social consequences: AIDS and the politics of public health.* New York: Free Press.

Bok, S. (1978). *Lying: Moral choice in public and private life.* New York: Vintage.

Bok, S. (1982). *Secrets: On the ethics of concealment and revelation.* New York: Pantheon.

Brandt, A. M. (1987). *No magic bullet: A social history of venereal disease in the U.S. since 1880.* New York: Oxford University Press.

Glaser, B. G., & Strauss, A. L. (1965). *Awareness of dying.* Chicago: Aldine.

Glaser, B. G., & Strauss, A. L. (1967). *The discovery of grounded theory: Strategies for qualitative research.* Chicago: Aldine.

Goffman, E. (1963). *Stigma: Notes on the management of spoiled identity.* Englewood Cliffs, NJ: Prentice-Hall.

Hafferty, B. (1988, November 4). A state by state breakdown of HIV confidentiality law. *American Medical News*, p. 28.

Jung, C. G. (1933). *Modern man in search of a soul.* New York: Harcourt Brace.

Keith-Lucas, A. (1977). Ethics in social work. In J. B. Turner (Ed.-in-chief), *Encyclopedia of social work* (17th ed., pp. 350–355). Washington, DC: National Association of Social Workers.

National Association of Social Workers. (1980). *Code of ethics.* Silver Spring, MD: Author.

Pellegrino, E. D. (1987). Ethics. *Journal of the American Medical Association, 258*, 2298–2300.

Presidential Commission on the Human Im-

18

munodeficiency Virus Epidemic. (1988). *Report of the Presidential Commission on the Human Immunodeficiency Virus Epidemic.* Washington, DC: U.S. Government Printing Office.

Sontag, S. (1989). *AIDS and its metaphors.* New York: Farrar, Straus & Giroux.

Volderding, P., & Abrams, D. (1985). Clinical care and research in AIDS. *Hasting Center Report, 15*(4), 16–18.

Walters, L. (1988). Ethical issues in the prevention and treatment of HIV infection and AIDS. *Science, 239,* 597–603.

THE PRIOR QUESTION: HOW DO SUPERVISORS LEARN TO SUPERVISE?

GIB AKIN, MARIE WEIL

IN SOCIAL WORK, SUPERVISION is considered part of professional practice.[1] It relates to agency-based professional practice and forms part of the ethical means for assuring competent and accountable practice with and for clients. The historical roots of social work supervision were grounded on efforts to assure a practice that adhered to board and donor standards.[2] Later, social work supervision moved from this assurance function to the adoption of a psychoanalytic model of supervision, to complement a psychoanalytic mode of practice. This shift was a stage in social work's drive for professionalization.[3] More recently, models of supervision based on learning theory, management and organizational content, and role theory have gained in stature, even though the psychoanalytic or supervision-as-metatherapy model still predominates.[4]

Supervision has received attention from notable social work theorists: Mary Parker Follett, Bertha Reynolds, Charlotte Towle, and Virginia Robinson.[5] With the exception of Follett, who stressed management and organizational competence, the earlier theorists concentrated on the development of professional and personal awareness and skills development for the supervisee.

The next phase of theoretical development for supervision focused primarily on delineation of basic roles. Alfred Kadushin's formulation has become a standard reference in the literature. Both Stewart Moore and Kadushin differentiate the practice of social work from the practice of supervision and note the role change. The new supervisor "is essentially entering a new occupation, not simply a new position. This occupation will have its own set of job specifications . . . precedents . . . expectations."[6] The new supervisor "is asked to make a transition to a new and unfamiliar role which requires implementation of functions that he [or she] has not as yet learned."[7]

More recent views, which draw from a variety of theoretical perspectives, broaden the base of issues to be considered in the practice of supervision. Although there is considerable literature about supervision, little has been written to date regarding how one learns to become a supervisor. What is the process of role change? How does the new supervisor learn what he or she needs to know to be effective? With the development of models of effective supervision, a framework for learning how to supervise is also needed. Following a brief review of the literature on the nature, roles, and skills of social work supervision, this article addresses the issues and assumptions surrounding supervisory learning.

Review of the Literature

Kadushin, in his presentation of supervision principles, identifies three components of supervision: (1) administrative, (2) educative, and (3) supportive. This framework is loosely followed here to organize a brief discussion of the current literature on social work supervision.[8]

The Role of Educator

Even though Kadushin does not introduce the role of educator as the first of the functions of the social work supervisor, the bulk of the current literature on supervisory practice can be categorized under this heading. Alex Gitterman and Irving Miller assert that the central part of the work of the supervisor is educational.[9] They present a set of pedagogical concepts to be used by the supervisor in the educational role, as well as examples of good supervisory techniques. In an earlier article, Gitterman argued that supervisory styles can be explained by differing models of education held by a supervisor. Three possible models were presented: (1) a subject-centered model, which focuses on the content that is to be learned by the supervisee, (2) a student-centered model, which concentrates on the development of the supervisee from within, and (3) an integrative model, which draws from the ideas of John Dewey and J. Bruner.[10] Gitterman clearly prefers the integrative model, which is addressed to the relationship between knowing, feeling, and doing.

Thomas D. Morton and P. David Kurtz offer a detailed technique for the supervisor who would like to implement more effective educational supervision.[11] Strategies for assessment, planning, and instruction are presented, based on a learning theory that is grounded on concepts of modeling and reinforcement.

The Supportive Function

The supportive function of supervision is acknowledged to be difficult to separate from the educational function. Effective education may require effective support. This aspect of supervision could be seen as even closer to educational supervision if a supervisor were to use what Gitterman calls the "subject-centered educational model."[12] Supportive supervision helps the supervisee to develop the ego strength needed to deal with the natural anxieties of the task at hand, and serves to remove road blocks to his or her personal development as an independent professional.

Although the literature of the 1960s and before frequently sounded as though the supervisor-supervisee relationship was analogous to the client-worker relationship, more recent writers have emphasized the importance of recognizing that the supervisor-supervisee relationship is not one of treatment or therapy.[13] Just as Gerald Caplan emphasizes the boundaries which hold in dealing with theme interference in mental health consultation,[14] Nathan Altucher suggests that the supervisor avoid establishing a psychotherapeutic relationship with the supervisee, despite helping the supervisee to remain open to his or her own experience.[15]

Counter to the trend of setting definite boundaries between supervision and treatment, Gene M. Abroms presents supervision as metatherapy, that is, the therapy of therapy. Metatherapy combines aspects of support and interpretation. Abroms counsels against "illicit psychotherapy," but in his formulation the boundaries are far less distinct than in other contemporary statements.[16]

In an approach that does delineate boundaries between supervision and treatment, Ilse J. Westheimer describes active supervisory support: "Indeed, the supervisor supports by asking challenging questions about the worker's performance, by stimulating his thinking, and by the very recognition that the worker has the strength and the capacity to respond and develop. Support also derives from a commitment to and a profound interest in the task of helping clients."[17]

The Administrative Component

This management-oriented approach to supervision is elaborated most extensively by Wilbur A. Finch. It emphasizes client-focused supervision and accountability. Finch takes an organizational management perspective: "Line supervisors must increasingly possess managerial skills and a knowledge of the dynamics of human behavior within an organizational context if they are to successfully guide and coordinate the provision of social services to clients."[18] The supervisory relationship takes place in, and is affected by, the organizational setting. The supervisor must have communication, negotiation, and conflict-management skills all of which go beyond the educational or supportive one-to-one relationship described in the previous two supervisory concepts.

Westheimer describes management and teaching as the key elements in supervision.[19] Dorothy E. Pettes stresses the administrative role of supervisor, highlighting the organizational base of social work, the linking role between management and operations, and issues of organizational accountability and professional responsibility. Supervision demands knowledge and skill in "both management and practice". She also states that the supervisor "must understand management roles and aims. He [or she] must see himself as part of the management team with all the responsibility this implies for assuring effective service at the organization level."[20]

The Need for Training and Development

Ione D. Vargus pinpoints three basic goals of supervision. These are: (1) to ensure that agencies provide adequate service, (2) to help workers function to the fullest of their capacity, and (3) to assist workers in their attainment of professional independence.[21] Vargus and Miller have noted with concern that a theoretical framework for social work supervision has been slow to develop.[22]

The literature on supervision that is available is characterized by assertions of what supervisors must do to be effective, or specifies the skills or knowledge they should have. Even less exists about the training and development of supervisors. The authors of this article found no systematic evaluation research on supervisory training programs or master's level courses. This absence of coherent theory, research, and evaluation raises fundamental questions about the nature of the learning process in becoming a supervisor. When and where, for example, should training for supervision take place—at the M.S.W. level, in post-M.S.W. programs, on the job, in formalized training, or through role incumbency? Also, what kind of training a supervisor should receive? The literature answers none of these questions; most supervisory training seems to be of the on-the-job variety.

How Do Supervisors Learn?

That very little has been written on the education of supervisors has not gone unnoticed. Joseph Olmstead and Harold E. Christensen conclude that "there appears to be a pressing need for supervisory training. The function of supervision is too critical to leave to trial and error learning. Systematic instruction in the fundamentals of supervision warrants a high place on any list of training requirements."[23]

While focusing on the educational aspect of supervision, Gitterman and Miller note that "skill about how to instruct others to provide services has received scant attention."[24] Sidney S. Eisenberg and Finch cite the need for the training of supervisors in the administrative area.[25] The key writers on supervision describe the concepts of effective supervisory practice, but do not focus on the processes by which a supervisor gains knowledge and skill. Even though Donald K. Granvold and Werner W. Boehm say that training is important, specific plans for the development of supervisors are in short supply. An exception is J.C. Hansen and R. Stevic, who propose a course on teaching how to teach.[26]

Nevertheless, supervisors do learn to supervise somehow, even though it is not clear how effectively. (A 1973 study cited by Kadushin found that one quarter of the supervisors questioned felt uncertain and anxious about their roles, and believed that they did not know enough to perform adequately.)[27] Although the literature reviewed here deals only with the content and structure of supervisory practice, embedded in these descriptions are assumptions about how supervisors learn to supervise, including some case examples of supervisory practice.

Seven basic processes emerge by which a competent social worker becomes an effective supervisor. These are: (1) role adoption; (2) emulation or modeling; (3) reframing current skills; (4) acquisition of new skills; (5) formal education—role preparation; (6) exhortation or prescription; and (7) selection.

Role Adoption

Probably the simplest and most primitive way of thinking about how a person moves into a supervisory position is that he or she is formally assigned to or takes on a role available in an organization. Presumably, the person begins to enact that role at once, even though there may be little thought given as to how the knowledge needed for a reliable performance is attained. Although quesionable in its wisdom, the approach of creating a supervisor by assigning a title still appears to be the most frequent means by which one becomes a supervisor: "There appear to be few provisions made for the formal induction of supervisors into their new role. . . . Perhaps the assumption is that if a person is experienced enough to be selected for the position, he or she should be able to operate independently."[28]

Part of the underlying process by which a role is successfully adopted is the learning that comes through experience on the job—what many supervisors call "flying by the seat of my pants." Learning is accomplished through trying out solutions to problems, encountering new situations and responding to them, through a trial and error process. In fact, almost all organizational experiences contain role-learning information.

Morton and Kurtz present a learning-theory approach to understanding the processes by which the direct service worker might become more effective. However, in their presentation, the social work supervisors described seem to learn in other ways. In one case, a supervisor learns from a role failure experience, and in another through consultation with a peer about a practical problem.[29] Although informal, on-the-job experience is an important way of attaining reliable role performance.

Emulation or Modeling

Emulation implies a sort of master-apprentice relationship as the primary process for learning. Modeling infers a trying out of roles and styles adapted from other role incumbents. These processes are probably not clearly distinguishable from role adoption, although there is some indication in the literature that this process accounts for much of the learning on the part of the supervisor. Alfred J. Kutzik suggests that most supervisors supervise others in the way that they have been supervised.[30] This behavior is probably relatively independent of what the emulated supervisor is espousing as content. The style and method—that is—*how* one supervises, is what gets copied most frequently.

Many of those writing about supervision provide demonstrations that they consider to be effective, thereby assuming that readers will find something useful to emulate. Kadushin's interview data contain both supervisory practice as described by supervisors, and responses to supervisory practice by supervisees. Numerous accounts of concrete situations are presented and labeled as either "good" or "bad" examples.[31]

Even when presenting abstract theories of the supervisory process, which case examples are usually meant to illustrate, emulation is the apparent process of learning that is hoped for. For example, Gitterman's presentation of three different educational models, and their influences on supervision, concludes with a strong recommendation to utilize one of the three models.[32] Morton and Kurtz hope that supervisors will enact their learning theory model. The reader is asked to adopt a particular view of the situation and then act accordingly, that is, to see things as the authors do and, thus, be like them.[33]

Reframing Current Skills

Some people assume that all of the skills needed by the supervisor have already been developed in the process of becoming a competent direct service worker. The problem is merely to reorient the use of these skills in the supervisory role. "Service delivery skills have been generally assumed to be similar or readily adaptable to the skills for teaching and helping others to deliver the services."[34]

Altucher sets parallel goals for supervision and for treatment—in both instances, the counselor should remain open to his or her own experiences. The roles and extent of experience change, but the skills of supervisor and worker are considered to be different only in degree of expertise.[35] Similarly, Carlton E. Munson believes that the key attribute of a supervisor is skill at the task being supervised.[36]

Within a presentation of supervisory roles that emphasizes accountability and administrative ability, Pettes also states that the "knowledge and skills needed for supervision are basically the same as those on which the supervisor will have relied as a social worker. However, the way in which he uses his knowledge is different, and the skills upon which he calls must meet rather different demands. Skills must be further developed in some areas rather than others."[37]

Even though these authors present supervisory practice as distinct from direct service, clearly they assume that the basic skills are the same.

Acquisition of New Skills

Eisenberg and Finch, Pettes, Westheimer and Finch assert that the supervisor must master new skills in order to be effective.[38] The needed skills relate to management, accountability, and administration. The ability to understand and interpret policy, to organize work flow, to handle administrative decision making, and to deal with complex organizations are all cited.

Although Eisenberg and Finch propose a framework for the content of training, focusing on program objectives and task statements, and Pettes presents a task-centered model for supervision, the means by which supervisors should learn the needed organizational and personnel management skills are not addressed. The supervisor who believes in the importance of these new skills usually studies independently, or takes courses in business, public, or social work administration offered through a continuing education or advanced degree program.

Formal Education as Part of Role Preparation

With changing societal and program needs, increasing numbers of master's programs now contain at least one course in supervision. Some such courses are part of a macro-practice track, while others are more clinical in their focus. Part of the reason for this development was both acceptance of the B.S.W. as the entry level professional degree, and resulting concerns about differential use of social work manpower.[39] Master's level courses in supervision frequently focus on issues of role learning and content regarding supervisory functions and responsibilities.

A limitation of this approach is, however, that unless the student is simultaneously involved in field practice, which includes experience in supervising, no opportunity exists to try out what is being learned. In this situation, students may master concepts but much of the learning is anticipatory guidance—preparation for future experiences.

Exhortation or Prescription

The lack of formal education and training for supervisors means that most new supervisors learn about their functions and roles, in part, from reading articles and books. There is considerable professional literature that not only provides information on the roles and norms of supervision, but is filled with specific directions about what to do and how to do it. Commonly, statements in articles take a form like: "The supervisor must realize that . . ." or, "The supervisor needs to . . . ." It is curious that although some writers present elaborate and sophisticated models of how direct service workers learn, they fail to apply their own learning models to supervisors. The expectation seems to be that supervisors will learn in a different way. Apparently, it is assumed that they will learn from normative statements about how to be a good supervisor, that is, by being preached to or exhorted by an expert.

Research in adult learning suggests that professionals do indeed develop some motivation for continued learning,[40] and exhortative writing may well be seen as a resource by people who are already stimulated to learn. The body of literature on supervision provides considerable information and contributes to setting role definition standards for the profession. Readers are exhorted to adopt models of supervision as various as Abroms's metatherapy, Abels's synergistic approach to mutual development, Pettes's task-centered orientation, or Eisenberg and Finch's or Westheimer's managerial approach.[41] Whether the reading is directed or haphazard, broad or narrow, the assumption is that supervisors can learn from being told what it is they should be doing.

Selection

The process of finding good supervisors is not always one of education, but is occasionally one of selection; that is, the identification of people on the basis of attributes that are needed to be a good supervisor. This is the trait-based personnel selection approach to staffing organizations that has come out of industry, and is sometimes alluded to by the authors writing in the field of supervision. For instance, Towle presents a list of qualifications for the supervisor that are probably beyond the direct scope of education.[42] It is assumed that having such attributes as a social conscience, a capacity to meet dependency, a capacity for cooperation, a clear sense of identity, and intellectual qualities are necessary, even if not sufficient, to be an effective supervisor. This kind of thinking, however, begs the question of how a person learns to become an effective supervisor.

Developing Effective Supervisory Models

Seven assumptions about learning being used by those who are concerned about social work supervision have been described. It is not clear to what extent any one or any combination of these assumptions are appropriate, much less optimal, for the task of increasing the effectiveness of supervisory development.

The number of social workers employed in supervisory and administrative roles has increased markedly.[43] Although Kadushin, Moore, and Scurfield have documented the role-transition tensions and conflicts experienced by clinicians who become supervisors,[44] insufficient attention has been given to these role tensions and the process of supervisory learning. There has been no systematic evaluation of learning by supervisors, even though, ironically, much of the content which is disseminated to supervisors concerns how their supervisees learn. The question remains: What do supervisors learn and how do they learn it most effectively?

This article has identified and made explicit the assumptions embedded in the current literature regarding how supervisory learning takes place. What is called for now is the specification of the supervisory learning process and the development and testing of supervisory learning models.

The following areas for investigation form an integrated methodological framework that should be considered in the process of model development and testing:
1. Anchoring and testing of the assumptions about supervisory learning.
2. Examining the process of learning the supervisory role.
3. Developing of the theory of supervision through integration of concepts from (a) management theory, (b) organizational behavior theory, (c) adult-learning theory, (d) socialization and role theory, and (e) supervisory practice theory.
4. Developing and testing of supervisory learning models in which process and content are integrated.

Toward these ends, the authors are engaged in research on *how* effective supervisors have learned to supervise. The study is focused on actual learning experiences described by supervisors as a means (1) to specify the role-learning process in becoming a supervisor, (2) to identify the learning needs that can be expected to occur on entry into supervisory positions, and (3) to build a taxonomy of effective responses for the learning needs encountered.

Approaches grounded on this kind of naturalistic research need to be refined and tested in educational and practice settings. The evolution of a coherent and comprehensive theory, based on knowledge of both the content and the process of learned supervision, provides logical and conceptual support for models of supervisory education. Work is now needed to develop and test models of supervisory learning, appropriate for master's level and beyond, and in-service programs, to assure the formulation of models that prepare supervisors for competent practice.

1. Alfred Kadushin, *Supervision in Social Work* (New York: Columbia University, 1976); Alfred J. Kutzik, "The Social Work Field," in *Supervision, Consultation, and Staff Training in the Helping Professions,* ed. Florence Kaslow et al. (San Francisco: Jossey-Bass, 1977); and Eugene Cohen, "Supervision in a Large Federal Agency: Psychiatric Setting," in *Issues in Human Services,* ed. Florence Kaslow et al. (San Francisco: Jossey-Bass, 1972), p. 39.

2. Kutzik, "The Social Work Field."

3. Roy Lubove, *The Professional Altruist* (New York: Atheneum, 1972).

4. See Kutzik, "The Social Work Field"; Paul A. Abels, *The New Practice of Supervision and Staff Development* (New York: Association Press, 1977); Gene M. Abroms, "Supervision as Metatherapy," in *Supervision, Consultation, and Staff Training,* ed. Kaslow et al., pp. 81-99.

5. Mary Parker Follett, *Dynamic Administration: The Collected Papers of Mary Parker Follett,* ed. Henry Metcalf and L. Urwick (New York: Harper and Brothers, 1942); Bertha Reynolds, *Learning and Teaching in the Practice of Social Work* (New York: Farrar and Rinehart, 1942); Charlotte Towle, *The Learner in Education for the Professions* (Chicago: University of Chicago Press, 1954); Virginia P. Robinson, *The Dynamics of Supervision under Functional Controls: A Professional Process in Social Casework* (Philadelphia: University of Pennsylvania Press, 1949); and Robinson, *Supervision in Social Case Work: A Problem in Professional Education* (Chapel Hill: University of North Carolina Press, 1936); and Stewart Moore, "Group Supervision: Forerunner or Trend Reflector? Part 1—Trends and Duties in Group Supervision," *The Social Worker: Le Travailleur Social* 38 (November 1970) 16-20.

6. Moore, "Group Supervision," 16-20.

7. Kadushin, *Supervision in Social Work,* p 253.

8. Ibid.

9. Alex Gitterman and Irving Miller, "Supervisors as Educators," in *Supervision, Consultation, and Staff Training,* ed. Kaslow et al., pp. 100-114.

10. Alex Gitterman, "Comparison of Educational Models and Their Influences on Supervision," in *Issues in Human Services,* ed. Kaslow et al., p. 18.

11. Thomas D. Morton and P. David Kurtz, "Educational Supervision: A Learning Theory Approach," *Social Casework: The Journal of Contemporary Social Work* 61 (April 1980): 240-46.

12. Gitterman, "Comparison of Educational Models."

13. Ione D. Vargus, "Supervision in Social Work," in *Supervision of Applied Training,* ed. D. J. Karpius (Westport, Conn.: Greenwood Press, 1977), p. 153; and Kadushin, *Supervision in Social Work.*

14. Gerald Caplan, *Principles of Preventive Psychiatry* (New York: Basic Books, 1964), chaps. 8 and 9.

15. Nathan Altucher, "Constructive Use of the Supervisory Relationship," *Journal of Counseling Psychology* 14 (March 1967): 165-70.

16. Abroms, "Supervision as Metatherapy."

17. Ilse J. Westheimer, *The Practice of Supervision in Social Work: A Guide for Staff Supervisors* (London: Ward Lock Educational, 1977), pp. 19-20.

18. Wilbur A. Finch, "The Role of the Organization," in *Supervision, Consultation, and Staff Training,* ed. Kaslow et al., p. 63.

19. Westheimer, *Practice of Supervision in Social Work.*

20. Dorothy E. Pettes, *Staff and Student Supervision: A Task Centered Approach* (London: George Allen and Unwin, 1979), pp. 8-9.

21. Vargus, "Supervision in Social Work."

22. See Vargus, "Supervision in Social Work"; and Irving Miller, "Distinctive Characteristics of Supervision in Group Work," *Social Work* 5 (January 1960): 68-76.

23. Joseph Olmstad and Harold E. Christensen, *Effects of Agency Work Contexts: An Intensive Field Study: Research Report No. 2* (Washington, D.C.: Department of Health, Education, and Welfare, 1973), p. 6.

24. Gitterman and Miller, "Supervisors as Educators," p. 100.

25. Sidney S. Eisenberg and Wilbur A. Finch, "Supervision in a Public Welfare Agency," in *Issues in Human Services,* ed. Kaslow et al., p. 229.

26. See Donald K. Granvold, "Training Social Work Supervisors to Meet Organizational and Worker Objectives," *Journal of Education for Social Work* 14 (Spring 1978): 38; and Werner W. Boehm, "Social Work Education: Issues and Problems in Light of Recent Developments," *Journal of Education for Social Work* 12 (Winter 1976): 20; and J. C. Hansen and R. Stevic, "Practicum in Supervision: A Proposal," *Counselor, Education, and Supervision* 6 (Spring 1967): 206.

27. Kadushin, *Supervision in Social Work.*

28. Ibid., p. 264.

29. Morton and Kurtz, "Educational Supervision: A Learning Theory Approach."

30. Kutzik, "The Social Work Field."

31. Kadushin, *Supervision in Social Work.*

32. Gitterman, "Comparison of Educational Models."

33. Morton and Kurtz, "Educational Supervision: A Learning Theory Approach."

34. Gitterman and Miller, "Supervisors as Educators," p. 101.

35. Altucher, "Constructive Use of the Supervisory Relationship."

36. Carlton E. Munson, "Supervising the Family Therapist," *Social Casework: The Journal of Contemporary Social Work* 61 (March 1980): 131-37.

37. Pettes, *Staff and Student Supervision,* p. 4.

38. Eisenberg and Finch, "Supervision in a Public-Welfare Agency"; Pettes, *Staff and Student Supervision;* Westheimer, *Practice of Supervision in Social Work;* and Finch, "Role of the Organization."

39. See Vargus, "Supervision in Social Work"; National Association of Social Workers, "Standards for Social Service Manpower," in *Social Administration: The Management of the Social Services*, ed. Simon Slavin, (New York: Haworth Press and the Council on Social Work Education, 1978).

40. A. Tough, *The Adult's Learning Projects* (Austin, Texas: Learning Concepts, 1979).

41. See Abroms, "Supervision as Metatherapy"; Abels, *New Practice of Supervision and Staff Development*; and Pettes, *Staff and Student Supervision*.

42. Towle, *Learner in Education for the Professions*.

43. Alfred M. Stamm, "NASW Membership: Characteristics, Deployment and Salaries," *Personnel Information* 12 (March 1969): 1-45.

44. Kadushin, *Supervision in Social Work*; Moore, "Group Supervision: Forerunner or Trend Reflection"; Raymond M. Scurfield, "Social Work Administrators: A Study of Their Preparation, Value Orientation, Role Transition and Satisfaction" (doctoral diss., School of Social Work, University of Southern California, 1979).

MALPRACTICE: FUTURE SHOCK OF THE 1980'S

BARTON E. BERNSTEIN

THE SOCIAL WORKER HAS been largely immune from malpractice actions. Indeed, one rarely hears or reads about a formal malpractice action of any type in which a social worker has been held liable or even sued by an unhappy client or patient. At a time when doctors, and to a lesser extent lawyers and psychologists, are being sued, the social worker remains aloof and removed from this tumultuous scene. This does not indicate that the time will never come, and the 1980s might be the time. The potential cause of action exists, and let a social worker overstep the bounds of propriety or professionalism and the cause of action will be asserted, established, and, probably, much publicized.

Every practicing social worker should have a basic knowledge of the elements of negligence and malpractice. Because the legal relationship between social worker and client is similar to that of psychiatrist and patient, these legal concepts may be examined from the point of view of the psychiatrist to extrapolate general rules. This is not to suggest or imply that the social worker and the psychiatrist have similar credentials or similar tools, or operate in identical fields handling identical problems. Nevertheless, there are many clear and obvious analogies between the social worker and the psychiatrist concerning professional conduct and the results desired and achieved. In fact, the definition of psychotherapy, as it appears in Black's Law Dictionary, shows that in many relationships, especially that of client and therapist, the definition applies to many aspects of work done by the social worker as well as to that of the psychiatrist:

A method or system of alleviating or curing certain forms of disease, particularly diseases of the nervous system or such as are traceable to nervous disorders by suggestion, persuasion, encouragement: the inspiration of hope or confidence, the discouragement of morbid memories, associations, or beliefs, and other similar means, addressed to the mental state of the patient without (sometimes in conjunction with) the administration of drugs or other physical remedies.[1]

Although social workers do not and cannot administer drugs, they do work in a sophisticated arena of practice that places on them the same or similar obligations to the public regarding their personal legal liability. Thus, social workers may find that, in their work with clients, an act, if negligent, may lead to embarrassing, professionally harmful, and often costly litigation.[2]

Elements of Malpractice

What are the elements of a malpractice suit? What can malpractice suits against psychiatrists teach the social worker? Henry B. Rothblatt and David H. Leroy have set out the basic test of any malpractice action as follows:

To recover in any malpractice action, the patient-plaintiff must prove four elements by a preponderance of the evidence:
1. That the doctor owed him a duty to conform to a particular standard of conduct;
2. That the doctor was derelict because he breached that duty by some act of commission or omission;
3. That because of that dereliction the patient suffered actual damage;
4. That the doctor's conduct was the direct or proximate cause of the damage.[3]

The elements in a negligence suit are, therefore, (1) duty, (2) breach of duty, (3) injury or damage, and (4) proximate cause (that is, the breach of duty caused the injury).

It is the breach of duty that is the basis of malpractice suits. The social worker must keep this in mind at all times. This is difficult because the measure of standard of care expected is somewhat vague and hard to define. However, the recent trend of the courts increasingly is to impose a higher standard of care.[4] At one time, the standard was measured by the norm within a particular locality. Now, with the arrival of the "specialist" on the scene following the medical model, the norm is the standard as established by the expert testimony of a fellow social worker. "Expert testimony, therefore, must be utilized to determine standard of care, deviation therefrom, and causation between the psychiatrist's misdeed and his victim's injury."[5] The courts, therefore, will look to the expert social worker to define the proper standard of care.

The higher standard of care imposes a higher standard of training: "Professional men in general, and those who undertake any work calling for special skill, are required not only to exercise reasonable care in what they do, but also to possess a standard minimum of special knowledge and ability."[6] Social workers are expected to have proper training from a creditable institution before offering care reserved for specialists. They must be properly trained over and above tender, loving, and compassionate care in order to undertake the problems of clients who come before them. Keep in mind that as soon as a social worker-client relationship is established, the social worker acquires legal obligations that give rise to potential liability. This is not to suggest that all conferences between a social worker and other individuals are therapy. It is to suggest that once the scales tip and consultation becomes therapy, the obligations change. The individual then becomes a "client" of the counselor. It is certainly established where a fee is charged on a per session or on a time basis.

The law of damages in malpractice actions parallels other negligence cases involving personal injury. Thus, a finding of negligence will result in liability for all injuries proximately caused by negligence, including pain and suffering, mental anguish, physical disfigurement, and economic losses.

Understanding Negligence

In its introduction to the law of negligence, American Jurisprudence defines negligence as follows: ". . . the failure to exercise the degree of care demanded by the circumstances, or as the want of that care which the law prescribes under the particular circumstances existing at the time of the act or omission which is involved. . . ."[7] Thus, there is a somewhat vague but still measurable standard that must be applied to each fact situation.

The Areas of Potential Danger

In reviewing the literature on psychiatric malpractice, within the realm of psychotherapy, general categories of potential danger are in the nature of faulty diagnosis and treatment.[8] Some of the categories below may appear ludicrous and absurd to the professionally minded social worker. Others will have a hint of reality, while still others will touch a tender nerve and perhaps suggest that a whole new approach to the practice of social work is needed.

Commitment

Negligence cases are often founded on the wrongful commitment of an individual to a hospital. This area is not of overwhelming concern to the social worker because usually a doctor would be consulted, although the social worker might conceivably recommend commitment to a family member. However, basic concepts do apply to both the social worker and the psychiatrist. It is essential that the social worker take a proper history when interviewing a client initially. Accurate records of all modes of therapy or further interviews should be maintained, together with a regular review of these records.

If hospital commitment is deemed necessary, a specialist should always be consulted, and accurate transcripts should be kept of the dialogue and consultation that takes place between the doctor, the social worker, and the family. In this way, if the social worker becomes party to a suit, he or she will be armed with evidence to substantiate his or her recommendations. The file must indicate, at all times, a current diagnosis, prognosis, treatment plan, and confirmation by a professional person able to make the final decision.[9]

Radical Treatment

Recommending radical treatment or "far out" therapy is a source of potential danger. The method of treatment does not have to be one thought to be best by the majority. It is enough that it is accepted by a respected minority. But, departure from any standard practice must be justified.[10] Were a client to initiate an action against a social worker for radical treatment, his or her attorney would concentrate efforts to show that the methods used, even those of a respected minority, were inappropriate in the present case.[11] Thus, where treatment is given, the method *must* be capable of defense. This does not mean that all clients with similar problems are treated equally, but deviation from a norm must have support in either experience or literature.

When sued for using a radical type of treatment, the social worker must be prepared to defend him or herself by showing that the treatment used was not negligent under the circumstances. One way to avoid such a pitfall might be to secure an informed consent, such as that used by surgeons to protect against malpractice. Remember, although one can consent to treatment in advance, one cannot consent to the therapist's negligence.

Accordingly, the social worker should explain the proposed therapy or treatment, its advantages and disadvantages, as well as its risks and results that may reasonably be anticipated. The client can either accept or reject the course of treatment.

Confidentiality

The social worker becomes privileged to his or her client's innermost secrets. These cannot be shared with third parties without a specific written release and permission of the client. There is some exception where there is a clear potential injury to a third party and, in this situation, a professional option will have to be exercised. However, when making this type of decision, the social worker is in the horns of a dilemma. On breaching confidentiality, he or she could be liable, or where a third party is injured and the social worker could have prevented such injury by reasonable diligence, that is, warnings, there is also a possibility of liability. The California Evidence Code imposes a general duty of confidentiality on nonmedical specialists as well as psychiatrists, including licensed psychologists, authorized school psychologists, licensed clinical social workers, and licensed marriage, family, and child counselors.[12]

If a controversy arises over whether disclosure is necessary, the social worker's action strikes a delicate balance between the probability of harm resulting to the client and its seriousness and society's interest in knowing the confidential information.[13]

Failure to Warn Others

The counterpart of confidentiality is the duty to warn others. A social worker might be negligent if he or she fails to warn third parties likely to come in contact with a client known to have violent tendencies.[14] A recent California case, *Tarasoff v. Regents of University of California*, has set a monumental precedent that the professional has a duty to breach the role of confidant when the public safety is in danger:

The court does not require routine disclosures of confidential information when the psychotherapist, in his best judgment, believes the patient

is not a threat to anyone. It requires doctors to exercise that degree of skill, knowledge and care possessed by other members of their profession under similar circumstances. ... It is the risk of danger to another within the range of foreseeability which defines the duty to be obeyed in any given case.[15]

In *Merchants National Bank and Trust Company v. United States*, a psychologist was found to have been negligent in failing to make an employer aware that a recently released mental patient had dangerous propensities.[16] Thus, the social worker should be aware that there are times when a breach of confidentiality is not only necessary to protect third parties, but also necessary to protect the social worker from suits against him or her by injured third persons. The confidentiality versus duty to warn others balance is a delicate one; whichever way the decision goes, the social worker could be held liable. In this particular area, any option should be weighed carefully.

There are major difficulties in suing a psychotherapist or other professionals for damages caused when his patient killed or injured another person. First, it must be established that the therapist had a duty towards the injured [third] party. Second, it must be proved that the therapist knew or should have known of the patient's dangerous propensities. Third, it must be proved that the therapist's [failure to] act was the proximate cause of the injury. Presumably, if these three elements can be established, there will be little difficulty in establishing damages, for the concern here is the patient's violent acts resulting in the victim's bodily harm or death.[17]

Assault and Battery

In supervising groups using fight techniques, the social worker becomes vulnerable to assault and battery liability. There is an increasing proliferation of group encounters in which people hit each other with paper or cloth bats or are dragged across lines or touch each other in various ways. This may all be under the social worker's supervision, guidance, and control, and may be in the context of or during group therapy.

Should someone be hurt, however, the social worker might be held liable if he or she were negligent in some respect. The test is clear. The application of the facts to that test is more obscure and would be a question for the jury to decide. One should not give up a solid theory or treatment or training because of a possibility, yet one should be aware.

Sexual Relationship

"It seems fair to state that the greatest number of actions are brought by women who lead lives of very quiet desperation, who form close attachments to their therapist, who feel rejected or spurned when they discover that relations are maintained on a formal and professional level, and who then react with allegations of sexual improprieties."[18] In this area, a long dissertation might be redundant, whereas a word to the wise is sufficient. The conduct of a social worker must clearly be above reproach.

Social workers are as available to temptation as are those of any other discipline or calling. They are probably no more or less susceptible than are the psychologists referred to in the general statement quoted above. Because this is an area of obvious concern and ruinous consequences, the rule is simple: Thou shall not. . . .

Abandonment

There are many instances when the social worker is not available to the client. Social workers leave town, are transferred, and give up social work practice. Further, they become ill, take vacations, sabbaticals, and, occasionally, just do not go to work. At such times, the social worker must take precautions so that his or her behavior will not be construed as abandonment of the client. For example, when a social worker leaves town, he or she should obtain someone else to substitute temporarily. The person covering temporarily must have a sufficient background to be able to help each client if a crisis arises. This is especially true if the client has dangerous propensities to himself or to others. Once again, the importance of good record keeping becomes apparent. The substituting social worker must be able to get a clear picture of the clients and their problems by reviewing the records. A pertinent fact, such as suicidal tendencies, if omitted, could leave the social worker open to liability.

Often social workers in private practice have a fetish about not reducing items to writing because such notes might be subpoenaed into court. Remember, the social worker is protected only if a replacement can make a true diagnosis from the available record. If the available record is misleading, either by absence of facts or incorrect data, it is the referring social worker who is negligent.[19]

Interestingly, there comes a time when a therapist in a sense owes it to a client to abandon him or her. An English decision[20] enunciates a duty by a psychiatrist to terminate or release his or her patient when lengthy and costly treatment has not borne fruit. This is broad enough to encompass a duty to consult or refer.

The social worker does not guarantee a client will get well. During some phase of the treatment, the social worker owes it to him or herself and the client to recognize that the particular therapeutic undertaking is not fruitful, and the client should either be referred to another professional, or a qualified professional should be called in for consultation.

Limitations on Ability

The social worker is not equipped to treat all problems. Often, the situation will require a psychologist or psychiatrist or medical specialist. Social workers should be aware of the limitations of their ability and training and, when appropriate, refer the patient to a discipline with more specialized knowledge or seek the aid of a consultant.

Termination of Treatment

As in all therapy situations, transference and countertransference could become sources of malcontent and, therefore, lawsuits. The client who forms a deep attachment to the social worker during the course of counseling may feel rejected or abandoned when the social worker suggests discontinuing therapy. Conversely, the social worker who forms a deep attachment to the client and extends counseling beyond the point that is productive is also subject to liability.

In addition, sources of liability arise on termination of treatment if treatment is no longer needed and the therapist continues merely to collect additional fees, or if therapy is concluded too soon and the client suffers a relapse or perhaps a greater setback as a result. Termination must be at the proper time with proper safeguards.

Professional Protection

What might a social worker do to become insulated professionally, personally, and financially from liability?

Insurance

Malpractice insurance is generally available and inexpensive, although there are often requirements or prerequisites. The social worker who practices publicly without a blanket policy or privately without an individual policy is in a precarious position. The policy will not only cover damages, but also the cost of defense, usually by a prestigious law firm. Malpractice insurance is the first essential for social workers, and it is relatively inexpensive.

Awareness of the Legal Entity

Most social workers in individual practice are responsible only for themselves. Social workers in a common practice of four or five can often face partnership liability, in which one can be responsible for the actions of another: "The Texas Uniform Partnership Act (an Act similar to most jurisdictions) provides that partners are liable jointly and severally for all debts and obligations of the partnership, including those arising from wrongful acts or omissions of a partner chargeable to the firm or from a partner's breach of trust."[21]

Further, often without any thought of liability, social workers join together in ventures, usually oral and often very loose, where seminars, workshops, or other services are provided. Conceivably, an individual attending a seminar could become irate and sue. Any attorney knows that the more defendants sued the better. Thus, unknowingly social workers can make themselves and their associates subject to a lawsuit and liable for damages by associating with other parties in a venture that has little supervision or control, and where appearance to the public is that of a single cohesive group performing a particular task. Under the agency theory, a social worker who is negligent regarding a client creates liability for the agency itself under the time-honored theory that "the actions of the agent are the actions of the principal when acting in the scope of his employment."

Releases

The social worker should always obtain releases. If there are audio or video tapes, and these will be used in a classroom for purposes of training or available to any third party, a release must be obtained so that this breach of confidentiality is explained to the client and he or she can make an informed consent concerning the sharing of a personal problem with other people. In fact, whenever a particular client is to be discussed with any third party, under any circumstances, a release is required. Confidentiality goes to the essence of the counseling procedure, and a breach of this confidentiality, in the nature of the relationship, can create personal liability.

Conclusion

Social work is a unique helping profession because of its involvement in mental health. As such, there is an increased exposure to lawsuits by dissatisfied clients both due to actions of commission and omission, that is, not doing what they should have done or doing what they should not have done. At a minimum, the social worker should have malpractice insurance and consult his or her attorney as to the consequences of all ventures, be they alone, under the auspices of an agency, or in concert with others. The relationship with a client should be contractual where appropriate, and releases are needed whenever a third party is to be consulted in reference to a client or where treatment is terminated.

In treatment, the social worker should have various problem areas in mind, and take such action so as to avoid even the thought of suit or liability. Each decision concerning treatment is a professional decision and, as such, must be capable of defense. The social worker must maintain a professional relationship and take a complete history, provide for adequate treatment personally, and provide for adequate treatment by others when the social worker is absent. Further, the social worker should realize personal, educational, and professional limitations and refer clients to another when the problem at hand exceeds his or her ability, training, or competence.

Although few social workers have been sued by clients, this lack of activity should not be used to conclude that no liability exists. The social worker should heed suggestions and insulate him or herself from what could be a professionally hazardous experience. To the social worker who already has these items in mind instinctively, this article is perhaps redundant. However, it is thought that for many, the concept of a social worker's liability is indeed the future shock of the 1980s.

Epilogue

Two recent events are appropriate red flags for the concerned social worker. One concerns the duty to warn third parties and the other concerns the criminal indictments of three social workers in El Paso, Texas.

Concerning the duty to warn third parties, the New Jersey Superior Court held recently that a psychotherapist who determines—or should have determined pursuant to the standards of his or her profession—that a patient presents a probability of danger to a third party has a duty to take reasonable steps to protect the potential victim. . . . Asserting that its decision would have a minimal impact on the confidentiality of the therapist-patient relationship, the court analogized the psychotherapist's duty to the established responsibility of physicians to warn those exposed to dangerous, contagious diseases.[22]

In El Paso, Texas "a child died under mysterious circumstances [an autopsy did not reveal the cause of death], charges of neglect were filed against the social workers handling the case even though the social workers involved had closely followed agency procedures."[23]

Although the charges were dismissed, the ramifications are enormous: the publicity was embarrassing and nationwide. The time and expense consumed in establishing and presenting a legal defense were enormous. The emotional drain on the social workers involved was incredible. Malpractice policies will not usually protect an insured person involved in a criminal case. This is an area of concern, recently established, that must be carefully watched.

1. See *Black's Law Dictionary*, 4th ed. (St. Paul, Minn.: West Publishing, 1951).

2. M L. Plant, "Recent Developments in Medicolegal areas," *ALI-ABA Course Materials* 1 (March 1976): 41-43.

3. Henry B. Rothblatt and David H. Leroy, "Avoiding Psychiatric Malpractice," *California Western Law Review* 9 (Winter 1973): 263.

4. Ibid., 261.

5. John G. Sauer, "Psychiatric Malpractice—A Survey," *Washburn Law Journal* 11 (Spring 1972): 461.

6. William Prosser, *Handbook of the Law of Torts*, 4th ed. (St. Paul, Minn.: West Publishing, 1971), pp. 30-161.

7. 57 Am. Jur. 2nd 333, Sec. 1.

8. James L. Hale and Gayle R. Podell, "Medical Malpractice in New York," *Syracuse Law Review* 27 (Spring 1976): 753.

9. See Patrick Sean Cassidy, "The Liability of Psychiatrists for Malpractice," *University of Pittsburgh Law Review* 36 (1974): 108-37.

10. Donald J. Dawidoff, "The Malpractice of Psychiatrists," *Duke Law Journal* (Summer 1966): 696.

11. Carl B. Tarshis, "Liability for Psychotherapy," *University of Toronto Faculty Law Review* 30 (August 1972): 85.

12. Marjory Harris, "Tort Liability of the Psychotherapist," *University of San Francisco Law Review* 8 (Winter 1973): 405-36.

13. Joseph A. Latham, Jr., "Torts—Duty to Act for Protection of Another—Liability of Psychotherapist for Failure to Warn of Homicide Threatened by Patient," *Vanderbilt Law Review* 28 (April 1975): 631.

14. See Berry V. Moench, 8 Utah 2d 191, 331 P. 2d 814.

15. Susan Merakean, "Tort Law: California's Expansion of the Duty to Warn," *Washburn Law Journal* 15 (Fall 1976): 499-501; and Alan A. Stone, "The Tarasoff Decisions: Suing Psychotherapists to Safeguard Society," *Harvard Law Review* 90 (December 1976): 358. See also Ralph Schindler, "Malpractice—Another New Dimension of Liability—A Critical Analysis," *Trial Lawyers Guide* 201 (1976): 129-51; Ralph Slovenko, "Psychotherapy and Confidentiality," *Cleveland State Law Review* 24 (Winter 1975): 375-96; and Tarasoff v. Regents of University of California, 131 Cal. Rptr. 14, 551 P. 2d 334 (1976).

16. 272 Fed. Supp. 409, D.M.D. (1967).

17. Harris, "Tort Liability," P. 425.

18. Jay Brownfain, "The APA Professional Liability Insurance," *American Psychologist* 26 (July 1971): 651.

19. Rothblatt, "Avoiding Malpractice," p. 203; and Harris, "Tort Liability," p. 419.

20. Landau v. Werner, Q.B. March 1, 1961, 105 S01, J. 257 (A.B. 1961), aff'd Sol, J. 1008 (CA 1961).

21. Texas Jurisprudence, Sec. 67.

22. McIntosh v. Milano, 168 N.J. Super. 466 (1979), *American Journal of Law and Medicine* 6 (Summer 1980): 190.

23. *NASW News* 26 (January 1981): 8.

Barton E. Bernstein is a partner in the firm of Hochberg, Bernstein, and Skor, Attorneys and Counselors, Dallas, Texas, and adjunct professor of social work, University of Texas at Arlington, Arlington, Texas.

DEVELOPING EMPIRICALLY BASED MODELS OF PRACTICE

BETTY J. BLYTHE, SCOTT BRIAR

FOR OVER a decade, social work practitioners have been urged to apply single-case methodology in their work with clients.[1] The most frequently given reason is that the methodology will allow practitioners to determine their effectiveness with clients, something that is important as a matter of ethical practice and for accountability purposes. Another common argument in support of the use of single-subject methodology is that practitioners will be able to design and validate new, effective social work methods.[2] It is also argued that because they are continually searching for new and better models of practice, practitioners should turn their talents to developing the models themselves. By conducting single-case evaluation, they can document the effect of particular interventive techniques and begin to form a knowledge bank about effective practice methods. Taken together, the work of one or more practitioners can result in the discovery of new, empirically based models of practice.

In this article, the authors examine the use of single-case methodology for developing empirically based models of practice. Following a definition of "model of practice," the article discusses the lack of well-defined models that have empirical support and explains how this situation developed. The ability of single-case methodology to build practice models is reviewed. Finally, the bulk of the article identifies problems that are likely to be encountered as practitioners attempt to generate practice knowledge with single-case methods and suggests ways of surmounting these problems.

DEFINITION

A model of practice, or a treatment model, prescribes what a practitioner should do in a given situation. Reid and Epstein have provided a useful definition:

In our terminology a model is a coherent set of directives which state how a given kind of treatment is to be carried out. A model is basically definitional and descriptive. It usually states what the practitioner is expected to do under given conditions. Casework models normally include some delineation of the kinds of problem or disorder for which they are intended, methods of diagnosis and assessment, desired ways of relating to clients, and statements of treatment goals, strategies, and techniques.[3]

There are two kinds of models of practice: (1) empirically based models that are derived from clinical research, and (2) theoretically based models that are extracted from theory. In testing specific interventive methods with single-case methodology, practitioners are not necessarily trying to test theory, although their findings may have implications for theory. In fact, the methods under investigation may not have been derived from theory but may have been drawn from practice wisdom or from existing research, or they may be adaptations of methods used with clients with similar problems. Although the two kinds of models are not mutually exclusive, there has been a shift in emphasis from theoretically based models to empirically based models over the past ten years.[4]

NEED FOR EMPIRICALLY BASED MODELS

Although practitioners are frequently urged to use only practice methods with demonstrated effectiveness, few comprehensive, empirically based models of social work practice have actually been articulated. Until the 1960s, social work methods were largely assumed to be effective even when there was little or no evidence to support this assumption. Over the past decade, however, reviews of numerous large social work field investigations suggested that this assumption was incorrect.[5] Subsequent analyses of these investigations have led some authorities to argue that part of the reason that the research was faulty was because the researchers did not understand the practice methods being examined.[6] Moreover, a review of effectiveness studies conducted since 1973 indicated that some of the recently developed social work methods are effective.[7] However, this same review suggested that many of the studies do not adequately delineate the specifics of the interventions being tested. Although they admitted that the more recent studies are much clearer about the nature of the treatment programs used, the reviewers nonetheless concluded that "with a few exceptions, the recent crop of experiments do only little better than their predecessors in presenting data on how the interventions were actually done."[8] Hence, we still are faced with a scarcity of well-explicated treatment models that are grounded in research.

There are several reasons why this dilemma continues to exist. First, most of the effectiveness studies are conducted by researchers who tend to be more interested in the dependent variables, the results, and the statistical significance than in the independent variables or treatment methods and clinical significance. Second, clinical research findings are typically disseminated in research journals that traditionally give only limited attention to describing the interventive methods being tested. Finally, clinical research today often examines differences in outcomes between a treatment and a control group and provides relatively little information about what practitioners should do under certain conditions or with particular clients. Group-design studies aggregate data from a number of clients and only describe average outcomes for the sample as a whole. This obscures the different responses to treatment exhibited by individual clients. Some clients may improve but others may get worse. Practitioners, of course, are more interested in the progress of individual clients and in the specific associations between certain characteristics of clients and the outcomes of the treatment. These characteristics include such variables as age, severity of the problem, and motivation to change. Group-design studies not only reduce information about the outcomes of the treatment to averages but they also tend to collect this information about clients at only two points in time—before and after treatment. Measures of changes in clients over time are rarely taken; hence, what happens to clients over the course of treatment is unknown. Thus, the types of information that facilitate selection of an interventive method for a particular client or that describe the conditions under which a method should be applied—both of which are important and necessary ingredients of a model of practice—are not readily available from group-design studies.

NEW ROLE FOR SOCIAL WORKERS

Because of the paucity of empirically based practice models and because it is unlikely that group-design studies conducted by researchers will produce such models in the near future, practitioners might begin developing practice models through their own clinical research. The results of single-case evaluations conducted by practitioners can be used to discover ways of maximizing the effectiveness of social work interventions. To make their research task more manageable, practitioners should aim to develop problem-specific models rather than generic models like task-centered casework. For example, if a given practitioner works primarily with shoplifters, then the model could be built around this target problem. Furthermore, it may be more realistic for practitioners to attempt to develop only one or two components of the practice model, such as a treatment

strategy applicable to adolescent girls engaged in petty shoplifting or a particular way of relating to court-referred, adolescent clients who are reluctant to receive services. Developing an entire model of practice, particularly a generic one, is an awesome task for an individual practitioner. Yet, the results of one, two, or three single-case studies can lead to the discovery of a new practice component or to the improvement of an existing component of a practice model. When the efforts of several practitioners are combined, they can produce a treatment model that is well-defined and coherent, and that describes what practitioners should do in specific situations with specific clients.

Reid has identified several strategies in which single-case research can be used to develop and revise empirically based models of practice.[9] In one developmental research strategy, a particular interventive method can be tested and refined. Then a second method is applied to determine if the combination improves on the results of the original, single method. This continues until a practice model is built. Alternatively, one can begin with a full model or treatment package and systematically alter and test various configurations, perhaps replacing less effective components, until the maximally powerful practice model is identified. Finally, a model could be tested with several different problems of clients, perhaps beginning with less difficult ones. A single practitioner might enter into one of these approaches at any given stage but would not be expected to carry out development of the entire model. Or, a group of practitioners working in the same organization or with similar client populations but in separate locations might collaboratively work on one segment of a particular developmental research strategy.

OVERCOMING VARIOUS IMPEDIMENTS

Even if a small number of practitioners were to work toward building empirical practice knowledge as described here, some problems would still remain. Although the methodology is becoming increasingly sophisticated, practitioners are likely to encounter certain impediments as they attempt to develop practice models based on single-case evaluations. For one thing, few guidelines exist for assimilating

findings from individual cases to form treatment models. Perhaps more serious is the lack of clear-cut rules to use in attempting to answer various statistical, logistical, methodological, and other questions that invariably arise. In addition, because few practitioners actually attempt to develop practice models through the process of single-case evaluation, those who do are largely traveling in uncharted territory.[10]

Rigor

Effectiveness studies conducted before the 1970s were often criticized for not offering sufficient rigor in their research.[11] How can practitioners using single-subject methodology avoid the same fate? Single-case research already has been attacked by some for providing inadequate control for extraneous variables that might influence clients' improvement.[12] Moreover, when the methodology is applied in clinical settings, certain compromises are frequently necessary. Debates about how these compromises should be made are only beginning to be heard in this relatively young field. Practitioners currently using single-subject methodology to develop knowledge for practice models will be faced with decisions about what designs to enlist, how to interpret data, and what constitutes adequate external validity.

An increasing number of single-subject designs are available to practitioners, but few guidelines exist for selecting a design for a particular situation. Some beginning attempts have been made to organize the designs according to degree of rigor.[13] The less rigorous designs, however, tend to be best suited to clinical applications. For instance, the AB design, which entails continuous measurement of the client's target problem before and during intervention, can be applied in most clinical situations with little or no effect on practice concerns. Yet this design offers little control for most threats to internal validity or alternative explanations for a client's progress or lack of progress. Rather than criticize the design for insufficient rigor and suggest that practitioners use more complex designs, greater emphasis should be given to the importance of routinely looking for and attempting to rule out alternative hypotheses that might explain a client's response to treatment. Practitioners already do this anyway. They observe and take note of events in the client's life, other than treatment, that might account for changes in the client's feelings, behaviors, or cognitions. We simply need to recognize the value of these activities and to encourage practitioners to be especially attentive to possible rival hypotheses when using less rigorous designs.

Another way of building confidence that a client's improvement is due to intervention rather than to other influences is through testing the same intervention with one or more additional clients who exhibit the same problem. Again, practitioners often apply the same intervention to different clients. By following certain guidelines for replication that are discussed later, practitioners can compensate for the lack of control of internal validity inherent in some of the designs that are most easily applied in clinical settings.

Even more helpful in dealing with the issue of design is the notion of flexibility in design selection proposed by Hayes.[14] He argued that we should think in terms of design elements rather than entire designs and urged practitioners to be creative in putting together the design elements to fit specific clinical situations or questions. Hayes presented in table form a helpful delineation of the types of clinical questions that can be answered by various combinations of the design elements. Thus, practitioners who want to know which components of a given treatment method account for its effectiveness can build a design that both answers the question and fits the client's needs for service and situation.

Another area of single-case research in which the issue of rigor may present problems is that of interpreting the data. Statistical analysis of single-case data by practitioners is rare. Although the appropriateness of statistically analyzing single-case data has been debated, the fact remains that many practitioners lack the requisite skills or simply the time to do the computations.[15] In other instances, statistical analysis is not possible because there are not enough baseline data points or because the data have pronounced trends. Yet visual inspection of graphed data, the analysis method that is most often adopted by practitioners, is subject to error unless the data patterns are very clear.[16]

In view of the current state of the art, it seems unwise to advise or ex-

hort practitioners to use statistical techniques. To do so would be likely to reduce the number of single-case evaluations carried out by practitioners and, because of the controversy surrounding the use of statistics in single-case research, it probably would be of little benefit. Instead, efforts should focus on strengthening visual analyses. As discussed earlier, the need to consider alternative explanations, particularly if the data patterns are unclear, should be stressed. Replication with additional clients will help to provide a more accurate understanding of the effect of a given interventive method. Finally, more attention must be given to determining if changes are clinically significant. Clinically significant improvement refers to those instances in which the client or those around the client note meaningful progress or improvement. An example in a depressed client might be increased appetite, reduced crying, general cheerfulness, and more enjoyable interactions with others. This progress may or may not be detected by quantitative measures. Guidelines are being developed to bring a higher degree of objectivity to determining clinical significance, but they cannot be applied to all client problems.[17] Meanwhile, an important step would be simply to acknowledge that good practice involves regular scanning for indicators of clinically significant improvement.

For practitioners interested in contributing to the development of empirically based models of practice, the question of external validity is a crucial one. The issue here is whether the findings of one single-case study apply to other cases. Once a positive outcome is achieved, the practitioner wants to know if the same intervention will produce the same response in other clients with similar problems. Other practitioners will wonder if they can achieve the same outcomes with their clients. Indeed, practitioners will have little reason to attempt to develop empirical models of practice with single-case evaluation tools unless the findings from one case have implications for their work with other clients. Yet an intervention that works with one client may or may not have relevance for other clients.

For the results of single-case evaluations to be applied by other practitioners, it is obviously essential that the practitioner conducting the evaluation be specific about descriptions of client characteristics, treatment

methods, and agency variables when writing case notes and reporting the case to others. Further, whenever an intervention fails to bring about improvement in a client, this information also needs to be shared with other practitioners. In this way, practitioners can estimate whether a particular treatment method is likely to help a given client.

The most frequently suggested means of increasing the generalizability of the findings from single-case evaluations to other cases is replication. Here, clear guidelines have been proposed. Hersen and Barlow recommended three repeated testings once a new method produces a successful outcome with an individual client.[18] As much as possible, intervention, critical characteristics of the client, target problem, setting, and practitioner should be uniform in each replication. If the results are similar each time, the method should then be subjected to systematic replication in which only one variable is manipulated at a time. Admittedly, systematic replication would be difficult for most practitioners to accomplish. Given common interests and adequate communication channels, however, it might be feasible for a network of practitioners working with clients with similar problems or using similar treatment methods to conduct systematic replication.

Tripodi has suggested applying a test of statistical significance to determine the generalizability of replicated single-case evaluations of a given intervention.[19] In addition to the above-mentioned conditions that must be held constant in clinical replication, the same criterion of success or failure must be administered with each client. Unless there is information to the contrary, Tripodi advises using the binomial distribution. Thus, if the probability of having the observed number of successes in a given number of replications is greater than a predetermined critical value, the effect of chance can be eliminated. This more rigorous approach to replication should be applicable in many clinical situations.

Obviously, there are many other elements in single-case methodology that affect the degree of rigor present in any given study. The ones discussed here seem especially pertinent to developing models of practice. In any event, the importance of methodological requirements must be tempered by clinical realities and by the need for empirically based practice models. Practitioners should not be held back from testing a treatment method because they do not have ideal research conditions. It is more important to begin the process of building a knowledge bank, being careful to specify the conditions under which each trial of a treatment method was conducted.

Aggregating Data

As soon as practitioners begin carrying out single-case evaluations to test treatment methods, another problem will surface: How can single-case data, emphasizing client-specific measures of change, be combined across several clients so that meaningful statements can be made about the efficacy of a particular treatment method? How can a Beck Depression Inventory score, a daily self-rating of depression, and a frequency count of self-critical statements be aggregated?[20] Unfortunately, little has been written about this problem although some clues can be gleaned from related projects.[21]

Developers of clinically oriented management information systems have had to find ways to represent specific outcomes of work with clients. The most frequent solution is to reduce the data to statements about attainment of goals or success. For example, Woods described a management information system in a small agency for autistic children that sorted treatment outcomes into categories based on whether each treatment goal was accomplished, was not accomplished, became irrelevant, or was still being pursued.[22] Although it reduces specific data to general statements, this approach is feasible and easy to apply. Other management information systems specify that particular outcome measures be used with each problem exhibited by clients.[23] The same measure or measures are used for every client with a drinking problem, for instance. However, this approach hinders one of the important features of single-case evaluations, the specificity of measurement. Moreover, the use of common, standardized outcome measures is impractical if several practitioners are working in different agencies to validate a model of practice. But it may be a viable approach for use in large agencies.

Single-subject methodologists have begun to develop procedures for applying meta-analysis strategies to single-case data. At least two formulas have been suggested for deriving an effect size, which is a quantitative estimate of the efficacy of a given intervention.[24] A careful scrutiny of these applications of meta-analysis, resulting in clear recommendations for practitioners, must be made. Nonetheless, it is encouraging to note that methodologists are developing easy-to-apply formulas and are considering the realities of conducting single-case evaluations in clinical settings (such as short baselines and unequal length of phases). Meanwhile, the uncertainty about the best way to aggregate outcome data should not prevent practitioners from beginning to conduct evaluations of treatment methods. The authors agree with Barlow that simply knowing if a particular treatment method was a success or a failure and how this outcome is associated with certain client variables will be an important advance for social work.[25]

Dissemination

Critical to the notion of several practitioners independently testing treatment methods to build models of practice is an effective means of communicating the findings. Sadly, there are too few channels for this dissemination. Clinical and research journals alike infrequently report single-case studies, especially those in which treatment failed. Furthermore, the format of these journals usually does not allow the necessary specificity about the client's diagnosis or about problem assessment and treatment methods.

One option, as yet unexplored, is for one or more professional associations to sponsor a newsletter describing systematic case evaluations. If publication of such a newsletter were undertaken, a standardized format for reporting the case would make the practitioner's task easier and would ensure that an adequate description was provided. The format should make provision for inclusion of important variables associated with the client and the problem being treated as well as a full description of treatment methods. Most of this information is routinely gathered by practitioners but would be time-consuming to report in narrative form. Rather, a checklist with uniform descriptors of client, problem, and setting is envisioned. Less easy to describe succinctly and yet fully would be the interventions, especially those growing out of treatment approaches that are difficult to specify. Even techniques that may seem fairly straightforward, such as role playing, can be carried out in several different ways. Considerable effort should go into developing a framework for describing treatment methods that is easy to understand and use. The newsletter might also include limited reporting of new assessment strategies and single-case design innovations.

Such a newsletter would have several advantages besides facilitating communication among practitioners testing similar practice methods. It is likely that many nonevaluating practitioners would subscribe simply to learn about new treatment strategies. Moreover, social workers' knowledge about treatment methods could be updated easily. From time to time, and depending on the state of the art, a detailed treatment protocol describing a particular model of practice developed through the cumulative empirical work of a number of practitioners could be published.

BUILDING MODELS

Rather than waiting for empirically based models of practice to be developed, practitioners can and should be involved in building their own models, using single-case methodology. Building practice models from the ground up is tedious work, but it is likely to result in models that are immediately applicable to the practitioner's own work with clients. The methodology affords enough flexibility to allow its use in clinical settings without having a negative effect on practice concerns. Research methodologists should give increased attention to examining ways in which single-case evaluation tools can be adapted for clinical application while the tools maintain sufficient research rigor. Meanwhile, practitioners should not hesitate to use single-case designs to develop practice knowledge. The results from simple, straightforward, single-case evaluations by a number of practitioners would provide a major contribution to our knowledge of what constitutes effective models of practice.

Notes and References

1. S. Briar, "Effective Social Work Intervention in Direct Practice: Implications for Education," in *Facing the Challenge* (New York: Council on Social Work Education, 1973), pp. 17–30; and M. Howe,

"Casework Self-Evaluation: A Single Subject Approach." *Social Service Review.* 48 (March 1974), pp. 1–23.

2. S. Briar. "Research and Practice: Partners in Social Work Knowledge Development." in J. W. Hanks. ed., *Toward Human Dignity: Social Work in Practice* (Washington, D.C.: National Association of Social Workers, 1978). pp. 15–25: and R. L. Levy and D. G. Olson. "The Single-Subject Methodology in Clinical Practice: An Overview." *Journal of Social Service Research.* 3 (Fall 1979). pp. 25–49.

3. W. J. Reid and L. Epstein. *Task-Centered Casework* (New York: Columbia University Press. 1972). pp. 7–8.

4. J. Fischer. "The Social Work Revolution." *Social Work,* 26 (May 1981). pp. 199–207.

5. See J. Fischer. "Is Casework Effective? A Review." *Social Work,* 18 (January 1973). pp. 5–20; Fischer, ed., *The Effectiveness of Social Casework* (Springfield, Ill: Charles C Thomas, 1976). and E. J. Mullen and J. R. Dumpson and Associates. *Evaluation of Social Intervention* (San Francisco: Jossey-Bass, 1972).

6. See, for example. W. J. Reid, "Research Strategies for Improving Individualized Services." in D. Fanshel, ed., *Future of Social Work Research* (Washington, D.C.: National Association of Social Workers, 1980). pp. 38–52.

7. W. J. Reid and P. Hanrahan. "Recent Evaluations of Social Work: Grounds for Optimism." *Social Work,* 27 (July 1982). pp. 328–340.

8. Ibid., p. 330.

9. Reid. "Research Strategies for Improving Individualized Services."

10. Those who have suggested this course of action include C. A. Richey. B. J. Blythe. and S. B. Berlin. "A Follow-Up Study of the Educational Unit: Do Our Graduates Evaluate Their Practice?" Paper presented at the Annual Program Meeting. Council on Social Work Education, New York, N.Y., March 1982.

11. Fischer. "Is Casework Effective?"; Fischer, ed., *Effectiveness of Social Casework;* and Miller and Dumpson, *Evaluation of Social Intervention.*

12. J. D. Kagle. "Using Single-Subject Measures in Practice Decisions: Systematic Documentation or Distortion?" *Arete.* 7 (Winter 1982). pp. 1–9; and E. J. Thomas. "Research and Service in Single-Case Experimentation: Conflicts and Choices." *Social Work Research and Abstracts.* 14 (Winter 1978). pp. 20–31.

13. R. P. Barth. "Education for Practice-Research: Toward a Reorientation." *Journal of Education for Social Work.* 17 (Spring 1981). pp. 19–25; and M. J. Mahoney. "Experimental Methods and Outcome Evaluation." *Journal of Consulting and Clinical Psychology.* 46 (August 1978). pp. 660–672.

14. S. C. Hayes. "Single Case Experimental Design and Empirical Clinical Practice." *Journal of Consulting and Clinical Psychology.* 49 (April 1981). pp. 193–211.

15. W. J. Gingerich. "Significance Testing in Single-Case Research." in A. Rosenblatt and D. Waldfogel. eds., *Handbook of Clinical Social Work* (San Francisco: Jossey-Bass, 1983). pp. 694–720; and A. E. Kazdin. "Data Evaluation for Intrasubject-Replication Research." *Journal of Social Service Research.* 3 (Fall 1979). pp. 79–97.

16. A. DeProspero and S. Cohen. "Inconsistent Visual Analyses of Intrasubject Data." *Journal of Applied Behavior Analysis.* 12 (Winter 1979). pp. 573–579.

17. N. S. Jacobson and W. C. Follette. "Clinical Significance of Improvement Resulting from Two Behavioral Marital Therapy Components." *Behavior Therapy.* 16 (June 1985). pp. 249–262.

18. M. Hersen and D. H. Barlow. *Single Case Experimental Designs* (New York: Pergamon Press. 1976). pp. 334–336.

19. T. Tripodi. "Replication in Clinical Experimentation Research Briefs and Notes, Social Work Research and Abstracts. 16 (Winter 1980). p. 35.

20. A. T. Beck. *Depression* (New York: Harper & Row. 1967).

21. S. Briar and B. J. Blythe. "Agency Support for Evaluating the Outcomes of Social Work Services." *Administration in Social Work.* 9 (Summer 1985). pp. 25–36.

22. T. W. Woods. "Developing a Computer-Assisted Data-Management System." *Education and Treatment of Children.* 4 (Winter 1981). pp. 71–86.

23. M. Spevack and S. Gilman. "A System for Evaluative Research in Behavior Therapy." *Psychotherapy: Theory, Research, and Practice.* 17 (Spring 1980). pp. 37–43.

24. W. J. Gingerich. "Meta-Analysis of Applied Time-Series Data." *Journal of Applied Behavioral Science.* 20 (January 1984). pp. 72–79; and K. J. Corcoran. "Aggregating the Idiographic Data of Single-Subject Research." *Social Work Research and Abstracts,* 21 (Summer 1985). pp. 9–12.

25. D. H. Barlow. "Behavior Therapy: The Next Decade." *Behavior Therapy.* 11 (June 1980). pp. 315–328.

ANALYZING THE FORCES FOR CHANGE
GEORGE BRAGER, STEPHEN HOLLOWAY

PROFESSIONAL PROBLEM SOLVING is characterized in part by the consideration of relevant alternatives and conscious selection from among them on the basis of understanding and knowledge.[1] In social work, assessment has tended to focus either on the service needs of specific individuals and groups or on the technical aspects of services and systems affecting categories of clients. While these are significant areas of professional activity, we believe that a set of concerns that might be called "political"—including the tasks of identifying potential opposition and support, negotiating an exchange of rewards, and the like—is no less important although it has been largely neglected.[2]

The politically oriented data required for organizational change purposes are especially difficult to obtain and appraise. Much of the information is uncertain or incomplete, and the wide assortment of the data further complicates the task. Information regarding dissimilar entities, at different levels of abstraction, having different direct or indirect impact on a change must be equated and weighed. Such disparate categories of data as the acceptance of or hostility toward the organization by its environment, the agency's structural constraints and opportunities, the interests of various individual participants, and the like must be integrated to allow even a tentative and approximate prediction about whether and how practitioner intervention will influence change.

Force-Field Analysis

Several devices for organizing data have been developed by behavioral scientists for practitioner use,[3] but, as noted in the introduction to Part I, we believe that the most useful conceptual tool for organizational change purposes is Kurt Lewin's force-field analysis.[4] Force-field analysis is a construct, at once both simple and comprehensive, that enables the practitioner to organize information in terms of its relevance for change. After the data have been considered in the context of a particular change goal, force-field analysis aids in highlighting areas of uncertainty, determining the feasibility of the change, and evaluating alternate interventions.

A brief summary of Lewin's ideas bears repeating. At the heart of his "field theory" is the conception that stability within a social system is a *dynamic* rather than a static condition. Seeming stability among the elements of social systems is, in this view, the result of opposing and countervailing "forces" that continuously operate to produce what we *experience* as stability. Change occurs when the forces shift, thus causing a disruption in the system's equilibrium.

Lewin called the systematic identification of opposing forces a "forcefield analysis." In analyzing a field of forces, a range of variables is identified which have a probability of influencing the preferences of significant organizational participants with respect to the desired change. Some of these variables constitute *driving forces* which, when increased, alter preferences in such a way that organizational participants act to support the planned change. Other variables constitute *restraining forces* which, when increased, reinforce an actor's commitment to the status quo or move him to resist the change; conversely, when decreased, they modify actor behavior in the direction of the desired change. By means of a force-field analysis, a practitioner can identify the range of driving and restraining forces critical to his goal and assess the interventions necessary to move them in the desired direction. The emphasis of this chapter is on the use of the analysis as a means of organizing data so as to permit educated—though necessarily tentative and approximate—predictions regarding the likelihood that a given organizational innovation will gain acceptance. Consideration of potential interventions is reserved for Chapter 6.

A number of steps are necessary to construct a force-field analysis in sufficient detail to guide the initial planning of a change. First, a change goal must be specified to deal with the problem or set of problems the worker hopes to solve. A second task is to identify those actors who are critical to achievement of the chosen goal. The worker is then able to specify the driving and restraining forces as they impinge on the relevant actors. Finally, he has to evaluate each of these forces in terms of their change-disposing characteristics. We detail each of these four steps in the following sections. First, however, we look at the matter of data collection, since the validity of the analysis depends on the accuracy of the information on which it is based.

Collecting Data

Since one is ultimately concerned about how organizational actors will behave with reference to a change proposal, the focus of data collection is on the meaning a potential change has for the relevant participants. In Chapter 4 we suggested that inferences can be drawn about an actor's preferences on the basis of his interests, that informed speculation is possible regarding the intensity of commitment for or against a potential proposal, and that initial judgments can be made about the influence respective parties have or might be willing to commit to affect an outcome. But these are only inferences, informed speculations, and initial judgments. They need to be researched, "felt out," probed, and revised before they become a foundation for action. The practitioner must engage in a search, employing the full range of information sources to which he has access.

The breadth of relevant information is wide indeed. As one gathers data, it is necessary to move from the general to the specific, increasingly narrowing the range of information that has special significance. The worker must also try to gather information in ways that will not commit him to a course of action until his change goals and strategies are well formulated.

Important sources of data are frequently a matter of record, an open file within the organization, and they may commit the worker to little more than the time they take to read. Statements of organizational mission and agency promotional material fall into this category and reflect what agency directors believe will impress significant publics. Past and present funding proposals are similarly representative of the agency's administration "putting its best foot forward" and may also be descriptive of program characteristics relevant to a particular change. Program evaluations, whether done internally or by outside researchers for reasons unrelated to the change, may reveal agency vulnerabilities related to the change proposal. They are often an excellent source of political information as well.

Administrative material is also useful. Annual budgets reflecting patterns of change over time highlight developmental trends and suggest the relative power positions of different actors and units. Personnel practice codes reveal a number of potentially important issues: formal authority arrangements, patterns of accountability, and sources of task ambiguity. Finally, policy manuals indicate not only the agency's rules but also which policies are in disuse and which rules are differentially applied depending on whether it is in someone's interest to apply or ignore them (and whose interest that is!). As a matter of fact, a critical element of information is the extent to which there are significant inconsistencies between the agency's self-descriptions and the agency's practice.

Another source of data useful in refining initial assumptions is the prior behavior of various organizational participants. Much can be gleaned from their past comments on organizational matters, the values they have espoused, and the positions they have taken. Further, generalizations can be drawn from patterns of an actor's associations within and outside the organization, his position on issues relevant to the change effort, instances of his creativity concerning change issues, and the degree of risk-taking he has demonstrated (and on which issues).

Observation at meetings is often a useful way of collecting relevant political data. In the meeting format those who possess a high degree of functional power tend to stand out. They are not necessarily the same actors who hold formal authority in the setting. High-power actors tend to talk more than others, their communications include more influence attempts, and they more often win their way.[5]

Another means of organizational assessment is to listen for complaints. They often pinpoint an organization's malfunctioning, or at least illuminate the bases of dissatisfaction, and therefore are revealing of possible forces for change. Similar data can be inferred by assessing what appear to be sources of difficulty workers experience in performing their jobs. In the same vein, expressions of hope, aspiration, or vocal "daydreaming" about how things might be are often reflective of potential actor interest in change. In listening to complaints or aspirations, however, sensitivity is required to distinguish between what people would *like* to happen and what they believe they have a right to *expect* to happen.[6] They are more likely to act in the latter instance than in the former.

These methods require no more of the practitioner than that he observe, listen, and hear. When observation is not possible or yields insufficient data, however, one must become more active in the exploration. The refinements of skill which are required to ask the right question and recognize the right leads in organizational practice are similar to those required in effective interviewing in social work, although the unit of attention is different and the information to be gathered is more politically sensitive. For this reason, the practitioner will try to obtain perspectives from a number of different sources before he draws a conclusion.

An illustration of active exploration, as well as of the risk inherent in this type of interviewing, is provided by the mental health worker from the Monrad Community Mental Health Center, to whom we referred in the previous chapter (pp. 80–81). The worker's goal, it will be recalled, was the development of a day hospital, and he was uncertain regarding the position Dr. N., the director of hospitalization services, might take. He used the occasion of a drive home from a conference to explore the matter with his friend Robert, who was also a trusted confidant of Dr. N.

> I began to discuss Robert's relationship with the Director of Hospitalization Services. Robert mentioned that he felt close to Dr. N., who trusted Robert's advice. He said that Dr. N. was concerned about the Center Director's plans for reorganization and how this might affect Hospitalization Services. I asked Robert what he thought Dr. N. would do, and he answered that Dr. N. was always looking for a new job in the event that he might suffer a loss in power.
>
> I asked him about the workshops we had attended. Did he feel that it was a good conference? He wondered why I was asking him so many questions. I said that I was curious if there were presentations from other psychiatric institutions about programs that we might use at Monrad. He said, "You mean a Day Hospital?" I responded affirmatively, and asked what he thought. He said that it seemed like a good idea from both a clinical and an administrative standpoint. Did he think Dr. N. would go for it? Robert answered that he might; it was hard to know. I asked how he would suggest I proceed. He said, "You need to plant seeds," and agreed that he would water them for me.[7]

The Monrad worker revealed his change interests in the interview, although he seems not to have intended to do so at the start. Because of his relationship with Robert and the positive nature of the latter's replies, the worker could move beyond exploration to forming an alliance. As workers begin active exploration, however, they also run the risk that they will reveal their change plans before they have sufficiently prepared for the effort. Depending on their audience, therefore, they must be circumspect in what they reveal. Had it been necessary for the worker to conceal his plans, he might have conducted the same conversation with Robert in segments that were extended over time, thus not arousing Robert's curiosity regarding a potentially hidden agenda. Practitioners must choose carefully—as did the Monrad worker—from whom they elicit information and opinion. The general rule of thumb is to go to friends first, neutrals next, and unknowns with decision-making authority last.

One other point is worth noting. The Monrad worker was well along in his thinking before he consulted with Robert. He had identified an agency problem that impinged negatively on a group of clients—the fact that day patients "fell between the cracks" of the impatient and outpatient departments—and had formulated a solution, the establishment of a day hospital. This highlights the fact that data collection, although logically a beginning step, continues throughout the change process and that exploration ultimately engages the worker in a series of actions and reactions, requiring further information, then action again, and so on. As we have noted, the same dynamic is true of assessment as well. Our discussion of the procedures in constructing a force field requires that we "stop time" to explicate the concepts, but we do not mean to imply that practitioners can do similarly.

The Change Goal

The force-field analysis starts when the worker has defined a change goal which has emerged from his identification of a problem in current practice. In conceptualizing a goal, elements are added or eliminated, behavior altered, or circumstances rearranged so that some future state of affairs is imagined which "solves" the problem.

Analysis is necessary, of course, prior to fixing upon even an approximate goal. In practice, analysis varies in the degree to which alternative goals are systematically addressed or emerge "intuitively" from long association with the problem. Ordinarily, some alternatives are dismissed out of hand as impractical or ineffective. This leaves a range of goals with varying potential for solving the problem and at the same time being acceptable to the organization. Force-field analysis might be employed at any point in this process of goal development (i.e., whenever the worker has an approximate notion regarding what he would like to achieve) or it may be used more than once to help him choose among alternate possibilities.

An example will make the point clearer. A worker in the social services department of a Veteran's Administration hospital identified as a problem the fact that patients had inordinate difficulty in obtaining welfare assistance. In addition to welfare-system obstacles, there were a number of internal reasons for the problem. The social service department of the hospital was unfamiliar with the application procedures; the social workers in the department were disinterested in the task, viewing treatment as a more appropriate call on their time; and the hospital itself was overly "tender" in its concern for how a sister public agency might view its pressing for patient interests too assertively.

One program in particular, the hospital's substance-abuse program, seemed a veritable Catch 22 to the worker. The inpatient phase of the program did not permit patients to leave their locked ward for thirty days, following which they were discharged and subsequently seen as outpatients. But many needed welfare assistance to begin on the day of discharge, so that they could find a place to stay, have money to tide them over until they could get a job, etc. This required that they apply in person—but because of their lockup, they could not do so in advance. Hence, they were unable to obtain the immediate help they needed. Unfortunately for her ability to have an impact on the problem, the worker did not have an assignment relating to the substance-abuse program. How to proceed?

The choice of goals was virtually limitless, and the worker had to begin to sort them out in a time-conserving way. Some goals were not even considered because they were patently overambitious. For example, as a Veteran's Administration line worker, the practitioner could not hope to reform welfare assistance policies, though this was clearly necessary, nor could she even expect to mobilize higher-ranking hospital officials to engage in a campaign for more sympathetic attention to their veteran clients. Typically, then, these goals did not even occur to her.[8] It is true that some workers think of taking on "the world" even when they are aware of the inevitability of failure. This approach, however, probably has more to do with powerful ideological or personal commitments than with an immediate goal such as helping the hospital and its substance-abuse patients. Such an approach often serves more to buttress the worker's idealism than to accomplish a specific outcome.

There was another range of goals, less ambitious than the first, which she did consider, but these were discarded relatively quickly as impossible to attain. The V.A. worker did not need a force-field analysis to know, for example, that a transfer of the substance-abuse program from the hospital's Department of Psychiatry to another department more responsive to patients' concrete needs was not within her grasp, although she believed that such a transfer would increase attention to their nonpsychological life problems.

It was as the worker developed potentially realistic goals—goals that were only as ambitious as the resources for influence she could muster to achieve them—that the force-field analysis became a valuable device. The V.A. worker's initial notions were twofold: (1) to work toward allowing substance-abuse patients to receive passes to leave the hospital at least one week prior to discharge in order to establish their welfare eligibility before resuming residence in the community, and (2) to ensure that all patients were adequately prepared for the welfare application process (i.e., knowing what questions to anticipate, what forms to bring). So that staff could better serve their clients, her secondary goal required the preparation of a manual on welfare procedures for staff use.

As she examined the driving and restraining forces for each of her goals, the worker realized that her wish to permit patients to obtain passes prior to discharge was *at that time* doomed to failure. Two major restraining forces were her own lack of legitimacy (she had no assignment in the substance-abuse program) and her lack of connections with staff in or relevant to the program.

Even so modest a goal as developing a manual posed significant restraining forces which might not be subject to reduction, as well as driving forces whose increase was uncertain. On balance, however, her assessment in this instance was to try, an attempt that was successfully accomplished. Significantly, her decision to work on the manual served to increase her own resources for influencing and thus to decrease some of the restraining forces that had prevented movement on the policy in regard to patients receiving passes. She developed a reputation as an expert in the welfare area, thereby legitimating her attention to welfare issues anywhere in the organization, and she also developed a close relationship with the social worker in charge of the substance-abuse program through contacts necessitated by working on the manual. In effect, the force-field analysis helped the practitioner to successfully engage a modest change effort and then to apply the acquired resources to take on a larger task.

There are several characteristics of goals which affect the likelihood of their adoption [9] and which must, therefore, be considered as the practitioner explores alternate possibilities. First, the more radical the goal—that is, the more it departs from common practice in the organization—the more difficult it will be to move to adoption. Conversely, the more a goal reflects current values, the easier it is to win support for it. A goal's complexity also affects the likelihood of acceptance. Innovations that require highly technical operations or call for coordinating the efforts of various specialities are, for obvious reasons, more difficult to attain than less complex innovations.

Relatedness to the problem to be solved is another characteristic of goals. The more directly a goal impinges on a generally recognized problem and the more obvious are its advantages over current practice, the easier it is to win its adoption. Goal relatedness is dependent on how the problem in question is experienced by other participants, but it has another aspect as well. When a goal's impact on a problem is immediate and direct, the goal is easier to implement after it has been adopted (see Chapter 9).

The issues of scope and reversibility are also important. The broader is the scope of a change goal, the more widespread is its impact on other organizational actors, and the larger the number of levels or functional subgroupings that must approve it; hence, the more resistance one might expect. Conversely, the more likely it is that the goal can be implemented on a limited basis or that its implementation can be reversed if necessary (as in a demonstration project, for example), the greater are its chances of acceptance. Finally, goal attainment is enhanced if the implementation of a goal requires a lesser use of scarce resources.

Keeping this range of goal characteristics in mind, the practitioner must attempt to refine his change notion into a goal (or goals) which can be operationalized. In the Veteran's Administration example, the worker's concern about the difficulty encountered by substance-abuse patients was translated into concrete conceptions of specific changes. Both the idea of obtaining a policy change that would allow patients to receive passes and the notion of developing a welfare-procedures manual were precise and specific, in contrast, for example, to a more global and nonoperational concern of "helping the substance-abuse patients deal with the welfare problem." The more specific the goal and the more it can be cast in operational terms, the more useful the force-field analysis becomes in determining its feasibility.

Similarly, goals often have to be partialized to allow effective intervention. A goal may be partialized by reducing its scope, thus reducing the number of people involved in or affected by its adoption. Or the content of the goal may be divided into developmental components (e.g., a two-, three-, or four-step process). In the previous example, the worker partialized the goal into two components. The development of a welfare manual was useful in its own right, but it also greatly increased the likelihood that the other component—obtaining a change in hospital policy concerning passes for the patients—would subsequently be accepted.

Once a goal has been considered with regard to its ambitiousness and defined operationally, the concern of the assessment process is then to locate the individual or group of individuals who have the influence to effect the goal and to identify the set of forces which, when altered, will modify the "meanings" of organizational events for the critical organizational actors so that the desired change will be supported. Thus, the initial assessment question once the goal has been determined is "What alterations in meanings for which organizational actors will result in the behavior changes that are necessary to effect the desired change goal?"

Critical and Facilitating Actors

For any change effort there is an individual or group of individuals who *must* support the effort in order for it to become a reality. "Critical actors" for a given change effort may include the agency administrator, the worker's peer group, or a supervisor who, if convinced of the efficacy of the change goal, *will be able to effect its adoption.* In any organization, the critical actors for a particular change effort will shift depending on the change being considered.

The critical actor is located by asking the question: "Who (or what group) has the power to deliver my change if he perceives it to be in his own or the organization's interest to do so?" Typically, though not inevitably, this is the individual who has administrative responsibility for the area of the organization affected.

We distinguish here between those who have the power to put a change into effect (the critical actors) and those who might be called facilitators. The latter are participants of two types. There are, first, those whose approval must be obtained before the matter reaches the attention of critical actors. (In some instances, to be sure, they are hardly facilitators in the sense that they may need to be circumvented to gain the notice of a critical actor.) The second category of facilitating actors are those whose approval, disapproval, or neutrality has a decisive impact on critical actors.

For example, in the case of Charter House, which we have discussed in prior chapters, the critical actor was the agency's priest-director, since only he had the authority to revise the discharge policy. But the practitioner who sought the change needed the approval of the social services department before the issue could even reach the director for his consideration. It was also clear that, because of the informal influence arrangements at Charter House (i.e., the long and close association of the director and child-care staff), the director would not approve a change if there was strong opposition from the child-care workers. In this case, the facilitating actors were the social-service and child-care staffs, or, more precisely, informal leaders and opinion setters within the two groups.

It is important both to distinguish between critical and facilitating actors and to recognize the part each plays in the change process. In large measure, critical actors are easier to identify since ordinarily they have responsibility for the area affected by the change. It is sometimes true that their authority is unclear or has eroded over time to be replaced by a less clear "common law." But who the critical actors are is ordinarily apparent to organizational participants after a minimum of exploration of the agency's authority system. The identity of facilitating actors, particularly those without formal influence (e.g., the child-care workers), requires more subtle exploration and understanding of the organization's dynamics. Since they influence the critical actors, however, the feasibility of the change and the actions that must be taken in pursuing it are importantly determined by the correct identification of facilitators as well as critical actors.

Who becomes the critical actor for one's change effort is partly a function of the nature of the change goal and partly a function of the structural characteristics of the organization in question. With regard to structure, our discussion in Chapter 3 is germane. The more complex the organization, the more likely it is that the critical actors will be numerous. As the task structure becomes more complex and the range of different professionals increases, the resulting interdependent responsibility necessitates collaborative decision making. By the same token, the more formalized and centralized the organization structure, the fewer critical actors one would expect to be involved in any given change effort.

Identification of the critical actors is also influenced by the nature of the change goal. Consider, for example, the situation where a change goal turns out to involve a critical actor who seems inalterably opposed to the change. It is possible to alter the goal so that it focuses on an aspect of the problem that is outside the purview of the nonsupportive critical actor and related to a critical actor who is more open to the effort. Perhaps more common is the situation where a worker enjoys high credibility with a particular agency official and consciously tailors the change effort so that it directly relates to this official's area of concern. In this situation the change is designed to have the "built-in" support of a critical actor.

In the Monrad case, for example, the worker developed his goal so that the proposed day hospital would be located administratively within hospitalization services rather than the organization's outpatient department. Among other reasons, he did so because of his greater access to Dr. N., the head of hospitalization services, than to Dr. B., the chief of the outpatient department. Another reason was his awareness that Dr. N. was more sensitive than Dr. B. to matters relating to his department's influence within the center and would be more assertive in pursuing the department's interests.

Developing the "Balance Sheet" and Analyzing Force Attributes

The force-field analysis proceeds with the elaboration of a "balance sheet" of forces, driving forces on one side and restraining forces on the other, as well as a specification of the actor or actors upon whom they are presumed to have an effect (Figure 2). In Part I we considered variables that influence organizational change—those elements of the environment and the organization, as well as the interests and influence of participants, that act as driving and restraining forces. The task for the worker at this stage of change planning is to translate these general ideas into a listing of particular forces that appear directly or indirectly to influence the preferences of relevant organizational actors with respect to the change goal.

The listing of forces must be as specific as possible. While a variable such as "the organization's ideology" may seem to be a driving or restraining force, it is too general to suggest interventions that might increase or decrease the force. Identification of a specific aspect of the ideology and of the particular actor or set of actors on whom it impinges is required to provide the necessary focus for practice efforts. Thus, the worker might note instead that "the executive director's belief in preventive rather than

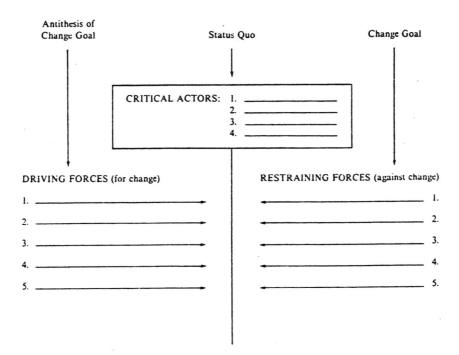

Figure 2. The Field of Forces[10]

treatment services and his commitment to increasing services to a low-income clientele" are driving or restraining forces, depending on the nature of the worker's goal.

To illustrate how this balance sheet is developed, we review some of the forces that influenced the Charter House worker's change effort. It will be recalled that the critical actor at Charter House was the priest-director, and that the worker's change effort involved revision of the existent informal discharge policy, which in effect enabled child-care staff to recommend discharge without substantive grounds and ensured that such recommendations would be approved. The worker's goal was to develop specific criteria for discharge and to involve the clinical staff in a broadly constituted case committee to pass on discharge recommendations.

A partial list will serve to indicate the range of driving forces: (1) The city's Bureau of Child Welfare, a major funding source, mandated the use of clinicians and was concerned with the maintenance of "standards" in its constituent residential settings. In light of the bureau's funding significance, this was a driving force for the critical actor. (2) The humanistic mission of the agency and staff led to an emphasis on the quality rather than the quantity of care. A proposal that improved quality of care would be predisposed to acceptance. (3) The absence of a definitive discharge policy created a vacuum which a new policy could fill, and the informality of the agency's rule system reduced the probability of fixed positions on the part of many participants. (4) The projected goal would have the effect of increasing the influence of the director of social services, and this self-interest feature was likely to move the director to support the change. (5) The idiosyncratic nature of current discharge decision making ignored the individual needs of the adolescents, violating the professional values of the clinical staff. It might thus be assumed that the clinical staff, an important set of facilitating actors, would support the proposal. (6) The change in policy would increase the esteem in which clinicians were held by increasing their importance within Charter House. This suggested that it would be in the clinicians' interests to support the proposal. (7) Child-care workers used the help of clinicians in handling difficult client behavior, and to the extent that they perceived themselves as dependent on clinical staff, their responsiveness to the clinicians' wishes might be anticipated.

Counterbalancing these forces were the restraining forces. Five may be noted: (1) The Bureau of Child Welfare was tentative in its relations with the city's major religious groupings and consequently granted latitude to many of its constituent agencies. This had the potential effect of blunting the possible impact of the bureau's professional orientation. (2) The love-care ethic that infused Charter House equated professionalism with a bureaucratic environment that was unloving and indifferent to clients. This would predispose the actors who shared the ethic (primarily the child-care staff and some of the administrators) to respond adversely to proposals that had a "professional standards" rationale. (3) A number of executives shared the nonclinical orientation of other organizational actors. This orientation was a restraining force since the proposal would be supported by clinical staff and involved clinical criteria. (4) An increase in professional influence posed a threat to the influence and esteem of the religiously oriented staff. Such staff might well associate any increase in the influence of clinicians with a decrease in their own influence. (5) The current discharge policy allowed child-care staff to control "acting out" children, thus enhancing their autonomy. The worker therefore expected the child-care staff to resist a proposal that reduced their autonomy in this area. Other restraining forces were at work as well, but these suffice to illustrate what might be included in a force-field balance sheet.

It may be noted that these forces conform to the environmental, organizational, and participant variables discussed in Part I. It ought to be clear as well that the interests and values of organizational actors can serve simultaneously as driving and restraining forces. For example, the need of the child-care workers for help from clinicians was a driving force, and their presumed desire for autonomy was a restraining force. Often a force field will incorporate a variable on both the driving and restraining sides simultaneously, since the variable may impinge on an actor's interests and commitments in conflicting ways. Similarly, the role of factors external to the organization may reflect two-sidedness on the balance sheet. As is the case with actor interests, the impact of a given external variable upon the change proposal in both a driving and a restraining fashion typically has to do with different aspects of the same variable. In the above example, the Bureau of Child Welfare's mandate of professionalism vs. its responsiveness to the religious community illustrates the point. The fact that these "ambivalences" exist offers potential leverage to practitioner change efforts. We refer here to the fact that each force, even if it simply involves a different aspect of the same variable, theoretically holds the potential for being increased and/or decreased.

Since the purpose of the initial assessment is the collection and evaluation of data in order to develop a strategy for the accomplishment of the change effort, once one has identified the range of probable forces related to the change, he is faced with the question of which forces to influence and in what fashion. We approach this question through a closer look at the attributes of the driving and restraining forces. Three are particularly important for practice purposes: (1) the forces' amenability to change, (2) their potency, and (3) their consistency.

AMENABILITY TO CHANGE

Amenability to change refers to a force's potential for modification, particularly the likelihood that the worker will be able to alter it—to increase it if the force is a driving force, or to decrease it if it is a restraining force. Forces may be amenable to worker influence directly or through the intercession of others (e.g., at Charter House, either the worker or other social service staff might become the primary actors in reducing pejorative judgments of professionalism). An objective fact may be involved in altering the force, or the modification may entail perception of that fact (e.g., the attention of the Bureau of Child Welfare to maintaining standards might be increased or the priest-director's perception of the bureau's interest in standards might be heightened). Since the concern of the force field is the reaction of critical or facilitating actors, for purposes of assessing a force's amenability to influence, changes in objective reality and in the perception of that reality may be equally relevant. Furthermore, a force may be increasing or decreasing as a result of "natural" (other than practitioner-initiated) causes—for example, if the Bureau of Child Welfare's interest in standards was increasing independently of the Charter House worker. A naturally increasing or decreasing force is as good as (indeed, sometimes better than) a worker-influenced force and therefore should be assessed as amenable to change.

It is difficult to generalize about criteria for determining the amenability of a particular force to worker influence because it is dependent on variables specific to the situation at the time of the initial assessment. Broadly, however, it is determined by the interaction of the nature of the forces and the resources for influence to which the worker has access.[11]

Our discussion of goals earlier in this chapter suggests some of the characteristics of forces that affect their amenability to change (e.g., the extent to which an increase or a decrease in the force will bring it into conformity with current values or practice, whether its modification requires the action of a few or many actors, etc.). Most significant, however, is the fact that a force is most amenable to worker influence when the proposed modification supports the interests of critical and facilitating actors—or when it may be made to *seem* in their interests. When changes are consistent with the interests of those who must take action or are perceived to be so, the less threatening the changes will be and the less resistance they will induce. Conversely, the more threatening the change is or is perceived to be, the more resistance. And the greater the resistance is, the more power, or resources for influence, that must be brought to bear by the practitioner. In other words, the characteristic of the force and the worker's resources for influence vary in tandem and, in their interaction, determine a force's amenability to worker influence.

Although it can be only approximate, an estimate must be made with regard to the probability that the force will increase or decrease as a result of the worker's efforts or of independent "natural" causes. On the basis of the worker's exploration, his experience with similar matters in the past, and his evaluation of the resources at his disposal compared to the resources of potential opponents, forces may be judged on a continuum from "high" to "low" in amenability to worker influence.[12] Thus, the Charter House worker defined the forces generated by the child-care workers as high in amenability to her influence; that is, their need for clinical assistance might be increased and the threat to the child-care worker's autonomy might be reduced. On the other hand, she deemed it beyond her resources to decrease the nonclinical orientation of the top executives.

If the worker cannot make the judgment of "high" or "low" amenability with relative assurance, he must consider the force's amenability to his influence "uncertain." The "uncertain" determination has implications which will be discussed later.

POTENCY

The potency of a force refers to the impact it will have on effecting the goal. To what extent will an increase or decrease in the force contribute to the desired outcome? Essentially, this is a measure of the potential strength of a force in effecting a goal. Once again, we may turn to Charter House for an example. If the worker's projected goal was not perceived as threatening by the child-care staff, the change in discharge policy would have a high likelihood of adoption because of the director's special relationship and sensitivity to the child-care group. The threat to their autonomy was therefore a highly potent force. Conversely, increasing the agency's commitment to the goal of quality care would have had a limited impact on the projected change in discharge policy, thus constituting a force of low potency.

Indicators of force potency are assessed by considering the sensitivities in the system. Which are the elements in the organization's ideology or goals that most move administrators, staff, or other critical actors for the anticipated change? Is their primary orientation to client service, esteem from colleagues, the maintenance of the agency or subunit, the advancement of a "cause," or self-protection? What is the range of possible pressure points (e.g., external and/or internal individuals and groups), and to which are they most responsive? The potency of a force will appear "intuitively" obvious to the worker who has done his organizational homework and who is sensitive to the impact of the economic and political variables explored in earlier chapters.

When considering the amenability of a force to change, the worker is measuring the probability of increasing or decreasing a force. When considering the potency of a force, the worker is assessing the potential strength of that force, once increased or decreased, in effecting the desired goal. Thus a force might be high in amenability and low in potency, or low in amenability and high in potency, or similarly high or low on both attributes.

Consistency

The third attribute of forces that is significant in estimating whether or how to commence the change project is their consistency. This is a measure of the extent to which the practitioner can depend on a force's remaining relatively stable as he moves into the change effort. If the practitioner hopes to increase or decrease the force, consistency refers to the extent to which the force will remain "increased" or "decreased" once the intervention has taken place. If the practitioner does not intend to manipulate the force, consistency is a measure of the extent to which the force will remain unaltered as one moves into the change effort. In the case of a naturally increasing or decreasing force, consistency would measure the extent to which the force could be expected to *change* at a stable and predictable rate.

In the Charter House example, the worker could expect that if the clinical staff's feeling that the discharge policy violated their value system became more intense, this increase of the force would be a constant one (particularly since it would be supported by other forces such as the boost in clinical prestige that her policy change would bring). The force thus had high consistency.

Consistency is the most difficult of the three attributes of forces to measure since it requires a fix on a continuously moving target, whereas amenability to influence and potency can be measured on the basis of the likelihood of their moving from one set position to another. Consistency in a force may ordinarily be designated as "high," "low," or "uncertain" in only gross terms. In deciding whether to proceed with a change effort, therefore, the practitioner would designate a force as having high consistency when there was no reason for assuming otherwise. For example, on the basis of sparse data, the Charter House worker had no way of knowing whether the Bureau of Child Welfare's responsiveness to its religious community would increase or decrease and therefore had to judge the consistency of the force as potentially high. If, on the other hand, there are trends or events that suggest the contrary, the force's consistency would be rated "low" or "uncertain" depending on an evaluation of specific elements in the trend or the significance of the event.

Past experience is the best predictor of a force's consistency. It is more easily evaluated as applied to the behavior of individuals than to structural elements. In regard to behavior, the practitioner can take account of the person's "track record" and the ways in which the change issue impinges on him. The worker may also engage in politically sensitive exploration regarding the actor's opinions and commitments.

Categorizing the Forces to Decide Next Steps

Having assessed the forces' amenability to change, their potency, and their consistency, the practitioner is in a position to begin to estimate the likelihood of success if he launches his change effort. His next step is to consider the *types* of forces that make up the force field so that he can judge the strength of the change-producing forces in relation to his goal. The likelihood of success depends on a fine balance between the nature of the goal (i.e., its scope, complexity, reversibility, etc.) on the one hand and the strength of the change-producing forces on the other. The more "difficult" the goal, the stronger the change-producing forces will have to be, and vice versa.

On the basis of his judgments concerning the attributes of forces, the practitioner has implicitly assessed the critical characteristics of the forces with regard to their usefulness and dependability in service of his desired goal. His estimate of their strength is advanced by an understanding of the categories into which they fall. There are three types: (1) working forces (i.e., potentially usable forces that the practitioner can try to increase or decrease or can otherwise count on to advance his goal); (2) framing forces (i.e., those that structure the change arena but are not directly useful in moving the goal); and (3) unpredictable forces (i.e., those that represent the measure of uncertainty or turbulence in pursuing the change).

WORKING FORCES

We define working forces as those that have been judged moderate to high in amenability to worker influence, potency, and consistency, and are thus the variables in the force field that can be put to use in a change attempt. The Charter House worker, as we found, deemed a reduction of the threat to the autonomy of child-care staff amenable to her influence and potent in its effect on moving her change in discharge policy, and she had no reason to question the force's consistency. Clearly, then, this was a working force.

Occasionally one finds a working force in his force field that is independently increasing or decreasing *and* is also judged to be potent and consistent. Even though the increase or decrease in the force is due to some factor other than worker intervention, since it is potent and consistent, it can be counted on nonetheless. If, for example, the Bureau of Child Welfare had been increasing its insistence on maintaining professional standards in its residential institutions independently of the worker's intervention, it might have had a significant impact on how the Charter House director would respond to the inclusion of clinicians in discharge planning and would thus constitute such a force. Other examples might be an increase in community good will as a new agency develops or a decrease in staff resistance to new forms of service as the merits of the new forms become clearer through the experience of related institutions.

There are also some occasions when a force is high in amenability to influence and consistency but low in its impact on the goal (potency), but the worker decides to try to influence it nevertheless. One such case is when there are a significant number of low-potency forces which, in accumulation, could have an impact on the change goal. The other is when there is little cost to the worker in intervening, other forces are not manipulable, and the low-potency force constitutes a step in the direction of his ultimate goal, albeit a short step.

The likelihood that a practitioner will reach the desired goal is directly related to the strength of working forces relative to his goal. Ordinarily, as workers assess a force's attributes, they are also implicitly considering the actions they might take to influence it. However, once a force has been defined as a working force, a systematic exploration of how to proceed and which strategies will be most effective becomes possible, since working forces constitute the core of a change strategy. The greater the percentage of working forces in the force field, the more likely is the practitioner to be successful.

FRAMING FORCES

Framing forces structure the field within which the change takes place. They provide a predictable context for the worker's efforts but cannot contribute independently to the accomplishment of the goal. They are, in our definition, forces that are high in consistency and low in amenability to change.[13]

Let's assume that a practitioner has informally scanned his organization and believes it possible to initiate a particular change. If the force field he develops involves only framing forces, the change is unlikely to occur since the forces are not manipulable and therefore offer no opportunity for worker intervention.

Framing forces may, however, be a dependent resource for change. When a force field is composed *mostly* of framing forces but there are driving or restraining forces that are amenable to change, the likelihood of movement toward the goal is increased due to the imbalance resulting from changes in these driving or restraining forces. The goal-directed pressure of a framing force on the "driving" side of the force field will no longer be so strongly opposed if a working force on the restraining side is reduced.

An example will make the point more sharply. Let us imagine that the Bureau of Child Welfare's interest in professional standards was neither increasing nor decreasing. Imagine too that it was not subject to worker modification. High in consistency and low in amenability to influence, it represents a framing force. But suppose, further, that one of the restraining forces in the situation—for example, the Charter House administration's nonclinical orientation—was reduced. In such a case, it is possible that the bureau's interest in professionalism might now affect the Charter House director in such a way as to advance the cause of the discharge-policy change. Although the bureau's position in itself was not amenable to the worker's influence and remained stable, a decrease in the nonclinical orientation on the part of Charter House directors might well move them to accept the bureau's standards and, by extension, the worker's goal.

In sum, framing forces structure the change arena and in isolation do not influence the accomplishment of a goal. When located in a field that includes some forces that can be modified, however, framing forces can contribute to goal achievement.

UNPREDICTABLE FORCES

We refer to forces of two types as unpredictable. The first are those that have been designated "uncertain" on any of the three attributes (i.e., amenability to change, potency, or consistency). The second are forces that have been ranked "low" on consistency (i.e., any force, however high in amenability to influence or potency, that the practitioner has reason to believe is unstable).

Where the attributes of the forces are uncertain, the practitioner may need to collect further information before he moves ahead. Indeed, one of the advantages of force-field analysis is that it impels a narrowing of the worker's focus to areas about which additional data must be gathered. Sometimes, too, when the amenability to change, potency, or consistency of a force is unknown, the worker is required to "test the waters" in order to glean the information he needs before he can make the decision to move on his goal. He would do well in such a case to proceed circumspectly, however.

Uncertainty is, of course, a fact of organizational life, and planning and decision making in the context of uncertainty have received considerable attention in the organization literature.[14] Nevertheless, for the practitioner who has exhausted the information available to him and remains uncertain after "testing the waters," a high degree of unpredictability puts the feasibility of his change and the advisability of proceeding into question. The greater the uncertainty, the less he is depending on skill and the more he is trusting to luck. In some change efforts, where the stakes are low for either the worker or the organization, this may be all right. Even here, however, there is some risk since a series of failed attempts has consequences for the judgments others will make about the practitioner's technical competence, political acumen, or both. When the stakes are high, on the other hand, ignorance of the major dynamics related to a proposed change poses too great a risk to proceed. Thus, when a significant percentage of the data related to his scheme has eluded the practitioner's assessment, it may be the better part of wisdom to revise the goal, postpone the effort until a more thorough assessment can be completed, or significantly extend the timetable, hoping that with the passage of time the field will alter sufficiently to make critical data available for assessment.

When the unpredictable forces represent a judgment of low consistency, the practitioner is provided with an index of the degree of turbulence in the system. A large number of such unpredictable forces augers ill for a successful change. As noted in Chapter 3, in an extremely turbulent setting it is unlikely that one can mobilize and maintain support for a planned change. And the more turbulent the setting, the greater may be the risk to both the worker and the organization of pursuing a change. A force field characterized by substantial instability or turbulence is thus not conducive to planned innovation.

To summarize: by going through the steps of force-field analysis—

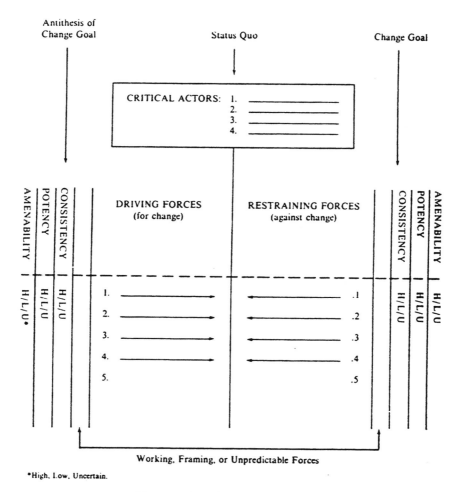

Figure 3. The Force Field Analysis

choosing a realistic goal, identifying the critical actors to accomplish that goal, listing the driving forces for and the restraining forces against, evaluating each force from the standpoint of its amenability to change, potency, and consistency (summarized in Figure 3), and then weighing the number and strength of working forces, as well as the potential impact of framing forces and the degree of unpredictability in the system—the practitioner can estimate his chances of success in seeking a particular goal.

It ought to be underscored, however, that the estimate will be a rough approximation; he will know, in other words, only whether his effort is "in the ball park." This is the case because force-field analysis attempts to systematize data that are at best incomplete or only partially systematic. Its usefulness is considerable but is also limited. For one thing, our current knowledge does not allow the full development and refinement of the variables employed in the tool. For another, the worker gains fuller understanding of the variables only as he starts his attempt to influence the process. As in all human processes, it is wise to anticipate the unexpected, and continuous re-evaluation is therefore necessary. Force-field analysis provides a significant theoretical starting point, however, and offers vast potential since its precision will increase with continued use, advancing knowledge, and refinements in practice skill.

In addition to its applicability in estimating the likelihood of success of a change attempt, the device offers a number of other advantages. Practitioners who invest the time and thoughtfulness in constructing a force field gain considerably greater understanding of the *overall* situation they face (i.e., the interrelations among discrete variables in the system) than if they had not done so. With continued use, workers also develop a *way of thinking,* a politically "conscious use of self," which adds to their tactical acumen in both current and future efforts. Finally, the analysis sharpens their focus on next steps. It allows the search for alternatives in regard to intervening to increase or decrease working forces, the subject to which we turn in the next chapter.

[1] This paraphrases the argument of Allen Pincus and Anne Minahan, in *Social Work Practice: Model and Method* (Itasca, Ill.: Peacock, 1973).

[2] While the technology is significantly different from that presented in this book, the field of organizational development represents an important trend in professional concern with issues of organizational change. See Richard Beckhard, *Organizational Development: Strategies and Models* (Reading, Mass.: Addison-Wesley, 1969).

[3] Harvey A. Hornstein et al., *Social Intervention* (New York: Free Press, 1971), pp. 531–52.

[4] Kurt Lewin, *Field Theory in Social Science* (New York: Harper & Row, 1951).

[5] Barry E. Collings and Harold Guetzkow, *A Social Psychology of Group Processes for Decision-Making* (New York: Wiley, 1964), p. 154.

[6] David Silverman, *The Theory of Organizations* (New York: Basic Books, 1971), p. 158.

[7] Alan Boyer, "Change at the Monrad Community Mental Health Center," unpublished paper, 1977.

[8] A disclaimer is necessary. We are describing the process as we believe it happens and indeed as we believe it must. We are not prescribing the procedure, however.

[9] Some of these concepts are detailed in Gerald Zaltman et al., *Innovations and Organizations* (New York: Wiley, 1973), Chapter 1.

[10] The figure oversimplifies the relationship of forces to critical actor; unrepresented is the fact that all forces do not affect critical actors equally. While some forces (e.g., strong consumer pressure or threats to continued funding) are so significant that they will have an impact on nearly all relevant actors, many forces (e.g., actor self-interest) affect critical actors differentially. In diagramming the force field, readers may find it useful to note which critical actors are affected by particular driving and restraining forces. Occasionally, the same variable will operate as a driving force for one actor and a restraining force for another.

[11] See Chapter 4 for a discussion of a worker's resources for influence.

[12] For purposes of decision making, we categorize forces as only "high" or "low." The "moderate" range must be judged to be either "higher than low" or "lower than high," thus facilitating a dichotomous judgment.

[13] From a practice viewpoint, the potency of framing forces is somewhat hypothetical. Although a framing force could have a major impact on a change goal *if* it increased or decreased, intervention is ruled out with regard to that particular force by definition since framing forces are both consistent and not amenable to influence.

[14] James G. March and Herbert Simon, *Organizations* (New York: Wiley, 1958).

CONCEPTUALIZING SELF-EVALUATION IN CLINICAL PRACTICE

WILLIAM D. ELDRIDGE

ALTHOUGH self-evaluation of clinical counseling has received increasing attention in the behavioral science literature, the research, discussions, and analyses are from a relatively narrow and premature perspective. (Clinical counseling is defined as face-to-face interviews with clients "to provide direct, diagnostic, preventive, and treatment services to individuals, families, and groups where functioning is threatened or affected by social and psychological stress."[1] It addresses itself to "the internal life of the client, seeking to modify maladaptive defenses and increase ego strengths . . ." and includes concern with "the client's interactions and transactions within his social orbit."[2]) Many articles on evaluation of clinical counseling have not demonstrated an understanding of the complexity of the subject or an appreciation of the individual process of self-evaluation. This article, therefore, points out some components of self-evaluation missing from the literature and discusses the complexity of self-evaluation. It then presents data that further clarify the dynamics by which clinical counselors approach and deal with their evaluative experiences. The growing concern among all behavioral sciences about professional accountability prompted the author to conduct a study of the process by which self-evaluation of clinical counseling occurs, because it represents one dimension of "accounting" for direct services.

STATEMENT OF THE PROBLEM

Self-evaluation of clinical counseling constitutes the relationship among the feelings, thoughts, and behaviors through which the clinician gathers and analyzes facts and makes decisions about personal competence and capability.[3] A study of the literature reveals that discussions of clinical self-evaluation have largely been restricted to descriptions of evaluative techniques, with little concern for the psychological gestalt or framework of the counselor's perceptions within which a self-evaluative technique is applied. Instead, the literature contains statistical procedures for behavior modification, single-subject (ABAB) design, contingency contracting, one-way analysis of variance for single subjects, and testing for means in single-subject experiments.[4] Although each technique is grounded in a traditional scientific theory of evaluation, the presentations often overlook the emotional and intellectual processes that counselors use in evaluating their work.[5] These processes constitute the personal framework within which methodological technique plays an interdependent and limited part. Proponents of self-evaluative techniques apparently assume that clinicians will simply insert the method into preexisting systems of cognitive decision making and reach conclusions once the evaluative process is somehow completed in the counselor's head. The erroneous hypothesis is that evaluative decisions occur in a step-by-step process of (1) establishing indices of client outcome, (2) premeasuring baseline behaviors, (3) conducting treatment, and (4) posttesting to note degree of change. However, there is no definitive evidence that clinicians make evaluative decisions in a systematic manner or that self-evaluation has anything at all to do with changes in a client's behavior. Indeed, the literature suggests that self-evaluation is an extremely complex and subjective phenomenon, not yet accurately defined, which is a function of numerous intervening psychological, social, and biological variables (in client, therapist, and treatment situations) whose relationships are also undefined.[6]

Scientific evaluation actually may not permit consideration of the full range of experiences and conceptualizations constituting self-evaluation, so that trying to use standardized evaluative techniques in a nonsystematic evaluative structure may be like trying to put a square peg in a round hole:

> Too often, social work professionals have relied heavily on [traditional scientific] research at the expense of evaluation. While the importance of research is indisputable, it alone cannot solve all problems and therefore should not monopolize the attention of social work professionals.[7]

The current crisis in accountability has illuminated the failure of traditional research to provide sufficiently relevant, effective, and efficient modes of inquiry into social services [p. 426.] . . . . The classical, academic "model" of research may be typified, according to its critics, as restrictive and unrealistic for examining and evaluating the issues, roles, functions and products of actual programs [p. 436].[8]

If one views evaluation as a systematic process of personal decision making that involves numerous components, at least two questions must be addressed: first, When are the evaluative techniques actually plugged into the practitioner's psychological system? and second, How do they interact with other components with which they are dynamically interdependent? Without an understanding of the process of clinical decision making, the introduction of specific techniques of measurement becomes a premature and possibly irrelevant contribution to the evaluative network.

SELF-EVALUATION

In their excellent book on single-subject evaluation, Hersen and Barlow emphasize that self-evaluative operations should be "clearly specified" and that measurements should be "done with exacting and totally standardized conditions with respect to measurement devices used [and] personnel involved."[9] These stipulations suggest that a standardized and organized decision-making paradigm undergirds the evaluative process. However, the subjective and complex nature of the clinician's thought processes makes it difficult to fathom exactly how to introduce evaluative techniques so that they both complement the decision-making structure and provide useful information for making critical judgments. Howe notes that the knowledge base for the evaluation of direct practice is "insufficiently conceptualized and inconsistently investigated" and that a strategy must be developed to study "what case-workers actually do in particular situations with particular clients having particular problems. . . ."[10] He might have added that knowing how they do it, and why, is also directly related to self-evaluative judgments.

In approaching the subject of self-evaluation, one must first abandon the notion that traditional scientific theory is the only framework for understanding the evaluation of clinical practice. Yet, as Suchman's statement shows, the highly standardized, formal, systematic, and mathematically precise principles of traditional science have spearheaded the development of single-subject and group-research methodologies:

> . . . we do not view the field of evaluation as having any methodology different from the scientific method; evaluative research is, first and foremost research, and as such must adhere as closely as possible to currently accepted standards of research methodology.[11]

In reality, however, many practitioners have not used single-subject or group-research methodologies, finding them irrelevant.[12] Although clinicians may understand the cognitive processes involved in scientific evaluation, they may be stymied in their attempts to insert scientifically based methods into nonscientific patterns of personal evaluation, an impasse

that may result in the rejection of the alien phenomenon—the scientifically based evaluative method.

Another approach to understanding self-evaluation is to view it as evaluative decisions that reflect interaction between personal "attitudes, values, and aspirations" and the sociocultural learning environment of the practitioner.[13] Each practitioner is a unique learner whose learning processes involve complex decision-making hierarchies and patterns. These patterns interweave social rewards for learning, psychological uncertainty about the value of the learned phenomena, the practitioners' feelings about their own level of knowledge, cognitive ability for different types of abstract and concrete learning, and philosophical differences concerning the relative values of learning "facts" as opposed to appreciating the "processes of thinking" for their own sake.[14]

The integration of learning and self-evaluation occurring at different stages of life changes the number of explanatory factors that are relevant, suggesting that the decision-making processes of scientific methodology may simplistically ignore the complex "how" of self-evaluation. The function of evaluative techniques may be drastically altered by the ways in which they are philosophically and cognitively linked to other facets of the learning process. Thus, the final decision is the result of the mixture rather than directly related to any one ingredient, much as a cake is the result of the combination and heat-induced interaction of eggs, flour, milk, and sugar, rather than the result of one ingredient alone.

The individual's personality development also contributes to self-evaluative action, motivation, and feeling, particularly as it concerns self-esteem and individual perceptual orientation. It has been suggested that self-evaluation is the key process in determining self-concept and personal esteem.[15] As internal and external (that is, feedback from others) evaluative experiences are combined, the individual develops esteem by achieving personally relevant goals, functioning in concert with certain values, and fulfilling standards of either personal or social origin. Self-evaluative processes, therefore, can mark complex relationships among internal psychological forces (that is, id, ego, and super ego) as well as between the individual and the social milieu.

As the self is being evaluated, the self-perception that evolves can be shaped by a combination of external and internal determinants that are interpreted by unique cognitive screening mechanisms within each individual. According to Brisset, competence is not only assessed in terms of goal achievement in the objective world but is also assessed in terms of the symmetry between one's conception of self and the manifestation of this self-concept through actual or fantasized behavioral outcomes.[16] It is not easy to acquire this ability to discriminate between behavioral goals for competence, as defined by self and others, and actual or fantasized outcomes, as these phenomena are somehow maneuvered through the psychodynamic system, to arrive at judgmental decisions.[17] Yet clinicians are expected to use evaluative techniques containing an inherent decision-making process, with total disregard for their own creative contribution to evaluation and on the supposition that evaluative techniques and the intrapsychic process of building self-esteem do not interact.

Marolla suggests that self-evaluation is a process whereby the individual "associates" (1) self-defined intents for action with (2) actual behavioral outcomes (for self—not for clients) and then assesses the feedback from significant others in the social environment as the outcomes are considered to conform or deviate.[18] He postulates that the environment has a significant influence on self-defined intents for action as one learns what one wants to do or how one wants to behave (based on personal and professional needs) to complete one's identity. Self-evaluation is the practitioner's mental measurement of the degree of congruence between intents and outcomes, and self-esteem increases as the two converge.

Although it is unclear where systematic measurement of change in a client would fit into this subjective evaluative scheme, it appears to add a fourth dimension or measurement index to the decision-making system, which can be set out in the following steps:

1. How do I want to behave? (desired clinical skills)
2. How do I actually behave? (demonstrated clinical skills as input to treatment)
3. How do significant others expect

me to behave? (relationship to consultant, clinical supervisor, or client)

4. How does the client behave? (results of treatment outcome through single-subject research)

The complexity, obviously, occurs as each practitioner attempts to weigh the categories and to compare their dimensions to one another for a final decision about personal competence.

Finally, the individual's philosophical orientation to evaluation itself as one independent variable affecting how self-assessment is actually conducted must be taken into account. Clinicians' characteristic ways of perceiving themselves, the world, and their interaction with the environment influence particular attitudes or methods of self-evaluation. Combs reports that effective counselors can be distinguished from ineffective ones by their "characteristic perceptual organizations," such as a "people versus thing" orientation to reality or a "growth versus controlling" orientation, because these and other perceptions represent the basic patterns that individuals use to view themselves and their world.[18] He suggests that counselors with self-revealing as opposed to self-concealing orientations are more likely to be effective in counseling relationships, are inclined to use different types of self-evaluative methods, and are more likely to interpret the self-evaluative findings in different ways. This theory points to the counselors' creative interpretation of evaluative experiences as a function of their psychological and perceptual orientations, and it means that evaluation is a subjectively interpreted synthesis of new and existing knowledge used to arrive at decisions about competence.[20] The use of a particular scientific methodology would only have relevance and meaning if clinicians chose to interpret or filter it through their individual perceptions of self and external reality:

> In general, inquiry has its origin in a conceptual structure. This structure determines what questions we shall ask in our inquiry; the questions determine what data we wish; our wishes in this respect determine what experiments we perform. Further, the data, once assembled, are given their meaning and interpretation in light of the conception which initiated the inquiry.[21]

The preceding discussion has attempted to illustrate the complexity of self-evaluation and to stimulate the reader to think critically about the relationship between scientific evaluative techniques and the psychosocial decision-making framework of the individual, within which these techniques are employed and interpreted. That the existential subjectivity of each clinician has an important part to play should now be obvious.[22] What part this is and how cognitive patterns deal with evaluative data have yet to be adequately questioned and investigated.

Clinical practitioners themselves struggled with the author to describe their own methods of evaluative decision making. A brief description of this research project follows, with a subsequent discussion of clinicians' responses to case study interviews as these responses reflect the difficulty in defining and explaining the experience of self-evaluation.

THE STUDY

The research goal of this study was to describe how clinical counselors evaluated their own performance and made decisions about their capability to deliver counseling services. Because self-evaluation is a subject that few researchers have studied, an exploratory descriptive design was used to "begin where the counselors were" in their unique approaches to self-evaluation.[23] The basic research questions guiding the inquiry were these:

• What were the processes by which counselors made decisions about their competence on the job?

• What types and sources of information were used, and how were they assessed and employed in reaching self-evaluative conclusions?

• What particular methods or types of thinking were required to assess evaluative data and to deal with various types of information to arrive at judgments about professional practice effectiveness?

A research sample of forty-five counselors with master's degrees in social work or psychology volunteered for the study.[24] They represented a wide range of ages, experience, employing agencies, and practice orientations (which were primarily ego-psychological and psychosocial). The majority had been in direct practice for five to ten years, with a few having less than two years of experience and one having more than fifteen years of experience. Their agency settings were varied, but mental health settings and mental health practice in other host settings predominated. All the practitioners were active in individual, family, or group therapy involving face-to-face, clinically oriented interviews with clients around a variety of psychological and social problems. No one refused to participate as all saw the research as a learning experience for themselves.

Although forty-five counselors answered a questionnaire describing how they evaluated their practice, fifteen of them also participated in intensive case study interviews to report self-evaluative thoughts, feelings, and specific behaviors. Nearly three hundred separate responses of these therapists were analyzed and categorized to describe varying methods of self-evaluation. Once these groupings were formulated through content analysis, a study of the frequencies of counselors' responses within each category enabled the author to draw conclusions about various components of self-evaluation.[25] Although the findings concerning types of performance evaluated and types of feedback from clients were interesting, this report primarily focuses on the counselors' personal descriptions of the process they used to appraise evaluative indices and to make decisions about their on-the-job competence. The findings are considered particularly reliable because of the extensive amount of time subjects spent in case study interviews and because of the advantage of the author's observations and interactions with the counselors as they struggled to describe their self-evaluation.

In none of the cases were the clinical counselors able to describe their specific thoughts, the interrelationships between ideas, their schemes for ranking or correlating different types of data, or the rational deductions by which they arrived at specific judgments about personal competence. Many of the counselors began by simply listing types or sources of information they used in clinical practice to form diagnostic opinions or to assess client change—for example, "clients' anxiety level," "specific pathological behaviors," "amount of delusional thought content observed during interviews," or "clients' reports of feeling better about relationships." Although these data were often precisely delineated and carefully collected, most counselors were then unable to describe how they assigned qualitative or quantitative values to various types of data for use in setting priorities on information so that decisions about degree of pathology, change, improvement, or regress, for example, could be made. Among the subjects who could describe systems for assigning quantity or quality to diagnostic indices (that is, numbers to represent frequencies of observed behavior or their cognitive ranking of degree of looseness of associations—"more abstract than yesterday's thoughts"), none could precisely describe qualitative or quantitative dimensions of their own input into treatment. Yet all agreed that they made self-evaluative decisions based on what they said or did during the interview process. Many practitioners said they felt competent when they "worked hard" in treatment, "listened attentively," or "confronted" clients—but how they related this input to clients' specific behavior remained unclear. All practitioners affirmed that input did, indeed, relate to client change, but they were hard pressed to explain how they related it to make evaluative decisions.

In some cases, the clinicians asserted that they felt competent in professional practice if they were successful in personal pursuits (for example, in "being a good father," "developing close personal relationships," or "staying physically fit"). What they were unable to delineate, however, was how they connected the three variables of professional input, client behaviors, and personal life accomplishments—whether through ordering, correlation, causality, significance, induction, deduction, congruence, deviation from norms, or some other means of associating one varying phenomenon to another. This was particularly evident as the researcher posed hypothetical changes in any one index of competence (for example, what would happen if the client began to get worse rather than better): the clinicians were confused as to how a change in one index would be connected with changes in other indices in their decision-making chain. They did "know" in their own "minds" that they could still feel competent when some clients got worse, but how they substituted other, more positive indices or altered perceptions of existing negative feedback was unexplainable.

Many of the subjects admitted that they had learned "in this business" to feel good about their work generally and that they knew they distorted facts, used fantasy, or perceived selec-

tively to make evaluation come out more positively. Again, however, they could not tell the author exactly how it happened that they knew it was time to alter their perceptions or how they used defensive maneuvers to block out some types of data or to boost the value of other, more positive information about practice.

From an interpersonal perspective, many practitioners used feedback from consultative, supervisory, or professional peer relationships for self-evaluation. But again, they could not describe the mental processes they went through to categorize and set priorities on external feedback, nor were they clear as to how this information was integrated with other types of internal feedback to arrive at logically derived decisions about competency. Most practitioners alluded to this process as a circular and abstract amalgamating of factual information and intuitive feelings, with decisions resulting almost randomly rather than through rational choice. Linear progressions of thoughts containing logical inductions and deductions, summarizations, and distinct points of decision making were never described.

The process of self-evaluation was, and remains, a complex and confusing interchange among verbal and behavioral observations, selective perceptions based on psychological needs, unexplained cognitive associations between ideas, interpersonal relationships, and perhaps numerous other factors that have not yet been identified. It is subjective, existential, possibly random, and certainly multivariate in its origin and operation—a difficult phenomenon to understand through either the introspection of the clinician or external observations by the researcher. Evaluating one's own practice is certainly a process within which research and evaluative methods and techniques can play an integral part, but where they are interjected and how they contribute to evaluative decisions remains to be seen. Any attempt to equate evaluative methods with self-evaluation is a serious oversimplification that can distort and obscure the actual validity and utility of the method.

CONCLUSIONS

One of the most important implications of the foregoing exposition is that clinical counselors and ther-

apists must become more fully aware of the total cognitive, emotional, and physical environment within which self-evaluation is carried out. This requires an appreciation and probing by individuals of the multivariate influences on how they define professional competence and how they cognitively and operationally pursue the process of self-evaluation. Because psychological and social influences differ for each clinician, introspection about the process of evaluation marks an important and difficult personal challenge for each evaluator. Defensiveness about personal competence needs to be reduced so that honest self-awareness can develop, and the practitioner must redesign personal prerequisites for reward so that credit can be given for the questioning process rather than for desired competency outcomes. The counselor must identify all beliefs, values, norms, and behaviors that stimulate feelings of competence, and then rank and qualify their degree of influence on the self-evaluative process. This personal framework for evaluation becomes the backdrop for comparing, contrasting, and blending each evaluative technique as a component of an evaluative scenario for each individual.

Directly related to the first implication is the need for practitioners, educators, and researchers to examine cognitive decision making to determine the degree to which counselors can be expected to make logical and systematic self-evaluative decisions. This examination is particularly important in honestly deciding whether evaluation of self can *ever* be a valid and relevant approach to evaluation of performance and whether self-evaluation has any real meaning as a measure of professional accountability to the consumers of counseling services. Personal decision making should also be compared to technical decision making using traditional evaluative methods, particularly in determining the success with which systematic methods can be integrated into less systematic and possibly even illogical processes of self-evaluative thought. All behavioral science professionals should be cautious in postulating the use of evaluative techniques for clinical counseling, particularly as preoccupation with the specifics of techniques can lead to spurious assumptions of validity by obscuring more basic questions suggested here.

Finally, educating is an important role for professors of clinical counseling in psychology, social work, psychiatry, and other counseling and human service areas. Clinical education must balance traditional concentrations on diagnostic and treatment methods or techniques with the strong emphasis among students on personal attitudes and on processes of evaluating those treatment approaches. To maintain a balance, the educator must resist student pressures to supply easy skills and techniques for therapy. It requires personal fortitude to examine skeptically those areas of self-evaluation that are more comfortably taken for granted. The educator must reject the enticement to seek realms of abstract and complex thought and must embrace the basic, simple, unasked questions that are the commonsensical foundation for the counseling professions: How do we evaluate? What influences the evaluative process? and How are evaluative decisions made?

Notes and References

1. Herbert Strean, *Clinical Social Work Theory and Practice* (New York: Free Press, 1978), pp. 35–36.
2. Ibid., p. 37.
3. William Eldridge, "Practitioner Approaches to Self-Evaluation," Ph. D. dissertation, University of Denver, School of Social Work, 1978.
4. See Thomas Kratochwill, "A Perspective on the Controversy over Employing Statistical Inferences and Implications for Research and Training in Behavior Modification," *Behavior Modification*, 2 (July 1978), pp. 291–307; Michael Howe, "Casework Self-Evaluation: A Single-Subject Approach," *Social Service Review*, 48 (March 1974), pp. 1–23; Sharon Hall and J. Cooper, "Contingency Contracting as a Therapeutic Tool with Methadone Maintenance Clients," *Behavior Research and Therapy*, 15 (December 1977), pp. 438–441; Lester Shine and S. Bower, "A One-Way Analysis of Variance for Single-Subject Designs," *Educational and Psychological Measurement*, 31 (1971), pp. 105–113; and James Higgins, "A Robust Model for Estimating and Testing for Means in Single Subject Experiments," *Human Factors*, 20 (December 1978).
5. Edward Suchman, *Evaluation Research: Principles and Practice in Public Service and Social Action Programs* (New York: Russell Sage Foundation, 1967); and Carol Weiss, *Evaluation Research: Methods of Assessing Program Effectiveness* (Englewood Cliffs, N.J.: Prentice-Hall, 1972).
6. Tony Tripodi, *Evaluative Research for Social Workers* (Englewood Cliffs, N.J.: Prentice-Hall, 1982), pp. 15–32.
7. Man Keung Ho, "Evaluation: A Means of Treatment," *Social Work*, 21 (January 1976), p. 24.
8. Melvin Brenner, "The Quest for Viable Research in Social Sciences: Development of the Ministudy," *Social Service Review*, 50 (September 1976), pp. 426–436.
9. Michel Hersen and David H. Barlow, *Single Case Experimental Designs* (Elmsford, N.Y.: Pergamon Press, 1976), p. 70.
10. Howe, op. cit., pp. 1–2.
11. Suchman, op. cit., p. 12.
12. Stuart A. Kirk, Michael J. Osmalov, and Joel Fischer, "Social Workers' Involvement in Research," *Social Work*, 21 (March 1976), pp. 121–124; and Aaron Rosenblatt, "The Practitioner's Use and Evaluation of Research," *Social Work*, 13 (January 1968), pp. 53–59.
13. Van Cleeve Morris, *Existentialism in Education* (New York: Harper and Row, 1966), p. 106.
14. See Pamela Landon, "A Correlational Study of Diffusion Theory in Social Work Practice," Ph. D. dissertation, University of Denver School of Social Work, 1975; Malcolm Knowles, *The Modern Practice of Adult Education: Andragogy versus Pedagogy* (New York: Association Press, 1970); and Cyril Houle, *The Inquiring Mind: A Study of the Adult Who Continues to Learn* (Madison: University of Wisconsin Press, 1961).
15. Martin Bloom and Joel Fischer, *Evaluative Practice: Guidelines for the Accountable Professional* (Englewood Cliffs, N.J.: Prentice-Hall, 1982), p. 483.
16. Dennis Brisset, "Toward a Clarification of Self-Esteem," *Psychiatry*, 35 (August 1972), pp. 255–263.
17. Lewis Leitner, "Discrimination of Counselor Interpersonal Skills in Self and Others," *Journal of Counseling Psychology*, 19 (November 1972), pp. 509–511.
18. Joseph Marolla, "A Study of Self-Esteem as a Two Dimensional Construct," Ph. D. dissertation, University of Denver School of Social Work, 1974.
19. Arthur Combs, *Florida Studies in the Helping Professions* (Gainsville: University of Florida Press, 1969), pp. 10–18.
20. H. Murray, "Vicissitudes of Creativity," in H. Anderson, ed., *Creativity and Its Cultivation* (New York: Harper and Row, 1959), pp. 96–118.
21. Joseph Schwab, "Problems, Topics and Issues," in Stanley Elam, ed., *Education and the Structure of Knowledge* (Chicago: Rand McNally & Co., 1964), p. 9.
22. Marie Wirsing, *Teaching and Philosophy: A Synthesis* (Boston: Houghton Mifflin Co., 1972).
23. Claire Selltiz, Lawrence Wrightsman, and Stuart Cook, *Research Methods in Social Relations* (New York: Holt, Rinehart & Winston, 1976), pp. 90–101.
24. Eldridge, op. cit.
25. Bernard Berelson, *Content Analysis in Communication Research* (Glencoe, Ill.: Free Press, 1952).

RELATIONSHIP: THE CORNERSTONE OF CLINICAL SUPERVISION

RAYMOND FOX

SUPERVISION IS A critical activity in social work. It serves as the nexus for the practical, personal, and theoretical elements of professional functioning. Much attention has been directed recently to the managerial functions of supervision. Numbers and accountability are highlighted, but little attention has been focused on the development of self-awareness and interpersonal clinical skills—the very lifeblood of professional practice. It is time that professionals reexamine and reaffirm the central goal of professional supervision—the enabling of clinicians to function to their fullest capacity as disciplined practitioners who have integrated the key dimensions of the helping role. This goal requires that supervisors interact with clinicians in such a way as to create a paradigm of the helping relationship. The medium is the message. In supervision, the clinician should experience firsthand the interest, empathy, acceptance, freedom, and openness from the supervisor that he or she is expected to deliver to clients.

The impact of supervision is dependent on how well the supervisor uses him- or herself and employs sensitivity to guide the clinician's journey in developing a professional self. The most important vehicle for this professional development is the supervisor's ability to model behavior, reflect attitudes, and explore thoughts and feelings that the clinician is expected to draw upon in his or her work with clients.

Supervision is a helping relationship. In the context of this relationship the clinician learns about the special form of listening that is the hallmark of professional intervention. If it is true, and this writer believes that it is, that clinicians must try to identify with their clients and somehow give them the feeling that they are understood, it is equally true that supervisors must identify with clinicians and somehow give them the feeling that they are understood.

The essence of successful supervision is nurturing the clinician's ability to trust him- or herself as a therapeutic instrument. For trust to occur, the clinician needs to experience his or her relationship with the supervisor as a process similar to that which he or she experiences with clients. If this experience does not occur, the outcome of supervision will be thwarted. If it does occur, stability and identity as a professional helper are achieved.

Insights into the Supervisory Relationship

Clinical practice and supervision are more than interconnected processes; they are isomorphs. The goals of both are to facilitate changes in thinking, feeling, and behavior by means of knowledge enhancement, example, analogy, and experience. Both rely upon the same premises regarding influence and change. Other similarities have been identified:

Both require a good relationship between a more knowledgeable "expert" and a learner. Both cognitive and emotional capacities are engaged in the two transactions, as an attempt is made to translate knowing into doing. The same psychodynamic principles apply to the two sets of relationships. In both instances, the learner re-experiences *vis-à-vis* the expert old established patterns regarding dependency, autonomy, submission to authority, hostility, competitiveness, fear of criticism and failure, as well as affection, idealization, and pleasure at accomplishments. Both are characterized by anxiety, fear, and resistance to change on the part of the learner. In both instances, the expert is prone to countertransference feelings, such as improper exercise of authority, displaced hostility, excessive narcissism, or need to nurture, all of which, if unrecognized, will interfere with the relationship. In both supervision and treatment there is an interpenetration of life and work which must constantly be scrutinized.[1]

Another similarity between supervision and clinical practice is that the conduct of the supervisory session resembles that of the therapy session. The supervisor listens and responds to what the clinician says, as does the clinician to the client. In the supervisory session, the clinician, in the role of client, is responsible for leading the session by providing relevant material, process recordings, and audio- or videotapes for review. The clinician is also responsible for raising questions. The supervisor, who plays the clinician role, tries to help the practitioner amplify the presented material and thereby gain insight into him- or herself.

The professional literature from the 1970s spoke of relationship as the vehicle through which both supervision and treatment occur.[2] Attention was also given to the "parallel process" whereby the relationship between the client and clinician is reflected in and has a direct effect on supervision.[3] In other words, when a clinician has trouble with a client, he or she may actually act like that client during his or her session with the supervisor in an unconscious effort to have the supervisor understand what is occurring in the clinician/client relationship. Other authors emphasized the therapeutic nature of the supervisory relationship, which may facilitate the clinician's continuing personal and professional growth.[4]

Although the supervisory relationship includes the various facets described above, it is also more and greater that what has been described. The supervisory relationship is the quintessential means for (1) self-development as a professional helper and (2) learning to comprehend the client. In brief, the clinician learns how to treat the client from the way the supervisor "treats" him or her.

Through the supervisory relationship, the supervisor helps the clinician to understand more fully and to use effectively his or her personality and patterns of interaction to help clients understand and express their own. The supervisor accomplishes this by providing an actual *in vivo* experience of empathic resonance for the clinician. The supervisor thereby offers a firsthand sense of the rich depth of the human mind, an appreciation of the strength of inner or intrapsychic forces, and a grasp of the power of the helping relationship.

Self-Awareness

Separating personal from professional roles and responses is a constant challenge for clinicians. This endeavor is especially difficult because clinical practice involves an interrelationship between life and work. Supervision helps clinicians understand and facilitate this task. It acts as a kind of quality control in the profession.

When clinicians are aware of who they are and what they are doing, they are sufficiently relaxed, clear, and open-minded in their efforts to understand the client.[5] In other words, it is impossible to be tuned into the feelings of others without first being attuned to one's own self. The clinician's personality, values, and sensitivity are the tools that help make him or her an effective therapeutic instrument. How the clinician uses these tools determines what happens in the clinician/client interaction. The clinician's own past and present conflicts may interpose themselves on functioning. They may hinder effective work as they compel and censor behavior, or may govern what the clinician perceives. Unless the clinician knows what is happening within him- or herself, it is tempting for him or her to blame clients for problems in therapy. When clinicians acknowledge and monitor their denying, distorting, and projecting behaviors and recognize their inner stirrings, they are able to use these processes to enhance their work with clients. To be helpful to others, the clinicians must resolve their own conflicts and problems so that these issues do not interfere with their ability to understand others. The capacity "to perceive one's behavior as objectively as possible, to have free access to one's own feelings without guilt, embarrassment, or discomfort, is a necessary, if not sufficient, prerequisite for the controlled subjectivity the helping process demands."[6]

Clinicians face a difficult challenge in their efforts to be responsive to clients without letting their own feelings intrude. To draw upon their feelings as a guide to understanding and intervention with clients, clinicians must know themselves well so that their capacity for developing relationships is increased, their ability to react consciously is intensified, and their freedom to make deliberate choices about how to respond to clients is enhanced. By knowing him- or herself, the clinician is able to creatively use feelings, thoughts, intentions, and motives to optimize the helping process.

Supervision enhances this opportunity by allowing clinicians to examine their beliefs and attitudes, to find compatibilities between feelings and behavior, and to expose and to scrutinize their basic assumptions. The goal of supervision is to develop self-awareness so that more disciplined and clearly directed work is established.

Through supervision, clinicians are helped to avoid the pitfalls of omnipotence and countertransference. They are helped to avoid feeling that they must solve all problems, feeling overwhelmed by elusive and unconscious responses to the client, and being discouraged by client reactions that seem uncooperative and ungrateful. When such feelings are left unexamined, clinicians may unwittingly reinforce clients' feelings of passivity and helplessness. Supervision helps clinicians avoid taking on the problems of the world as their own. In exposing to the supervisor their own reactions to clients, clinicians are free to attend to what is happening with the client.

Five Levels of the Supervisory Relationship

Supervision is an intensive interpersonal relationship that facilitates the development of therapeutic competence. Its principal goal is not merely training workers in skills or techniques to "do therapy," but rather enabling them to become therapeutic with others. Emphasis is placed on who one is, not what one does. Indirectly, supervision goes beyond conducting therapy by simply telling the clinician what to do or say. As with clinical practice, supervision involves a gradual modification of behavior and cognitive processes through the development of a relationship. The nature and quality of this relationship influences and shapes the clinician's professional self.

The effectiveness and success of supervision depends largely upon the ability of the supervisor to institute and to sustain a helping alliance with the clinician, which in turn serves as a paradigm for the helping process. Thus the relationship between the supervisor and clinician is not just a way to facilitate the acceptance of supervision; it is integral to the therapeutic process. Every action between the clinician and supervisor creates structures and patterns of learning and awareness from which arise organized, internalized representations of self-with-other. The clinician transforms interactions with and characteristics of his or her supervisor into inner regulations so that what is internalized becomes part of the structure of self and is integrated into the professional persona.

Supervision helps the clinician achieve this advanced state through five interrelated processes of internalization—intellectual learning, imitation, introjection, identification, and idealization.

Intellectual Learning

At its most obvious and uncomplicated level, supervision involves intellectual learning and didactic teaching. Its goal is knowledge enhancement. At this level, the supervisor appeals to the cognitive and conscious processes within the clinician. The supervisor involves the clinician in a maieutic dialogue whereby the clinician becomes aware of latent knowledge, ideas, and hunches. Supervisors provide clinicians with information, hints, concrete suggestions, and advice regarding case situations. The worker receives a direct and realistic critique of his or her ongoing interactions with clients as well as the effect of self on clients. This level of intellectual learning is analogous to advice giving, direct guidance, and concrete assistance in the treatment situation. Its purpose is to nourish a sense of mastery over the rational and tangible aspects of the client–worker interaction. In the supervisor's role of teacher and coach, he or she provides the clinician with technical assistance for developing and improving skills of treatment and recognizing the impact of "self" on that process. The supervisor performs this function by reviewing recordings, asking key questions, providing challenging and new experiences, highlighting inconsistencies, suggesting modifications, proposing theoretical formulations, reframing, focusing, and contracting.[7]

The supervisor also encourages the clinician to read relevant literature and research and to confer with available experts. Supervision involves asking the clinician to look at and talk about clients, particularly his or her interchange with them. Intellectual understanding is a necessary component in the process. It not only fosters "proper technique," it bolsters skills while focusing on increased self-appraisal and self-criticism.

Imitation

The supervisor also acts as a role model for clinicians by continually demonstrating his or her own practice competence. The clinician observes the supervisor in his or her dealings with clients, staff, and colleagues. Inevitably, the clinician appraises and assesses the supervisor's ability to facilitate communication, manage anxiety and dilemmas, encourage mutuality, and foster cooperation in working associations with others. The clinician is likely to ask, "Does the supervisor demonstrate how to be the kind of helper that he or she expects me to be? Is the supervisor keenly attuned to timing and aware of nuances? Does he or she identify and verbalize tension openly and deal with it? Does he or she behave as someone who has mastered the dynamics that characterize the helping process?" In other words, does the supervisor demonstrate warmth, acceptance, permissiveness, respect for the client, understanding, interest, tact, maturity, belief in one's own ability to help, trust, and generalized reinforcement?[8]

Thus the supervisor serves as an example of clinical excellence. When clinicians apprehend the supervisor's expertness, coupled with an intellectual understanding of the process, they are likely to emulate this behavior when working with their own clients. Imitation is reinforced when the supervisor shares with the clinician how he or she is affected by what is happening and inquires about the impact of his or her actions on the clinician.

Introjection

The third interconnected level of internalization is introjection. It pertains to the supervisor's management of the supervisor/clinician relationship itself, which involves mutual reflection on the dyadic exchange and how the supervisor handles the dynamics of their encounter.

The supervisor maneuvers to reduce anxiety and to convey an atmosphere of trust. He or she invites the clinician to share reflections about work with clients and, more importantly, about their immediate relationship. The clinician is asked to experience, examine, and talk about the problems, strains, and tensions in their relationship. Open discussion creates an atmosphere of mutuality and collegiality and promotes reflection and discussion about the meaning and the mechanics in the establishment and maintenance of their relationship. Through this kind of dialogue, supervisors assist clinicians in liberating themselves from responses that limit their work with clients. Together they are able to explore questions such as, "What can we gain from this experience?" and "What can we give to each other?" Building a warm, supportive environment with a sense of security leads them to an alliance that eventually permits the expression of the clinician's doubts and apprehensions without fear of harsh judgment.

No significant human relationship proceeds without conflict, stress, and stalemates. However, these problems can be moderated by the supervisor so that they do not constitute a constant or repeated threat and are tolerated and reasonably well integrated within the overall harmonious functioning of the relationship. In good supervisory relationships, anger can be expressed and responded to without overwhelming anxiety and can be resolved on a collaborative basis. The supervisor encourages mutuality and reciprocity so that barriers to their relationship can be examined and substantial growth can occur.

At this level the supervisor's role is that of medium—a channel of deep expression and responsiveness for the clinician. Immediacy and self-disclosure between the supervisor and clinician about their own conscious and transferential reactions to others and to each other enhances understanding of the therapeutic process. It helps clinicians recognize their own emotional reactions to clients and the supervisor, which in turn facilitates more objectivity in the clinician's work.

This firsthand experience of rapport in a relationship helps clinicians to analyze critically their own work. Beyond the specific factors of skill, method, and strategy, the process of establishing a relationship allows the worker to perceive and understand the helping relationship. The clinician integrates and assimilates the supervisor's finesse, which alters the way the clinician perceives him- or herself and interacts with others.

Identification

The fourth level of internalization, identification, is less conscious than those discussed above. Identification involves the way in which the supervisor establishes an alliance, stays in touch with the nature of the clinician's experience, and handles the clinician's vulnerability within this experience. It pertains to the clinician's sensitivity to the supervisor's empathic resonance, the supervisor's response to the clinician's subjective experience, and the way the supervisor conveys understanding of the clinician's prejudices, feelings, attitudes, and ideas. Through identification, the worker learns appropriate helping behavior. The worker "soaks up" the manner in which the supervisor empathizes with him or her and thus establishes the core conditions for change.

These conditions are described by Carl Rogers as congruence, empathy, and unconditional positive regard; by Hans Strupp as respect, interest, understanding, tact, maturity and firm belief in the ability to help; and by Beulah Compton and Burt Galaway as concern for the other, commitment and obligation, acceptance and expectation, empathy, authority and power, and genuineness and congruence.[9] The clinician absorbs and identifies with the supervisor's facility in emotional exchange as well as with the supervisor's ability to deal with sensitive matters such as dependence, conflict, and power in the clinician's relationships with clients and the supervisor. Identification involves transference on the part of the clinician and deals with his or her induced feelings of anxiety and guilt arising from the array of voyeuristic, autocratic, and saintly facets he or she experiences in the work.[10]

In essence, the supervisor serves as a mentor. Mentoring is like apprenticeship. What cannot be conveyed in direct ways is introjected by association. The way the supervisor manages his or her own as well as the clinician's complex mixture of roles, tasks, and emotions serves to instruct the clinician. More important, it impels the clinician toward greater resolution and compassion in his or her own functioning. The manner in which the supervisor relates to the clinician affects the clinician's perspective on the helping process and deepens his or her view of how a professional helper should behave.

By "tuning in" to the clinician, reflecting the clinician's emotional and intellectual state, and tracking the process of change in their relationship, the supervisor helps shape clinician's professional self. The clinician recognizes, expects, and predicts the supervisor's mode of operation, which ideally becomes an internal part of the clinician's own generalized professional identity. Over time, the clinician becomes increasingly discriminating in what he or she identifies with and begins to focus on features and qualities that are compatible with and enhance his or her talents. The attributes and qualities of the supervisor are integrated and are transformed into the clinician's own therapeutic style. Some degree of identification is essential for eventual individuation in the process of professional development.

Idealization and Mirroring

This dimension of supervision occurs at a nonconscious level in the clinician. It involves how the clinician intercepts the supervisor's accessibility to and utilization of his or her own vulnerability within the context of the relationship and how the clinician uses this to overcome self-doubt and develop a firm sense of identity. In addition to experiencing trust, warmth, and empathy, the clinician needs to perceive the supervisor's conscious and disciplined attention to his or her role as a helper. The clinician needs to experience the supervisor's vulnerability and sensitivity to intimacy.

As the supervisor transforms vulnerability into awareness and creativity, he or she provides a mirror for the clinician. Clinicians need to feel understood and experience a sense of affirmation, safety, and comfort as well as a sense of identity with the supervisor. Some of these needs for validation and affirmation are met through professional accomplishments. However, the supervisory relationship also fulfills these needs through the process of mirroring. Heinz Kohut pointed out that the healthy adult needs to experience the mirroring of the self by self objects as well as targets for his or her idealization.[11] The clinician internalizes the functions provided by the self object, that is, the supervisor. By drawing freely on his or her inner life, the supervisor reinforces and corroborates the clinician's self and role as a helper; by sharing his or her perceptions and subjective reactions, the supervisor makes it possible for the clinician to expose his or her own perceptions and reactions. In so doing, the clinician develops confidence. The supervisor provides a vehicle by which the clinician can internally maintain self-esteem and tolerate unavoidable mistakes and failures. As the clinician becomes more confident, he or she requires less support from the supervisor.

Idealization allows the worker to emulate the supervisor's own accessibility to self and consequently the clinician becomes more confident and flexible. The qualities of the supervisor are internalized and utilized for inner guidance and regulation.

Distinguishing Supervision from Personal Treatment

Professional development and personal individuation are inextricably intertwined processes. They are fostered in supervision by processes of intellectual understanding, imitation, introjection, identification, and idealization. However, to become a competent clinician certain personal needs, response patterns, and attitudes need to be examined. In the supervisory relationship, some confusion may result when dealing with these needs.

The goal of therapy is to enable clients to deal constructively with problems or symptom manifestations for which they are seeking help. The goal in supervision is to learn to become a professional practitioner. Although supervision is not therapy, it should, like many good human relationships, be therapeutic. Its goal is to alter behavior, attitude, thinking, and feelings so that the clinician can master specific techniques and develop a sensitive and understanding professional self. Thus supervision is analogous to the development of insight in therapy, although there are distinctions between the two.

One distinction is that personal change occurs indirectly as a by-product of the supervisory process. Supervision refrains from exploring internal dynamics and their genesis and is restricted to examination and analysis of current job-related interpersonal transactions. The clinician's self-awareness arises from his or her opportunity to discuss issues that arise in work with clients. The supervisory relationship focuses on professional identity, as opposed to personal identity.

The supervisor's function is to encourage frank discussion of the clinician's attitudes, actions, and reactions to clients and situations. By discussing the clinician's patterns of learning, self-awareness is facilitated. How far the supervisor goes in clarification of these patterns of learning depends on a number of variables, including the personality of the learner, the goal for learning, and so forth. The supervisor's role is to identify personality difficulties in the clinician and to enhance the clinician's alertness to what is occurring in the self and their relationships with clients. Ideally, the supervisor shuns the clinician's personality background and underlying conflicts and attempts neither symptom alleviation nor exploration of all personal feelings and thoughts. Rather, the supervisor addresses the clinician's blocks in functioning as a therapist by encouraging examination of the clinician's feelings toward the supervisory relationship when these feelings interfere with the clinician's effectiveness with clients and interaction with the supervisor.

Another significant distinction between the supervisory relationship and therapy involves professional standards and criteria of performance. The supervisor, unlike the clinician, does not suspend critical judgment. The supervisor continually measures the growth and development of the clinician against established professional standards—ethical, educational, performance, and practice. These professional credentials are established by governmental agencies and service organizations to assure quality in service through normative and operational controls. The supervisor is guided by these standards and controls in establishing expectations for the clinician to meet. This situation does not apply in clinical practice.

The character of the supervisory relationship is defined by its purposes, standards, and controls. In order to create the most effective climate, certain boundaries are established by the supervisor to ensure that standards are met and maintained. Nevertheless, the supervisory relationship is a human relationship developed through the mutual interactions of two individuals.

The supervisory relationship is the cornerstone in the development of effective clinicians. It serves as a paradigm for the clinician in his or her own helping relationship and as a vehicle through which essential knowledge is transmitted. In fact, the relationship provides the quintessential learning experience for the clinician. In the supervisory relationship emphasis is placed on the immediacy of the supervisor's presence and attitudes, rather than on skills or techniques. The relationship enables the clinician to enhance his or her observing ego and to integrate experiences into a meaningful system. The relationship does not merely facilitate the clinician's learning values, attitudes, and capabilities—it is *equivalent* to the learning.

1. Eva Kahn, "The Parallel Process in Social Work Treatment and Supervision," *Social Casework* 60 (November 1979): 520.

2. Rudolf Ekstein and Robert Wallerstein, *The Teaching and Learning of Psychotherapy* (New York: International Universities Press, 1972).

3. M. J. G. Doehrman, *Parallel Process in Supervision* (Topeka, Kans.: Menninger Clinic, 1976); Kahn, "The Parallel Process in Social Work Treatment and Supervision."

4. Harold Moses and John Hardin, "A Relationship Approach to Counselor Supervision in Agency Settings," in *Counselor Supervision: Approaches, Preparation, Practices,* ed. John D. Boyd (Muncie, Ind.: Accelerated Development, Inc., 1978).

5. Hilde Bruch, *Learning Psychotherapy* (Cambridge, Mass.: Harvard University Press, 1974).

6. Alfred Kadushin, *Supervision in Social Work* (New York: Columbia University Press, 1976), p. 152.

7. Raymond Fox, "Contracting in Supervision: A Goal Oriented Process," *Clinical Supervisor* 1 (Spring 1983): 37–49.

8. Enola Proctor, "Defining the Worker–Client Relationship," *Social Work* 27 (Spring 1982): 430–35.

9. Ibid.

10. Carl Goldberg, *On Being a Psychotherapist* (New York: Gardner Press, 1986).

11. Heinz Kohut, *The Analysis of Self* (New York: International Universities Press, 1971).

A FRAMEWORK FOR PROMOTING ORGANIZATIONAL CHANGE
GERALD A. FREY

Managing a social service agency is a dynamic process that requires ongoing modifications and changes in organizational policies. Policy makers, administrators, and direct service practitioners are responsible for finding innovative ways to improve services to clients. Because organizational changes may shape delivery of services, direct service practitioners are in a critical position to identify how the policies and practices of their organization influence the practice environment, and consequently, to identify issues and propose changes that will improve service delivery to their clients.

Unfortunately, promoting organizational change is sometimes viewed as a top–down process in which workers are the target of change (French, Bell, & Zawacki, 1978). Moreover, much of the literature on organizational change focuses on helping administrators achieve compliance from lower-ranking staff members for administratively designed changes, although a growing body of literature emphasizes change from below or from within (Brager & Holloway, 1978; Resnick & Patti, 1980; Weissman, 1973; Finch, 1976; Pawlak, 1976; Wasserman, 1971). Nevertheless, both administrative and line staff share the goal of effective service delivery, and the support of both are needed to promote effective change. Although practitioners may have viable ideas about how to improve services, many of them have no training in organizational dynamics and a limited awareness of how to promote change effectively from below. As a result, sound, creative ideas for organizational improvement are lost when they are needed the most.

The present article is designed to help direct service practitioners become more effective agents for organizational change by providing them with a framework for assessing the potential support or resistance that any change proposal may encounter. Although the article is specifically designed to help lower-ranking members become more effective, it is also useful for policy makers and administrators.

Assumptions

The framework presented here is based on several assumptions. Although some social agencies may have a clear set of policies and procedures that practitioners use to promote change, some authors assume that organizations are predisposed to resist change (Morris & Binstock, 1966; Hall, 1972; Johns, 1973). In order to develop an effective plan of action, direct service practitioners must be able to identify and assess those factors that are likely to support or inhibit the acceptance of a proposal. Consequently, a preliminary assessment of potential resistance is critical; such an assessment forms the basis for developing a plan of action that will gain support for change.

Second, it is assumed that every change proposal is unique. In theory, an infinite number of change proposals can be introduced to solve an organizational problem, because any organizational problem can be resolved in a variety of ways. Even proposals that are designed to solve the same organizational problem vary in their complexity, size, content, and costs. Furthermore, because organizations change in time, an organization's receptivity to change may also vary; a change proposed at one time may be accepted at another time simply because attributes of the organization have changed. Thus every change proposal needs to be viewed in its own particular situational context.

Third, it is assumed that the content and substance of a change proposal will provide the practitioner with clues to assess the relative impact that organizational factors will have on the proposal. This assumption highlights the need for each change proposal to be assessed independently of all other change proposals. One cannot assume that the factors that caused the rejection (or adoption) of one proposal will necessarily be the same for another proposal. Furthermore, the same factor, such as expenditure of funds, may be a significant barrier for one proposal but relatively unimportant in another. Thus the content of the proposal provides the clues not only to assess what factors are important but to help identify the relative importance of individual factors.

Finally, it is assumed that the practitioner does have a change proposal. Here, the difference between a change goal and a change proposal should be understood. A change goal refers to the general end, that is, the direction of actions that need to be taken to solve some organizational problem. A change proposal, however, consists of a specific, concrete set of recommendations that potentially can be acted upon. For example, a group of practitioners may be concerned about an agency's waiting list. Their goal may be to reduce the time that clients must wait to receive service. A change proposal, however, might be to add additional staff, change the intake procedure, or emphasize short-term counseling. Change goals tend to be general and abstract, whereas change proposals tend to be concrete and specific (Resnick, 1978; Brager & Holloway, 1978). Although the goals of a given change are important, organizational issues or problems are resolved by acting upon a specific change proposal. The content of different change proposals will generate different sets of issues or questions that, in turn, will generate varying forms and degrees of organizational resistance. Consequently, a practitioner can assess and anticipate the resistance a proposal might encounter only by analyzing the content of the change proposal.

The Framework and Its Use

The framework consists of a set of variables or factors that the practitioner needs to assess in relation to a specific proposal for organizational change. These factors are (1) perceived advantage, (2) effort, (3) risk, (4) sunken cost, (5) understandability, (6) ability, (7) depth and distance, (8) idea and ideology, (9) need, and (10) generality (Davis, 1971). By systematically assessing each factor in relation to a specific proposal for change, practitioners are able to identify potential sources of organizational support or resistance. The framework can be used to assess a single proposal or to compare two or more proposals designed to achieve the same goal.

The framework requires the practitioner to make judgments on each of the variables, generally ranking each from high to low. In some instances, the practitioner may not be able to make a judgment because he or she lacks the necessary data. This is important to know because it suggests that additional information should be collected before proceeding. The process of making these judgments also forces the practitioner to ask very practical questions. For example, in order to assess the perceived advantage of a proposal, one is forced to answer the question "What are the benefits of the proposal and who benefits?" Once the process has been completed, the practitioner has, in effect, taken the first step toward the development of a plan of action. As points of resistance are determined, the practitioner can begin to design alternative strategies to deal with the resistance. The framework focuses primarily on those internal factors that are likely to generate resistance. It should be noted that external factors may also need to be taken into consideration (Brager & Holloway, 1978).

Although the framework emphasizes potential organizational resistance to change, it must be noted that some organizations may not only encourage practitioners to identify organizational issues and problems that need to be changed, but may also have formal policies and procedures to initiate change. In such environments, the presumed resistance to change may be tempered by the philosophy and policies that promote change.

Perceived Advantage

The perceived advantage of a proposal refers to the benefits that a particular proposal has for the organization. However, not all proposals will have benefits for all groups in an organization (Brager & Holloway, 1978; Kouzes & Mico, 1979; Patti, 1982). In fact, a proposal may produce positive benefits for one group and negative benefits for another group. For example, a proposal to reduce the amount of paperwork may be perceived by line workers as a positive proposal because it reduces the amount of administrative work and allows more time for direct client contact. But decision makers may evaluate the proposal negatively because they believe that paperwork provides them with the information they need to justify programs and to secure adequate funding. Consequently, in order to understand the benefits of a proposal fully, the practitioner needs to assess the proposal from the perspective of three different organizational groups:

1. The decision makers: those individuals who have the formal authority to accept, modify, or reject the change proposal

2. The implementors: those individuals who will have responsibility for translating the proposed change into operations[1]

3. The staff: those individuals who will actually carry out or be directly affected by the change once it is implemented

It may be quite difficult to identify precisely how a proposed change might be viewed by different organizational groups, especially by administrative personnel with whom the practitioner may have limited contact. Nevertheless, efforts should be made to list the positive and negative consequences of a proposed change for each segment of staff, and, if appropriate, across organizational units. Unless the change can be shown to have a clear benefit to the organization and to the clients it serves, the proposal is likely to be resisted.

Effort

This factor refers to the amount of time and energy it will take to secure the adoption and implementation of a proposed change. Effort can be thought of as an organizational cost. Consequently, it needs to be demonstrated that the benefits of a proposal—its perceived advantage—outweigh the efforts (the costs) of the proposal

(Human Interaction Research Institute, 1976).

The more a change proposal requires a heavy investment of time and energy on the part of various organizational actors, the more difficult it is to sustain a high level of interest in and commitment to the proposal. Thus, its chances for adoption diminish. Although the literature on organizational change suggests that the participation of organizational members in the development of the change process is a critical variable in successful change efforts (Glaser, Abelson, & Garrison, 1983), it is also important to note that change proposals that require long, sustained efforts are more difficult to manage than are proposals that require less effort.

Risk

Organizational change creates uncertainty in an organization because administrators and staff can never be sure that a proposed change will meet its intended objectives. Risk refers to the relative costs that might be incurred if a proposal fails to meet its objectives. Once a proposal is adopted, unanticipated problems may occur during the implementation phase that may result in the termination of the proposal. One should pose the question "How easy will it be to return to a normal state of affairs if the change does not work or if too many problems are encountered during implementation?" Risk, then, emphasizes the potential negative consequences of a proposal (Glaser, Abelson, & Garrison, 1983).

In general, there are three types of "high risk" proposals. The first type includes proposals that, once adopted, cannot be terminated or reversed without incurring a substantial cost to the organization. Such proposals incur costs as soon as the decision is made to adopt them. For example, proposals that call for the purchase of expensive equipment such as computers, audiovisual equipment, or training materials are high-risk proposals because they involve up-front costs. Proposals that call for the creation of entirely new organizational units, such as an intake or evaluation unit, are similarly risky.

The second type of high-risk proposal must be implemented in its entirety. Proposals that can be implemented in stages are more likely to be adopted because they reduce risks to the organization (Brager & Holloway, 1978; Rothman, 1978). Initiating a proposal in stages can be done by introducing the changes sequentially so that each stage can be evaluated before proceeding to the next step, thus allowing termination of the proposal if unanticipated problems occur. Another way of introducing a proposal in stages is to introduce it on an experimental or demonstration basis in one unit or department of the organization. Proposals that can be partialized are less likely to be resisted (Rothman, Erlich, & Teresa, 1981; Resnick, 1977).

The third type of high-risk proposal conflicts with the dominant values of the organization and its members or the public at large. These proposals are perceived as too "radical" or "controversial," although such definitions are relative. Controversial proposals can potentially generate internal conflict among organizational members or cause loss of support from segments of the community. Thus the more radical a proposal, the more likely it is to be resisted (Rogers, 1962; Brager & Holloway, 1978).

Sunken Costs

A sunken cost refers to an organizational investment to support a particular institutional practice. Such investments may consist of money, time, or energy that cannot be converted into another type of resource for the organization (Patti, 1974). For example, an agency may have spent considerable time and money on staff training in a particular mode of therapy; such an investment represents a sunken cost because the cost cannot be converted into another type of resource. In contrast, the purchase of a bus is an asset because the bus can be sold and the funds used for other purposes. Proposals that challenge sunken costs are more likely to be resisted than are those that do not.

Understandability

This factor emphasizes the importance of communication skills in promoting organizational change. It has two major dimensions. The first dimension involves explaining the results one hopes to achieve and the sequence of actions that need to be taken to achieve those results. Proposals that require very complex explanations are more likely to be resisted than are those that do not. Consequently, it is important that one be able to summarize and condense complex proposals into simple language. In part, then, the degree of resistance a proposal may encounter is related to the ability of the practitioner to communicate its content in clear, understandable language (Glaser, Abelson, & Garrison, 1983).

The second dimension involves the audience to whom the proposal is being presented; that is, the practitioner needs to describe the proposal in language that is compatible with the values of the audience (e.g., technical vs. nontechnical language) and that will address their major concerns. For example, a proposal to establish socialization groups in a mental health clinic might be presented to the director on the basis that it could potentially serve more clients without increasing organizational costs. However, the same proposal might be presented to the staff on the basis that it allows for differential treatment plans. Both arguments are valid, yet each addresses an important concern of the two groups. Thus both the content (what is proposed) and the language (how it is proposed) can be important factors in reducing or creating resistance to a change proposal.

Ability

Ability refers to the capacity of the organization to carry out a proposed change. As a general rule of thumb, the practitioner should assume that any proposal that requires additional funds is likely to be resisted. In an era of scarce resources, many excellent change proposals are likely to be shelved simply because funding is not available. One way to help overcome this problem is to identify realistic funding sources.

However, the ability of an organization to carry out a proposed change is not always dependent upon funds. Sometimes specialized personnel are required (e.g., a psychiatrist to provide case consultation) or new skills may need to be developed among the staff (e.g., understanding how to use a new information system). In part, the ability of an organization to implement a proposal is related to the resources required and the extent to which these resources are available within the organization. In some cases, the ability to carry out a proposal may depend on practical issues such as the availability of space.

Depth and Distance

The depth of a proposal refers to the extent in which it changes the organization. There are three levels of depth or targets of change.

1. Procedural: proposed changes that seek to alter the rules and procedures guiding the day-to-day behavior of employees who carry out the policies or programs of the agency

2. Programmatic: innovations aimed at modifying the existing policies or programs that implement the basic purpose and objectives of the organization

3. Basic: efforts that are aimed at changing the core goals and objectives of the organization (Patti, 1974)

As the depth of a proposal increases, that is, as it moves from procedural to basic change, resistance to the proposal is also likely to increase. The more a change proposal affects the basic goals and objectives of an organization, the more likely it will also involve changes in programs and procedures.

The organizational distance a proposal travels is also an important factor in assessing potential resistance. Organizational distance refers to the number of administrative levels between the practitioner who makes a proposal and the administrator who must ultimately decide upon it. The greater the distance a proposal must travel, the greater the likelihood it will meet with resistance. In part, this phenomenon is due to the fact that as a proposal moves up the organizational ladder, it tends to become condensed, summarized, and perhaps distorted or altered (Patti, 1974).

Idea and Ideology

Idea refers to the existing knowledge about the content of the proposal. Innovations that have been tested are less likely to be resisted because data about costs, effectiveness, and implementation are available. In contrast, ideas that have not been tested increase the potential risk to an organization (Glaser, Abelson, & Garrison, 1983).

Proposals also need to fit the ideology of an organization or at least be cast in language that is compatible with the ideology of the organization. An organization's ideology consists of the belief system or assumptions that guide its overall operations. For example, some organizations value communalism wherein tasks are widely shared by all members. Other organizations may have strong commitments to various causes, such as the rights of ethnic minorities, women, or homosexuals. Change proposals need to fit the ideology of the organization in order to preclude resistance (Brager & Holloway, 1978).

Need

Need is an ambiguous term because it reflects subjective feelings and values. The "need for change" reflects organization members' sense that something ought to be done to correct a problem. Operationally, need can be viewed as the extent to which members of the organization share similar perceptions regarding a problem.

Need for change emphasizes the goals of a change proposal. It is entirely possible, for example, to have considerable agreement on the need to change certain procedures, but disagreement on the new procedures that should take their place. If the need for change is supported by a variety of members of the organization, change goals are less likely to be resisted and proposals more likely to be considered.

Generality

Generality refers to the scope of a proposal or the size of the organization unit that will be affected by a proposed change. Patti (1974) suggests three levels of generality:

1. *Component*: change efforts that seek modifications in organizational arrangements or operations that have relevance primarily for the change agent or for a small group with whom the change agent interacts on a day-to-day basis (e.g., supervisory unit)

2. *Subsystem*: efforts aimed at altering the arrangements or operations of an entire unit or class of organizational members (e.g., a department or all caseworkers)

3. *System*: efforts aimed at changing some aspect of the organization that will consequently affect all members

The more a proposal affects larger systems, the more likely it will be resisted. When the factor of generality is combined with the factor of depth, it is apparent that proposals that affect the goals of the organization and have direct ramifications for the entire organization will be resisted the most.

Summary

The framework presented here offers a practical tool for analyzing various resistance factors. Although more research is needed on the subject of organizational resistance, the framework has a number of practical uses for practitioners interested in becoming more effective agents of change. First, it alerts the practitioner to potential points of resistance or support for a given change proposal. Second, after points of resistance have been identified, the practitioner is able to think about ways to overcome resistance, which sets the stage for developing a logical plan of action. And finally, analysis can be conducted before a change proposal is formally introduced to decision makers, thus allowing the practitioner to anticipate potential resistance and to develop a rational, practical approach to overcoming resistance.

1. This organizational group is included because it is possible for an administrator to delegate the responsibility for the implementation of a proposal to a group of subordinates (e.g., middle managers, a task force, or committee). In many instances, however, the staff implement a proposed change.

REFERENCES

Brager, G., & Holloway, S. (1978). *Changing human service organizations: Politics and practice.* New York: Free Press.

Davis, H. R. (1971). A checklist for change. In National Institute of Mental Health, *A manual for research utilization.* Washington, DC: U.S. Government Printing Office.

Finch, Jr., W. A. (1976). Social workers versus bureaucracy. *Social Work, 21,* 370–375.

French, W. L., Bell, Jr., C. H., & Zawacki, R. A. (Eds.). (1978). *Organizational development: Theory, practice, and research.* Dallas: Business Publications.

Glaser, E., Abelson, H. H., & Garrison, K. N. (1983). *Putting knowledge to use.* San Francisco: Jossey-Bass.

Hall, R. H. (1972). *Organizations, structure, and process.* Englewood Cliffs, NJ: Prentice-Hall.

Human Interaction Research Institute. (1976). *Putting knowledge to use: A distillation of the literature regarding transfer and change.* Rockville, MD: National Institute of Mental Health.

Johns, E. A. (1973). *The sociology of organizational change.* New York: Pergamon Press.

Kouzes, J., & Mico, P. (1979). Domain theory: An introduction to organizational behavior in human service organizations. *Journal of Applied Behavioral Science, 15,* 449–469.

Morris, R., & Binstock, R. H. (1966). *Feasible planning for social change.* New York: Columbia University Press.

Patti, R. J. (1974). Organizational resistance and change: The view from below. *Social Service Review, 48,* 367–383.

Patti, R. J. (1982). Analyzing agency structures. In M. J. Austin & W. E. Hershey (Eds.), *Handbook on mental health administration* (pp. 137–162). San Francisco: Jossey-Bass.

Pawlak, E. J. (1976). Organizational tinkering. *Social Work, 21,* 370–380.

Resnick, H. (1977). Effecting internal change in human service organizations. *Social Casework, 58,* 546–553.

Resnick, H. (1978). Tasks in changing the organization from within. *Administration in Social Work, 2,* 29–44.

Resnick, H., & Patti, R. J. (Eds.). (1980). *Change from within: Humanizing social welfare organizations.* Philadelphia: Temple University Press.

Rogers, E. M. (1962). *Diffusion of innovation.* New York: Free Press.

Rothman, J., Erlich, J. L., & Teresa, J. G. (1981). *Changing organizations and community programs.* Beverly Hills, CA: Sage Publications.

Rothman, J., Teresa, J. G., & Erlich, J. L. (1978). *Fostering participation and promoting innovation: Handbook for human service professionals.* Itasca, IL: F. E. Peacock.

Wasserman, H. (1971). The professional social worker in a bureaucracy. *Social Work, 16,* 89–95.

Weissman, H. H. (1973). *Overcoming mismanagment in the human services.* San Francisco: Jossey-Bass.

STRENGTH OR PATHOLOGY: ETHICAL AND RHETORICAL CONTRASTS IN APPROACHES TO PRACTICE

HOWARD GOLDSTEIN

LANGUAGE, WE WANT TO BELIEVE, is precise. And if we append the adjective "scientific" to the language we use and hear, we credit it with even greater reliability. These beliefs are necessary to the extent that they help maintain the needed illusion that there is a semblance of order and logic in the world we inhabit.

Experience tells us, however, that language is neither precise nor transparent. More often than not, our words either do not reveal exactly what we want to say or our listener doesn't understand them. As an imperfect representation of what occurs—either in our minds or in the social, material, or organic world—the ambiguities of our verbal messages are accepted as part of living. In fact, the frailties of human communication add spice and richness to life; they press us to search for meaning and understanding of the nuances and subtleties that underpin our relationships with others. Indeed, there would be no poetry, art, literature, or biography—and perhaps no science—if words were literal representations of reality. The eminent physicist Werner Heisenberg (1958) observed more than 30 years ago that even the concepts, axioms, and laws represented by a mathematical scheme are actually *idealizations* that can be compared with the development of an artistic style. In both art and science, language is a product of the interplay between self and world that enables us to speculate about the remote parts of reality.

All this is by way of introducing the central theme of this essay: Tied to the ethical, humanistic, and professional issues that arise when we enter the lives of our clients are questions of the language that is employed (expressed in theories, concepts, and frameworks) to describe, explain, and deal with our clients' problems of living. Depending on culture, region, and other factors, ordinary people might make use of a wide variety of terms and images to account for their own or others' unusual actions or feelings. In the helping professions, descriptive/explanatory schemes typically express two contrasting points of view: one, a humanistic perspective that is concerned with processes of strength and survival; the other, a medicoscientific model that centers on classifications of pathology and disability. Clearly, each perspective poses critical implications for our work with people.

Given the polarities that each perspective represents, controversies about the strengths and weaknesses of either position have flourished in the literature. In this article, the argument (or perhaps more accurately, the polemic) focuses more on the rhetoric, the ethics, and to some extent the politics of each position. The basic assumption is that each frame of reference persists not because either can claim any real evidence of essential "goodness," "truth," or "effectiveness," but rather because each stands for a disparate set of assumptions about the nature of the human state expressed in language forms that typically are unquestioned and ingrained in our lexicon.

Consider, first, that the term "psychopathology" is a misnomer. Its literal meaning is "illness of the mind" (or if we use Freud's definition of "psyche," "illness of spirit or soul"). Because "mind" is an elusive and fuzzy concept that, in one definition, refers to the emergent properties of the brain (Gazzaniga, 1988), it would seem that the more precise term "neuropathology" should be used. However, this term is equally inappropriate because it refers only to the physical properties of the brain.

Yet, for political and other reasons that will be discussed, the term persists. In the *Diagnostic and Statistical Manual of Mental Disorders* (DSM-III-R) (American Psychiatric Association, 1987) the doctrine of the pathological model is inscribed chapter and verse, expressing the finely wrought elements that characterize human frailties and flaws. The resulting taxonomies become ever more persuasive and respectable, expressed as they are in the medical idiom. For example, in section 301.82, the Avoidant Personality Disorder classification commands more regard than do the more commonly used descriptions of self-consciousness, fearfulness, or shyness. Other nonmedical attributions pretend to be less pathological in scope; however, ascriptions such as "defense mechanism," "denial," "resistance," and "dysfunction" convey a quality of morbidity and defect on the part of the client.

On the other hand, "strength" and its many synonyms—competence, wellness, effectiveness, for example—is a more modest term that owns little of the authority of the tenets of pathology. As an approach to practice, it is not systematized or standardized by a comparable handbook such as the DSM-III-R. Its vocabulary, relatively free of jargon, sounds a lot like the language most people use in everyday circumstances.

Despite these sharp differences, the two perspectives do have something in common: Neither is securely anchored in fact—whether it be scientific proof, empirical evidence, or conformity with some established truth. As will be shown, both "strength" and "pathology" are terms that fall into the linguistic class of metaphor. These terms allow us to relieve confusion and say something meaningful and intelligent about otherwise baffling human conditions, which themselves are typically expressed in metaphorical terms. Rather than presenting objective facts, the client offers an account, a story, that is often peppered with all sorts of figurative statements: similes ("I feel like a lost dog"), symbols ("my mind is just a blob of nothingness"), irony ("my husband is such a sweet bastard"), euphemisms ("I'd call it social drinking"), and metaphors of all shapes and sizes.

Such vague and obscure statements require interpretation by the caring listener. It is when we ask *how* they are interpreted that the differences between the pathological and strength orientations come into sharp relief. And the "how" of interpretation is directly related to the "what for" of it. If the intent is to achieve the illusion of neutral and scientific objectivity—based on the assumption that the human state can, in fact, be rationally ordered—then the medicoscientific, psychopathological framework will suffice. If, however, the listener's purpose is to gain some grasp of the meaning and themes contained in the client's message—based on the assumption that understanding is inevitably subjective and tentative—then the humanistic strength orientation is called for.

The point of this preliminary overview is to suggest that our professional activities are not, as we would prefer to believe, rational consequences of a set of established and tested theories, constructs, and techniques. Rather, we are the inheritors of abstractions and concepts—a professional language comprised of value-laden metaphors and idioms. This language has far more to do with philosophic assumptions about the human state, ideologies of professionalism, and, not least, the politics of practice than they do with objective rationality. In general, the rhetoric expressed by the two perspectives inevitably takes the form of prescriptions for action. That is, they dictate (at least in broad terms) the professional's role *vis-à-vis* that of the client. In so doing, unavoidable ethical questions arise concerning the allocation of power and authority (and the matter of self-determination) in the helping experience. In the case of a medicoscientific approach to practice, what are the limits of power and authority that ought to be assumed by the expert? Or in the case

of the humanistic, strength-oriented approach, how much power and authority, seen as natural conditions of the helping process, can reasonably be shared by client and worker?

With these questions in mind, the balance of this article will attempt to cast light on the premises sketched thus far. First, I will develop the proposition that neither the concepts of pathology nor those of strength are objective facts but are, instead, social constructions that reflect public and professional attitudes and beliefs. Second, I will consider how well each of these models and their constructions serve us in our work with people, that is, the extent to which they approximate the types of human circumstances we encounter in practice. As a consequence of this analysis, consideration will be given to the influence of these models on the ethical and political climate of the practitioner–client relationship.

Before proceeding with this analysis, it is important to qualify the discussion of how these models might affect practice (taking account of the practitioner's role, status, and actions). First, the comparison of the two models is framed in polar terms to elucidate their essential contrasts. Second, they are considered in prototypical terms in order to show what each form of practice would look like if its contours and roles were adhered to by the practitioner. It is doubtful, however, that these conditions would actually reflect any one practice event. A considerable gap exists between workers' expressed commitment to a particular theory and the way they implement such theory in practice.

Strength and Pathology as Social Constructions

As defined by Gergen (1985), social constructionist inquiry attempts to understand the processes by which people explain and define themselves and their world. Dismissing the notion that a firm and objective basis exists for conventional knowledge and language, social constructionism argues that the terms by which the world is understood are social artifacts, the products of cultural, symbolic, and historical interchanges among people. Such artifacts have currency only as long as there is consensus about their value: Quite simply, we continue to depend on conventional knowledge and language as long as they serve our varied social, adaptive, and professional purposes.

Consider, from a social constructionist perspective, the language of the two models in order to determine what they imply about the human condition. By definition, "strength" and "pathology" denote antithetical states of being. According to *Webster's Third Dictionary*, the former refers to moral courage, fortitude, physical force, and vigor, among other qualities. Pathology, in contrast, covers abnormality, disorder, and disease.

With regard to the current usage of these

terms, the contrasts become even more striking when we examine their root derivations. "Strength" derives from Anglo-Saxon, an earthy and unadorned language that depicts the natural world of living. Etymologically, it is related to other terms that express normalcy, assertiveness, proactivity, and integrity. Pathology, in contrast, derives from the early Greek, which tends to be more scholarly, abstract, and in some ways detached from worldly experience. Its root is *pathos*, which connotes suffering, endurance, and sorrow.

Because the social constructions we inherit are rarely subject to inquiry it is important to ask how the biomedical term "pathology" came to be applied to something as ambiguous as human mental states. Although the term has a long history of use in general medicine, it was not used by medical psychiatry until the mid-19th century. At that point, the adoption of the term pathology by the psychiatric profession was based more on political than medical reasons. It had the effect of abolishing the perspectives of strength and normalcy that had characterized the way psychiatry was practiced up to that time.

Until the mid-19th century, psychiatry was somewhat philosophical and romantic. In ways that we might now see as quaint and arcane, various forms of prescientific psychiatry anticipated modern humanistic and cognitive psychology. Some of its practitioners used forms of what now is called psychodrama for "reeducation of perceptions." Others viewed health as being consonant with freedom and perfectibility; thus, mental illness was considered to be a result of loss of freedom and self-control. Still others considered one's mental state to be inextricably linked to personal morality. Although psychiatry was certainly idiosyncratic during this era, its various practitioners did share a common conviction that mind and body constituted an inseparable whole (a system), that psychiatric classifications should not be trusted, and that each individual deserved to be understood in his or her own right (Ellenberger, 1970).

By mid-century, however, the work of these pioneers fell into disrepute or oblivion as the study of brain anatomy took over and the positivistic sciences came into ascendance. During this scientific revolution, medicine became institutionalized and standardized, and mental disorders were formalized under medical terminology (Ellenberger, 1970).

Becker (1964) sums up these events in tracing the ascendance of medical psychiatry and its annexation of mental malfunctioning as a medical prerogative.

Nineteenth-century diagnosticians redoubled efforts to keep man under medical wraps and dress his behavior disorder in Greco-Latin cant. Thus the science that knew least about total symbolic man and most about the animal body fully established its sacrosanct domain. We are coming to know that it had no business there . . . The result of this lopsided jurisdictional development was that human malfunction has continued to be treated largely in nineteenth century disease categories up to the present day (pp. 9–10).

In contrast, strength as a social construction did not have to be invented and therefore offers less historical or political interest. Nevertheless, this unpretentious term, tied as it is to judgments of virtue, willpower, integrity, and fortitude, has long been used by individuals, groups, and cultures as a metaphor to define character and worth. Often, we use the term in private moments to rate and evaluate our ability to cope with and survive the travails of living. It is a universal, unsophisticated term that requires little interpretation. And, as an estimate of personal worth and ability, it is a powerful term. We are, for example, more cautious about telling a troubled friend that he or she lacks the strength to cope than in suggesting that he or she may be suffering from depression, anxiety, or some other psychological disorder.

In this regard, the two metaphors clearly stand for much more than their semantic and rhetorical differences. More than just speculative theoretical abstractions about the human state, they have a functional purpose insofar as they are intended as guides for how practitioners ought to think about and therefore deal with the circumstances they encounter. For example, the medico-diagnostic labels that are appended to particular mental states or behaviors purport to be purely descriptive and, therefore, meaning-less and value-free. In other words, the diagnosis of schizophrenia or behavior disorder ought to have the same order of scientific objectivity accorded to it as, say, a diagnosis of arthritis or anemia. We know, however, this is not the case; as Sontag (1977) observes, even physical illnesses such as cancer and tuberculosis have long been used as metaphors for all sorts of social and political purposes. Such uses are possible as a result of the reductionistic quality of the diagnostic process, whereby utterly complex human conditions are narrowly enveloped in a specific category.

Labeling theory tells us that people bearing particular psychiatric diagnoses are likely to be subjected to judgments and attitudes that further embellish the caste in which the patient has already been installed. Such attributions may be outwardly benign, as when we see the individual as a patient, a victim, or in need of care; or they might be alienating, as when a person is seen as deviant, dangerous, or just plain crazy. In short, medicoscientific classifications are readily transformed into yet other powerful social constructions. They not only define one's station, but can also serve as a justification for control of the client and the right of the practitioner to determine how the client ought to be regarded and treated.

On the other hand, the metaphor "strength" is frankly a value-laden, subjective term in that it reflects a judgment made in accord with certain personal or social norms and standards. At the same time, it is an expansive rather than a reductionistic concept. When we attempt to gauge another person's attributes in a fair and caring fashion, we are bound to take into account a number of mitigating human and social factors. Some examples include *context* (the peculiar circumstances surrounding the person), *history* (awareness of how he or she has coped with dilemmas in the past), *potential* (indices of untapped capabilities), *expectations* (what the individual hopes for and wants), *meaning* (personal interpretations of his or her state), and *relationship* (how we perceive and value one another). Overarching these judgments is the process of *introspection*, our personal and humble reflections about the extent to which we can really comprehend another's life.

It follows that because our language of perception and understanding determines how we act, the worker's active role in the helping process is influenced by his or her choice of model and metaphor. Out of this choice emerges a peculiar social arrangement (more commonly called therapy, counseling, or treatment relationship) that begins to inform and influence the client in ways that are not immediately apparent.

For example, if I, as the worker, focus more on your problems and disabilities than on your strengths, my perceptions will narrow as I search for clues and causes to figure out what you and I will need to do to resolve or cure your malaise. However, if I am persuaded by your strengths and fortitude, then my scope will broaden as I attempt to learn from you how you have survived thus far and where you believe we ought to be heading in our work together. Although I am not uninterested in your distress, my inquiry would include and reach beyond the central problem to understand what keeps you going. If how we understand determines how we act, how we act, in turn, influences the response of the other in the human relationship that begins to take shape.

In the first instance, the focus on problems and inadequacies creates an analogue of distance and control. The posture of detached objectivity required to construct a "case history" and diagnose another person's condition poses the risk of creating an aura of separateness. Such an approach becomes even more elitist if I intimate that I have the special knowledge of professionalism, which grants me the authority to define your problems and, from this definition, determine the plan that should produce the desired results. A *moral* and *ethical* distance might also result from such an outlook, particularly when questions of personal responsibility are diffused by my clinical lens.

Conversely, a more egalitarian relationship becomes possible when I am intrigued by the remnants of hope and vision that you harbor as faint shadows of your strength. Your story interests me, not as a set of facts to be ordered into a rational explanation of your problem, but as a personal narrative that expresses the meaning of your existence. Thus, I invite you to regard me as a comrade moreso than as an expert in our endeavor to set the ethical, moral, and value terms of our relationship.

Thus far, I have tried to show that within the culture that we call social work and human service, the ritual terms that shape theory and practice are not precise concepts purified by the scientific method but rather socially constructed abstractions. These constructions have something to say about the allocation of power, authority, personal rights and obligations, and self-determination. As well-meaning as a preoccupation with problems and deficits may be, this focus can lead to an uneven distribution of power and control. In its most elemental form, a relationship that focuses on one member's failings or pathology must, in some way, elevate the other's power and status. Conversely, a strength-oriented relationship by its nature and intent presses for equality and sharing. The helping relationship, typically thought of as benign and altruistic, can also embrace the political attributes of authority and control.

Pathology and Strength as Models Of Practice: Which Fits Better?

The argument takes a different turn, however, when we ask which model more accurately corresponds with the structure and processes of the change experience itself. This question leads to an even more elemental question that, as yet, has not produced conclusive answers: What is the nature of the change experience and how does it unfold?

Over the past decades, the evolution of systems of change has shown a greater resemblance to the fashion industry than to progress in science. Rather than progressing in an incremental manner built on research and scholarship, a series of alternating shifts in prevailing paradigms—or more accurately, ideologies, styles, and fads—has occurred.

In his book *A Dialectical Psychology*, Buss (1979) explains the complexities of these swings by observing that they involve radical shifts between two prototypical statements: (1) person constructs reality and (2) reality constructs person. To illustrate this argument, he shows that in psychology, early structuralism was replaced by Watsonian behaviorism, which in turn was succeeded by cognitive psychology—a shift from person creates reality to reality creates person and back again. At the same time, humanistic or third-force psychology (person constructs reality) was a reaction to psychoanalysis and behaviorism, both of which, in their respective ways, express the statement that reality constructs the person. Each of these shifts represented something less than an improvement in theory or research. More to the point, they posed contrasting ideological or philosophical positions about questions of brain versus mind, biology versus culture, determinism versus free will, cause versus function, and reality as fact versus reality as a construction.

This dualistic, either–or debate has proved to be futile. It is apparent that person and reality have a dialectical rather than a linear relationship. Our best understanding of how people live and change (in and out of the helping relationship) comes from our appreciation of the process that is created when person and environment converge.

One reason that the either–or debate has persisted is because the dynamics of this convergence are easier to label than they are to define and comprehend. To be sure, we have a number of handy terms such as interface, dialectic, person-in-situation, and transaction to describe this dialectic, but these terms are about as informative for social work purposes as are terms such as Big Bang, quarks, and black holes are for understanding the universe. In both instances, the use of these terms shows more sophistication than substance.

The dilemma, it seems to me, reflects the tacit problems of language, concepts, and the assumptions that have been willed to us. First of all, although any one human experience is a unitary, holistic event, the language that we use to report it is, by its nature, linear: the description follows a sequential line, *as if* thoughts, feelings, and actions unrolled like a carpet. Not by coincidence, our horizons of understanding are also cramped by the concepts that we have inherited, which are also linear in nature. If life is defined as a chain of events, then this chain is forged by the idea that every effect must have its cause. In other words, if one behaves, thinks, or feels in a peculiar way, then we naturally assume some predisposing conditions exist and that this cause—whether we call it repression, trauma, conditioning, or deprivation—must be identified if we are to determine how we might bring about change. To be sure, we have had a romance with a social systems or ecological model that intends to capture the interplay of forces within the human field. Informative as these models are, they offer no prescriptions for what to do, and all too often the practitioner falls back on traditional methods to get something done.

Second, standard theories support the myth that the human state is relatively uniform, consistent, and, as we find in the more empirical approaches to research and practice, predictable. These assumptions are evident in concepts of personality, traits, syndromes, measurement variables, and scales as well as in the very notion of diagnostic categories.

Consistent with the first two assumptions about cause and effect and uniformity, a third assumption presumes that the ideal for whatever we call well-being—adaptation, adjustment, freedom from stress, absence of symptoms, or working through—is commensurate with balance, equilibrium, or even homeostasis. In other words, the ideal state of being is the absence of stress and the presence of rest, stability, and symmetry.

Are these assumptions valid? Do they explain in useful ways what human and social experiences are really about? Common-sense reflection on how we get through an ordinary day tell us that our lives are not linear sequences of events, each episode a precondition of the next. Surely our minds can and do invent scenarios in which we conveniently order reality in a way that makes it look like one happenstance seemed to predict another, but this is the mind's way of simulating order, a process that can be revised any time we decide to think about our circumstances in another way.

In addition, we are acutely aware that our patterns of living are neither uniform nor consistent. Despite the habit patterns that roughly characterize the way we go about the ordinary tasks of living, the next novel situation we encounter is likely to evoke responses that are surprising even to ourselves. And to most of us, predictability as it pertains to ourselves is an abhorrent idea because it suggests possible control and power on the part of the one who predicts. Thus we would prefer to be seen as enigmatic and opaque as opposed to transparent.

Finally, given the contingencies, quirks, and the occasional risks of daily life, it is safe to say that mind and body are altogether restless, in motion, at least slightly out of balance, and watchful in an effort to monitor and cope with whatever may come along next. Interestingly, although the human sciences persist in pursuing the myth of linear cause–effect relations, notions of lawful uniformity, predictability, and stability, the physical sciences—particularly quantum and mathematical physics—provide us with a new and radical picture of what the universe and its material, organic, and human elements are like. The newest of these sciences, aptly called *chaos*, marks the end of the compartmentalization and reductionism of science (Gleick, 1987). It suspends the illusion that science will finally provide us with universal laws that will reinforce our need to believe that the universe is ultimately comprehensible and manageable. In fact, the systems around us (ecological, physiological, economic, for example) lack the order, regularity, and predictability long characterized by the Newtonian version of reality. If we are to come to terms with this chaotic version of reality, then we must settle for a revision of reality that allows us to search for variable and unpredictable patterns in the human state. In so doing, we would need to give up our illusion of regularity and predictability in our work with humans and their predicaments.

Returning to questions regarding the nature of the change process, the preceding discussion offers yet another perspective on the attributes of the psychopathological and the strength approaches as they bear on practice. The former can be seen as a relic of an earlier scientific era of positivism and reductionism. Essentially, the complexities of the personal, cultural, physiological, and environmental conglomeration that mark the human state tend to be reduced to narrow compartments of a diagnostic scheme and, thus, are treated accordingly.

In contrast, a health or strength perspective, although rooted in the philosophy of humanism, is sympathetic to the knowledge and findings of the new science. It is less concerned with control, classification, and precision. With its emphasis on capability and potential, it discards notions of causality that may define the client as a hapless victim of conditions beyond his or her control in favor of an approach that centers on the client's values, hopes, and desired goals.

The idea that life is a chaotic and unpredictable venture means that the strength of the individual or collective is not tied to the wistful hope for a static state of tranquility; rather, strength is found in the vital, dynamic search for at least some periodic states of security and structure within the turbulence of life.

In these terms, one's strengths cannot be cataloged, compared, or measured in line with one scale or another. In response to the same dire circumstances, strength for one person may be merely an active hope for survival; for another, it may be evident in the willingness to risk untried solutions. Accordingly, a strength approach to practice does not impose plans and programs; rather, it encourages clients to discover their own abilities, to explore possibilities, and to discover the richness of choice, the cornucopia of opportunity. Importantly, such an approach also frees workers to be at ease with their own humanness, liberating them to share their understanding of the challenge of finding meaning in a baffling world.

The Worker–Client Relationship

When we peel back the layers of theory, technique, style, and other characteristics that give the change experience its character and movement, what we find is two or more human beings engaged in conversation. This is the core of the therapeutic experience. More than likely this is how it is perceived or sensed by the client; having no explanatory theoretical framework, he or she would see the activity in a natural and unsophisticated way.

If all goes well, a relationship will grow out of this conversation. And, as is true of all important human relationships, the relationship is (or should be) governed not by professional methods or protocols alone but by ethics in a broader sense. In this instance, ethics are the personal In these instances, the worker must be certain that her or his ethics stand in tension with the politics of helping. Because the political dimension of the helping relationship risks encroachment of unwarranted influence and control as a result of

an unbalanced relationship, the ethical dimension serves as the conscience of the helping experience by jogging the worker's awareness of the need for prudence and care regarding how the politics of the helping relationship are handled.

In *Ethical Dilemmas in Social Work Practice* (1986), Rhodes covers many of the same issues raised in this essay. Her fine book, in fact, has inspired many of the ideas herein.

> . . . the ideal of value-free counseling is impossible and dangerous. The non-political stand is misleadingly political, and the detached worker conveys values despite her detachment. If we do not recognize these assumptions, we (and our clients) cannot fully examine or challenge them (p. 87).

This brief foray into the political–ethical domain of practice is not a side trip from or an add-on to the preceding arguments in this essay. Rather, these assumptions, which touch on the risks of power and the centrality of ethical awareness, in themselves call for a strength-oriented approach to our work with people. Our work with clients is fundamentally an ethical and moral enterprise—one that is all too often camouflaged by technical, faddish, or theoretical embroidery. All the jargon and pseudotechnology become irrelevant, however, once we are willing and able to enter the client's metaphoric and moral world.

Symptoms or defects are not expressed by these metaphors; rather these metaphors often reflect a struggle with moral anguish, value conflicts, or the conditions of living that impede growth and achievement. As a colleague and perhaps as a mentor, the worker appreciates that in most instances it is not a disorder of the psyche or mind that is at the root of suffering or a personal sense of failure. Instead, it is the discord and strife that come into being when life seems too chaotic and out of control, when the integrity of self is at risk, and when former values and beliefs no longer seem reliable.

A Personal Footnote

If we put aside our cherished theories and other presumptive notions about the human state and listen carefully to how people frame and define their own lives, we might truly learn something about the meaning of strength and the limits of a medicoscientific framework. Moreover, we might understand better the ethical and moral incentives that shape one's quality of life. The most reliable text cannot be found in the universal and abstract features of theory; rather, it is contained within the stories our clients tell us about their individual lives.

Currently, I am involved in a study of lives of a number of people, now in their later years, who spent most of their childhood in an institution for dependent children that existed for many years prior to the end of World War II. Although the early experiences of the respondents varied, they agreed completely on one point: life in the institution was harsh and deprived. Physical punishment was not uncommon, parental care and professional services were lacking, as were other conditions necessary for proper development.

Contradicting standard developmental theories is the remarkable evidence that, almost without exception, all who endured their years in this institution succeeded in building lives that were and are successful by most standards. The lives of most were ordinary and uneventful. Some did well in business, others entered the professions, and a number of respondents became social workers. Their families appear to be close-knit and secure; their own children are now achieving further successes.

In my conversations with these people, I ask why they think things turned out so well for them—timing my question after they have recounted vivid recollections of pain and hardship in institutional life. Their responses are fascinating, revealing personal sketches of strength, mastery, and will fortified by commitments to certain values—some religious, others having to do with caring for and obligation to others.

A few were puzzled by my question, as they had never considered any other alternative but to do well. Others gave the question some thought and observed, "It was hard, but it was also good since I learned that I had to depend on myself" or "I learned how important self-discipline is" or "Because religion was so heavily stressed, I did get some values that helped me when I became an adult" or "It helped me understand how people should be treated." Still others who vividly recalled how hurt and angry they were as children said things such as, "I had to do OK, in spite of the way I was treated" or "I promised myself that I would do the best I could just to show them."

One exception to these fairly consistent stories leaves me wondering whether the good fortune of these people had something to do with the absence of mental health services. This exception was a woman, whom I will call B, who is now in her early sixties. By all accounts, her life was fulfilling and secure. I could see that her home was lovely, that her husband adored her, and that both had great pride in their children's success. B was nearly ready to retire from her long and rewarding career as a teacher of handicapped children.

However, when she finally spoke about her childhood years in the home, she did so with unexpected bitterness and resentment, pouring forth a litany of hurts and rejections. Puzzled and surprised, I asked the inevitable question: Then how did things turn out as they did? How did she view the connection between her wretched past and the pride that she expressed about her current life?

She started to respond, then paused, obviously reflecting on what she had just told me. A bit bewildered, she mentioned, almost out of context, that she had been seeing a therapist for a while. Her beloved father had died a few years ago and since that loss, which she felt so deeply, she had not been able to shake off some feelings of depression. Then she added, as a rather solemn response to my question, "You know, I had never given much thought to my childhood in the home until I went into therapy. It never seemed that important to me until my therapist asked me about my childhood. When I told her about the institution, my therapist got really upset and told me that I had the most pathological childhood she had ever heard!" She thought for a moment, and then wistfully asked of no one, "Was it?"

REFERENCES

American Psychiatric Association. (1987). *Diagnostic and statistical manual of mental disorders* (3rd ed., rev.). Washington, DC: Author.

Becker, E. (1964). *The revolution in psychiatry*. New York: Free Press.

Buss, A. R. (1979). *A dialectical psychology*. New York: Irvington Publishers.

Ellenberger, H. (1970). *The discovery of the unconscious*. New York: Basic Books.

Gazzaniga, M. S. (1988). *Mind matters*. Boston: Houghton Mifflin.

Gergen, K. J. (1985). The social constructionist movement in modern psychology. *American Psychologist*, *40*, 266–275.

Gleick, J. (1987). *Chaos: Making a new science*. New York: Viking.

Heisenberg, W. (1958). *Physics and philosophy: The revolution in modern science*. New York: Harper & Brothers.

Rhodes, M. (1986). *Ethical dilemmas in social work practice*. Boston: Routledge & Kegan Paul.

Sontag, S. (1977). *Illness as metaphor*. New York: Farrar, Straus and Giroux.

GAMES SUPERVISORS PLAY
LILLIAN HAWTHORNE

WHAT ARE GAMES? Why do people play them? Is game-playing honest? Is it an effective strategy?

Games are defined by Berne as "an ongoing series of complementary ulterior transactions . . . often superficially plausible . . . and progressing to a well-defined, predictable outcome."[1] Four components of this basic statement warrant further definition.

First, the desired outcome of the game is to achieve a payoff for its initiator. For this reason, the essential function of all preliminary moves is to set up conditions that will insure this outcome. The purpose of the payoff is to obtain some internal or external advantage leading to a new or confirmed homeostasis.

A second factor is the ulterior quality of the transactions. This means that "by definition . . . games must have some element of exploitation in them."[2] That is, the initiator seeks to achieve maximum reward at minimum cost and directs his strategies toward this purpose regardless of the effects on his partner in the game.

A third component of the definition is complementarity. The game requires the participation of a responsive, active partner if it is to proceed toward its desired conclusion. As if in contradiction, there must also be some benefit to the partner. Despite the initiator's achievement, the partner must derive a secondary gain, or he will be unwilling to continue playing.

The fourth factor is superficial plausibility. The strategies of the game are not conjured up out of fantasy but have some connection with reality. This connection may be selective in that it can be distorted or misinterpreted to serve the purpose of the game and, at the same time, can be exploited to justify its perpetuation.

DEFENSIVE GAME-PLAYING

Kadushin relates games that are played in the supervisory situation to "the kinds of recurrent interactional incidents between supervisor and supervisee that have a payoff for one of the parties in the transaction."[3] Although his article focuses chiefly on games initiated by supervisees, he does suggest as a possible motivation for supervisors' games the need for defenses against

> . . . felt threats to their position in the hierarchy, uncertainty about their authority, reluctance to use their authority, a desire to be liked, [or] a need for the supervisee's approbation. . . .[4]

In this article, the author will focus on certain games that are played by supervisors and relate principally to problems concerning the supervisors' definition and use of authority. The material presented is based on reading, observation, and personal experience. The author has witnessed these games being played, has been induced to play them, and has even initiated them herself.

Many supervisors, especially new ones, have difficulty adjusting to their new authority. As Reynolds notes, "The balance which they have worked out for their personal lives between dominance and submission is upset by the new responsibility."[5] The supervisory relationship is complex, intense, and intimate. Within this framework, the supervisor must exercise several different kinds of authority—administrative, evaluative, educational, paren-

tal, and consultative. It requires effort and experience to integrate these into a comfortable and effective identity. Sometimes the effort is hampered by the supervisor's unfamiliarity with the requirements of his role, by difficulties stemming from personal experiences with authority, or by discomfort in the one-to-one relationship.

The games that will be described are attempts on the part of supervisors to deal with the difficulties surrounding authority. They do not, however, actually resolve the problem, but merely deal with it through different and seemingly contradictory kinds of avoidance. These games fall into two general categories that use almost opposite kinds of strategies but are motivated by the same payoff—the avoidance of a clear definition and exercise of supervisory authority. The first category is referred to as "games of abdication" and the second as "games of power."

In games of abdication, the supervisor deliberately relinquishes authority, manipulates the circumstances so that he is unable to exercise authority, projects the responsibility elsewhere, or uses inappropriate kinds of authority. Perlman describes professional authority as "carrying those rights and powers that are inherent in special knowledge and are vested in special functions."[6] Although she associates this with the casework process, her point is equally valid in the supervisory relationship. There too, "it is the very assumption that the person carries this authority which infuses the relationship with safety and security and strengthens the response to guidance."[7]

In the second type of game, the

supervisor sees his authority as omnipotent and sets up a closed system where every member participating has a fixed assignment from which deviation or negotiation is not permissible. Towle refers to this as "the cult of passivity" in which supervisors deliberately generate helplessness or submission on the part of their supervisees, "perhaps because they themselves experienced this kind of supervision, or because for varied reasons they are not secure in their responsibility. . . ." [8]

Although seemingly contradictory in the techniques used, both types of game, if successful, achieve the same payoff for the supervisor. His authority is never clearly defined or validated and, at the same time, his position as supervisor is retained and reinforced.

GAMES OF ABDICATION

One of the most common games of abdication is "They Won't Let Me." Here the supervisor expresses the desire to take or permit some requested action, but does not do so and does not even attempt to explore the possibility of doing so, because his superior in the agency, the regulations, or customary practice will not allow it. "I know this family might be eligible for a special allowance but the deputy won't approve it." "I'd really like to let you make an evening home visit, but no one in the agency does that." "I know this meeting is covering material you're already familiar with, but you're required to attend anyway." The supervisor protects himself from making decisions, from taking risks, from becoming involved in change by projecting onto others the responsibility for his inaction and indecision. By doing this, he accomplishes two things at the same time. He preserves his image by expressing the desire and willingness to take some action and he avoids risking that image by surrendering his authority to anonymous, superior powers. "I'd really like to do it if I could, but they won't let me."

Another common game in this category is "Poor Me." Here the supervisor is so involved with the details of administrative requirements—statistics, reports, surveys—that he has no time for other supervisory tasks. "I wish I had time to discuss that case with you, but I have to complete this report for the deputy." "We'll have to postpone the unit meeting because I was just handed this survey that has to be done immediately." "I'm sorry about having to cancel our weekly conference, but you have no idea how busy I am with these monthly lists for the director."

This results in a reversal of roles in which the supervisor instructs the worker to sympathize with him and not to impose any additional demands. By using these techniques of role reversal and environmental manipulation, the supervisor achieves a double payoff—he retains his positive and sympathetic image and avoids his role responsibilities toward his supervisees.

A third example of a game of abdication appears in two basic variations, "I'm Really One of You" or "I'm Really a Nice Guy." In the first variation, the supervisor seeks approval by supporting his supervisees in all complaints against agency policy, requirements, or expectations. He even relates incidents from his own experience in which he successfully ignored or circumvented agency practices. However, none of his past experiences involved direct confrontation of the disputed issues, nor does his attitude imply any planned action directed at changing regulations.

In the second variation, the supervisor seeks approval and even affection on the basis of personal qualities rather than professional competence. He is an attractive and affable person who socializes freely with his supervisees, or he is a devoted husband and father who relates compassionate and endearing anecdotes about his family. Once the supervisor has been accepted as "one of the crowd" or "really a nice guy," no reasonable supervisee could be critical or demanding of him or become dependent. Whatever variation is used, a double purpose is achieved—the supervisor establishes a benevolent image and is not called on to exercise his supervisory authority.

Another classic game of abdication is referred to by Kadushin as "One Good Question Deserves Another." Here the supervisor invariably responds to questions by asking the worker what he thinks. This transfers the responsibility back to the supervisee at the same time as the supervisor retains his reputation for omniscience. Other ploys are to assign the worker to do some research on the question or to schedule it for fuller discussion at a later date. The worker is thus made to feel that he has raised a significant issue and that his independence of thought and action are being fostered. At the same time, the supervisor has avoided answering, instructing, clarifying, or deciding anything.

There is some essential validity in each of these games, which is what makes them so difficult to deal with and also makes it possible for supervisors to be unaware that they are even playing these games. There are agency policies, requirements, and limitations that restrict supervisory authority and prohibit certain practices. There are administrative requirements that may be demanding and time consuming. Certainly it is pleasant for a supervisor to be personable as well as proficient, to be democratic as well as authoritative. Indeed, encouraging independent solutions is a valuable teaching technique. The point is to what extent has the reality of the situation been manipulated to justify or perpetuate the game? Have other options been attempted or even considered? To what extent do the advantages of playing the game outweigh the benefits of solving the problem?

The supervisee acquiesces in these games for various reasons: he is in a vulnerable position in the relationship, he recognizes the essential reality in some of the situations, he likes the supervisor, or he senses the possible advantages that participation gives him. As Kadushin points out:

> The simplest and most direct way of dealing with the problem of games . . . is to refuse to play. The supervisee can only successfully enlist the supervisor in a game if the supervisor wants to play for his own reasons. Collusion is not forced but is freely granted. Refusing to play requires the supervisor to be ready and able to forfeit self-advantages. [9]

He also adds that agreeing to play the game implies a mutual face-saving agreement. By not challenging the other, the player insures that he will not be challenged in turn. For the supervisee, the payoff in games of abdication is that few demands or expectations are made of him, few controls are placed on him, few pressures disturb him. He is effectively freed—or abandoned—to do whatever he wishes.

GAMES OF POWER

Games of power can be further divided into subgroups that are distinguished by the degree of benevolence involved. The first two games in this category are less benevolent than the last two, although their strategies are similar and their motivations identical.

The first game is called "Remember Who's Boss." Here the supervisor defines his role as one of absolute power and permits no contradictions, disagreements, or negotiations. The supervisor is the critical parent who insists on undeviating obedience. "This is the way things are always done in my unit." "My workers always notify me before leaving for home visits and after coming back." "Everyone in my unit knows I expect them to be at their desks on time." This supervisor implements his control in two ways: (1) explicitly, by frequent reminders of his power, especially in preparing evaluations, and (2) implicitly, by establishing a possessive relationship with his supervisees that clearly delineates his position as master ("my workers," "my unit").

The supervisor who is most successful at this game is generally one who is a veteran in the agency and who has an impeccable reputation for meeting bureaucratic requirements. The payoff is that the supervisor never has to defend or validate himself because he has placed himself beyond reach. His omnipotence is unquestioned and his closed system remains tightly locked.

"I'll Tell on You" is the name of the second game. It is similar to the first, except that it relies on a second-hand use of power. The supervisor exercises control by repeated threats of reporting to a higher power—the deputy, director, or administrative board. The

supervisor places himself in a weaker position than he held in the first game because he has delegated his power of punishment to the next highest level of authority. For this second-hand control to be effective, he must periodically carry out his threats and is therefore dependent on the hierarchy to validate his power. The payoff in this game would appear to be less effective than in "Remember Who's Boss" because of the supervisor's diminished power. However, many supervisors prefer playing this game because they achieve sufficient power to preserve their status and, at the same time, the burden of disciplinary responsibility is transferred to others. Also the supervisor enjoys the advantage of power by association, which is both flattering and safe.

The next two games are more benevolent in their techniques than the preceding ones, but are similar in that they establish an inflexible and unvalidated relationship of authority. The first is called "Father Knows Best" or "Mother Knows Best," depending on the sex of the supervisor. The supervisor cloaks his control in the garment of parental wisdom and experience. "I'm only telling you this for your own good." "I've had years of experience, so I know what I'm talking about." "This is what has always worked for me, so I know it will work for you." The supervisor is using not his professional competence or knowledge to validate his authority, but his external position—his status, seniority, and past experience.

In this game he assumes the role of wise and guiding parent, and the supervisee the role of helpless, dependent child. But beneath the benevolent role of parent, the superior-subordinate relationship is clearly structured. Any potential threat to the supervisor's power becomes translated into an implicit attack on the act of parenting. As a result, the supervisee is effectively disarmed, and the supervisor retains both his image as benign parent and his undiminished control.

The last game in this category either takes the form of "I'm Only Trying To Help You" or "I Know You Really Can't Do It Without Me." Both are

variations of the pseudo-benevolent approach to power and both are based on the assumption of failure or incompetence on the part of the partner. In these variations, control is exercised in the disguise of help, but success is never actually expected or even sought. If anything goes wrong, it is the supervisee's fault because he did not use the proffered help or used it incorrectly. Success is due solely to the supervisor's intervention and not to the worker's action, because recognition of success would threaten their positions in the game. The supervisor assumes that the supervisee is helpless and inadequate and therefore expects little of him. He offers to share the work load because otherwise it would not be properly handled. All this is presented in the form of concern and help.

The message of lowered expectations is clear; the supervisee is instructed not to be competent or independent. He thereby safeguards the supervisor's own need to be effective and indispensable. The success of this game depends on the supervisee's inability to be "helped" or to conform to the supervisor's lower expectations. Towle distinguishes this supervisor from the effective one who "does not waive demands, but . . . affords a relationship oriented to current reality on the assumption that the worker can use it." [10]

The element of reality in each of these situations must be acknowledged. The supervisor does have a responsibility to serve as critic, judge, and controller of the supervisee's actions. The supervisor does have an obligation to keep the administration reliably informed about workers' performances. The supervisor generally does have more professional experience, greater familiarity with and knowledge of agency operations, and often more personal maturity than the worker. The supervisor should attempt to help workers with particular problems and, if necessary and appropriate, adjust their expectations. Again the question is to what extent these realities are exploited as part of the game instead of used as part of the process of resolving problems.

There is also the fact of the supervisee's acquiescence in the games. The supervisee may agree to play the game because he has little alternative in dealing with an authoritarian supervisor. Or he may derive a payoff himself—the benefits of the passive and dependent role. He is relieved of responsibility; he is absolved from making plans or decisions; he escapes all risks. By accepting this role of child toward the powerful parent, the worker reaps the advantages of dependence and irresponsibility. As Scherz points out:

> Dependence is not in and of itself evil, but the unwholesome childish dependence which is stimulated when job responsibilities are ill defined and ill used has created problems in both casework and supervisory practice. Mature interdependence, which results from the appropriate use of the strengths of others without loss of self-identity, is actually highly desirable. . . .[11]

RESPONSES TO GAMES

Responses to games can come from the supervisee or from the supervisor himself. The supervisee is generally in too vulnerable a position to deal with games through open confrontation, which Kadushin defines as "a refusal to accept the game being proposed by seeking to expose and make explicit what is being done." [12] To this point, Austin suggests that "if supervisors are not fearful themselves, they can let workers tell them what helps them and what bothers them in their ways of working." [13] But it can be seen that the supervisor's very need to play these games implies the absence of the kind of relationship or environment that would make such an exchange possible. If the supervisee is also willing to forego his own advantages and assume some risks, there are other ways in which he can refuse to play the game.

With the abdicating supervisor, he can present his needs for professional help explicitly, persistently, and in a nonthreatening way. He can clearly and honestly share with the supervisor his professional needs and his concerns about fulfilling them effectively. He can use the countergame "I Know You Can Help Me," thus appealing to the supervisor's expertise and experience, or the one "I Know You Can Help Me Get Help," appealing to the supervisor's parental instincts to direct him to other appropriate sources of help. This last countergame must be practiced with caution for fear that it could impugn the supervisor's ability or undermine his role. Or the worker can turn to an available consultant-adviser or specialist in staff training—for intervention. In this case, the supervisee must be clearly aware of his real needs and be able to present them objectively and without recrimination.

With the authoritarian supervisor, confrontation is probably inadvisable, but a process of gradual interpretation may be possible. The supervisee can attempt to expand the constraints by testing independent ideas and by validating his right to independence through achievement. In following this course, he must be meticulously careful to operate within agency policies and procedures.

He can counteract the threat of "I'll Tell on You" by honestly acknowledging the supervisor's responsibility to evaluate him and accepting responsibility for his own actions. Or he may play the countergame "I Learned Everything I Know From You," which will preserve the supervisor's influence at the same time as it validates his own independent performance. At all times, the supervisee must be careful to focus his attention on the professional problem and not on the dynamics of personal behavior.

For the supervisor to deal with his own games is a more complex and subtle task. He may not be consciously aware that he is playing these games, because each one is partly rooted in reality and may appear superficially reasonable and appropriate. The supervisor who plays these games consciously may be doing so to protect himself from feelings of insecurity. He will understandably be reluctant to

> . . . risk and deal with supervisee hostility and rejection. . . . In declining other games the supervisor denies himself the sweet fruits of flattery, the joys of omniscience, the pleasures of acting the therapist, the gratification of being liked. He has to incur the penalties of an open admission of ignorance and uncertainty and the loss of infallibility.[14]

The supervisor must examine his own feelings and needs concerning his professional role. He must decide what he wants to give as a supervisor and what he wants to get, and whether these are appropriate and congruent. He must be sensitive to the responses of the supervisee and the meaning his behavior communicates. Is the worker generally acquiescent or open? Is he conforming or concerned? Is he anxious or active? The supervisor must examine to what extent his own behavior has programmed these kinds of responses and what benefits he has derived from those responses. In other words, he must become aware of the payoffs from the games he plays and he must assess honestly whether these are compatible with his supervisory role. He must explore whether a professionally responsible position can be better maintained through other kinds of behavior, such as "good" games. Berne defines these as games

> . . . whose social contribution outweighs the complexity of their motivations . . . and which contribute both to the well-being of the other players and to the unfolding of the one who is "it." [15]

The supervisor who experiences discomfort in his role and dissatisfaction with his gamesmanship may also turn to a consultant for help. Unfortunately, this rarely happens unless the games are not working, at which point intervention is sought as a corrective measure by the other person in the game. The more aware of and comfortable with himself the supervisor is, the less need he will have for gamesmanship. As Reynolds wrote:

> Once a supervisor has given up trying to answer all questions, and knows that his skill consists in drawing others out, clarifying responsibilities, contributing what is known from theory and experience, his position is no longer terrifying but rather exhilarating. A leader, no less than those who are led, is sustained by the sharing of responsibility, not only with those who may be above him but just as truly with all those with whom he works.[16]

82

The supervisor who continues to rely on these games to defend himself actually loses by winning, for he deprives himself of both the tasks and the joys of his role.

NOTES AND REFERENCES

1. Eric Berne, *Games People Play* (New York: Grove Press, 1964), p. 48.
2. Ibid., p. 163.
3. Alfred Kadushin, "Games People Play in Supervision," *Social Work,* 13 (July 1968), p. 23.
4. Ibid., p. 30.
5. Bertha Reynolds, *Learning and Teaching in the Practice of Social Work* (New York: Farrar & Rinehart, 1942), p. 305.
6. Helen Harris Perlman, *Social Casework* (Chicago: University of Chicago Press, 1957), p. 69.
7. Ibid., p. 69.
8. Charlotte Towle, "The Place of Help in Supervision," *Social Service Review,* 37 (December 1963), p. 404.
9. Kadushin, op. cit., p. 31.
10. Towle, op. cit., p. 405.
11. Frances Scherz, "A Concept of Supervision Based on Definitions of Job Responsibility," *Social Casework,* 39 (October 1958), p. 442.
12. Kadushin, op. cit., p. 321.
13. Lucille Austin, "Basic Principles of Supervision," *Social Casework,* 33 (December 1952), p. 416.
14. Kadushin, op. cit., p. 31.
15. Berne, op. cit., p. 163.
16. Reynolds, op. cit., p. 305.

VIOLATIONS OF THE SUPERVISORY RELATIONSHIP: AN ETHICAL AND EDUCATIONAL BLIND SPOT

CATHY JACOBS

THE HISTORICAL investment of social workers in challenging issues of power and oppression has not facilitated the examination of abuses of power within the social work profession. Sensitivity to these issues actually may have increased resistance to such painful self-examination.

The student-supervisory relationship is a complex interpersonal one. Alonso (1985) described the role of supervisors as "professional parents" who instruct, support, and nurture students in the formative phases of their professional development. The teaching and caretaking components of the relationship are hierarchical functions wherein the more powerful person (supervisor) is entrusted with the well-being of the less powerful individual (trainee). Alonso noted that professional helpers can experience

anxiety about the sadistic instincts stimulated by the power inherent in the [supervisory] role. Committed to a non-judgmental healing stance as clinicians, the responsibility of judging the trainee's personal and professional competence is a real departure, and the subsequent discomfort may be difficult to address in public. (p. 6)

Pinderhughes (1989) defined power as "the capacity to produce desired effects on others" and identified "a sense of power [or interpersonal mastery] as critical to one's mental health. Everyone needs it" (pp. 109–110). Thus, supervisors are vulnerable to using their power to gratify self-esteem needs of their own. Furthermore, Pinderhughes (1983) wrote, "power and powerlessness operate systematically" (p. 332); "the cyclical nature of power is demonstrated when individuals who feel powerless and oppressed cope with it by assuming a power stance over others" (p. 125). In situations where a "supervisor feels un-supported, uncherished or underpaid by the institution, there is serious potential for these conflicts to spill over into the supervisory hour" (Alonso, 1985, p. 103). A supervisor may use the "helping role to reinforce . . . [his or her] own sense of competence by keeping subordinates in a one-down position" (Pinderhughes, 1989, p. 111). Therefore, students are vulnerable targets for dumping behavior by acting-out supervisors. Students also may replicate aspects of harmful interactions (modeling effect) with supervisors in a parallel process with clients, thereby extending the influence of the dysfunctional supervisor onto succeeding generations of clients.

Students who are devalued, humiliated, coerced, frightened, ignored, or criticized in a nonconstructive way by supervisors are unlikely to protest because of their power disadvantage: "In any hierarchical situation, the people in power define reality. . . . Men have done this for women—parents for children" (Pinderhughes, 1989, p. 136). Thus, supervisors can refute or pathologize student reactions, including healthy, assertive behaviors, without threatening their own reputations or institutional base of support. As "experts," their power advantage includes enhanced credibility. Even in clear-cut conflicts such as student complaints of insufficient supervision time, student credibility is at risk in a my-word-against-yours presentation of events. Supervisors who are well liked and respected may be particularly invulnerable to student complaints.

A member of a graduate social work student support group described one experience: Sally's supervisor liked to tell Sally about her own cases during supervision. At first Sally enjoyed hearing about her supervisor's work, but gradually she began to get frustrated at not having enough time to review cases she had questions about during her supervision. When the supervisor began using the time to tell Sally about some problems she was having with her children, Sally became alarmed. She recognized that the supervisor was acting inappropriately but she wasn't sure how to address the issue. To complicate matters, the supervisor had also disclosed to Sally that she was a personal friend of Sally's faculty adviser for the placement. Sally was concerned that if she raised the matter with either instructor, the two of them would join forces against her and undermine her credibility.

Exploitation of student by supervisor is associated with role reversals or "parentification" of the student, whereby the needs of the supervisor supersede those of the student. Dual role relationships and boundary violations are hallmarks of even more serious exploitation (Stout, 1987; Strohm-Kitchener, 1988). Stout (1987) identified two markers of exploitive supervisory relationships: sexual contact and personal counseling of the supervisee. These activities are prohibited "because the supervisee is in a position of diminished consent (meaning that he or she is unable to provide voluntary consent to be a part of any dual relationship)" (Stout, 1987, p. 90). Consensual sexual or psychotherapy relationships between supervisors and trainees do not exist according to this definition. Sexual relationships present the most difficulty. In a study by Glaser and Thorpe (1986), female psychologists who became sexually involved with educators during their graduate training reported substantial changes in their judgments about these relationships over time: "On the average, evaluations at the time of contact [were much less negative]; many currently perceive the contact as extremely exploitive and harmful" (p. 43). The authors suggested "that these [judgment] changes in part reflect a consenting involvement by many students at the time as well as an increased current sensitivity to the problems involved in such relationships, a sensitivity that was not present at the time of contact" (p. 49). Conroe and Schank (1989) found that "sexual involvement between persons in positions of unequal power [appears to] render greater harm than other boundary violations" (p. 246).

Alonso (1985) noted that when a student and supervisor find themselves at an impasse, "the common assumption is that the dyad is stimulating powerful transferential and countertransferential reactions in one another" (p. 103). Pope, Keith-Spiegel, and Tabachnick (1986) pointed out that

> virtually all mistakes committed by well-trained and experienced therapists are caused directly by countertransference. . . . Failure to acknowledge and examine countertransference blocks its therapeutic potential and unleashes its destructive effects. (p. 149)

Similarly, unchecked countertransference reactions of the clinical supervisor encourage power abuses within the supervisory relationship.

Hazards of the Student-Supervisor Relationship in Clinical Training

Transference and Countertransference Reactions

In a lecture on clinical supervision for first-year graduate social work students that the author attended, the speaker commented that many students have had difficult experiences with supervisors in previous work settings, which could contribute to student anxiety about relationships with supervisors in academic situations. The lecturer suggested that students let go of such experiences and start clinical training with a clean slate. This view, however, ignores the role of the unconscious and its interpersonal manifestations, including transference and countertrans-

ference phenomena, in the supervisory relationship.

In the context of the supervisory relationship, transference refers to feelings that the student experiences in association with a supervisor that are actually displaced—that is, feelings that originated in an earlier significant relationship (often with a primary caretaker) in the student's life. Countertransference refers to displaced feelings that the supervisor experiences in association with a student that have their origin in an earlier relationship in the supervisor's life.

Failing to alert the student to such forces can contribute to a student's confusion if transference or countertransference reactions begin to disrupt the working relationship with a supervisor (Gartrell, Herman, Olarte, Localio, & Feldstein, 1988; Halgin, 1985). A student who is not cognitively prepared is more likely to question his or her own emotional functioning than the interactional component of the experience. It is important for the student to know that people's interactions are rarely free of past influences. Everyone grows up in families or under some sort of supervision and may recapitulate conflicts in these early relationships with different authority figures in various settings. This repetition compulsion is an unconscious effort to master unresolved feelings and to feel empowered in current interpersonal relationships. People fill up their slates with historical data, and the concept of an ability to erase them at will is not psychodynamically valid. People do not have cognitive control over what they feel; ids have their own agendas.

This lecturer's attitude was not atypical; her statement reflected a generalized denial or selective inattention that has become institutionalized within the psychodynamically oriented educational system (Pope, Levenson, & Schover, 1979). Students often are not encouraged to explore, within an educational context, feelings generated within their supervisory relationships. Some clinical programs suggest students undergo psychotherapy during their training; few schools make it a formal requirement.

During their first year of clinical in-

struction, students often experience significant anticipatory and transitional anxiety (Schmidt, 1976), but it generally is considered normative by educators. Students who feel anxious, intimidated, frightened, or overwhelmed at this time typically are reassured by instructors that such reactions are reasonable to an unfamiliar and inherently stressful situation. Unfortunately, this partially empathic response generally ends the dialogue; once uncomfortable feelings have been labeled normal, instructors seem to say, what more is there to discuss? Few students want to admit how abnormal they feel at times during their training, let alone argue the point, particularly with representatives of a system that is academically evaluating them (Schmidt, 1976). The instructor's unconditional reassurance communicates the message that uncomfortable feelings that occur in the supervisory relationship do not warrant further discussion and that serious exploration of such feelings could appear to be like therapy rather than education, thereby jeopardizing the boundaries of the academic relationship.

But whose interests—the student's or the educator's—actually are being protected? Presumably, the restrictions are intended to protect the student's safety; in practice, the opposite may be true. The following case example illustrates this point: John's supervisor would frequently cancel his supervision and usually arrived late or ended supervision sessions early. At first John thought that his supervisor needed the time to attend to other work-related duties of a more urgent nature. One day, however, the supervisor canceled their meeting explaining that she had to go to her dry cleaner. At this point, John realized that he had been acting out his resentment around the repeated cancellations by not handing in his process recordings on a regular basis, and he shared this observation with his supervisor the next time they met. On his final evaluation, the supervisor wrote, "John has been resentful about doing his process recordings. His resistance seems to be related to an ongoing struggle with autonomy and control issues."

One student at the lecture on clinical supervision asked whether the one-way mirror, an observational tool sometimes imposed on clients during therapy, could be imposed on her in the course of her training. Her question symbolically demonstrates how client-student roles can fuse experientially and create confusion and even paranoia. Students feel unsure about what actually is going on behind the mirror (for example, academic evaluation or analysis), and this uncertainty generates a precarious emotional climate for learning (Schmidt, 1976; Zetzel, 1953).

Rosenblatt and Mayer (1975) described an analogous blurring of boundaries from the standpoint of the clinical supervisor in the following common scenario:

> The supervisor believes that certain actions or feelings of a student, whether in relation to himself or his clients, are inappropriate. He then ascribes the difficulty, not to some aspect of the situation or context, but to "deficiencies" in the student's personality. These then are explored in considerable detail. . . . Students did not necessarily object to some of their transactions being labeled inappropriate. Rather, it was the designated source of the shortcoming and its subsequent exploration that caused them concern. (p. 186)

Interaction Replication

At the beginning of clinical training, the student is introduced to a power relationship that is emotionally loaded in three major respects. First, the student-supervisory relationship replicates aspects of early parent-child interactions and may generate feelings similar to those experienced as a child, such as helplessness, dependency, disappointment, and rage. The following types of students may engage in interaction replication:

- students who grew up in a parentified role in the family and fear overburdening already overworked supervisors by acknowledging their own learning needs
- students who felt criticized or unsupported in childhood by their parents and have difficulty tolerating any criticism from their supervisors
- students who as small children tried to please their parents and now try to ingratiate themselves with their supervisors
- students who were emotionally deprived as children and feel enraged at supervisors who are not available to meet their learning or emotional needs.

Second, the training process involves renegotiation of the developmental task of separation and individuation in a professional arena (Halgin, 1985; Horner, 1988). Adult students accustomed to functioning autonomously in other life roles may feel regressive reworking developmental issues.

Third, students in supervision may try to conceptualize the very phenomena they are experiencing and emotionally defending themselves against, with both didactic and reactive processes operating in the same supervisory relationship. This conflict arises because the student-supervisory relationship is structurally similar to the patient-therapist relationship they are striving to understand in the following ways:

- Both relationships are hierarchical and involve a significant power differential.
- In both situations, the more powerful individual (therapist or supervisor) is entrusted with the care of the less powerful individual (patient or student), which means that the therapist or supervisor is solely responsible for maintaining interpersonal boundaries that ensure the emotional safety of the patient or student within the context of that relationship.
- Implicit in a patient or student's acceptance of the less powerful role in these relationships is the trust placed in the therapist or supervisor to use that enhanced power position on the patient or student's behalf. This trust actually increases the power of the therapist or supervisor to manipulate the situation to his or her own advantage and to perpetrate abuse.
- Beginning students may know no more than patients about therapy. They depend on their supervisors to define the therapeutic process just as patients rely on their therapists to determine what is therapeutic.
- Both relationships can provide support to the less powerful partner, but the therapist or supervisor should not be using the patient or student relationship to meet his or her own emotional needs.
- The student as well as the patient emotionally processes information: "the student is often expected to participate in . . . forms of supervision that encourage the student to analyze, in the formal sense of the word, his own feelings and behavior" occurring in the course of his interactions with clients (Pope, Schover, & Levenson, 1980, p. 159). Exploring such material can stir up intense feelings in the student about unresolved personal issues. Supervisors differ on how much to process these feelings with students, but the boundaries in the processing roles of supervision and therapy can be unclear and confusing for both student and supervisor.
- Because of the therapy-supervision overlap, students can feel emotionally vulnerable in the presence of their supervisors much as patients feel vulnerable in the presence of their therapists. Abusive treatment by therapists or supervisors can exacerbate a patient or student's emotional regression and intensify a sense both of helplessness in the relationship and of general feelings of personal or professional incompetence.
- Both relationships have an unusual emotional intensity (Halgin, 1985; Zetzel, 1953).

For these reasons, relationships between students and supervisors can feel similar to relationships between therapists and patients (Goguen, 1986; Zetzel, 1953); both are susceptible to the formation of strong transference and counter-transference phenomena (Pope & Bouhoutsos, 1986). Students can experience strong transference reactions to their supervisors and supervisors may experience strong transference reactions to their students as they project unresolved internal conflicts, especially related to early parent-child interactions, onto their supervisory relationships, much as patients recapitulate early childhood conflicts in the transference of the therapeutic relationship.

Students' reactions can be completely unconscious. They would experience the transference simply as feelings toward supervisors indistinguishable from the feelings associated with other relationships, unless the feelings have an unusual level of intensity or atypical impact on their functioning in the clinical setting. Subjectively, students may feel they are overreacting to supervisors for reasons that are not understood. Another member of the graduate social work student group shared this incident: Sarah, a 26-year-old graduate student, noticed that she had become very attracted to her 42-year-old clinical supervisor. She was embarrassed by this schoolgirl-type crush and determined not to disclose these feelings to the supervisor. She continued working with him uneventfully for another three months, at which time a male client Sarah was working with began talking about his feelings of attraction to her. Sarah was unsure about how to manage this situation clinically but she was also afraid to bring it up in her supervision. Not only was she concerned that her supervisor might think she had been sexually provocative with the client in some way, but the whole idea of trying to discuss dispassionately the issue of sexual attraction with a man she was feeling attracted to seemed overwhelming to her.

Supervisory relationships can become sexualized. Working with oneself and one's feelings can generate an intimacy that is distorted by transference. Students can become attracted to their supervisors, supervisors to their students, or both. Often, graduate students are treated more like colleagues than students during their training. Although this presumed parity tends to feel more comfortable to older, adult students, it can complicate, confuse, and distort the boundaries between student and supervisory roles. Sexual involvement between supervisors and their students is dangerous and unethical because of the confusion of roles and the level of transference in such relationships (Pope & Bouhoutsos, 1986). Supervisors are considered responsible for ensuring that boundaries are respected. Because of their level of training, they are expected to know the problems in violating these boundaries and the importance of obtaining adequate supervision for themselves should difficulties arise. Pope et al. (1986) remarked that

> educators must display the same frankness, honesty and integrity regarding sexual attraction that they expect their students to emulate. . . . [Clinicians] need to acknowledge that they may feel sexual attraction to their students as well as to their clients. They need to establish . . . and maintain . . . unambiguous ethical and professional standards regarding appropriate and inappropriate handling of these feelings. (p. 157)

Violations can have severe emotional repercussions for both supervisor and student (Gutheil, 1989). Students who become sexually involved with supervisors can suffer psychological consequences similar to those experienced by victims of incest because of the betrayal of trust (Kong, 1989; Sonne, Meyer, Borys, & Marshall, 1985).

Students may file sexual harassment charges if they are willing to risk the personal and professional exposure of a legal investigation. However, students who ostensibly consented to a sexual relationship may be particularly reluctant to file charges of harassment, even if their experience with the supervisor became abusive. Profound shame and self-blame, fear of condemnation by others, and a sense that they got what they deserved strongly deter students from making public grievances or legal complaints.

Student Inexperience with the Supervisory Experience

Because students are emotionally vulnerable in the context of their supervision, they are in a poor position to advocate for themselves should the boundaries of that relationship break down. When the student is a woman and the supervisor is a man, heterosexual cultural factors exacerbate the power base of the dominant male/supervisor (Pope et al., 1979).

The frequent result of the student's disempowered position over time is impaired self-esteem. Supervisors are in a position of trust; consequently, students are more likely to identify themselves as the problem in a dysfunctional situation, at least emotionally, than to identify the interactional component of the experience. Supervisors also may ascribe the problem to the student and use the power of the transference and knowledge of the student's personal history to disguise a blame-the-student process (Rosenblatt & Mayer, 1975). Self-blame is a hallmark of any victimization experience and a major obstacle to disclosure of actual incidents of abuse (Kong, 1989). Clinical programs that provide students with a comprehensive understanding of the supervision experience before the fact, including the signs of dysfunction, will better enable students to identify any dysfunctional transference and countertransference aspects of their training experience before an abusive relationship develops

(Bouhoutsos, 1985; Pope et al., 1979). Such programs also are more likely to engender a level of trust enabling students to seek help in the event of difficulties. Disclosure is a critical step in the healing process; healing cannot proceed in isolation.

The numerous articles on psychodynamic thinking about the student-supervisory relationship and its analogues typically are written for educators or clinical supervisors. The technical level of the material makes it largely incomprehensible to most beginning graduate students, who lack the linguistic competence and psychodynamic theory base. Pinderhughes (1989) suggested that failing to share this information directly with students further weakens the already seriously disempowered position they must negotiate in relation to their clinical supervisors. Students must struggle alone with feelings that they cannot understand and that they must prevent from disrupting academic functioning.

Contribution of Secrecy to a Dsyfunctional Relationship

Silence about important issues creates a secretive atmosphere similar to that in dysfunctional families; indeed, transference and countertransference in supervision have remained a secret within the family of psychotherapists. That is one reason why violations of the student-supervisory relationship are so dangerous; they carry the heavy burden of secrecy, which constitutes the major obstacle to getting help.

Providing information to students, on the other hand, is an invitation to a dialogue (Halgin, 1985). It validates the "crazy" feelings that students may be experiencing within a dysfunctional supervisory context and gives them permission to share these feelings. Pinderhughes (1989) noted that failing to share information with disempowered individuals "about how they can cope with external systems and with victimizing structures can be a way of perpetuating their dependency and trapped position" and their victimization (p. 134).

Talking about transference and countertransference in the supervisory relationship can be difficult and hazardous for both student and supervisor. The topic may seem seductive and can be a particularly stressful sort of interaction for the clinical supervisor, whose professional role includes the ethical responsibility for maintaining safe boundaries in the relationship. Often, students quickly get an intuitive sense of their supervisor's comfort level and then cooperate to protect these boundaries, just as children may modulate expression of needs to accommodate the emotional resources of the adults they depend on. Furthermore, many individuals enter the helping professions partly to fill strong caretaking needs. Thus students may take on caretaking roles even in a relationship that is intended to meet their own emotional or learning needs. In this way, students collude with the silence established about transference and countertransference issues by enabling their educators to feel safe in their roles and by attempting to manage conflictual feelings in isolation.

Consequences of a Dysfunctional Relationship

There are two major consequences of this impaired communication process: first, students miss an extraordinary opportunity to learn about their own interactional style with people in positions of authority (Halgin, 1985), and second, a situation is established that is particularly conducive to the development of abuse in the supervisory relationship. One study suggested that 25 percent of female graduate psychology students become sexually involved with their teachers or clinical supervisors and that the rate of sexual contact in student training relationships appears to be increasing (Pope et al., 1979). Glaser and Thorpe (1986) acknowledged "the reality of a population of women of unknown numbers who, after gaining keenly competitive admission to doctoral studies in psychology, take leave of that effort and goal not through lack of ability and diligence but through disgust, dissuasion and misuse" (p. 50). Pope's study concluded that "clearly, issues of sex with educators are prominent and difficult to avoid for women who are currently psychologists in training" (p. 688).

Bettelheim (1988) suggested that many of the ways adults parent children are derived from how they incorporated early interactions with their own

parents. Similarly, supervised students are not just assimilating knowledge about becoming therapists; they also are engaged in the first phase of training to become supervisors themselves. To protect students as they negotiate this complex training relationship, social work educators must empower them to talk about their experiences in clinical supervision and listen to their stories.

Evaluation of Supervisory Relationship

Although supervisors are ultimately responsible for the maintenance of an emotionally safe working relationship, students must be encouraged to monitor their feelings in reaction to all aspects of their supervision experience to ensure their own emotional protection and well-being throughout the course of their training. The following questions may help students identify signs of dysfunction in their relationship with clinical supervisors:

• Is the student having any feelings about his or her supervisor that the student feels uncomfortable about or that may be interfering with the ability to work comfortably with the supervisor?

• Does the student feel comfortable with the ways his or her supervisor interacts with the student?

• Does the student find himself or herself reacting to his or her supervisor in confusing ways or differently than the student normally reacts to other people?

• Is his or her supervisor generally available to the student? Will the supervisor find time for the student if he or she communicates that something important has come up?

• Does the student ever feel judged or labeled by his or her supervisor? Does the supervisor ever make the student feel like there is something wrong with him or her?

• If a conflict arises, can the supervisor acknowledge a role in the difficulty, or does the student tend to feel blamed or identified as the cause of the problem?

• Does the student ever feel exploited or abused by his or her supervisor?

• Does the supervisor ever discourage the student from sharing information with his or her fieldwork adviser?

If the student has any concerns related to this material, he or she is encouraged

to contact the fieldwork adviser or a trusted faculty member for assistance. Alternatively, some chapters of NASW provide social workers' assistance networks that offer confidential consultation and referral services for social workers and students.

Implications for the Profession

At present, the *Code of Ethics* of the National Association of Social Workers (NASW, 1990) does not address the ethical responsibilities of clinicians in relation to the students they supervise. A protected status for clients is well established; the code includes the principles that "the social worker should avoid relationships or commitments that conflict with the interest of clients" and under no circumstances may the social worker "exploit relationships with clients for personal advantage" (p. 4) or "engage in sexual activities with clients" (p. 5).

It is not clear whether these principles also apply to students or whether a student is considered a client, colleague, or friend in this context. Student-supervisor relationships can develop qualities associated with all three relationship types (Goguen, 1986). Their boundaries often are unusually fluid to accommodate the multiple roles and functions. Boundaries may become particularly unclear as the student disengages from the training process, either prematurely under stress or naturally in the termination phase of the experience. Students who remain at an agency in which they trained or who choose to maintain some work-related contact must negotiate a transition from student to collegial status. Although such circumstances may seem to complicate defining the student's status in relation to the clinical supervisor, ultimately the overt or covert power differential throughout and beyond the life of the training process will make it clear. Herman, Gartrell, Olarte, Feldstein, and Localio (1987) addressed the "timelessness of unconscious processes, including transference" (p. 168). Individuals enter a supervisor endeavor with expectations that differ according to their preconceptions of the possibility of extending the boundaries of the relationship to accommodate a personal level of intimacy.

The supervisory role is a powerful one

(Halgin, 1985), and the power differential between the supervisor and student generates the force behind the transference that warrants a protective client status for the student/partner in training. If social work educators fail to address this issue directly in the context of the primary teaching relationship, then they must not be surprised when it is reincarnated as ethical violations, including sexual abuse, of patients by therapists (Gartrell et al., 1988; Pope et al., 1986).

References

Alonso, A. (1985). *The quiet profession—supervisors of psychotherapy.* New York: Macmillan.

Bettelheim, B. (1988). *A good enough parent.* New York: Vintage Books.

Bouhoutsos, J. C. (1985). Therapist-client sexual involvement: A challenge for mental health professionals and educators. *American Journal of Orthopsychiatry, 55,* 177–182.

Conroe, R. M., & Schank, J. A. (1989). Sexual intimacy in clinical supervision: Unmasking the silence. In G. R. Schoener, J. H. Milgrom, J. C. Gonsiorek, E. T. Luepker, & R. M. Conroe (Eds.), *Psychotherapists' sexual involvement with clients: Intervention and prevention* (pp. 245–262). Minneapolis, MN: Walk-In Counseling Center.

Gartrell, N., Herman, J., Olarte, S., Localio, R., & Feldstein, M. (1988). Psychiatric residents' sexual contact with educators and patients: Results of a national survey. *American Journal of Psychiatry, 145,* 690–694.

Glaser, R. D., & Thorpe, J. S. (1986). Unethical intimacy: A survey of sexual contact between psychology educators and female graduate students. *American Psychologist, 41,* 43–51.

Goguen, T. (1986). Psychotherapy supervision: Clarifying a complex task. *The Clinical Supervisor, 4*(4), 69–76.

Gutheil, T. (1989). Borderline personality disorder, boundary violations, and patient-therapist sex: Medicolegal pitfalls. *American Journal of Psychiatry, 146,* 597–602.

Halgin, R. P. (1985). Pragmatic blending of clinical models in the supervisory relationship. *The Clinical Supervisor, 3*(4), 23–46.

Herman, J. D., Gartrell, N., Olarte, S., Feldstein, M., & Localio, R. (1987). Psychiatrist-patient sexual contact: Results of a national survey, II: Psychiatrists' attitudes. *American Journal of Psychiatry, 144,* 164–169.

Horner, A. J. (1988). Developmental aspects of psychodynamic supervision: Parallel process of separation and individuation. *The Clinical Supervisor, 6*(2), 3–12.

Kong, D. (1989, August 7). Pain lingers after sexual abuse ends. *The Boston Globe,* pp. 25, 26.

National Association of Social Workers. (1990). *Code of ethics.* Silver Spring, MD: Author.

Pinderhughes, E. B. (1983). Empowerment for our clients and for ourselves. *Social Casework, 64,* 331–338.

Pinderhughes, E. B. (1989). *Understanding race, ethnicity & power.* New York: Free Press.

Pope, K. S., & Bouhoutsos, J. C. (1986). *Sexual intimacy between therapists and patients.* New York: Praeger Publishers.

Pope, K. S., Keith-Spiegel, P., & Tabachnick, B. (1986). Sexual attraction to clients: The human therapist and the (sometimes) inhuman training system. *American Psychologist, 41,* 147–158.

Pope, K. S., Levenson, H., & Schover, L. R. (1979). Sexual intimacy in psychology training: Results and implications of a national survey. *American Psychologist, 34,* 682–689.

Pope, K. S., Schover, L. R., & Levenson, H. (1980). Sexual behavior between clinical supervisors and trainees: Implications for professional standards. *Professional Psychology, 11,* 157–162.

Rosenblatt, A., & Mayer, J. E. (1975). Objectionable supervisory styles: Students' views. *Social Work, 20,* 184–189.

Schmidt, T. M. (1976). The development of self-awareness in first-year social work students. *Smith College Studies in Social Work, 46,* 218–235.

Sonne, J., Meyer, B., Borys, D., & Marshall, V. (1985). Clients' reactions to sexual intimacy in therapy. *American Journal of Orthopsychiatry, 55,* 183–189.

Stout, C. E. (1987). The role of ethical standards in the supervision of psychotherapy. *The Clinical Supervisor, 5*(1), 89–97.

Strohm-Kitchener, K. (1988). Dual role relationships: What makes them so problematic? *Journal of Counseling and Development, 67*(12), 219–221.

Zetzel, E. R. (1953). The dynamic basis of supervision. *Social Casework, 34*(4), 143–149.

Cathy Jacobs, OTR, MSW, CSW, is Clinical Social Worker, The Addiction Treatment Center of New England, 77F Warren Street, Brighton, MA 02135.

CLIENTS DON'T SUE: THE INVULNERABLE SOCIAL WORKER

JAMES A. JONES, ABRAHAM ALCABES

DESPITE THE COGENT ANALYSIS of malpractice vulnerability among social workers by Douglas Besharov[1] and the increased attention paid to malpractice issues in the professional literature,[2] the rate of suits against social workers has remained extraordinarily low, both in absolute terms and relative to other professions (see Table 1). Comparative data, in fact, show that social workers are far less vulnerable to malpractice claims than are members of nearly all other professions. What has been virtually ignored in the spate of articles, news stories, and conferences devoted to malpractice is the fact that rates of malpractice suits vary enormously among professions and from specialty to specialty within each profession.

Explanations for the increase in malpractice suits range from charges of professional incompetence to professional cannibalism by lawyers seeking clients to a society turned more litigious. However, these explanations fail to take into account the differences from profession to profession and specialty to specialty in the prevalence and increase in the rates of malpractice suits. Even the appealing thought that malpractice suits are directed toward those with "deep pockets" is shattered by Besharov's data showing that 60.3 percent of the defendants in 373 social work malpractice claims from 1965 to 1985 were individuals rather than agencies.[3]

In contrast to the foregoing explanations, the present article argues that help seekers (the authors prefer this term to "client" or "patient" in this context) no longer believe that the majority of professionals are committed to the welfare of their clients. According to one observer of medical education, for example, today's physicians have difficulty providing patients with the "trusting, caring feeling [that] people like to get from a doctor."[4] This loss of faith has led to the help seekers withdrawing authority and legitimation from the professional, with a consequent increase in the number and rate of malpractice suits.

Differences in the rate of malpractice suits can best be understood as a consequence of a clash between the service-ideal model, which traditionally has governed the professional–client relationship, and a reemerging fee-for-service model, which is similar to the tradesperson–customer relationship. Until one or the other model becomes dominant, professionals will remain vulnerable to lawsuits. Social workers have, by and large, escaped the flood of malpractice suits because their practice has remained fairly true to the service-ideal model.

How do social workers convince help seekers of their commitment to the service-ideal model? They do so through the process of socializing applicants into the role of clients. When that process is successfully completed and the applicant assumes the role of client, social workers become less vulnerable to malpractice suits. True clients do not sue.

The present article (1) contrasts the service-ideal and fee-for-service models, (2) shows how socialization into the role of client reduces the threat of malpractice suits, (3) addresses the impact of specialization upon the rise in malpractice suits, and (4) predicts that the service-ideal model will continue to guide social work practice, unless the private practitioner comes to typify the profession.

The Service-Ideal Model

The essence of the service-ideal model is characterized best by Hippocrates: "where there is love of man, there is also love of the art of healing."[5] The relationship between any professional and help seeker is predicated upon the confidence that the client has in the professional's skill in and devotion to solving the help seeker's problem. Although the professional cannot guarantee success, he or she guarantees to do the very best for each help seeker that the technology of the profession permits, regardless of whether that person can pay.

Under this model, the professional dedicates his or her expertise to the service of the client. In the words of one help seeker, "I found that [my social worker] was quite interested in me.

It seemed to her more than just a job. I think you can usually pick it up if it's just a job."[6] When such dedication and concern are present, few help seekers ever consider suing their practitioners. One survey found

that most [clients]—virtually all those interviewed—said they would not have considered suing if their doctor had shown them consideration and sincere regret. All complained about what they saw as the arrogance, distance, and coldness of the medical professionals who treated them. The doctors' refusal to admit anything wrong—and in some cases, the doctors' outright lies—fed a simmering rage that eventually resulted in legal action.[7]

The Fee-for-Service Model

The fee-for-service model offers a quality service (for example, eliminating a phobia) in exchange for a fee set by the professional.[8] In

TABLE 1. Rate of malpractice claims by profession.

	1981–85	1976–80	1971–75	1966–70
Physicians	11.5[a]	7.4[a]	6.7[b]	2.8[a]
Lawyers	3.2[c]	no data	1.4[d]	1.2[d]
Social Workers	0.2[e] (for entire time span)			

[a]Patricia M. Danzon, "Frequency and Severity of Medical Malpractice Claims: New Evidence," *Law and Contemporary Problems* (Spring 1986). Estimated from data presented in Table 1.

[b]John Guinther, *The Malpractitioners* (Garden City, N.Y.: Anchor Press/Doubleday, 1978). Estimated from data presented on pp. 4–5.

[c]William H. Gates, "The Newest Data on Lawyers' Malpractice Claims," *ABA Journal* 70 (April 1984). Estimated from data presented on p. 78.

[d]Werner Pfennigstorf, "Types and Causes of Lawyers' Professional Liability Claims: The Search for Facts," *American Bar Foundation Research Journal* (Spring 1980). Estimated from Figure 1.

[e]Douglas J. Besharov, *The Vulnerable Social Worker* (Silver Spring, Md.: National Association of Social Workers, 1985). Estimated from data presented in Chart 1-1.

this model, as in any economic exchange, the client is free to shop around for the best value that can be obtained. Although the professional is reluctant to post the prices of various services (as is done in laundries, clothing stores, and other service establishments), an implicit "price list" exists. Like many customer–tradesperson relationships, it is often assumed that the more expensive the service, the higher its quality and effectiveness. Thus, unlike the service-ideal model, the fee-for-service model implies a promise of a "cure." Under this model, the help seekers expect their competent doctors to cure their high blood pressure, their competent lawyers to win their malpractice suit, the competent teacher to keep their child reading far above grade level, and their competent social worker to eradicate their

child abuse.

In the fee-for-service model, the authority and legitimation of the professional does not reside in his or her technical competence, as reflected in degrees and certifications; it resides, instead, in the outcome of the service that the professional delivers. Prospective clients do not select a professional whom they feel is devoted to their welfare and who will do his or her best. Rather, prospective clients buy a product that, like other products, they feel should be guaranteed by the seller. Like other products, buyers believe that the higher the cost, the higher should be the quality and effectiveness of that product. As in all tradesperson–customer relationships, the judge of the quality of the product is the customer, not the tradesperson or the tradesperson's colleagues.

In the fee-for-service model, authority essentially lies with the professional. Help-seekers can, of course, refuse to defer to the authority of the professional or can sabotage the professional's efforts, as is indicated in the extensive literature on medical noncompliance.[9] In this model, problems are seen solely through the eyes of the professional; it is the professional who decides what can and should be done about the help seeker's problems.

In the service-ideal model, on the other hand, authority lies with the help seeker, and the professional must get the help seeker to share that authority. The social worker does this through a socialization process in which the help seeker comes to believe that the professional is operating solely in the help seeker's best interests. Furthermore, through this process, the help seeker comes to believe that the professional defines problems in the same way as does the help seeker.

Becoming a Client

Persons seeking professional help must enter a role relationship—doctor–patient, lawyer–client, therapist–patient, minister–parishioner, social worker–client, teacher–student, and so forth. Entry into the role relationship imposes a set of mutual obligations upon the help seeker and the help provider that specify what each must do in order for help to be offered and received. It is a mistake to presume that one's appearance in a lawyer's waiting room, a social worker's office, or a hospital bed means that a professional–client role relationship has been established. As is true with other roles, the norms of the patient or client role must be learned. These norms cover a variety of complex matters such as the way in which fees, if any, are to be paid; agreement on what will be done to help the applicant; the simultaneous use of two or more professionals; complying with the professional's directives; providing the professional with pertinent information; acquiring pertinent information from the professional; ascertaining what can legitimately be expected of the professional; defining the client's right to self-determination; explaining the rules of confidentiality; assuring that the professional is acting only in the client's behalf; defining the circumstances under which either the help seeker or the professional may terminate the relationship.

Sociologists point out that norms are learned through a socialization process that occurs prior to or very shortly after an individual moves into a new status.[10] So it must be with the help seeker as well. The help seeker becomes a client only after learning and agreeing to conform to the appropriate norms, and only clients can be successfully treated or served. Although social workers, more than other professionals, strive to establish a "helping relationship," they have "not clearly specified who is a client, [or] the process by which individuals become clients."[11] Helen Perlman distinguishes an applicant as "one who makes a request for something he wants" versus a client as "one who employs the services of a profession or business."[12] This distinction identifies two roles that are crucial in determining who is receiving professional help and who is not.

We would add a third role—that of novitiate—to Perlman's roles of applicant and client. An applicant cannot employ the services of a profession or business—that is, become a client—until the norms for the role of client have been inculcated through the socialization process. During socialization to the role of client, an individual occupies the status of novitiate. If one closely examines the list of malpractice claims against social workers provided by Besharov,[13] it appears that "novitiates" (our term) are far more likely to sue professionals than are true clients (Table 2). Although translating the legal categories provided by Besharov into the three stages of socialization is hazardous, it appears that nearly half of the malpractice claims reported in his data are a consequence of not having successfully completed the novitiate phase of socialization. Further support for such an hypothesis can also be gleaned from data reported by William Gates for the Lawyers Professional Liability committee of the American Bar Association.[14] He reports that fully 15.6 percent of the malpractice errors of lawyers involve "client relations." He has in mind such errors as "failure to obtain client's consent," "failure to inform client," or "failure to follow client's instructions." These errors, however, constitute only part of the failure to socialize clients. Other data drawn from a report of malpractice

suits against Arkansas lawyers can more easily, but far from perfectly, be translated into the

TABLE 2. Malpractice claims against social workers according to stages of socialization ($N = 225$).*

	Complaints (N)	%
Applicant	15	6.7
Improper or incorrect diagnosis	13	5.8
Failure to refer	2	0.9
Novitiate	110	48.9
Incorrect treatment	27	12.0
Improper child placement	18	8.0
Breach of confidentiality	16	7.1
Improper removal from placement	13	5.8
Countersuit—due to fee collection	10	4.4
Defamation (libel/slander)	8	3.6
Breach of contract	7	3.1
False imprisonment	6	2.7
Failure to supervise client properly	5	2.2
Client	36	16.0
Improper death of client or others	15	6.7
Violation of civil rights	9	4.0
Suicide of client	9	4.0
Abandonment of client	2	0.9
Failure to cure, poor results	1	0.4
Unclassifiable	64	28.4
Sexual impropriety	34	15.1
Miscellaneous	17	7.6
Bodily injury to client	7	3.1
Assault and battery	3	1.3
Accident on premises	2	0.9
Licensing or peer review	1	0.4

*Data compiled from Douglas Besharov, *The Vulnerable Social Worker: Liability for Serving Children and Families* (Washington, D.C.: National Association of Social Workers, 1985): Chart 1-1, p. 3.

stages of socialization.[15] These data, presented in Table 3, show that more than two-thirds of the complaints from 1981 to 1986 represented miscommunication of the norms of the lawyer–client relationship.

The authors' previous work indicates that becoming a client is not simply a transaction between two people—the helper and the help seeker.[16] Socialization takes place within a wider context that structures the interaction between them. First, society must conceive of the help seeker's behavior or situation as requiring professional intervention. Second, the profession must have and be willing to apply the technology that will ameliorate the help seeker's condition. Third, the help seeker must legitimate the authority of the professional and comply with the norms of the client role. Fourth, the help seeker's family and peers must provide social support. The latter point is especially important for understanding the socialization process. Lawsuits are sometimes filed by relatives rather than by the help seekers themselves, particularly in suits alleging improper death, solicitation, failure to supervise a client, or improper removal from placement. That the support of relatives and friends is important in treatment is well known. Their support is also required if novitiates are to be successfully socialized and practitioners are to avoid malpractice suits.

Until socialization is completed, the applicant has not entered the client–worker relationship. Unless an individual has graduated from the roles of applicant and novitiate, that individual cannot be the client of a lawyer, social worker, architect, teacher, and so forth. Many lawsuits are brought by help seekers who are still in the novitiate phase of the socialization process. These novitiates have not as yet legitimated the right of the professional to engage in treatment or service delivery. Consequently, efforts to provide such services would often be seen by novitiates as malpractice.

The Emerging Profile of the Profession

As professional technology and specialization have increased, so too has the need for more training, more staff, and more sophisticated equipment. Because of these increases, the cost of providing professional services, especially in the medical field, has skyrocketed.[17] Data (see Table 4 for examples from medicine and the law) have clearly shown that specialists are more likely to be sued for malpractice than are generalists.

The specialist, particularly, often justifies high fees on the basis of the cost of attaining his or her skill, the cost of the sophisticated equipment used, and, most important, the high quality of the service rendered.

Specialists are also vulnerable to overconcentrating on the technical problems brought to them and ignoring the socialization requirements for inducting applicants into the role of client. They make the common mistake of assuming that applicants who are referred to them are clients. Consequently, the help seeker has no opportunity to perceive the professional as a helping, caring, devoted individual. Furthermore, the specialist's failure to socialize clients means that the client–professional relationship, which might protect the specialist from malpractice suits, does not develop.

Because of these costs, a feeling has begun to emerge among clients that the professional cares more about the fees than about the help seeker's welfare. Rather than assuming that the doctor, lawyer, social worker, or other professional is devoted to his or her welfare, the help seeker begins to assume that the quality of the service is directly related to the size of the fee,[18] which quickly leads to a "show me that you are

TABLE 3. Malpractice complaints against lawyers in Arkansas 1982–1986 according to stages of socialization (N = 3,483).*

	Complaints (N)	%
Applicant	34	1.0
Refusing to withdraw	14	0.4
Advertising	12	0.3
Solicitation	8	0.2
Novitiate	2406	69.1
Failure to perform	551	15.8
Neglect	517	14.8
Failure to communicate	438	12.6
Undue delay	283	8.1
Fee dispute	277	8.0
Failure to turn over file	146	4.2
Conflict of interest	100	2.9
Harassment	49	1.4
Improper withdrawal	13	0.4
Acquiring interest in litigation	12	0.3
Communicating with adverse persons	10	0.3
Commingling of funds	7	0.2
Revealing confidential information	2	0.1
Dividing fees with nonlawyer	1	<0.1
Client	250	7.2
Incompetence	100	2.9
Misappropriation of funds	60	1.7
Failure to perfect an appeal	51	1.5
Allowed statute of limitations to run	35	1.0
Ineffective counsel	4	0.1
Unclassifiable	793	22.8
Deceit, fraud, misrepresentation	404	11.6
Bonding	289	8.3
Engaged in illegal conduct	59	1.7
Failure to pay debts	36	1.0
Omitting practice	5	0.2

*Data compiled from Walter R. Niblock and Ann R. Henry, "Complaints against Attorneys on the Rise," *Arkansas Lawyer* 21 (July 1987): Table II, p. 109.

worth the fees that I am paying" attitude. The higher the cost of the service, the more likely the help seeker is to expect a totally successful resolution of his or her problem(s).

Such an attitude would not be severely damaging were it not for the fact that high fees create an unrealistic expectation in the mind of the help seeker concerning the outcome of the service. Persons seeking legal assistance expect their case to be won, regardless of the merits of their legal position; patients having torn cartilage replaced expect to be made "as good as new"; and anxiety-ridden business executives expect a therapist not only to eliminate their anxiety, but to replace it with a zest for corporate life. When such expectations are not realized, help seekers assume that the professional has not carried out his or her end of the bargain and look for a reason to sue.

Social workers and other professionals, such as the clergy, are generally insulated from such expectations. Social workers often do not extract fees from the client for the services that they perform. When fees are paid, they are far more modest, even among those in private practice, than are fees charged by physicians and lawyers. This lack of obvious material reward for social workers enables help seekers to feel that services are controlled more by client need than by the fee to be paid to the professional. Consequently, help seekers are less likely to sue a social worker than they are a physician.

Conclusion

The fee-for-service model is gradually dominating delivery of professional services.

A variety of practitioners, agencies and even state governments have begun to require contract-like agreements for clients receiving services. Such agreements commonly include commitments by client, guardian, and therapist to specifically identified goals, procedures to be used, and methods to assess progress. Also included are mechanisms for periodic reviews and modifying the agreement. In some cases, fee arrangements and other elements of the overall treatment context are included.[19]

There may, in fact, be no alternative to such a development, given the explosion of technical knowledge requiring professionals to specialize if they are to reap the personal rewards of professional status.

Ironically, we see social work as being less likely to suffer a radical transformation of its service-ideal model because it has (1) shared less in the technological explosion among professions, (2) avoided inflated expectations of its powers of rehabilitation, (3) not rewarded its practitioners with the material wealth and comfort of many other professions, and (4) focused some of its energies on converting help seekers into clients. However, the social work profession may become more vulnerable to the fee-for-service model as the proportion of private practitioners increases. Private practitioners lack the aura of selfless service provided by an agency's social purpose and philosophy. Of all the professions (except religious ministry), social work appears most likely to retain clients' belief in their practitioners' selfless dedication to the welfare of humanity. If social work manages to retain this image and continues to socialize applicants into clients, it will be less vulnerable to the crippling effects of malpractice suits.

TABLE 4. Malpractice suits among physicians and lawyers*

Physicians (rate per specialist)	
Internists	14.0
Obstetricians and gynecologists	10.3
Psychiatrists	7.1
Pediatricians	6.0
Anesthesiologists	3.6
Opthalmologic surgeons	3.2
Orthopedists	3.2
Urologists	1.9
Neurosurgeons	0.5
Plastic surgeons	0.5
Lawyers (percentage of claims by area)	
Real estate	24.9
Personal injury—plaintiff	24.0
Collection—bankruptcy	12.3
Family law	7.8
Estates and probate	7.1
Corporations and business organizations	4.9
Criminal law	3.3
Personal injury—defendant	2.7
Worker's compensation	2.3
Security and exchange commission	2.0
Tax	1.7
Business transactions	1.3
Civil rights	1.1
All other	4.6

*The data for physicians and lawyers are not comparable. The physicians' data show the number of suits per specialist. Lawyers, however, are less likely to identify themselves as specialists in a particular branch of the law. Thus, the data for lawyers show the proportion of malpractice suits by the area of the law. Data sources: physicians—John Guinther, *The Malpractitioners* (Garden City, N.Y.: Anchor Press/Doubleday, 1978), Table B, pp. 8–9; lawyers—William H. Gates, "The Newest Data on Lawyers' Malpractice Claims," *ABA Journal* 70 (April 1984): 8C.

3. Besharov, *The Vulnerable Social Worker*, p. 3

4. Quoted in Paul M. Barrett, "The Premed Machine," *The Washington Monthly* 17 (May 1985): 44.

5. Hippocrates, *Precepts*, trans. Walter Jones (Cambridge, Mass.: Harvard University Press, 1972), p. 319.

6. Anthony Maluccio, *Learning from Clients: Interpersonal Helping as Viewed by Clients and Social Workers* (New York: Free Press, 1979), p. 59.

7. Bob Wyrick and Adrian Peracchio, "Malpractice/The Bitter Pill," *Newsday*, 25 October 1985, p. 28.

8. Interestingly, this model was proposed by the medical profession in early Colonial days. The model was rejected, however, when legislatures, particularly those in New Jersey and Connecticut, refused to accredit the medical societies as the sole purveyors of medical care. The reasons for the rejection were similar to current complaints about all professions: fee schedules were considered disreputable by the public and physicians were "bold in their frank and open acknowledgment of their economic motives." Consequently, political opposition to the incorporation of medical societies arose, based on the "danger of establishing monopolies [and on] contradictions between physicians' claims that they were disinterested men of science and the very real financial benefits that would accrue from state grants of incorporation of medical societies." It was only when physicians attached themselves to universities that an image of scientific objectivity and public service could be conveyed. Peter Dobkin Hall, "The Foundations of Professional Credibility: Linking the Medical Profession to Higher Education in Connecticut and Massachusetts, 1700–1830," in *The Authority of Experts: Studies in History and Theory*, ed. Thomas L. Haskell (Bloomington Ind.: Indiana University Press, 1984), p. 116.

1. Douglas Besharov, *The Vulnerable Social Worker: Liability for Serving Children and Families* (Washington, D.C.: National Association of Social Workers, 1985).

2. For the ten-year period 1978–87, *Social Work Research & Abstracts* lists eleven articles on malpractice. This contrasts with the ten-year period 1968–77, in which only two were listed.

94

9. See M. Robin DiMatteo and D. Dante DiNicoia, *Achieving Patient Compliance* (New York: Pergamon Press. 1982).

10. Bruce J. Biddle and Edwin J. Thomas. "Learning and Socialization," in *Role Theory: Concepts and Research* (New York: John Wiley, 1966), pp. 345–382.

11. Abraham Alcabes and James A. Jones. "Structural Determinants of Clienthood," *Social Work* 30 (January–February 1985): 49.

12. Helen Harris Perlman. *Persona: Social Role and Personality* (Chicago: University of Chicago Press, 1968), p. 166.

13. Douglas Besharov, *The Vulnerable Social Worker.*

14. William H. Gates. "The Newest Data on Lawyers' Malpractice Claims," *ABA Journal* 70 (April 1984): 78–84.

15. Walter R. Niblock and Ann R. Henry, "Complaints against Attorneys on the Rise," *Arkansas Lawyer* 21 (July 1987): 108–109.

16. Alcabes and Jones, "Structural Determinants of Clienthood."

17. Physicians' fees and hospital care, for example. have increased more than 40.000 percent and 80.000 percent. respectively, since 1948. See *Statistical Abstract of the United States: 1985* (Washington, D.C.: *Historical Statistics, Colonial Times to 1970* (Washington, D.C.: U. S. Government Printing Office, 1973), Series B 221–235. p. 73.

18. David Mechanic. "Physicians and Patients in Transition." *Hastings Center Report* (December 1985): 9–12.

19. Walter P. Christian, Hewitt B. Clark, and David E. Luke, "Client Rights in Clinical Counseling Services for Children," in *Preservation of Client Rights: A Handbook for Practitioners Providing Therapeutic, Educational, and Rehabilitative Services*, ed. Gerald T. Hannan, Walter P. Christian, and Hewitt B. Clark (New York: Free Press, 1981), p. 28.

GAMES PEOPLE PLAY IN SUPERVISION
ALFRED KADUSHIN

GAMESMANSHIP HAS HAD a checkered career. Respectably fathered by an eminent mathematician, Von Neumann, in his book *The Theory of Games and Economic Behavior,* it became the "Art of Winning Games Without Actually Cheating" as detailed by Potter in *Theory and Practice of Gamesmanship.*[1] It was partly rescued recently for the behavioral sciences by the psychoanalyst Eric Berne in *Games People Play.*[2]

Berne defines a game as "an ongoing series of complementary ulterior transactions—superficially plausible but with a concealed motivation."[3] It is a scheme, or artfulness, utilized in the pursuit of some objective or purpose. A ploy is a segment of a game.

The purpose of engaging in the game, of using the maneuvers, snares, gimmicks, and ploys that are, in essence, the art of gamesmanship, lies in the payoff. One party to the game chooses a strategy to maximize his payoff and minimize his penalties. He wants to win rather than to lose, and he wants to win as much as he can at the lowest cost.

Games people play in supervision are concerned with the kinds of recurrent interactional incidents between supervisor and supervisee that have a payoff for one of the parties in the transaction. While both supervisor and supervisee may initiate a game, for the purposes of simplicity it may be desirable to discuss in greater detail games initiated by supervisees. This may also be the better part of valor.

WHY GAMES ARE PLAYED

To understand why the supervisee should be interested in initiating a game, it is necessary to understand the possible losses that might be anticipated by him in the supervisory relationship. One needs to know what the supervisee is defending himself against and the losses he might incur if he

eschewed gamesmanship or lost the game.

The supervisory situation generates a number of different kinds of anxieties for the supervisee. It is a situation in which he is asked to undergo some sort of change. Unlike the usual educational situation that is concerned with helping the student critically examine and hence possibly change his ideas, social work supervision is often directed toward a change in behavior and, perhaps, personality. Change creates anxiety. It requires giving up the familiar for the unfamiliar; it requires a period of discomfort during which one is uneasy about continuing to use old patterns of behavior but does not, as yet, feel fully comfortable with new behaviors.

The threat of change is greater for the adult student because it requires dissolution of patterns of thinking and believing to which he has become habituated. It also requires an act of disloyalty to previous identification models. The ideas and behavior that might need changing represent, in a measure, the introjection of previously encountered significant others—parents, teachers, highly valued peers—and giving them up implies some rejection of these people in the acceptance of other models. The act of infidelity creates anxiety.

The supervisory tutorial is a threat to the student's independence and autonomy. Learning requires some frank admission of dependence on the teacher; readiness to learn involves giving up some measure of autonomy in accepting direction from others, in submitting to the authority of the supervisor-teacher.

The supervisee also faces a threat to his sense of adequacy. The situation demands an admission of ignorance, however limited, in some areas. And in sharing one's ignorance one exposes one's vulnerability. One risks the possibility of criticism, of shame, and perhaps of rejection because of one's admitted inadequacy. In addition, the supervisee faces the hazard of not being adequate to the requirements of the learning situation. His performance may fall short of the supervisor's expectations, intensifying a sense of inadequacy and incurring the possibility of supervisory disapproval.

Since the parameters of the supervisory relationship are often ambiguous, there is a threat that devolves not only from the sensed inadequacies of one's work, but also from the perceived or suspected inadequacies of self. This threat is exaggerated in the social work supervisory relationship because so much of self is invested in and reflected by one's work and because of the tendency to attribute to the supervisor a diagnostic omniscience suggesting that he perceives all and knows all.

The supervisor-supervisee relationship is evocative of the parent-child relationship and as such may tend to reactivate some anxiety associated with this earlier relationship. The supervisor is in a position of authority and the supervisee is, in some measure, dependent on him. If the supervisor is a potential parent surrogate, fellow supervisees are potential siblings competing for the affectional responses of the parent. The situation is therefore one that threatens the reactivation not only of residual difficulties in the parent-child relationship but also in the sibling-sibling relationship.

The supervisor has the responsibility of evaluating the work of the supervisee and, as such, controls access to important rewards and penalties. School grades, salary increases, and promotional possibilities are real and significant prizes dependent on a favorable evaluation. Unlike previously encountered evaluative situations, for instance working toward a grade in a course, this is a situation in which it is impossible to hide in a group. There is direct and sharply focused confrontation with the work done by the supervisee.

These threats, anxieties, and penalties are the losses that might be incurred in entering into the supervisory relationship. A desire to keep losses to a minimum and maximize the rewards that might derive from the encounter explains why the supervisee should want to play games in supervision, why he should feel a need to control the situation to his advantage.

Supervisees have over a period of time developed some well-established, identifiable games. An attempt will be made to group these games in terms of similar tactics. It might be important to note that not all supervisees play games and not all of the behavior supervisees engage in is indicative of an effort to play games. However, the best supervisee plays games some of the time; the poorest supervisee does not play games all of the time. What the author is trying to do is to identify a limited, albeit important, sector of supervisee behavior.

MANIPULATING DEMAND LEVELS

One series of games is designed to manipulate the level of demands made on the supervisee. One such game might be titled "Two Against the Agency" or "Seducing for Subversion." The game is generally played by intelligent, intuitively gifted supervisees who are impatient with routine agency procedures. Forms, reports, punctuality, and recording excite their contempt. The more sophisticated supervisee, in playing the game, introduces it by suggesting the conflict between the bureaucratic and professional orientation to the work of the agency. The bureaucratic orientation is one that is centered on what is needed to insure efficient operation of the agency; the professional orientation is focused on meeting the needs of the client. The supervisee points out that meeting client need is more important, that time spent in recording, filling out forms, and writing reports tends to rob time from direct work with the client, and further that it does not make any difference when he comes to work or goes home as long as no client suffers as a consequence. Would it not therefore be possible to permit him, a highly intuitive and gifted worker, to schedule and allocate his time to maximum client advantage and should not the supervisor, then, be less concerned about the necessity of his filling out forms, doing recording, completing reports, and so on?

For the student and recent graduate supervisee oriented toward the morality of the hippie movement (and many students, especially in social work, are responsive to hippie ideology, often without being explicitly aware of this), professional autonomy is consonant with the idea of self-expression—"doing your thing." Bureaucratic controls, demands, and expectations are regarded as violations of genuine self-expression and are resented as such.

It takes two to play games. The supervisor is induced to play (1) because he identifies with the student's concern for meeting client needs, (2) because he himself has frequently resented bureaucratic demands and so is, initially, sympathetic to the supervisee's complaints, and (3) because he is hesitant to assert his authority in demanding firmly that these requirements be met. If the supervisor elects to play the game, he has enlisted in an alliance with the supervisee to subvert agency administrative procedures.

Another game designed to control and mitigate the level of demands made on the supervisee might be called "Be Nice to Me Because I Am Nice to You." The principal ploy is seduction by flattery. The supervisee is full of praise: "You're the best supervisor I ever had," "You're so perceptive that after I've talked to you I almost know what the client will say next," "You're so consistently helpful," "I look forward in the future to being as good a social worker as you are," and so on. It is a game of emotional blackmail in which, having been paid in this kind of coin, the supervisor finds himself incapable of firmly holding the worker to legitimate demands.

The supervisor finds it difficult to resist engaging in the game because it is gratifying to be regarded as an omniscient source of wisdom; there is satisfaction in being perceived as helpful and in being selected as a pattern for identification and emulation. An invitation to play a game that tends to enhance a positive self-concept and feed one's narcissistic needs is likely to be accepted.

In general, the supervisor is vulnerable to an invitation to play this game. The supervisor needs the supervisee as much as the supervisee needs the supervisor. One of the principal sources of gratification for a worker is contact with the client. The supervisor is denied this source of gratification, at least directly. For the supervisor the principal source of gratification is helping the supervisee to grow and change. But this means that he has to look to the supervisee to validate his effectiveness. Objective criteria of such effectiveness are, at best, obscure and equivocal. However, to have the supervisee say explicitly, openly, and directly: "I have learned a lot from you," "You have been helpful," "I am a better worker because of you," is the kind of reassurance needed and often subtly solicited by the supervisor. The perceptive supervisee understands and exploits the supervisor's needs in initiating this game.

REDEFINING THE RELATIONSHIP

A second series of games is also designed to mitigate the level of demands made on the supervisee, but here the game depends on redefining the supervisory relationship. As Goffman points out, games permit one to control the conduct of others by influencing the definition of the situation.[4] These games depend on ambiguity of the definition of the supervisory relationship. It is open to a variety of interpretations and resembles, in some crucial respects, analogous relationships.

Thus, one kind of redefinition suggests a shift from the relationship of supervisor-supervisee as teacher-learner in an administrative hierarchy to supervisor-supervisee as worker-client in the context of therapy. The game might be called "Protect the Sick and the Infirm" or "Treat Me, Don't Beat Me." The supervisee would rather expose himself than his work. And so he asks the supervisor for help in solving his personal problems. The sophisticated player relates these problems to his difficulties on the job. Nevertheless, he seeks to engage the supervisor actively in a concern with his problems. If the translation to worker-client is made, the nature of demands shifts as well. The kinds of demands one can legitimately impose on a client are clearly less onerous than the level of expectations imposed on a worker. And the supervisee has achieved a payoff in a softening of demands.

The supervisor is induced to play (1) because the game appeals to the social worker in him (since he was a social worker before he became a supervisor and is still interested in helping those who have personal problems), (2) because it appeals to the voyeur in him (many supervisors are fascinated by the opportunity to share in the intimate life of others), (3) because it is flattering to be selected as a therapist, and (4) because the supervisor is not clearly certain as to whether such a redefinition of the situation is not permissible. All the discussions about the equivocal boundaries between supervision and therapy feed into this uncertainty.

Another game of redefinition might be called "Evaluation Is Not for Friends." Here the supervisory relationship is redefined as a social relationship. The supervisee makes an effort to take coffee breaks with the supervisor, invite him to lunch, walk to and from the bus or the parking lot with him, and discuss some common interests during conferences. The social component tends to vitiate the professional component in the relationship. It requires increased determination and resolution on the part of any supervisor to hold the "friend" to the required level of performance.

Another and more contemporary redefinition is less obvious than either of the two kinds just discussed, which have been standard for a long time now. This is the game of "Maximum Feasible Participation." It involves a shift in roles from supervisor-supervisee to peer-peer. The supervisee suggests that the relationship will be most effective if it is established on the basis of democratic participation. Since he knows best what he needs and wants to learn, he should be granted equal responsibility for determining the agendas of conferences. So far so good. The game is a difficult one to play because in the hands of a determined supervisee, joint control of agenda can easily become supervisee control with consequent mitigation of expectations. The supervisor finds himself in a predicament in trying to decline the game. For one, there is an element of validity in the claim that people learn best in a context that encourages democratic participation in the learning situation. Second, the current trend in working with the social agency client encourages maximum feasible participation with presently undefined limits. To decline the game is to suggest that one is old-fashioned, undemocratic, and against the rights of those on lower levels in the administrative hierarchy—not an enviable picture to project of oneself. The supervisor is forced to play but needs to be constantly alert in order to maintain some semblance of administrative authority and prevent all the shots being called by the supervisee-peer.

REDUCING POWER DISPARITY

A third series of games is designed to reduce anxiety by reducing the power disparity between supervisor and worker. One source of the supervisor's power is, of course, the consequence of his position in the administrative hierarchy vis-à-vis the supervisee. Another source of power, however, lies in his expertise, greater knowledge, and superior skill. It is the second source of power disparity that is vulnerable to this series of games. If the supervisee can establish the fact that the supervisor is not so smart after all, some of the power differential is mitigated and with it some need to feel anxious.

One such game, frequently played, might be called "If You Knew Dostoyevsky Like I Know Dostoyevsky." During the course of a conference the supervisee makes a casual allusion to the fact that the client's behavior reminds him of that of Raskolnikov in *Crime and Punishment,* which is, after all, somewhat different in etiology from the pathology that plagued Prince Myshkin in *The Idiot.* An effective ploy, used to score additional points, involves addressing the rhetorical question: "You remember, don't you?" to the supervisor. It is equally clear to both the supervisee and the supervisor that the latter does not remember—if, indeed, he ever knew what he cannot remember now. At this point the supervisee proceeds to instruct the supervisor. The roles of teacher-learner are reversed; power disparity and supervisee anxiety are simultaneously reduced.

The supervisor acquiesces to the game because refusal requires an open confession of ignorance on his part. The supervisee in playing the game well co-operates in a conspiracy with the supervisor not to expose his ignorance openly. The discussion proceeds under the protection of the mutually accepted fiction that *both* know what they are talking about.

The content for the essential gambit in this game changes with each generation of supervisees. The author's impression is that currently the allusion is likely to be to the work of the conditioning therapists—Eysenck, Wolpe, and Lazarus—rather than to literary figures. The effect on the supervisor, however, is the same: a feeling of depression and general malaise at having been found ignorant when his position requires that he know more than the supervisee. And it has the same payoff in reducing supervisee anxiety.

Another kind of game in this same genre exploits situational advantages to reduce power disparity and permit the supervisee the feeling that he, rather than the supervisor, is in control. This game is "So What Do *You* Know About It?" The supervisee with a long record of experience in public welfare makes reference to "those of us on the front lines who have struggled with the multiproblem client," exciting humility in the supervisor who has to try hard to remember when he last saw a live client. A married supervisee with children will allude to her marital experience and what it "really is like to be a mother" in discussing family therapy with an unmarried female supervisor. The older supervisee will talk about "life" from the vantage point of incipient senility to the supervisor fresh out of graduate school. The younger supervisee will hint at his greater understanding of the adolescent client since he has, after all, smoked some pot and has seriously considered LSD. The supervisor trying to tune in finds his older psyche is not with it. The supervisor younger than the older supervisee, older than the younger supervisee—never having raised a child or met a payroll—finds himself being instructed by those he is charged with instructing; roles are reversed and the payoff lies in the fact that the supervisor is a less threatening figure to the supervisee.

Another, more recently developed, procedure for "putting the supervisor down" is through the judicious use in the conference of strong four-letter words. This is "telling it like it is" and the supervisor who responds with discomfort and loss of composure has forfeited some amount of control to the supervisee who has exposed some measure of his bourgeois character and residual Puritanism.

Putting the supervisor down may revolve around a question of social work goals rather than content. The social action-oriented supervisee is concerned with fundamental changes in social relationships. He knows that obtaining a slight increase in the budget for his client, finding a job for a client, or helping a neglectful mother relate more positively to her child are not of much use since they leave the basic pathology of society undisturbed and unchanged. He is impatient with the case-oriented supervisor who is interested in helping a specific family live a little less troubled, a little less unhappily, in a fundamentally disordered society. The game is "All or Nothing at All." It is designed to make the supervisor feel he has sold out, been co-opted by the Establishment, lost or abandoned his broader vision of the "good" society, become endlessly concerned with symptoms rather than with causes. It is effective because the supervisor recognizes that there is some element of truth in the accusation, since this is true for all who occupy positions of responsibility in the Establishment.

CONTROLLING THE SITUATION

All the games mentioned have, as part of their effect, a shift of control of the situation from supervisor to supervisee. Another series of games is designed to place control of the supervisory situation more explicitly and directly in the hands of the supervisee. Control of the situation by the supervisor is potentially threatening since he can then take the initiative of introducing for discussion those weaknesses and inadequacies in the supervisee's work that need fullest review. If the supervisee can control the conference, much that is unflattering to discuss may be adroitly avoided.

One game designed to control the discussion's content is called "I Have a Little List." The supervisee comes in with a series of questions about his work that he would very much like to discuss. The better player formulates the questions so that they have relevance to those problems in which the supervisor has greatest professional interest and about which he has done considerable reading. The supervisee is under no obligation to listen to the answer to his question. Question 1 having been asked, the supervisor is off on a short lecture, during which time the supervisee is free to plan mentally the next weekend or review the last weekend, taking care merely to listen for signs that the supervisor is running down. When this happens, the supervisee introduces Question 2 with an appropriate transitional comment and the cycle is repeated. As the supervisee increases the supervisor's level of participation he is, by the same token, decreasing his own level of participation since only one person can be talking at once. Thus the supervisee controls both content and direction of conference interaction.

The supervisor is induced to play this game because there is narcissistic gratification in displaying one's knowledge and in meeting the dependency needs of those who appeal to one for answers to their questions, and because the supervisee's questions should be accepted, respected, and, if possible, answered.

Control of the initiative is also seized by the supervisee in the game of "Heading Them Off at the Pass." Here the supervisee knows that his poor work is likely to be analyzed critically. He therefore opens the conference by freely admitting his mistakes —he knows it was an inadequate interview, he knows that he should have, by now, learned to do better. There is no failing on the supervisor's agenda for discussion with him to which he does not freely confess in advance, flagellating himself to excess. The supervisor, faced with overwhelming self-derogation, has little option but to reassure the supervisee sympathetically. The tactic not only makes difficult an extended discussion of mistakes in the work at the supervisor's initiative, it elicits praise by the supervisor for whatever strengths the supervisee has manifested, however limited. The supervisor, once again, acts out of concern with the troubled, out of his predisposition to comfort the discomforted, out of pleasure in acting the good, forgiving parent.

There is also the game of control through fluttering dependency, of strength through weakness. It is the game of "Little Old Me" or "Casework à Trois." The supervisee, in his ignorance and incompetence, looks to the knowledgeable, competent supervisor for a detailed prescription of how to proceed: "What would *you* do next?" "Then what would *you* say?" The supervisee unloads responsibility for the case onto the supervisor and the supervisor shares the case load with the worker. The supervisor plays the game because, in reality, he does share responsibility for case management with the supervisee and has responsibility for seeing that the client is not harmed. Further, the supervisor often is interested in the gratification of carrying a case load, however vicariously, so that he is somewhat predisposed to take the case out of the hands of the supervisee. There are, further, the pleasures derived from acting the capable parent to the dependent child and from the domination of others.

A variant of the game in the hands of a more hostile supervisee is "I Did Like You Told Me." Here the supervisee maneuvers the supervisor into offering specific prescriptions on case management and then applies the prescriptions in spiteful obedience and undisguised mimicry. The supervisee acts as though the supervisor were responsible for the case, he himself merely being the executor of supervisory directives. Invariably and inevitably, whatever has been suggested by the supervisor fails to accomplish what it was supposed to accomplish. "I Did Like You Told Me" is designed to make even a strong supervisor defensive.

"It's All So Confusing" attempts to reduce the authority of the supervisor by appeals to other authorities—a former supervisor, another supervisor in the same agency, or a faculty member at a local school of social work with whom the supervisee just happened to discuss the case. The supervisee casually indicates that in similar situations his former supervisor tended to take such and such an approach, one that is at variance with the approach the current supervisor regards as desirable. And "It's All So Confusing" when different "authorities" suggest such different approaches to the same situation. The supervisor is faced with "defending" his approach against some unnamed, unknown competitor. This is difficult, especially when few situations in social work permit an unequivocal answer in which the supervisor can have categorical confidence. Since the supervisor was somewhat shaky in his approach in the first place, he feels vulnerable against alternative suggestions from other "authorities" and his sense of authority vis-à-vis the supervisee is eroded.

A supervisee can control the degree of threat in the supervisory situation by distancing techniques. The game is "What You Don't Know Won't Hurt Me." The supervisor knows the work of the supervisee only indirectly, through what is shared in the recording and verbally in the conference. The supervisee can elect to share in a manner that is thin, inconsequential, without depth of affect. He can share selectively and can distort, consciously or unconsciously, in order to present a more favorable picture of his work. The supervisee can be passive and reticent or overwhelm the supervisor with endless trivia.

In whatever manner it is done, the supervisee increases distance between the work he actually does and the supervisor who is responsible for critically analyzing with him the work done. This not only reduces the threat to him of possible criticism of his work but also, as Fleming points out, prevents the supervisor from intruding into the privacy of the relationship between the worker and the client.[5]

SUPERVISORS' GAMES

It would be doing both supervisor and supervisee an injustice to omit any reference to games initiated by supervisors—unjust to the supervisees in that such omission would imply that they alone play games in supervision and unjust to the supervisors in suggesting that they lack the imagination and capacity to devise their own counter-games. Supervisors play games out of felt threats to their position in the hierarchy, uncertainty about their authority, reluctance to use their authority, a desire to be liked, a need for the supervisees' approbation—and out of some hostility to supervisees that is inevitable in such a complex, intimate relationship.

One of the classic supervisory games is called "I Wonder Why You Really Said That?" This is the game of redefining honest disagreement so that it appears to be psychological resistance. Honest disagreement requires that the supervisor defend his point of view, present the research evidence in support of his contention, be sufficiently acquainted with the literature so he can cite the knowledge that argues for the correctness of what he is saying. If honest disagreement is redefined as resistance, the burden is shifted to the supervisee. He has to examine his needs and motives that prompt him to question what the supervisor has said. The supervisor is thus relieved of the burden of validating what he has said and the onus for defense now rests with the supervisee.

Another classic supervisory game is "One Good Question Deserves Another." It was explicated some years ago by a new supervisor writing of her experience in an article called "Through Supervision With Gun and Camera":

I learned that another part of a supervisor's skills, as far as the workers are concerned, is to know all the answers. I was able to get out of this very easily. I discovered that when a worker asks a question, the best thing to do is to immediately ask for what she thinks. While the worker is figuring out the answer to her own question (this is known as growth and development), the supervisor quickly tries to figure it out also. She may arrive at the answer the same time as the worker, but the worker somehow assumes that she knew it all along. This is very comfortable for the supervisor. In the event that neither the worker nor the supervisor succeeds in coming up with a useful thought on the question the worker has raised, the supervisor can look wise and suggest that they think about it and discuss it further next time. This gives the supervisor plenty of time to look up the subject and leaves the worker with the feeling that the supervisor is giving great weight to her question. In the event that the supervisor does not want to go to all the trouble, she can just tell the worker that she does not know the answer (this is known as helping the worker accept the limitations of the supervision) and tell her to look it up herself. . . .[6]

IN RESPONSE TO GAMES

Before going on to discuss possible constructive responses to games played in the context of supervision, the author must express some uneasiness about having raised the subject in the first place, a dissatisfaction similar to the distaste felt toward Berne's *Games People Play*. The book communicates a sense of disrespect for the complexities of life and human behavior. The simplistic games formulas are a cheapening caricature of people's struggle for a modicum of comfort in a difficult world. A perceptive psychiatrist said in a critical and saddening review of the book:

It makes today's bothersome "problems" easily subject to a few home-spun models —particularly the cynical and concretely aphoristic kind that reduces all human experiences to a series of "exchanges" involving gain and loss, deceit or betrayal and exposure, camouflage and discovery.[7]

There are both a great deal more sensible sincerity and a great deal more devious complexity in multidetermined human interaction than is suggested by *Games People Play*.

However, the very fact that games are a caricature of life justifies discussing them. The caricature selects some aspect of human behavior and, extracting it for explicit examination, exaggerates and distorts its contours so that it is easier to perceive. The caricature thus makes possible increased understanding of the phenomenon—in this case the supervisory interaction. The insult to the phenomenon lies in forgetting that the caricature is just that—a caricature and not a truly accurate representation. A perceptive caricature, such as good satire, falsifies by distorting only elements that are actually present in the interaction in the first place. Supervisory games mirror, then, *some* selective, essentially truthful aspects of the supervisory relationship.

The simplest and most direct way of dealing with the problem of games introduced by the supervisee is to refuse to play. Yet one of the key difficulties in this has been implied by discussion of the gain for the supervisor in going along with the game. The supervisee can only successfully enlist the supervisor in a game if the supervisor wants to play for his own reasons. Collusion is not forced but is freely granted. Refusing to play requires the supervisor to be ready and able to forfeit self-advantages.

For instance, in declining to go along with the supervisee's requests that he be permitted to ignore agency administrative requirements in playing "Two Against the Agency," the supervisor has to be comfortable in exercising his administrative authority, willing to risk and deal with supervisee hostility and rejection, willing to accept and handle the accusation that he is bureaucratically, rather than professionally, oriented. In declining other games the supervisor denies himself the sweet fruits of flattery, the joys of omniscience, the pleasures of acting the therapist, the gratification of being liked. He has to incur the penalties of an open admission of ignorance and uncertainty and the loss of infallibility. Declining to play the games demands a supervisor who is aware of and comfortable in what he is doing and who is accepting of himself in all his "glorious strengths and human weaknesses." The less vulnerable the supervisor, the more impervious he is to gamesmanship—not an easy prescription to fill.

A second response lies in gradual interpretation or open confrontation. Goffman points out that in the usual social encounter each party accepts the line put out by the other party. There is a process of mutual face-saving in which what is said is accepted at its face value and "each participant is allowed to carry the role he has chosen for himself" unchallenged.[8] This is done out of self-protection since in not challenging another one is also insuring that the other will not, in turn, challenge one's own fiction. Confrontation implies a refusal to accept the game being proposed by seeking to expose and make explicit what the supervisee is doing. The supervisory situation, like the therapeutic situation, deliberately and consciously rejects the usual rules of social interaction in attempting to help the supervisee.

Confrontation is, of course, a procedure that needs to be used with some regard for the supervisee's ability to handle the embarrassment, discomfort, and self-threat it involves. It needs to be used with some understanding of the defensive significance of the game to the supervisee. It might be of importance to point out that naming the interactions that have been described

as "games" does not imply that they are frivolous and without consequence. Unmasking games risks much that is of serious personal significance for the supervisee. Interpretation and confrontation here, as always, require some compassionate caution, a sense of timing, and an understanding of dosage.

Perhaps another approach is to share honestly with the supervisee one's awareness of what he is attempting to do but to focus the discussion neither on the dynamics of his behavior nor on one's reaction to it, but on the disadvantages for him in playing games. These games have decided drawbacks for the supervisee in that they deny him the possibility of effectively fulfilling one of the essential, principal purposes of supervision—helping him to grow professionally. The games frustrate the achievement of this outcome. In playing games the supervisee loses by winning.

And, if all else fails, supervisees' games may yield to supervisors' counter-games. For instance, "I Have a Little List" may be broken up by "I Wonder Why You Really Asked That?" After all, the supervisor should have more experience at gamesmanship than the supervisee.

1 John Von Neumann, *Theory of Games and Economic Behavior* (Princeton, N.J.: Princeton University Press, 1944); Stephen Potter, *Theory and Practice of Gamesmanship* (New York: Henry Holt & Co., 1948).

2 New York: Grove Press, 1964.

3 *Ibid.*, p. 81.

4 Erving Goffman, *The Presentation of Self in Everyday Life* (Garden City, N.Y.: Anchor Books, Doubleday & Co., 1959), pp. 3–4.

5 Joan Fleming and Therese Benedek, *Psychoanalytic Supervision* (New York: Grune & Stratton, 1966), p. 101. See Norman Polansky, "On Duplicity in the Interview," *American Journal of Orthopsychiatry*, Vol. 37, No. 2 (April 1967), pp. 568–579, for a review of similar kinds of games played by the client.

6 H.C.D., "Through Supervision With Gun and Camera," *Social Work Journal*, Vol. 30, No. 4 (October 1949), p. 102.

7 Robert Coles, *New York Times*, Book Review Section (October 8, 1967), p. 8.

8 Erving Goffman, *Ritual Interaction* (Garden City, N.Y.: Anchor Books, Doubleday & Co., 1967), p. 11.

THE PARALLEL PROCESS IN SOCIAL WORK TREATMENT AND SUPERVISION

EVA M. KAHN

THERE ARE BOTH SIMILARITIES and differences between treatment and supervision. Both require a good relationship between a more knowledgeable "expert" and a learner. Both cognitive and emotional capacities are engaged in the two transactions, and an attempt is made to translate knowing into doing. The same psychodynamic principles apply to the two sets of relationships. In both instances, the learner reexperiences vis-à-vis the expert old established patterns regarding dependency, autonomy, submission to authority, hostility, competitiveness, fear of criticism and failure, as well as affection, idealization, and pleasure at accomplishments. Both are characterized by anxiety, fear, and resistance to change on the part of the learner. In both instances, the expert is prone to countertransference feelings, such as improper exercise of authority, displaced hostility, excessive narcissism, or need to nurture, all of which, if unrecognized, will interfere with the relationship. In both supervision and treatment there as in interpenetration of life and work which must constantly be scrutinized.

The most important difference between treatment and supervision is one of goal. In supervision, a major goal is the promotion of professional learning and growth and attainment of a stable, professional identity on the part of the supervisee. Toward this end, the supervisor makes an educational diagnosis. For the client, the goal is personal growth, improved coping ability, and capacity to function in his or her life situation. To accomplish this end, the social worker makes a psychosocial diagnosis.

Furthermore, the supervisee is expected to have resolved personal problems sufficiently to have ego capacity available to be of service to others; ego capacity that can be engaged in the learning process. No such expectation is made of the client, whose ego capacity may be quite poor. In both supervision and treat-

ment an effort is made to provide a non-judgmental setting within which it is safe to show ignorance, make mistakes, and try out new behavior, although supervisees know they are periodically evaluated and clients are not. Hence, a judgmental element is inevitable in the supervisory relationship. Whereas in treatment all aspects of the client's personal dynamics are explored without reservation, most supervisors limit such explorations with their supervisees. When a supervisee's psychodynamic problem interferes with the treatment, supervisors will draw attention to it, making it as specific as possible. But the resolution of a supervisee's personality problem is usually not seen as a supervisory responsibility.

The Parallel Process

Treatment and supervision also share the simultaneous occurrence of similar psychodynamic processes in both relationships. This phenomenon, which has been variously called the parallel process, the reflection process, or mirroring[1] has been described in publications dealing with the training of psychotherapists and psychoanalysts, but rarely in social work literature. The concept of the parallel process refers to the simultaneous emergence of similar emotional difficulties in the relationship between social worker and client, social worker and supervisor, and postulates a link between these two relationships, whereby emotions generated in one are acted out in the other. The supervisor, social worker, and client are all actors in this scenario, which can create a treatment impasse that must be resolved if treatment or supervision is to continue satisfactorily.

It is the purpose of this article to demonstrate that the parallel process must be understood by supervisors if they are to be effective in helping supervisees treat clients successfully. An attempt will also be made to explore the causes of the parallel process and to describe a supervisory intervention designed to resolve this treatment impasse.

The Supervisory Relationship and Treatment

Rudolf Ekstein and Robert S. Wallerstein were among the first to recognize and study the connection between the supervisory relationship and treatment. They reserve the terms transference and countertransference for therapy and call the affective problems between supervisor and supervisee the student's "problems about learning" and the problems existing in the treatment relationship the student's "learning problems." They also draw attention to the supervisor's unresolved conflicts about the teaching role as a possible factor affecting the supervisory and, indirectly, the treatment relationship.[2]

Margery Doehrman, in her research study on the parallel process, emphasized the intensity of students' reactions to their supervisors and the considerable effect rather ordinary actions by the supervisor could have on therapists' feelings about themselves and upon the way they conducted their therapy. Old fears of inadequacy and criticism, of dependency and the wish for approval, and characteristic defenses and resistances to learning were called into play. Unlike the relaxed, collegial attitudes supervisors saw themselves as bringing to their supervisees, they were, according to Doehrman, often seen as admired teachers, but also as feared and powerful judges.[3]

The Transference Problem

Doehrman's study showed that the therapist's intense relationship with the supervisor had demonstrable effects on the treatment process. Each supervisor was quickly pulled into a transference relationship, and certain key problems of the therapist were awakened and acted out not only in supervision but in his or her relationship with clients. The transference paradigm was found to be consonant with a core neurotic problem or transference disposition of the supervisee and, to some extent, of the supervisor. Therapists behaved with clients in a manner that was either similar to or opposite from that which they experienced with supervisors in supervision. Only after transference problems with supervisors had been resolved could therapists help clients resolve similar binds in the treatment relationship.

In social work the cognitive and conceptual levels of teaching are well established and practiced by most supervisors. However,

although it is generally accepted that the relationship is the vehicle through which both supervision and treatment occur, insufficient attention tends to be given to the nature of the supervisory relationship and its effect on treatment. As in the cases described by Doehrman, strong feelings are inevitably aroused in both supervisor and supervisee in their relationship. Transferential problems frequently develop. The manner in which supervisor and supervisee negotiate these feelings will affect the nature of the social worker's relationship and intervention with the client. Unrecognized and unresolved difficulties in the supervisory relationship can impede successful treatment.

The Treatment Relationship with the Client

The other major relationship in which social workers are involved is the treatment relationship with clients. Social workers tune in to clients' latent as well as overt feelings, including unconscious communications, and are expected to develop some degree of self-awareness in order to recognize and react appropriately to these messages, and bring to bear on them a body of conceptual knowledge. The development of self-awareness is, however, not always given the attention it deserves, and too few social work supervisors carefully explore with their supervisees transference and countertransference feelings aroused in them by particular clients. Fortunately, the old idea that social workers must not have strong feelings about their clients, and that they must remain emotionally neutral and "objective," is no longer generally accepted, and most supervisors would agree that "the concept of casework objectivity has grown in the field to mean the awareness of one's own feelings as they are aroused by the client. An acknowledgement of the feeling, rather than a denial of it, is a sign of the worker's capacity for developing further skills."[4]

Source of Interlocking Feelings

Thus, not only does the client transfer to the worker feelings related to some significant person in the client's past (transference), but the worker may develop strong feelings about the client. It is important for the worker to know whether these feelings stem from his or her own past and are transferred to the client (countertransference), or whether they are aroused entirely by the client's behavior or feelings. Or, to quote Janet Mattinson, the worker's "psychological skin needs to be sensitive enough to pick up some of the psychic difficulties of his client but it needs to be firm enough round his own being to be able to distinguish between what belongs to him and what is, in fact, some feeling he has introjected from the client."[5] The worker must also ask whether these feelings stem from his or her relationship with a supervisor.

The supervisor's task, then, is to attempt to understand, and help the worker understand, the interlocking of three possible sets of feelings: feelings aroused by the client that are imperfectly understood by the worker and acted out in supervision; transference feelings of the worker (that is, feelings stemming from the worker's past) that become activated in the supervisory relationship; and countertransference feelings of the supervisor, activated in the supervisory relationship. When a difficulty in the supervisory relationship resembles an impasse in the client-worker relationship, the parallel process is probably operating and its resolution will depend upon an accurate recognition and resolution of the transferential factors being transmitted from one relationship to the other.

In this connection, Doehrman states that "the most effective supervision . . . depends upon active insight into the interplay of forces in the parallel processes of therapy and supervision. The resolution of an existing difficulty between a student and a supervisor will often free the therapist to look with more spontaneity and capacity for insight into the dynamics of the existing patient-therapist relationship."[6]

Harold F. Searles' "reflection process" in psychoanalytic supervision is related to, but not identical with, the parallel process. He postulates that a supervisee unaware of a patient's emotional difficulty may unconsciously act it out in the supervisory session, and that the supervisee's behavior in supervision and the feelings aroused in the supervisor offer important diagnostic clues to the supervisor about the dynamics occurring between therapist and client.[7] This would appear to presuppose that the therapist is well analyzed and the interaction is not seriously contaminated by reactions he or she brings from his or her own past.

This assumption cannot be made for social workers, whose training does not require personal psychotherapy and most of whom have not had a thorough psychoanalysis. Hence, it falls upon the supervisor to distinguish, and to help the supervisee distinguish, whether the reflection process is operating, or whether the problem originates with the supervisee and is being played out in the relationship with the supervisor. At the same time, the supervisor must be aware of his or her own transferential impact upon the supervisee and the supervisory relationship.

Examples of the Parallel Process

At one family service agency, five examples of the parallel process occurring in supervision and casework treatment were collected from three graduate students of social work and two caseworkers. The students had been placed with the agency for their fieldwork training; the caseworkers held master's degrees in social work and had several years of practice experience. All five had the same supervisor. An attempt was made to identify the parallel process when it was happening, make it overt, and attempt to resolve it with the supervisee, and then to observe the effect of this resolution on the supervisee's work with the client. The supervisor also sought to determine whether the parallel process originated with the client, the supervisee, or the supervisor.

Example One: Fear of Being Adversely Judged

Early in her placement, a highly responsible graduate student brought to supervision the case of a narcissistic woman who made her feel anxious and frustrated because of her superficiality, frantic jumping from one topic to another, and constant demands for answers. The student felt she was "not getting anywhere" because the client seemed unable to stay with any one subject. Although the supervisory session was supposed to deal with one case in depth only, the supervisee brought to the session a long list of questions and problems unrelated to the case. Her anxiety was evident in her rapid speech and impatience for answers to many practical matters.

The supervisor pointed out this frenzy and disjointedness to the supervisee and indicated that she felt somewhat frustrated, as the supervisee did with her client. The supervisor then suggested that the supervisee slow down, think before she answered, and get in touch with what she was feeling. The supervisor spoke slowly and leaned back in her chair to slow down the supervisee. The supervisee responded and became more reflective; after a while, she expressed her anxiety about not knowing all the answers and about being "pushed against the wall" by the demanding client. She related this to her own fear of not performing adequately and of being judged adversely by the supervisor. She was greatly relieved to express these feelings, and even more relieved when she was told that she was not expected to know all the answers, that it was not even good for the client to be given too many answers. The supervisee became more calm and was able to discuss the case in greater depth. In her next session with the client, she slowed down the therapy session in much the same way as her supervisor had. The client was able to focus better and got in touch with her lack of self-confidence and fear of not being approved of.

In this example, there was a similarity between the client's need for approval and praise and the supervisee's anxiety about meeting what she imagined were the supervisor's standards for performance in her fieldwork practice. It was necessary to resolve her anxiety and fears in the supervisory relationship before she could address herself to the client's insecurities. Hence, this example illustrates an unresolved problem a supervisee had with a supervisor that impeded the treatment of the client.

Example Two: "Goofing Off"

A graduate student, whose treatment of clients was of very high caliber, brought to supervision her discovery that one of her clients, who had been working well in treatment, had not paid his fee for several months. At about the same time, the supervisor became aware that the student was not producing the dictation of case material required of her. When the supervisor confronted her with this, the student admitted that she had indeed not completed it. She then reflected that it was her pattern, when she felt approved of by authority figures, to "goof off" to test out whether she would still be accepted. She thus spoiled her good relationship with those in authority and later had to work hard to regain acceptance. The supervisor listened to this explanation, but resisted the temptation to be overly understanding or accepting; she insisted that the problem must be corrected. A structure was set up within which the student was to do the missing work. The student was uncomfortable with this, but accepted the need to carry out her obligation if she was to become a self-disciplined caseworker.

The supervisor brought the apparent similarity between her behavior and that of her nonpaying client to the student's attention, and the latter agreed that the underlying theme of "unconditional acceptance" seemed to be similar. Just as the supervisor had set limits on the student's regressive acting out in supervision, the student expressed her disappointment to the client in his next session that he had "not kept his end of the bargain." The client became angry and told the student she should treat him free of charge because she worked for a nonprofit agency. However, when the student confronted him with his "goofing off" and firmly communicated her expectation that he pay his fee, he agreed to meet his obligation. He paid half of the fee immediately and obtained two part-time jobs to earn money to pay the remainder. He then volunteered to the student that their relationship had been strengthened as a result of this experience.

This example represents the supervisee's acting out of her wish for unconditional acceptance by an authority figure, which resembled the client's desire to be similarly accepted by the student without meeting his obligation. This example, like the previous one, represents an unresolved problem that the supervisee had in the supervisory relationship. The student caseworker could treat her client successfully only after her own feelings toward the supervisor as authority figure had been resolved.

Example Three: Defense Against Dependency

A mature graduate student who showed much sensitivity and creativity in her work with children brought to supervision difficulties she was having with an overly responsible, sad, masochistic twelve-year-old girl client, who was resistant to continuing in treatment. Although the girl at times enjoyed the therapeutic hour once it had begun, she told the supervisee that "coming was no good" and did not help her. No matter how hard and creatively the supervisee worked with her, the child maintained her negative position. In supervision sessions, the supervisee expressed her frustration about the client's rejection of her efforts to engage her and said that she felt "put down" by the child.

During the same period, the supervisor had become aware of some discomfort in supervising this student. At times, when the supervisor was discussing the dynamics of a case, the student would say to her, "I know this already," or "I have done this already," making the supervisor feel that her teaching efforts were fruitless and not valued. The supervisor finally brought this to the student's attention, together with her feeling that the student was impatient with what the supervisor was offering her, and that the supervisor was wasting the student's time. The student admitted her behavior and, in exploring it, became aware that it was a long-established pattern that stemmed from her relationship with her mother. She told the supervisor that she was indeed learning from her, but that it was characteristic of her to not let the supervisor know this. In this way, she would not have to acknowledge her dependency on the supervisor, or be beholden to her.

The supervisor commented on the similarity between their interaction in supervision and the student's experience with the young girl who, it appeared, would also not acknowledge that she was benefiting from the student's considerable efforts. The supervisee readily saw the parallel process and was then able to engage the client on this issue. There was a lessening of her resistance to treatment, which was, unfortunately, broken off when the girl departed on a trip overseas.

This example is similar to the first two in that the psychodynamic difficulty that appeared in the supervisory relationship resided in the supervisee and stemmed from an early, unresolved need to defend against dependency and subtly denigrate the mother figure. Once this student became aware of her own feelings and successfully resolved them in supervision, she was able to help her client examine a similar dynamic.

Example Four: Disorganization

A usually effective and capable social worker brought to supervision the case of a divorced mother with three children who was under serious chronic financial and emotional strain. This depressed, poorly functioning mother defied the worker's numerous efforts to help her plan an orderly life for her family and an orderly method of treatment. Some unforeseen disaster always seemed to strike, resulting in a continuing state of emergency. The worker responded "on demand" with financial assistance or with additional sessions for the children, whenever the mother thought they needed these.

In supervision, it became evident that the worker was having trouble formulating a treatment goal and the means to reach it. She stated that she felt disorganized, frustrated, and exploited by the client. The worker sounded disorganized and diffuse and the supervisor was unable to get a clear picture of the case. The supervisee's explanations seemed very different from her usual clear-thinking, insightful, and creative formulations. The supervisor finally shared her impression of this atypical behavior with the supervisee and suggested that there might be a similarity between her own feelings and those of the client. The worker readily agreed. She said that this client had aroused so much disorganized feeling in her that she felt almost helpless and in despair.

Once the supervisee recognized these feelings as unusual and alien for her, she was able to disengage herself emotionally and formulate a treatment plan with clear objectives and limits. The plan called for the mother and her three children to be seen regularly for family sessions, while the mother's own, unexpressed needs were to be borne in mind. No further financial assistance was to be given. The worker was able to confront the mother with the latter's disorganized mode of functioning and stay with her emotionally, while insisting on regular family sessions. The mother soon responded positively by directly requesting help for herself with a hitherto concealed drinking problem.

In this example, unlike the first three, the diffuseness, helplessness, and despair clearly did not originate in the supervisee, but were absorbed by her during sessions with the clients. Unable to adequately describe the emotional transactions in this case, the supervisee acted them out in her behavior with the supervisor. The supervisor's task here was to recognize the behavior as uncharacteristic, and help her externalize it, so that it could be understood and dealt with.

Example Five: The Frustrated Supervisor

An experienced, conscientious worker brought to supervision the case of a woman with a borderline personality organization whose difficulties with her husband, her boyfriend, and the worker seemed unclear and poorly defined. In supervision, the worker described the case in such a vague, fragmented manner the supervisor had difficulty understanding it. The more details the worker told the supervisor, the less the latter felt she knew. In an effort to get more clarity, the supervisor began to ask questions; the worker responded to them with more details, without providing a coherent diagnostic picture. The supervisor, getting frustrated and still searching for clarity, began to suggest hypotheses about the client, but to no avail. The worker became defensive and more diffuse and the supervisory relationship became strained. The impasse continued for a while, the supervisor aware that the difficulty lay in the supervisory relationship and that probably a parallel process was at work. However, she was unable to recognize the specifics.

Finally, the worker confronted the supervisor with the impasse. She told her that when the latter had persisted in asking questions, she had felt criticized and thought her angry. Upon reflection, the supervisor acknowledged that she had been very frustrated, both at the worker's inability to give a coherent view of the client and at her own inability to derive one from the material presented. In the circumstances, her frustration had succeeded only in making the supervisee more fragmented than before. The worker experienced considerable relief at the supervisor's admission of her frustration and was able to acknowledge her own problem of "not seeing the wood for the trees." Several sessions later, she told the supervisor that she had gained greater distance from the client and was able to see her more objectively. Her presentation was much clearer and she had a firmer hold on the case.

In this example, there was a parallel between the client's diffuseness and difficulty defining her personal problems and the worker's difficulty identifying the major diagnostic and treatment themes among the wealth of detail. The supervisor, who felt herself to be a structured person striving for clarity in order to teach well, became frustrated with both the supervisee and herself because of her inability to reach the desired educational goal. The resolution in the supervisory relationship was found when the supervisor, with the worker's help, could acknowledge to the worker her hitherto unrecognized frustration. This freed the worker to address her own difficulty of diffuseness and resulted in her becoming more definite in her relationship with the client, an indication of a resolution of the parallel process.

This example illustrates a parallel process that began with the client, was acted out by the worker, but was not recognized by the supervisor, who reacted instead with countertransference feelings that made the problem worse. The supervisor's acknowledgement of her feelings partially resolved the parallel process by releasing the worker from the supervisor's countertransference bind to the point where she could successfully address herself to her own difficulty with definition and integration.

Origin of the Parallel Process

There are puzzling questions concerning the origin of the parallel process and its simultaneous occurrence between supervisor and worker, and worker and client, respectively. The examples described seem to have originated in two different ways, four falling into one category and the remaining example into another.

Psychodynamic Patterns of Supervisors

As already discussed, the supervisees readily acknowledged that the troublesome feelings that interfered with treatment and were acted out in supervision represented aspects of their own psychodynamic patterns. The supervisor became the recipient of the supervisees' transference reactions toward parent and authority figures. But why did these transference reactions emerge only when the clients were dealing with similar emotional issues in their treatment with the supervisees?

Helene Deutsch, writing about psychoanalysis in 1926, offers a basis for an understanding of the parallel process when she suggests that under certain conditions affective psychic content emerging from the patient's unconscious becomes transmuted into an inner experience of the analyst, who may have a certain unconscious readiness to receive it. This content is recognized as belonging to the patient only in the course of subsequent intellectual work. Deutsch attributes this "intuitive attitude," that is the analyst's own process of identification, to "the fact that the psychic structure of the analyst is a product of developmental processes similar to those which the patient himself also experienced."[8]

David Sachs and Stanley H. Shapiro state that their "experience working with novice therapists ... has produced repetitive parallelisms which appear to derive from some general similarities among narcissistically vulnerable novices which, in turn, are congruent with anxieties found in most patients with regard to feelings of inadequacy, dependence on authority as a protection against helplessness, etc."[9]

The findings of the first three and the fifth examples described seem to confirm those of Sachs and Shapiro. The parallel process appears to begin with the client's relationship with the worker. If the client's transferential feelings unconsciously touch on a similar area of emotional vulnerability in the worker, they activate similar feelings in the supervisee who, thereupon, unconsciously acts out these feelings in supervision.

The nature of the feelings acted out and the type of identification varies with the individual. For instance, a very disorganized, undifferentiated client may temporarily stimulate this type of early, preoedipal identification in the worker, a state of development the worker has long outgrown. Grandiose expectations and a projected sense of entitlement can be similarly identified with and acted out in supervision. Characteristic defense mechanisms can be activated; for example, the worker, experiencing the supervisor as assaulting his or her autonomy, may transmit this to the client by way of identification with the aggressor. Or, the worker can identify with the client's denial of painful feelings, or sublimation of them into intellectual "discussions."

Thus, in the first example, the shallowness and demands of the narcissistic client, born of her insecurity and fear of rejection, stimulated similar feelings in the supervisee, whose own fear of being judged and found wanting by an authority figure were unconsciously acted out in supervision. In the second example, the client's dependent demand for unconditional acceptance (treatment without fee) induced a similar demand (supervision without dictation) in the supervisee. The crucial ingredient in this process of identification is the worker's unconscious familiarity with the emotion or defense mechanism, because it is part of his past or present personality structure. It is egosyntonic. The supervisor only learns of the process when the worker acts out in supervision what is experienced in treatment and explores this behavior with the worker. If the dynamic process with which the worker identified can be recognized, it can frequently be resolved, first in the supervisory relationship, and subsequently in treatment.

In the fifth example, the supervisor did not recognize the parallel process, thereby delaying its resolution. Although it did not occur in this example, a parallel process could begin with the supervisor's countertransference, remain unrecognized, and be acted out by the worker in treatment with adverse effects on the client. Some characteristic countertransference feelings with which workers might identify would include need to be loved (excessive narcissism), critical authority (identification with the aggressor), the omnipotent parent, and so on.

Reflective Pattern of Supervisee

In contrast to the preceding examples, the parallel process in the fourth example seems to have a different origin. The emotions acted out in this parallel process did not appear to stem from the supervisee's personality, nor were they derived from her childhood experiences; they were quite at variance with her customary behavior. This example of the parallel process seems to have been produced by what Searles calls the "reflection process," whereby the supervisee unconsciously assumes a temporary identification with aspects of the client's emotional life she does not comprehend, and then acts these out —"reflects them"—in supervision. In this connection, Searles states: "What I observed and was emotionally responsive to was, I believe, less an aspect of the therapist's own personality than a transitory unconscious identification occurring as a function of his relationship with the patient."[10]

This example differs from the preceding ones in that the psychodynamic material was ego alien to the worker. As far as could be ascertained, it was not "familiar." The feelings acted out appeared to the supervisor like a cloak that the worker wore and "showed" to the supervisor. When the supervisor commented on how atypical this behavior was for the worker, the latter recognized this immediately. It is probably no coincidence that this supervisee was not a trainee, but a worker with several years experience, who had also undergone a considerable amount of personal psychotherapy. Her greater self-awareness made it easier for her to distinguish between her transference feelings toward the supervisor and feelings absorbed from the client, and to draw the boundary clearly between the two.

Resolution of the Treatment Impasse Produced by the Parallel Process

The parallel process should be suspected whenever the supervisee appears to have reached an impasse in a treatment that does not yield to the usual exploration of case dynamics. Its detection requires considerable alertness on the part of the supervisor, who must be able to identify as parallel process what may at first appear to be inconsistencies or omissions in the supervisee's presentation or behavior or an emotional strain in the relationship with the supervisor.

The supervisor needs to know the supervisee well, must be familiar with the latter's customary functioning, and must have made a thorough educational diagnosis. The supervisor should know what kind of learner the supervisee is, and what type of client, problem, or relationship is likely to cause identification, stress, or resistance in the worker. The supervisor should look out for unusual or atypical behavior in the supervisee. In addition, the supervisor must constantly be sensitive to her own countertransference and the nature of the relationship with the worker. As indicated in the examples discussed above, both cognitive and experiential interventions proved to be useful tools for resolving the treatment impasse.

Eva M. Kahn is Casework Supervisor, Jewish Family Service of North Jersey, Wayne, New Jersey. At the time this article was written, she was a fieldwork instructor, Graduate School of Social Work, Rutgers University, New Brunswick, New Jersey.

1. For explanations of these terms, see Margery Jean Gross Doehrman, "Parallel Processes in Supervision and Psychotherapy," *Bulletin of the Menninger Clinic* 40 (January 1976): 9-20; Harold F. Searles, "The Informational Value of the Supervisor's Emotional Experiences," *Collected Papers on Schizophrenia and Related Subjects*, ed. Harold F. Searles (New York: International Universities Press, 1965), pp. 157-76; and Margaret J. Rioch et al., *Dialogues for Therapists* (San Francisco: Jossey-Bass, 1976).

2. Rudolf Ekstein and Robert S. Wallerstein, *The Teaching and Learning of Psychotherapy* (New York: Basic Books, 1958).

3. Doehrman, "Parallel Processes," pp. 10-11.

4. Richard Sterba et al., *Transference in Casework* (New York: Family Service Association of America, 1948), p. 28.

5. Janet Mattinson, *The Reflection Process in Casework Supervision* (London: Institute of Marital Studies, Tavistock Institute of Human Relations Research Publications Services, 1975), p. 31.

6. Doehrman, "Parallel Processes," p. 17.

7. Searles, "The Supervisor's Emotional Experiences," pp. 166-70.

8. Helene Deutsch, "Occult Processes Occurring During Psychoanalysis," in *Psychoanalysis and the Occult*, ed. George Devereux (New York: International Universities Press, 1953), pp. 133-46.

9. David Sachs and Stanley H. Shapiro, "On Parallel Processes in Therapy and Teaching," *Psychoanalytic Quarterly* 45 (March 1976): 409-10.

10. Searles, "The Supervisor's Emotional Experience," p. 161.

PART-TIME PRIVATE PRACTICE: PRACTICAL AND ETHICAL CONSIDERATIONS
PATRICIA KELLEY, PAUL ALEXANDER

SOCIAL WORK as a profession has long shown ambivalence over private practice as an appropriate method of service delivery.[1] Since 1964, the National Association of Social Workers has officially recognized private practice as a legitimate area for social workers but stated the position that practice within agencies should remain the "primary" avenue for the implementation of the goals of the profession."[2] In the 1970s, Kurzman argued that private practitioners can make an important contribution to the social work profession but that private practice should not replace agency-based work or be viewed as a superior delivery system as Levin, Piliavin, and others had suggested.[3] This view of private practice as an adjunct to agency work is paralleled by the reality that most private practice in social work is conducted on a part-time basis. In a 1975 survey of social workers, only 2.4 percent designated private practice as their primary mode of work, but 22.6 percent indicated a "second employment" (usually ten hours a week or less) in such practice.[4] Although there would seem to be some different issues for part-time as opposed to full-time practice, the authors found little in the literature to distinguish between the two. A recent study that did make such a distinction focused on the full-time practitioner.[5]

In this article, the authors examine issues and concerns regarding part-time private practice: they report the results of a survey of clinical social workers in private practice, focusing especially on those who work in it part time. Drawing on responses to this survey and on their own experiences, the authors discuss some advantages and special problems of such practice. They consider practical and ethical issues and offer alternative practice methods.

SURVEY OF CLINICAL SOCIAL WORKERS

In 1981 the authors conducted a survey of clinical social workers. Four percent of the approximately 10,500 names listed in the 1978 NASW Register of Clinical Social Workers were selected by random sampling techniques, and questionnaires regarding private practice were mailed to these persons.[6] The total number of persons who were mailed questionnaires was 420; there were 191 usable responses representing a 45.5 percent rate of return. Of these 191 responses, 21.5 percent reported maintaining a full-time private practice, and 34 percent reported engaging in part-time private practice (N = 66). Even if one considers that social workers listed in the Register are more likely than others to be in private practice, the figures are surprisingly high. The Clinical Register was chosen as a source of names on the authors' assumption that social workers listed in it were more likely to have given thoughtful consideration to the issues of private practice. Portions of the study differentiating part-time from full-time private practice are reported here; other aspects of the survey are reported elsewhere.[7]

ADVANTAGES

There are many advantages to a part-time private practice in social work. Agency practitioners may welcome the professional independence and additional income that private practice provides. Social workers who find themselves in supervisory or administrative positions may enjoy the opportunity to maintain continued contact with clients through private practice.[8] Educators may wish to have a practice through which they can maintain those skills that are being taught in clinical courses. Social workers who are parents of young children may wish to limit and choose their hours of work.

There are advantages to the profession as a whole and to individual clients as well. By fostering part-time practice, the profession can keep its main focus on agency service where there is a commitment to serve persons without regard to their ability to pay and where there can be a basis for social action and reform. At the same time, the profession expands it services to a wider range of clientele and also offers its members more room for creativity, autonomy, and skill building. Many agencies have eligibility requirements concerning who can be served and constraints on how clients will be served. Furthermore, some clients prefer the opportunity to choose their own practitioner and a service that they consider to be more personal and confidential. Thus private practice increases options for both workers and clients.

POTENTIAL PROBLEMS AND CONCERNS

In the survey, respondents were also asked to identify problems they had had in beginning and maintaining a private practice. Table 1 shows problem areas that respondents listed frequently. The authors categorized the responses into four broad areas: generating referrals, practical business issues, time management, and professional development and quality control. Personal competence and maintaining confidentiality are issues that underlie all these categories. The authors added one category to those identified by the respondents: interface between the agency and the private practitioner. In the sections that follow, the authors examine these is-

Table 1.
Problems of Part-Time Private Practitioners (N = 66)

Problems	Starting a Private Practice		Maintaining a Private Practice	
	Number	Percentage	Number	Percentage
Generating Referrals				
Getting a referral system	28	42.4	20	30.3
Becoming known, advertising	5	7.5	0	0.0
Other	2	3.0	0	0.0
Total	35	53.0	20	30.3
Practical Business Issues				
Locating an office	9	13.6	0	0.0
Financing, collecting fees	7	10.6	7	10.6
Third-party payments	5	7.6	3	4.6
Keeping records, business procedures	4	6.1	4	6.1
Total	25	37.9	14	21.2
No Problems	13	19.7	11	18.3
Time Management	5	7.6	20	30.3
Professional Development and Quality Control	5	7.6	6	9.1
Personal Competence	6	9.1	1	1.5

sues by category and discuss practice implications and alternatives.

Generating Referrals

As the authors' survey shows, generating referrals is a common problem of continued concern in beginning and keeping a practice. Because this is a key issue for private practice, the authors asked respondents to list their best sources of referral. See Table 2 for a summary of responses to this question.

Word of mouth and informal contacts are the most important sources for practitioners to foster. Professional colleagues come next as a referral source, followed by medical persons, organizations, and "other," in that order. The area of generating and receiving referrals raises ethical concerns that are special for the part-time practitioners. If the practitioner also works for an agency, it may be tempting to receive referrals from that agency. Some agencies will encourage this because it helps reduce their waiting lists; other agencies discourage this practice because it reduces the number of clients who are able to pay full fees. Regardless of the agency's position, however, the ethics of this practice are open to question, and the practitioner would do well to consider carefully before embarking on it. A referral concern for educators is the question of accepting students as clients. Some boundary and power issues exist that need to be carefully reviewed. Promotion is another related concern. When a practitioner announces the opening of a private practice, it is common to list agency affiliation. Does such an announcement imply agency sanction or responsibility? Clearly, agency and board approval should be obtained.

Practical Business Issues

The nuts and bolts of running a business was second to referrals as an area of concern for survey respondents. In the authors' experience, practical issues become especially difficult for the part-time practitioner. Office location is one such problem. A part-time practice is often not lucrative enough to justify renting office space, yet the common alternatives present certain practical and ethical issues. If the agency office is used, questions of insurance and liability are raised, as are questions about use of resources (for example, utilities and

secretarial assistance). Guidelines for good practice here would include securing the approval of the agency's board of directors and staff, a clear contract, and personal liability insurance. Some payment of rent would seem fair and justified, also. Another common practice for the part-time practitioner is the use of his or her own home. Here, there are boundary issues between personal and private life, zoning laws, and issues of confidentiality (for example, being observed by the practitioner's family or neighbors) to consider. If this option is chosen, the practitioner needs to consider zoning laws and insurance coverage carefully and would be wise to select an area for consultation separate from the living space. Another option is to share office space with several other private practitioners. There are fewer ethical and boundary issues here, but there are practical issues to consider such as scheduling, liability for others' practices, and the reputation of the other practitioners. Such a choice requires careful planning, and the authors recommend hiring a lawyer to prepare the contract. An attorney is likely to ask, Is this a business partnership or individuals renting joint office space?

An alternative practice method that the authors recommend for many situations is consulting with clients in their homes. For years, social workers have made home visits to agency clientele but have been reluctant to visit middle- and upper-class private clientele. Such a distinction suggests that agency visits may have been more investigative than therapeutic in nature. The authors have found home visits to private, full-paying clients to be useful and nonthreatening. The practice certainly reduces many of the problems of securing a meeting space. In family therapy, especially, home treatment has been viewed by some as superior because family dynamics can be observed in the home setting.[9]

Another business issue is that of maintaining records. This is an especially difficult issue for the part-time practitioner who does not have a secure office for storage or a secretary to type and file. Storage of records in either the agency office or in the therapist's home can present issues of confidentiality. Some clients choose private practitioners because they do not want their records stored in agency files. But private homes may not be secure either.

The authors offer an unusual proposal for maintaining records. The confidential clinical notes taken during an interview are recorded in a notebook, which the clients are asked to keep between sessions. Such a plan requires a different method of note taking, which in turn alters actual practice methods. Labels and impressions that have not been discussed with and validated by the clients are not written down. Maps of relationships (often called genograms) replace the listing of events. The practitioner lists problem formation, methods used, and hoped-for outcomes and writes down homework tasks assigned between sessions. The clients have access to these notes during the week and are asked to add more ideas as they think of them. Contracts and homework are clearly stated and in the clients' hands. What began as a practical solution to a confidentiality problem has become a new practice method that gives more control and responsibility to the clients for their own treatment. The clients are more involved between sessions, too. They are often asked to write in a journal between sessions about their thoughts and feelings; these are often written down in the case notebook. The beginning of each session is spent on reviewing the journal. The worker's records—separate from the case notebook—contain face sheet information, number of sessions, records of payment, and only minimal clinical data. The confidential material discussed in interviews is thus protected.

Fee collection is another business issue. One questionable practice is that of entering into an association with medical persons strictly for the benefit of receiving third-party insurance payments. Some practitioners will pay part of their fees to physicians who sign forms for them, although the physicians have no consultative relationship. Although this has been justified as a means of helping clients receive insurance payments, in reality it is fee splitting. (When there is a genuine partnership or consultative relationship, of course, it is a different matter.) Some private practitioners may find it ethically desirable to see some clients who pay lower or no fees, but this may not be practical for the part-time practitioner whose caseload is very low. Professional ethics require that such clients must be continually served until the case is closed or referred.

Time Management

The respondents to the survey in-

Table 2. Referral Sources of Clients for Part-Time Private Practitioners (N=68)[a]

Referral Sources	Number	Percentage
Informal Sources		
Former clients, word-of-mouth, friends, students	57	83.8
Professional Individuals		
Other therapists, clergy, attorneys, social workers	28	41.2
Medical Profession		
Physicians, psychiatrists	22	32.4
Organizations		
Social service agencies, schools, voluntary groups	14	20.6
Other Sources		
Yellow Pages, referral service	8	11.8

[a]Two additional responses were made by persons who had recently discontinued private practice. Most practitioners indicated multiple sources of referrals.

dicated that once their practice was established, one of the most important concerns was controlling their time. Although time management was a minor concern when practitioners were starting a practice, later on it was reported to be as important a problem as generating referrals. This issue is especially important for part-time practitioners who must balance their personal time and other employment with the demands of their private practice. These practitioners and their employers need to clarify their assumptions about what full-time professional employment means. Most social work positions require some time and effort after hours, out of town trips, and professional and community service work. Will private clients take a backseat to the full-time job? Who serves the client in distress when the worker is on call for the agency? To serve the private clients well, will the worker give less than full time to the primary employer? If the worker attempts to give both jobs top priority, what will the effects on the personal and family life of the worker be? What are the value implications of such time choices for human service professionals? A potential aid to this dilemma is for the social worker to arrange backup services for clients on a trade-off basis with other practitioners. Another alternative is to limit the private practice or to reduce time in the agency.

Professional Development and Quality Control

The remaining statements made by the respondents related to personal

competence and collegial relationships. Professional isolation and lack of opportunity for development are potential hazards of private practice in general. They are increased hazards for part-time practitioners who are less likely to have the resources to hire case consultants and to attend training institutes. In some situations, the part-time worker with an agency affiliation may have opportunities for professional development through the agency. Sometimes, however, staff development through agencies relates only to the specific job assignment (for example, administration), and persons in private practice often do not have clinical tasks in their agency job.[10] Certainly agencies will not hire consultants for private practitioners. Private clients, however, can be asked to pay for specific expertise, such as legal, medical, or psychological evaluations.

It is also important for the worker to form associations with peers in the profession. Members of such an association could report to each other on suggested readings, take turns attending courses and workshops, and share materials with each other. The associations can be informal, such as mutual case consultation, or formal, such as a partnership. Peer consultation among professionals can decrease isolation for the workers and increase the quality of services to the clients. If the professionals represent many disciplines, an even broader range of ideas and help is available to the clients. The allied professionals can refer clients to each other as well.

Association with psychiatrists or

other medical persons can be useful if the outcome is better service to clients. In fact, it would be unethical to see certain clients without medical backup or consultation. However, ethical concerns are raised if the social workers lose their identity and become "junior psychiatrists": this downgrades the social work profession and, by narrowing the approach, serves the client less well. Social workers who focus on intrapsychic or biological phenomena of clients to the exclusion of contextual issues are in danger of giving up their professional identity. The client is served better through mutual consultation and collaboration. A strength the profession can offer to interdisciplinary teams is the broad, systemic view of person-in-environment.

Interface with Agencies

A notable proportion of the respondents to the survey indicated that they had no problems in initiating or continuing their private practice. This suggests that one of the advantages of part-time private practice is that working in this manner is possible for practitioners to do while keeping the security of a full-time position. It also indicates that many social workers may wait until their professional reputation in a community makes it relatively easy to engage some private clients.

It is surprising, however, that none of the respondents reported any difficulties with their employing agency. Perhaps those who do encounter some resistance simply refrain from private practice. Nonetheless, important factors arise concerning the interface between the private and public practice of the part-time practitioner. The authors consider this to be a critical issue for the profession.

The authors have observed three levels of response by agencies to their employees' participation in private practice. In some cases there is a high level of involvement wherein the agency openly encourages private practice. The agency may participate in the private practice by allowing the use of office space and other resources. This alternative may be fortuitous for the practitioner but could easily create as many problems as it resolves. In particular it raises the issue of conflicts of interest both for the social worker and for the agency. Other agencies display a very low level of involvement. This is the situation in which the agency permits its employees to practice privately but generally disapproves. Sometimes the relationship becomes adversarial, and certain agencies explicitly prohibit their employees from participating in private practice. This situation is unfortunate, because it creates tensions or dissatisfactions that need not exist. Furthermore, this attitude fails to recognize the constant increase of private practice as a legitimate form of social work.

However, the most probable relationship is a medium level of involvement. In this case, the agency neither supports nor disapproves of private practice. In essence the agency states that the individuals are free to engage in whatever private activities they choose during nonwork time. The problem that arises here may be that administrators of the agency presume that the agency has priority over the worker's time. The conflicting priorities of agency and private practice could create serious complications.

It would be helpful if social workers and their employing agencies would negotiate the parameters for part-time private practice. Agencies can benefit by encouraging private practice; they will be more likely to keep their experienced staff if opportunities for creativity and additional income are allowed. Explicit discussions and agreements need to be negotiated between agencies and workers.

IMPLICATIONS

Private practice has become an accepted form of practice and has grown in the past two decades. It is important that the profession as a whole come to terms with this reality. Most social workers who conduct private practice do so on a part-time basis, which keeps the focus agency-based but with increased options for some clients and some workers. When private practice is viewed as a supplement to agency work, there is a wider continuum of service delivery. Although this is a laudable state of the art, there are issues that the profession needs to address to ensure practice excellence in the 1980s. Policy issues that need to be addressed include the relationship between agencies and private practitioners, state licensure and certification, determination of competency, relationships with other professions, enforcement of ethical standards, and how the profession presents itself to the public.

Decreasing public resources are being allocated to human services. On the one hand, this trend might bring an increase in entrepreneurial human services, with more social workers going into private practice. On the other hand, if fewer dollars are available to public agencies for purchase of services, private practitioners may find fewer referrals being made to them. The impact of the economic trend on private practice is not clear and represents an area for further study. It is clear, however, that private practice is a significant part of the profession.

Notes and References

1. See, for example, Robert L. Barker. *Social Work in Private Practice: Principles, Issues, and Dilemmas* (Silver Spring, Md.: National Association of Social Workers, 1984).

2. Margaret A. Golton. "Private Practice in Social Work." *Encyclopedia of Social Work*, Vol. 2 (16th issue: Washington, D.C.: National Association of Social Workers, 1971), p. 950.

3. Paul A. Kurzman. "Private Practice as a Social Work Function." *Social Work*, 21 (September 1976), pp. 363–368. See, for example, Arnold M. Levin. "Private Practice Is Alive and Well." *Social Work*, 21 (September 1976), pp. 356–362; and Irving Piliavin. "Restructuring the Provision of Social Services." *Social Work*, 13 (January 1968), pp. 34–41.

4. Manpower Data Bank Frequency Distributions (Washington, D.C.: National Association of Social Workers, 1975).

5. Marquis Earl Wallace. "Private Practice: A Nationwide Study." *Social Work*, 27 (May 1982), pp. 262–267.

6. National Association of Social Workers. *NASW Register of Clinical Social Workers* (2d ed.: Washington, D.C.: National Association of Social Workers, 1978).

7. Paul Alexander. "Social Workers and Private Practice." final examination project (Iowa City: University of Iowa, School of Social Work, 1981).

8. Michael Cohen. "The Emergence of Private Practice in Social Work." *Social Problems*, 14 (Summer 1966), pp. 84–93.

9. Marvin Bryce and June Lloyd, eds., *Treating Families in the Home: An Alternative to Placement* (Springfield, Ill.: Charles C Thomas, Publisher, 1980).

10. Cohen. "The Emergence of Private Practice in Social Work."

UNDERSTANDING TEAMWORK: ANOTHER LOOK AT CONCEPTS

JANE ISAACS LOWE, MSW, ACSW

MARJATTA HERRANEN, RN, MS

Discussion of interdisciplinary teamwork has mushroomed in direct response to the increasing complexities in the health care system. It is clear that no one individual can possess all the expertise necessary for the care of patients and families in the highly technical and specialized health care field. Thus, interdisciplinary teamwork has become *the* method most frequently utilized to provide an organizing and unifying framework for both health care delivery and for the work of health care professionals. Yet, considerable confusion surrounds the concept of teamwork. Teamwork evokes multiple, automatic and dissimilar responses in all professionals. To some, the word teamwork is synonymous with collaboration, to others with any group action. Many view teamwork as beneficial to patient care while others perceive teamwork as further fragmenting care making it difficult to get anything accomplished. (Dyer, 1977; Feiger and Schmitt, 1977; Kane, 1975; Rae-Grant and Marcuse, 1968.) A recent literature search turned up 635 references for teamwork indicating just how popular this concept has become. Popularity, however, is double-edged. It promotes general familiarity with the concept of teamwork but does not establish the standards, requirements and limitations of teamwork. Thus, expectations are raised and frustrations heightened as health care professionals attempt to practice a concept they are unclear about.

In pursuit of clarification of terminology an interdisciplinary team is defined as: "a functioning unit composed of individuals with varied and specialized training who coordinate their activities to provide services to a client or a group of clients" (Duncanis and Golin, 1979, p. 3.). These authors would add two additional points to this definition to increase its applicability: the functioning unit (1) holds a common purpose around which work is centered and (2) has a distinct method for communication.

Given the parameters etched by this definition of interdisciplinary team work, the following premises are presented: (1) teamwork is an evolutionary process with identifiable developmental stages; (2) teamwork can occur only when it is supported and sanctioned by the environment in which it exists; and (3) teamwork as a concept must be understood, practiced and studied in order to fulfill its potential. This paper discusses each premise delineating issues related to working together. Implications are drawn and recommendations made for social work and nursing practice.

Teamwork Is an Evolutionary Process

In 1976 the authors began to work together as practitioners on the Rena Treatment Center team at Mount Sinai Hospital, New York City. The group had little awareness of what it meant to be a "team" and consequently the word was used rather loosely. As a result, these authors systematically, over time, analyzed dyadic and group interactions utilizing five components: role expectations, decision-making, leadership, group norms, communication and goals. From this analysis emerged a model for the evolution of an interdisciplinary team. (Lowe and Herranen, 1978). The team development model has expanded since the first article was written to include a sixth and final stage that of team maintenance.

The Lowe-Herranen model traces the development of a group of people working together from the period of formation, through conflict and crises, to resolution, to team maintenance. Within each developmental stage, patterns of interactions, common emotions and individual-team productivity are delineated. The six stages are presented to highlight the evolutionary process of teamwork.

Stage I

The first stage is "*Becoming Acquainted*." This stage affects the way the individuals enter the team. Some enter into teamwork because they find themselves sharing intermittently in aspects of patient care while others enter because a team approach is mandated for the program. The method of entry is critical as it sets the tone for future interactions in terms of how the team functions within specific settings. During this initial stage leadership styles range from autocratic to democratic, or may be totally absent. The structure of the group tends to be hierarchical with the higher status professions assuming the position of leader. Decisions are made by individual professionals with the leader having the final say on group decisions. Patterns of interactions are polite and impersonal. Group norms are social in focus. The goals for patient care are those established by the individual professionals without group consensus or involvement. Emotions are repressed and neutralized with minimal conflict emerging. Individual productivity is high while team productivity is low.

Stage II

The stage of "*Trial and Error*" begins when there is an awareness of the need to work together towards a common goal for patient care. This awareness emerges when each individual becomes cognizant of the need to coordinate treatment plans on behalf of the patient. The most common pattern on interaction to emerge here is pairing: individuals seek an ally, usually someone who has a compatible personality, distancing those perceived as incompatible. The modus operandi becomes parallel play. As team members begin to test their boundaries, role conflict, role ambiguity and role overload result. There is no change from the first stage in the patterns of leadership, decision-making of norms. During this stage, emotions manifested are those of suspicion and a jealous guarding of turf. Group productivity is low while individual professionals continue to achieve stated goals. Dyads that have formed also increase individual productivity.

Stage III

"*Collective Indecision*," the third stage, occurs as the group attempts to avoid direct conflict and achieve an equilibrium. Boundaries for the group as a team are beginning to develop. There is an attraction in being part of the team but an ambivalence as well. Decisions are made by default and are characterized by the assumption that responsibilities are shared when in fact they are not. There is no group norm for accountability and thus little is accomplished. Frequently heard comments are, "I thought we agreed to do this last week," or "I thought you were going to do this." Leadership is largely absent. Group norms exert a pressure for individuals to conform. As a result, the predominant patterns of interaction are pseudo-consensus and scapegoating. Role conflict is present but is not dealt with directly. Emotions are those of covert anger and poor team morale. Team and individual productivity are low as there exists a feeling that no one is listening to the other or being heard.

Stage IV

The next stage, "Crisis," is precipitated when an internal or external event forces the team to face the issue of "collective-indecision." As a result of the crisis, this is the stage where boundaries begin to be drawn with more rigidity and where more definitive roles and responsibilities are delineated. Leadership is assumed both by a formal as well as informal leader. The focus shifts to the group as a team with more attention being paid to its internal processes rather than to patient care problems. The team is now able to begin to handle negative emotions. The issue of personality lessens and members begin to view each other in terms of knowledge and contributions to patient care. Emotions expressed are open anger, depression, guilt and recognition of conflict. While individual productivity is varied with team members assuming responsibilities for some aspects of patient care, team productivity remains low.

Stage V

From the crisis emerges the stage of "Resolution" with a group commitment to working together as a team. This stage is the first level of tangible teamwork. It is characterized by open communication, shared leadership, decision-making and responsibility. There are mechanisms for both individual and group accountability. Satisfaction is the predominant emotion with high individual/team productivity. However, this is a fragile stage and without ongoing evaluation by team members of their interactions and productivity it cannot be sustained. The goal of this stage is to move members towards team maintenance, the sixth and final stage of team development where the actual work of the team begins.

Stage VI

As a stage "Team Maintenance" is characterized by shared acknowledgment of team tasks: the paramount driving force finally becomes the client's health needs. There now exists an awareness that multiple variables influence the group's efforts to work together to manage their interdependence. The effectiveness of the team's work in this stage is directly dependent upon the internal group processes, the ways conflicts are managed and the client-team relationships.

The internal group processes now are geared towards an understanding of the interrelatedness of roles and functions and towards an ability to break down interprofessional rivalries through the management of conflict. In this stage both the internal and external expectations of the team are continuously clarified. Group norms of behavior are consolidated, validated and mutually accepted, allowing work to progress. Team members have a thorough understanding of their own special input as well as knowledge and recognition of the skills of other team members. There is accountability to the group and a willingness to share information. A common language evolves allowing for freer communication. Decisions are supported by the team even when there may not be complete agreement.

Team leadership is more flexible. While there may be a designated formal leader, the actual leadership role shifts to the person best equipped for carrying out the client care plan. The group's goals are both client and task-centered with the focus on the achievement of the stated goals rather than on who does what. The team's boundaries become more fluid without fear of loss of unity: members move in and out safely according to goals and use other groups and individuals as dictated by client needs. Rivalry is viewed as healthy and growth promoting rather than involving winning or losing Mechanisms for evaluation and change are built into the group process with flexibility and tolerance for ambiguity.

The complexities that make the existence of the interdisciplinary team necessary also contribute to role overlap and, thus, make conflict inevitable. The crux of this stage is that the team now manages this internal conflict positively. Members recognize and value the viewpoints of other disciplines: compromise and negotiation occurs in setting priorities and in redirecting the analysis of complex issues. New solutions to old problems are explored, tried out and outcomes are jointly evaluated. Role conflict is dealt with by jointly clarifying expectations, identifying competences, evaluating overlapping functions and renegotiating assignments. Flexibility, a sense of humor and resiliency in the face of conflict assist positively in its management. Defense of turf, focus on personality and scapegoating are not allowed by the group.

In this stage, it is the team goal to facilitate open communication between the patient and team members and to implement consistent treatment plans. The team is more accepting of a variety of patient behaviors and responses, and no longer expects all patients to respond in the same manner. Patient-team interactions center around joint information-giving, cooperation and participation in the decision-making process related to his/her treatment plan. Team members learn from the patients and thereby assist them in advocating on their own behalf.

There is a danger in this team maintenance stage which must be watched for; that of the team existing for the sake of the team. This is manifested in two ways: "group think" and enmeshment. Group think occurs when team members are more concerned about retaining the approval of fellow members than with creative problem-solving. The often hidden goal of this element of group process is to eliminate all ideas that do not appeal to the collective; the group's decisions are deemed more ethical and correct than those of individuals. There is a failure to reexamine initial decisions and a neglect in obtaining outside experts.

The group seals itself in and becomes a world of its own. Enmeshment occurs when a team becomes trapped in enchantment with each other (social benefits) and loses sight of its reason for existence, i.e., patient care. These two developments are signs that the team is no longer effective and that a refocusing of its efforts must occur. Further, the attractions of teamwork in this stage may obscure the issue of individual responsibility and accountability. Every problem in patient care is not necessarily one that requires the attention of the entire team. Many problems and tasks can be resolved by one or two individuals who can communicate solutions and outcomes to the larger team.

The evolutionary process of teamwork is fluid. The developmental stages can be observed when a new team is formed or when personnel change within an existing team. While each stage has distinct boundaries, one stage may blur into another with overlapping of the described interactions and emotions. Teams are subject to progression or regression through this model depending on the external environment, on resistances to moving forward and on the internal group processes. However, once team members are able to evaluate and assess on an ongoing basis their group and individual patterns of functioning, the team will be better able to maintain its equilibrium and work together successfully.

Teamwork Can Occur Only When It Is Supported and Sanctioned by the Environment

The hospital system is highly bureaucratic with an emphasis on the division of labor along departmental and professional lines, and on hierarchical patterns of communication, decision-making, leadership and rewards. Further, both the hospital, department and profession require that employees be loyal and uphold institutional goals. "Teams, on the other hand, are structured so as to emphasize the sharing of knowledge and communication across disciplines" (Ducanis and Golin, 1979, p. 174). Teams also require loyalty and a commitment from their members which often supercedes that required by the institution and department. Thus, the dichotomies between the hospital organization and the team structure require that the interface between the two be understood and evaluated in order to address those aspects which create conflict and are ultimately dysfunctional to patient care.

Any hospital organization which espouses the concept of teamwork must also support that concept with commitment. The hospital system can provide this commitment by shifting the rewards from hierarchical components to explicit positive recognition of the team delivery model. If this does not occur then the organization and the teams within it will be at constant odds with each other. Impediments to patient care will result for those who attempt to engage in teamwork sanctioned only on paper and not in practice. Therefore, the task for the team is to understand organizational procedures, rules and limits, to acknowledge the dilemma of double loyalties to the team and the institution, and to work towards management of organizational conflicts. The task for the hospital system is to deal with the conflict between the bureaucracy and the team by developing a matrix or dual organizational pattern. Each individual has a position in the matrix that permits communication on both a horizontal and vertical level (Ducanis and Golin, 1979) This allows for ongoing feedback between the organization and the team

To work on these tasks, the following questions should be considered: "What are the norms and values of the organization in relation to the team? Are the goals and objectives of the team and the organization shared? Does the arrangement of space enhance or detract from team efficiency? Are there organizational barriers to effective communication from and to team? How is the authority structure of the organization reflected in the team?" (Ducanis and Golin, 1979, p. 174). These questions provide a starting point for the examination of how the team interacts with the organization and for evaluation of where work needs to focus.

Teamwork Must Be Understood, Practiced and Studied to Achieve Its Potential

Teamwork is an ongoing process. It takes time, effort, evaluation, and a commitment to the concepts of teamwork. To work together effectively and efficiently individuals must be aware of: (1) what it takes to do the work, (2)

what is necessary to strengthen the team, and (3) how to effect individual and team accountability. Each individual must develop strong professional identity, self-awareness about his/her own collaborative style and interpersonal biases. The individual also needs to develop methods of coping with role confusion and conflict. In working with others, it is easiest to respond to professional stereotypes rather than to learn what other professionals actually do. The challenge here is to understand each professional's frame of reference so that roles and functions do not become rigid and non-flexible. Participation in teamwork also necessitates that professionals define for the team their specific expertise and how this is useful in the assessment and treatment of the patient and family. Through this process, professionals can clarify their respective thinking, become aware of each other's roles and responsibilities and develop collegial respect for the skills and contributions of others.

It is important to keep in mind that in working within a team cooperation is essential to fulfill one's professional role and function. Building alliances with other professionals not only enhances the individual's ability to deliver care but also contributes to strengthening teamwork through joint planning which takes into account the gestalt of patient and family. Inherent in shared planning and care delivery is the concept of professional and team accountability. Team members must guard against the blurring of these two forms of accountability: joint decision-making does not mean abdication of individual professional responsibility for patient care. Where conflict exists between professional and team standards of accountability this must be acknowledged openly. It is critical that the team's internal dynamics not require a lowering of professional accountability. Thus, team members should ask frequently whether accountability has to be sacrificed in order to hold the team together or to protect it from external and/or internal threats.

> (1) Who needs what information from whom? (Nature of interdependence); (2) What are the individual professionals trying to do together? (Function of a team); (3) Which professional does what? (Division of labor, role clarity); (4) How do tasks/goals get accomplished? (Leadership, decision-making); (5) How do professionals communicate with each other? (Authenticity, clarity); and (6) Is the stated task/goal accomplished by working together? (Feedback systems, accountability). (Weiner, 1978, p. 1)

These questions should form the basis for the practice of teamwork and should be utilized throughout the developmental stages in order to facilitate both team functioning and accountability.

Discussion

Ideally, the purpose of the team (e.g., to meet client needs) should determine its composition and life span. Yet in reality organizational constraints, service mandates, and staffing patterns determine how teams are constituted and utilized. Teamwork can take many forms and can fulfill many functions, i.e., teaching, consultation, liaison. These authors suggest that there are two predominant forms or models for teamwork: Integrative (long-term) and Coordinate (short-term) (Balassone, Briggs and Olson, 1981; Horowitz, 1970; Wise, 1974).

The integrative model of teamwork encompasses the team development framework as outlined in this paper. This form is functional for ongoing teams who care for patients over months or years, i.e., chronic illness or primary care. The coordinate model of teamwork applies to short-term care addressing specific acute health problems. This form is best suited for medical/surgical units where decisions often need to be made quickly. The designated leader is usually the physician, and professionals work together with clear delineation of roles towards a common objective. In this model, the nurse and social worker remain constant while the physicians, both housestaff and attendings, rotate frequently. As a result of the constantly changing personnel and patients, the integrative (interdisciplinary) approach is not applicable or congruent to the acute care setting. This short-term coordinate approach results in an ongoing and repeated reconstitution of the team; this closes off opportunities for team building and the consistent and constructive management of interdependence. Yet the care of patients is managed through the coordination of professional activities, particularly those of the nurse, social worker and physician. The nurse and the social worker, who are most often the permanent members of the coordinate team, can move together through certain of their own evolutionary processes. As a dyad they can influence the ongoing reconstitution of this type of team by taking responsibility for actively involving and reinvolving the physician in coordinating professional relationships to achieve patient care goals.

Recognition that these two forms or models of teamwork are different structures can help individuals minimize their frustrations, set more realistic goals for their interactions, and ultimately be more effective in patient care.

Implications for Social Work and Nursing

As professions, social work and nursing have grown out of many similar concerns which relate to the humanistic meeting of the needs of patients and families in a health care system. Because of shared values and goals, i.e., viewing oneself as *the* patient advocate, both professions perceive their roles and functions as competitive and the battle for turf results. In addition, both professions, largely female, compete for recognition by the higher status professional group, physicians, usually male. Nurses and social workers view themselves and each other as occupying the lower echelon of the power structure. These similarities in perceptions evoke the need to place distance between each other which results in failure to ally productively.

To end this battle for turf and power-seeking, nurses and social workers must view their roles as complementary rather than as overlapping and conflictual. What both professions have sometimes lost sight of is the value of alliances and strong dyads, and the opportunities they can develop jointly to influence teamwork, the hospital organization and ultimately patient care.

Nurses and social workers involved in the supervision and education of staff and students have a special responsibility to help those individuals understand the complexities of teamwork as well as the expertise of each other.

Both professions need to help students and staff develop a professional ego which is sturdy enough to be threatened by differing disciplinary viewpoints and capable of separating person from profession. This is essential for working together.

Conclusions

There are many frameworks for studying interdisciplinary teamwork. The developmental model presented in this paper represents one way in which a systematic analysis and understanding of the limitations and strengths of teamwork can be achieved. According to this model team maintenance or the management of interdependence is the essential stage. How well this is achieved will influence team productivity, patient satisfaction, and environmental supports.

While interdisciplinary teams as defined in this paper are not appropriate for all settings, working together in some form is now an integral part of the health care systems. Underlying any form of teamwork is the concept that no one individual possesses all the expertise necessary for the care of patients and families. In any form of teamwork being a team member requires an understanding of the interrelatedness of roles and functions, and the ability to break down interprofessional rivalries. Communication is the essential ingredient in the team approach. Social work or nursing cannot do teamwork alone, but by joining forces have a better chance for success. Working together in a dyad or triad may be the most effective and realistic method for delivering care.

As patients increasingly view themselves as consumers of care with certain rights, health professionals have begun also to acknowledge the need for greater participation of patients and families in their treatment planning. The nature of patient/family participation is unique from other team members in that they contribute from their own life experience and response to illness information pertinent to the planning and implementing of their care. As the patient and family are included in a partnership with the team this will inevitably effect team dynamics.

Education of health care professionals, nurses, physicians, social workers, etc., must include training in team skills.

> One of the most striking aspects of professional education is that we are presently training people for roles they will continue to fill 20 or 30 years from now. Not only must we make educated guesses about the skills and competencies that will be needed by professionals in the future, we must also develop in our students a flexibility that will allow them to shift roles and responsibilities as conditions in their fields change. (Ducanis and Golin, 1979, p. 166)

The literature on teamwork has reached a point where little new knowledge is being added to it. Health care professionals assume that teamwork means better coordination of care which in turn means better service to patients and families. This assumption is one that requires further legitimizing support. Research is needed that would develop and validate step-by-step the knowledge base and skills required for the practice of teamwork.

REFERENCES

Balassone, M L., Briggs, T and Olson, M M *Infusing a Male Dominated Medical Setting with Feminist Values: Intervention by a Social Work Team*. Manpower Monograph. No. 15. Syracuse: Syracuse University School of Social Work. 1981.

Ducanis, Alex and Golin, Anne K. *The Interdisciplinary Health Care Team A Handbook*. Germantown, MD. Aspen Systems Corporation. 1979.

Dyer, William G. *Team Building Issues and Alternatives*. Reading, MA: Addison-Wesley Publishing Company. 1977.

Feiger, S M and Schmitt, M.H "Collegiality in Interdisciplinary Health Teams Its Measure

Horwitz, John *Team Practice and the Specialist —An Introduction to Interdisciplinary Teamwork*. Springfield, Ill. Charles C. Thomas. 1970.

Kane, Rosalie *Interprofessional Teamwork*. Manpower Monograph No 8. Syracuse Syracuse University School of Social Work. 1975.

Lowe, Jane Isaacs and Herranen, Marjatta. "Conflict in Team Work Understanding Roles and Relationships," *Social Work in Health Care*, Vol. 3(3), Spring 1978. p. 323-30

Rae-Grant, Quentin and Marcuse, Donald. "The Hazards of Team Work." *American Journal of Orthopsychiatry*, Vol. 38(1), January, 1968, p. 4-8.

Weiner, Hyman J. Adapted from *Interdisciplinary Collaboration in Health Care*. Course Syllabus. Columbus University School of Social Work. November, 1978

Wise, Harold et al. (eds.) *Making Health Teams Work*. Cambridge, MA Ballinger Publishing Co., 1974.

WOUNDED HEALERS
THOMAS MAEDER

ALFRED ADLER, ACCORDING TO HIS SON, ONCE SAID, "I think I could make out of a sadist a good butcher—perhaps even a good surgeon." He would need to imbue the sadist with social interest and modify certain patterns of behavior, and he would end up with a constructive member of society who nonetheless retained the sadist's underlying personality pattern and motivations. One might wonder what sort of pathological type Adler would have selected as raw material for a psychotherapist.

One does not need to search for pathology to explain career choice any more than one needs underlying scatological or sexual explanations to understand every innocuous bit of behavior. Altruistic people, who work hard to help others, should not be suspected *ipso facto* of harboring ulterior selfish motives. Nonetheless, the "helping professions," such as nursing, charitable work, the ministry, and psychotherapy, attract people for curious and often psychologically suspect reasons. Something is a bit odd about people who proclaim "I want to help other people"—the underlying assumption being that they are in a position to help and that others will want to be helped by them. Such people may be lured, knowingly or unknowingly, by the position of authority, by the dependence of others, by the image of benevolence, by the promise of adulation, or by a hope of vicariously helping themselves through helping others. Though some helping professionals have humbly and realistically perceived that they have something to offer and are willing to accept the responsibilities inherent in their calling, others use the role to manipulate their world in a convenient, simplistic manner, ultimately failing to take responsibility and using authority precisely to avoid it. For such people their job is not merely a way to earn a living: it is the essence of their lives.

It is a commonplace that psychotherapists are crazy, and that this is probably what led them to their jobs. "What still strikes me," one woman I interviewed said, "is I'll go to a party in New York, and inevitably the craziest person there is a psychiatrist. I mean the person who is literally doing childish, antisocial things, making a fool of himself and embarrassing everyone else. I just shrug. That's the way it is." A president of the American Academy of Psychotherapists once said, in an address to the members of his organization, "When I first visited a national psychiatric convention, in 1943, I was dismayed to find the greatest collection of oddballs, Christ beards, and psychotics that I had ever seen outside a hospital. Yet this is to be expected: psychotherapists are those of us who are driven by our own emotional hunger."

Psychotherapists often take a perverse delight in criticizing their peers, and the amount of abuse I have heard them heap upon one another is truly astounding. Psychiatrists often say that analysts are crazy. Analysts say that psychiatrists, being unanalyzed, are crazy. Both of them say that social workers and psychologists, whose training is more limited and subject to fewer quality controls, are crazy, and are particularly harmful because a little bit of knowledge is a dangerous thing. Social workers and psychologists accuse psychiatrists and analysts of being pompous asses—pompous *crazy* asses, so puffed up with theoretical abstractions that they are out of touch with the real world.

"I very rarely have found a healthy, well-integrated, happy person *seeking* this profession," one training psychoanalyst says. Another man, a clinical psychologist, told me, "I questioned your calling it a myth that therapists are crazy because the *fact* is that most of them *are*. If you need any proof, let me tell you that every patient who comes into this office who has had a previous experience with another therapist has some kind of horror story to tell, about some *major* failing on the therapist's part, including, quite often, sexual abuse, verbal abuse, things that cross the boundary of mere bad technique and come pretty damn close to the criminal."

Various statistical surveys of the psychopathology of therapists have been published, but this literature yields inconclusive results. In one study 91 percent of psychiatrists surveyed agreed that psychiatrists had "emotional difficulties that are special to them and their work as contrasted with non-psychiatrists." The psychiatrists said, however, that some of these problems were related to the personalities of people who went into the field, and others stemmed from the nature of the work. Few considered their "emotional difficulties" to be diagnosable clinical problems. But an interesting Swiss study compared the military-conscription records of people who subsequently became psychiatrists with the records of those who became surgeons and internists, and found that significantly more of the eventual psychiatrists were declared unfit for military service because of psychiatric disorders.

In another survey, this one of psychologists, social workers, counselors, and other nonmedical psychotherapists, 82 percent of respondents said they'd had relationship difficulties, 57 percent had experienced depression, 11 percent admitted to substance abuse, and 2 percent said they had attempted suicide. Again, the survey does not make clear how serious the relationship difficulties and depression were, nor does it give comparable figures for a non-therapist population.

With respect to alcohol and drug abuse, a concrete measure of emotional problems, physicians in general show a higher incidence than nonphysicians, and a study that examined ninety-eight physician members of Alcoholics Anonymous found that 17 percent were psychiatrists, who constituted only 8 percent of physicians at the time. Though this has been interpreted to mean that a disproportionate number of psychiatrists (among physicians in general) are alcoholics, it may also mean that out of the total population of alcoholic physicians, psychiatrists are among the most likely to seek help. Other studies have found that alcohol-abuse rates among therapists range from 6 to 11 percent, but in the absence of proper controls such studies seem inconclusive. When therapists are asked about themselves, 4 percent of them report drug or alcohol abuse serious enough to affect their work. When asked about their colleagues, these same therapists say that 18 percent of them are so impaired.

Studies of suicide among psychiatrists also furnish contradictory results. "Among the specialties, psychiatry appears to yield a disproportionate number of suicides," said an article on suicide among physicians which appeared in the *British Medical Journal* as long ago as 1964. "The explanation may lie in the choosing of the specialty rather than its demands, for some who take up psychiatry probably do so for morbid reasons."

Physicians in general do not seem to commit suicide at a rate significantly different from that of their nonmedical peers, although, perhaps because of their knowledge of drugs and access to them, their methods of choice are characteristically nonviolent: doctors poison themselves more than twice as often as the lay public, and shoot themselves less often. Psychiatrists, however, show a markedly greater tendency to commit suicide than the population at large or their medical peers. After several conflicting and methodologically flawed studies of suicide among psychiatrists were published, the Task Force on Suicide Prevention of the American Psychiatric Association instigated its own study of psychiatrists' suicides. Investigators examined the records on nearly 19,000 physician deaths from 1967 to 1972 and calculated the ratio of suicides to members for each medical specialty. They found that psychiatrists killed themselves about twice as often as other physicians. No other specialty showed a frequency significantly greater than average. Moreover, when individual years of the time span were examined, the rate was found to be constant, "indicating a relatively stable over-supply of depressed psychiatrists from which the suicides are produced."

Some people have argued that many psychiatrists who commit suicide have good reasons for doing so. One view is that psychiatrists are more likely to kill themselves when they are terminally ill than are most other people, because they take a more realistic and enlightened view of human life and suffering. Some of the prominent early analysts are examples: Paul Federn shot himself when he was dying of cancer, and Wilhelm Stekel, faced with declining health, poisoned himself.

Others suggest that the strains of the profession, whether practical or emotional, may drive practitioners to despair. Judd Marmor, a well-known professor of psychiatry, points out that the burden of constantly associating with depressed people, the stress of the transference-countertransference situation, the problems of role uncertainty, the burden of continuing education, and economic difficulties might be expected to take their toll on anyone. Fritz Wittels, originally an antagonist of psychoanalysis but later an ardent supporter, wrote of analysts who

> involve their own unconscious in the dreams of others as in a distorting mirror; so that a gremlin catches them and drives them to death. Weininger was one of those who became involved in a bit of self-analysis, saw a distorted image of his unconscious that pressed a revolver into his hand. I have known three brilliant analysts, Schrötter, Tausk, Silberer, who voluntarily ended their lives. And in Vienna alone. Others will follow.

After Wittels changed his opinion of psychoanalysis, he retracted this view, saying that Weininger was not really a qualified psychoanalyst, that the others had not been properly analyzed, and that these facts, in the end, were to blame. "An analyst who has not himself been analyzed is in danger, be it suicide or otherwise."

On balance, however, with the significant exception of an apparent high suicide rate, the evidence that psychotherapists are disproportionately *impaired* is slight, and to accuse them of pervasive gross psychopathology would be foolish. Therapists are not crazy. Nonetheless, in terms of personality types, emotional weaknesses, and psychological motivations, a substantial majority of them may differ from the general population in ways more subtle than full-blown pathology yet more important than mere style.

WHAT FACTORS LEAD PEOPLE TO BECOME PSYCHO-therapists? On this, not surprisingly, such information as exists is poorly controlled, open to wide interpretation, and generally anecdotal, as is psychotherapy itself. A book by William Henry, John Sims, and S. Lee Spray, titled *The Fifth Profession*, presents statistics that are diverting but scarcely enlightening. Given a questionnaire asking why they had become interested in the field of psychotherapy, 15.8 percent of all polled therapists said they wanted "to help people," 14.4 percent wanted "to understand people," and 9.6 percent wanted "to gain professional status." Psychoanalysts and psychiatrists, which were considered separate groups, were more interested in "gaining an identity," whatever that means, than in any of the other possibilities, whereas this was of negligible concern to the clinical psychologists and social workers. And 24.4 percent of all therapists gave an "other" reason for their interest.

Once one gets past the responses that invoke benevolence and civic-mindedness, one finds reasons that tend to involve a search for compensations and cures for the therapist's personal unhappiness. Freud theorized that a strong desire to help others stems from longings that are the consequence of childhood losses. Indeed, several articles on related issues assert that many therapists grew up in rejecting or inadequate families and were thus led to what Karl Menninger has called a "professional interest in lonely, eccentric, and unloved people."

One book that examines the lives of twelve psychotherapists concludes that most of them felt responsible for maintaining family happiness during their youth. In the cases the authors studied, the mothers were seen as pallid or uninspired women, notably indifferent to their children except insofar as the children could be manipulated for the mothers' own gratification. The fathers were typically weak and estranged, though their children admired them. "Since every study shows that [therapists] mostly come from disrupted or disjointed families, often with the father physically or psychically absent, the therapists-to-be were delegated the task of assuring the fate and fulfillment of the family. They became, and are, the family nurturer."

Often the psychotherapist's secret goal is to continue in the role of family support. In analytic transference the analyst comes to represent aspects of the patient's parents, and the patient represents aspects of the therapist's earlier life. Unfortunately, however, patients are not trained to manipulate this curious relationship, nor is that what they have come and paid money to do. Meanwhile, the therapist treats a succession of patients not only for their own problems but also for other problems, belonging to another time and place in the therapist's life, that haunt his consultation room. One study describes several therapists who seem to have done this. A psychiatrist undergoing analysis became depressed when she realized that she would not be able to cure her mother, an idea that lay in the back of her mind and had been her most important motive for entering psychiatry. A psychiatrist who in childhood had been saddled with the burden of maintaining family harmony was found to harbor the fantasy that one day his father and mother would be happy together as a result of his efforts. Meanwhile, he had particular difficulty treating patients with severe marital problems, and his own marriage suffered from his tendency to treat his wife as if she were a patient. In a third case a medical student embarking upon his psychiatric residency broke under the strain of caring for his emotionally disturbed mother and dependent psychiatrist father; he had planned to work in child psychiatry, and was especially interested in helping doctors' families.

The children of psychotherapists seem to talk more than most people do about their parents' emotionally dismal childhoods. They portray their therapist parents as exceptionally lonely and unhappy, socially ostracized at school, and abused at home, either psychologically or physically. The parents were ill at ease with themselves and with others, and sought through association with the world of adults and a retreat into the world of the intellect, and ultimately through the field of psychotherapy, to understand and manage their misery and to protect themselves and, later, their families. In many cases, the therapist parents themselves had said that their unhappy early lives were the primary motivation for their choice of career. In others, the motive seemed so clear that the children drew the conclusion on their own.

A host of other less-than-selfless motives may enter into the choice of psychotherapy as a profession: sublimated sexual curiosity, aggression, the problem-solving pleasure of clarifying emotional confusions, and a voyeuristic interest in the lives of others. These factors, which have been discussed by other authors, are very likely important, but they seem to be secondary rather than determining characteristics and will be considered here only insofar as they enter into what I believe to be the primary one: that of the wounded healer.

The idea of the wounded healer has ancient roots. In Greek mythology, Chiron, the centaur who taught medicine to Aesculapius, suffered an incurable wound at the hands of Hercules. Saint Augustine was conspicuous but not alone among the Christian saints in using his own weaknesses and his struggle against them to help him find compassion and strength. Mythology and religion are fraught with figures who must learn to heal themselves before healing others—who must recognize and forgive their own sins before they can, with authentic humility and understanding, forgive anyone else. Many of Freud's significant early discoveries arose out of the scrutiny of his deeply buried memories and then heroic confrontations with the painful things he found. In case histories of his patients he drew upon his own experience often enough to show that he regularly put his own flaws at the service of the empathic process. Psychoanalysts in training are required to undergo analysis for two complementary reasons. First, they must try to rid themselves of their psychological problems, so that they will be less likely to project their preoccupations onto their patients and then mistake what they perceive in them for objective fact. Second, the painful analytic process is itself instructive: an analyst who ventures into the patient's world needs to know how analysis can hurt and how it can help, and to recognize that therapist and patient are made of the same mortal stuff. Having emotional problems may not actually be a prerequisite or an advantage for a psychotherapist, but, clearly, having had problems is not in itself a handicap, so long as these problems have been recognized, confronted, and successfully resolved.

The danger occurs when the wounded healer has not resolved, or cannot control, his own injury. The helping professional's career can follow either of two paths. The more difficult, but ultimately more satisfying, road leads to a painful confrontation with his own problems and weaknesses, and ultimately to self-knowledge. Ideally, he overcomes the difficulties; at worst, he is forced to resign himself to insuperable handicaps. In either case, though, the end result is a clearer perception of his ambitions and needs and their relationship to the task at hand. He can approach others with honesty, compassion, and humility, knowing that he is motivated by genuine concern, and not by some ulterior motive.

The other path is easier but often disastrous. The psychotherapist comes, consciously or unconsciously, to see in his profession a means of *avoiding* the need to deal with his problems. He gains authority and power to compensate for his weakness and vulnerability. He learns slippery techniques that enable him to justify his actions in almost all circumstances, and perhaps even to shift blame onto somebody else. In his work with his patients, the entire therapeutic relationship is perverted and turned to the service of his hidden purpose. The therapist is there not to treat the patient but, by circuitous and well-concealed means, to treat or protect or comfort himself. The patient is not an object of empathy and altruism but an unsuspecting victim who is taken into the therapist's realm of personal needs and subjective impressions and assigned a role there that he does not recognize and would not want. And in the course of this strange, unacknowledged process, the patient's own problems may be neglected.

In choosing his profession, the therapist-to-be may even make his problems much worse, because he discovers a justification for divorcing himself from the emotions that have caused him so much pain. He is to become a cold, accurate instrument instead of a sloppily warm and vulnerable human being. He may console himself with the heady deceit that he is martyring himself for the good of others: rather than live a happy and self-interested life, he says, he will forgo his own satisfaction in order to transform himself into someone who can do greater good. The flaw in this idea is that he is not being selfless at all but seeking, through the very medium of ostentatious self-denial, a perverse gratification of his personal needs. For such a therapist, the wound has become sealed off, prevented from causing pain but also left inaccessible to healing. Since his energy is directed toward defending the status quo, he is diverted from the arduous and humbling process of self-examination which might otherwise have made him whole, and is forced, continuously and forever, to work just to stay where he is. With this sealed-off problem now at the center of his personal and professional life, the further along he goes the more difficult and costly it becomes to try to correct the mistake. His situation is almost Faustian: he has sold his hopes of redemption in the future for power, comfort, and knowledge in the present.

THE PARALLELS IN THE WORLD OF RELIGION ARE conspicuous and instructive. The Church has often been regarded as a haven for the emotionally disturbed. Like studies on the mental state of psychotherapists, studies of the clergy are contradictory and emotionally charged. Overall, however, they suggest a high incidence of family problems and narcissistic disorders, and a host of other problems involving interpersonal relations and self-esteem. In the course of my research I spoke to several psychotherapists who had begun their careers as ministers, and who now specialize in treating the emotional problems of their erstwhile professional colleagues.

Some of these problems are incidental to the occupation, or result from its peculiar pressures and strains, but others seem to be both causal and recurrent enough to rate as a mild but characteristic clerical pathology.

One type of clergyman, like one type of psychotherapist, is a repentant sinner who has recognized his or her weakness and can therefore align himself with other mortal men in the search for salvation. Another kind, the sealed-off sinner in his most extreme form, is the rigid and damning preacher who exhorts and chastises his flock from above, who has no sympathy for their weaknesses, and who may hurt his congregants by condemning their transgressions, instead of helping by leading them, through understanding, to righteousness. These preachers are so deeply beset by uncertainty and unresolved problems that they have organized their external life through sheer brute force and imposture, but they have left their internal life untouched. They cannot understand their congregants because they cannot understand themselves, and they cannot constructively help with many emotional problems because the solution they have adopted themselves is to cap such tensions tightly and hold them unseen.

Perhaps the most interesting and significant problem shared by many "healers," which has been described by a number of therapists, is that of the person, often a first-born or only child, who was rushed through childhood too quickly, without the warmth, the protection, and the love that children deserve, and who was obliged to become a little adult. Such people grow up believing that hard work and responsibility are the only things that give them value in others' eyes. They have a chronically low sense of self-worth and a stunted ability to receive genuine love or friendship from others; only their selfishly selfless labors make them feel satisfied with themselves. As a result, they may be driven into a veritable frenzy of wholesale helping, which is motivated not by altruism but by a desperate need to fill an inner vacancy—an effort that ultimately helps very little, because, like trying to fill a bucket with a hole in the bottom, it can never succeed until they have attended to the necessary repairs. As one man, a Jungian analyst and an Episcopalian minister who has treated many clergymen, describes the problem: "They give too much, without knowing how to take, and it has an effect on them as well as on their families. They build up even more of an inhibition against being able to appropriately take things for themselves, which is taboo. They can justify this attitude with all sorts of theological jargon that says 'It is more blessed to give than to receive,' and so on. They are into loving their God and loving their neighbor, but they forget that little, crucial, additional thing: 'as thyself.'

"These people are pathological givers, and so they become servers, pastoral counselors, and so on, and they can even be good at it, to a degree, but they become impoverished after a while. They have given so much that they finally run out of spiritual and nervous energy, and what remains is the underlying resentment. You find a great deal of resentment and sourness among the clergy. Just go and interview your garden-variety Catholic priest in the parish. Get to know him a little bit, and you will find a lot of anger and bitterness, even though he will maintain a façade of benevolence and contentment. He has given more than he had to give, and gotten very little back."

In choosing the ministry as a profession, these wounded healers have embarked on an ultimately doomed quest, one that perverts the purpose of their work. One bishop summed up the issues quite neatly when he said that in screening candidates for the ministry, one of the questions he asks himself is, "Is this a whole person seeking to express his wholeness through the ministry? Or is this a person trying to *find* his wholeness in the ministry?"

William Dewart, a clinical psychologist who works primarily with clergymen, points out another interesting, common problem. One of the lures that drew these people to the Church was a position of authority that might help them to compensate for their feelings of inadequacy and emptiness and to escape from painful impositions by others. "Some go into the clergy believing that 'in the end, I answer only to God.' That is a very nice arrangement, they suppose, because God is a spiritual entity, after all, and His love is unconditional. They won't have to deal with a foreman or boss, no changes of administration. It's just you and God, who, after all, called you in the first place. At least that's what they believe when they begin. But before they know it, they find themselves running up against authority and issues of power everywhere, from the vestry of their own small parish all the way up to the bishop of the diocese. For example, in the Episcopal Church the canons provide for the bishop to make the final decision regarding the very question of one's calling to an ordained priesthood. So the poor individual unconsciously seeking the priesthood in hopes of circumventing issues of authority and power will certainly find himself walking straight into one of the more authoritative, political organizations in the world."

Among psychotherapists this is rarely a problem, except among those entering a psychoanalytic institute, who may feel that the institute's teachers and training analysts hold despotic power over their fate. Indeed, the psychotherapist in private practice is responsible to no outside authority. Information about what he does comes only from what he chooses to tell and from the perceptions of his patients, who tend to mistrust their own judgment. The therapist truly has the independence that the clergyman hoped for; he is the solitary ruler of his microcosmic domain. This unusual circumstance tends to exacerbate whatever problems he brought to his profession and to add novel difficulties.

IN AN IMPORTANT PAPER TITLED "THE GOD COMPLEX," published in 1913, Ernest Jones, a pioneer psychoanalyst now best remembered as Freud's biographer and chief English-language ambassador, described a set of character traits resulting from a pathological unconscious belief that one is God. People with this complex do not wander the streets proclaiming themselves the deity but have both a concealed, insidious faith in their own importance and entitlement, and an inability to conceive of others as comparably important, which color every aspect of their relations with the world.

The type in question is characterized by a desire for aloofness, inaccessibility, and mysteriousness, often also by a modesty and self-effacement. They are happiest in their own home, in privacy and seclusion, and like to withdraw to a distance. They surround themselves and their opinions with a cloud of mystery, exert only an indirect influence on external affairs, never join in any common action, and are generally unsocial. They take great interest in psychology, particularly in the so-called objective methods of mind-study that are eclectic and which dispense with the necessity for intuition. Phantasies of power are common, especially the idea of possessing great wealth. They believe themselves to be omniscient, and tend to reject all new knowledge. . . . The subjects of language and religion greatly interest them. . . . Constant, but less characteristic, attributes are the desire for appreciation, the wish to protect the weak, the belief in their own immortality, the fondness for creative schemes, e.g., for social reform, and above all, a pronounced castration complex:

Oddly enough, this comes very close to being a description of many psychotherapists, or even a job description for psychotherapy. Some of the qualities are ones that psychotherapists go out of their way to cultivate as part of their professional persona, and the training process may encourage them. Indeed, Jones said that people with God complexes were more likely than others to go into psychology and related professions. He hastened to add that they were not drawn to psychoanalysis, his own specialty, for it required intuition and an ability to empathize with others. A great many analysts and analytically oriented therapists, however, plod through their jobs on the basis of dogma, with little empathy at all. Jones himself was notable for his lack of psychological intuition, and was a curious mixture of radicalism and conservatism. He left medicine and Wales, his native land, which threatened in separate ways to hold power over him, yet once he had embraced Freudian psychoanalysis he became its most inflexible defender. His belief in the powers of psychoanalysis, by his own admission, bordered on grandiosity:

Perhaps, indeed, in centuries to be, the medical psychologist may, like the priest of ancient times, come to serve as a source of practical wisdom and a stabilising influence in this chaotic world, whom the community would consult before embarking on any important social or political enterprise. Mere megalomania, it may be said. Perhaps, but it is my living faith none the less, and only our descendants will be able to say if it was a misplaced one.

Freud himself had a strong element of grandiosity, insisting that he was not a man of science, an observer, an experimenter, or a thinker, but a conquistador. His bitter relations with Jung, Adler, Rank, and others who strayed from his patronage and guidance are in keeping with Jones's image of the man who can tolerate no god but himself.

In any psychotherapist, for that matter, an unusual degree of self-assurance is essential. After all, the therapist's patients are people whose attempts to conduct their own lives have failed, to some degree, and who are seeking help from another. However much therapists may wish to play the part of mere mediators rather than guides, the situation forces them into a position of superiority in which, by whatever direct or subtle means, they must assert their notion of what is good for their patients above what the patients may believe to be proper in the management of their own lives. Moreover, therapists need self-confidence and poise, combined with a great deal of humility, to withstand the emotional onslaught of the patients' unreasonable expectations and assumptions. Patients force therapists into a position of superiority through their idealization: the therapists must have wonderful marriages, perfect children, cultured and profound interests, clear and correct understanding of issues. Many patients want to be like their therapists, to adopt facets of their therapist's tastes and mannerisms, and some patients go on to become therapists or counselors themselves, because the profession has emerged in their minds as the most perfect of all occupations. Patients do not simply want advice from their therapists: as children, they expected magic from their parents, and often with their therapists— thanks to the transference—they entertain similarly unrealistic hopes that their fears will be soothed and their problems miraculously resolved.

The field of psychotherapy inevitably attracts people with God complexes, and it is custom-designed to exacerbate the condition when it exists. Psychiatrists sometimes expect, and are often expected by others, to address questions that lie well outside the range of their expertise.

They are expected to do so simply because they study human beings and, by erroneous implication, are therefore supposed to understand all things human. Psychiatrists comment on the law, politics, art, literature, and ethical questions, which nothing in their training has qualified them to comprehend any better than any other intelligent and educated person. Above all, within the therapeutic situation itself therapists who do not have the personal strength and equilibrium to resist the temptations of power and to see the patients' adoration as the epiphenomenon of their actions that it is may subside into self-importance.

Each profession carries its respective difficulties, and the danger of analysis is that of becoming infected by transference projections, in particular by archetypal contents. When the patient assumes that his analyst is the fulfillment of his dreams, that he is not an ordinary doctor but a spiritual hero and a sort of saviour, of course the analyst will say, "What nonsense! This is just morbid. It is a hysterical exaggeration." Yet—it tickles him; it is just too nice. And moreover, he has the same archetypes in himself. So he begins to feel, "If there are saviours, well, perhaps it is just possible that I am one," and he will fall for it, at first hesitantly, and then it will become more and more plain to him that he really is a sort of extraordinary individual. Slowly he becomes fascinated and exclusive. He is terribly touchy, susceptible, and perhaps makes himself a nuisance in medical societies. He cannot talk with his colleagues any more because he is—I don't know what. He becomes very disagreeable or withdraws from human contacts, isolates himself, and then it becomes more and more clear to him that he is a very important chap really and of great spiritual significance, probably an equal of the Mahatmas in the Himalayas, and it is quite likely that he also belongs to the great brotherhood. And then he is lost to the profession. We have very unfortunate examples of this kind. I know quite a number of colleagues who have gone that way.

This description by Carl Jung is probably exaggerated, which is fortunate in one obvious sense, though unfortunate in another, inasmuch as therapists of the sort described are not necessarily lost to the profession but may continue to practice. They can justify their attitude to themselves and to others—but someone who wields power in the name of some perceived ultimate good is always potentially dangerous. The zealot can find a moral excuse for oppressing others that is unavailable to the mere bully or the charlatan.

IF VIEWED CLINICALLY, THE GOD COMPLEX CAN BE RELATED to narcissism, a personality disorder whose chief features are well established. Those with narcissistic personality disorders have grandiose self-images, often entertain unrealistic notions of their abilities, power, wealth, intelligence, and appearance, and feel entitled to things they haven't earned, simply by virtue of their inherent greatness. This exalted view of themselves, however, lacking the comfortable and certain support of reality, is very fragile. Narcissists constantly need admiration and praise from others and can be incongruously devastated by relatively unimportant failures, which threaten the fragile tissue of their belief. A paradoxical indifference to the wishes and feelings of others, combined with a simultaneous dependency upon their praise, is a particularly striking feature of narcissists. Many of them have a deep-seated sense that they are frauds—as in many ways they are.

Narcissists are much more concerned with the appearance of things than with the reality; thus their ambitions tend to have a driven quality but to be empty of genuine sustained interest or pleasure. They are ethically empty, though their fundamental amorality is often masked by an intense but superficial show of morality and social, political, or aesthetic concern. Since these cosmetic ethics do not touch them personally, however, narcissists may readily change their views or entertain conflicting ethical beliefs.

Their relations with others tend to be emotionally hollow and exploitative, since narcissists are ultimately interested only in themselves (failing, in a profound way, even to perceive other people as separate from themselves) and are thus unable to maintain equal give-and-take relationships. They are insensitive and lacking in empathy; their views of others are chiefly projections from within themselves, and therefore vacillate between idealization and debasement. Frequently they believe other people to be basically unscrupulous, unreliable, false, and opportunistic. Though they may make an extravagant show of generosity and concern for others, this behavior inevitably proves to be just that—a show, which serves to polish the fine image they strive to hold of themselves.

Various schools of psychoanalytic thought postulate different origins for narcissistic disorders, but all agree on the fundamental outlines. Narcissists were deprived in infancy and childhood of the affection and the deep emotional interactions with their parents that would have allowed the normal development of a distinct sense of the difference between self and other and a feeling of personal value. According to the psychoanalysts Heinz Kohut and Alice Miller particularly, pathology in the parents (who are often narcissistic themselves) kept them from treating the child as an independent person and responding to him on his own merits, and led them instead to use the child for their own gratification. As a result, the child's sense of self was stunted and his sense of value was structured around his ability to comprehend and fulfill his parents' wishes. As

Miller comments,

> This ability is then extended and perfected. Later, these children not only become mothers (confidantes, comforters, advisers, supporters) of their own mothers, but also take over the responsibility for their siblings and eventually develop a special sensitivity to unconscious signals manifesting the needs of others. No wonder that they often choose the psychoanalytic profession later on. Who else, without this previous history, would muster sufficient interest to spend the whole day trying to discover what is happening in the other person's unconscious?

Thus the peculiar miseries of the narcissist's childhood have encouraged him to develop a sensitivity to others' needs and a knack for anticipating and dextrously catering to them. These are extraordinarily useful in the practice of psychotherapy, as is a need to exercise these talents and to achieve the approval of others. The very same qualities, however, ultimately hinder the therapist's ability to help patients or to raise children who are free of emotional problems, because the empathy and altruism are basically false. Meanwhile, the profession he has entered presses him further than ever from the chance of cure.

One of the best ways to avoid or counteract feelings of grandiosity is to cultivate genuine human loves and friendships. By dealing with people as equals, in symmetrical relationships in which the corners tend to get knocked off people's fantastic monuments to themselves, and in which they may grow comfortable with their shortcomings through others' acceptance of them, they can learn to be real, solid human beings who take true pride in genuine strengths and are able to recognize and deal with genuine weaknesses. Healthy, loving marriages, in particular, wean people from lonely grandiosity, and also mitigate the effects of their particular problems on their children.

Unfortunately, this is not the sort of marriage many psychotherapists seem to have or to seek out. When measured in superficial statistical terms, psychiatrists have a divorce rate insignificantly higher than the rate among other medical specialists, and considerably *lower* than the rate among the general professional population. Their marriages, however, according to one respected research team, often appear to be remarkably distant and formal, based on shared intellectual and recreational activities rather than on affectionate interaction. Moreover, considerable anecdotal evidence suggests that therapists, both men and women, tend to marry troubled and dependent partners who will not counteract their narcissistic disturbances but will supply the admiration they crave. It is said that they marry their patients—which is sometimes even literally true—and end up in relationships that are anything but equal. The psychiatrist Richard Robertiello, speaking from professional and personal experience, writes,

> [Therapists] tend to be drawn to partners who have rather serious emotional problems and who are looking for a wise understanding person who will help, support and perhaps "cure" them. . . . They are drawn by their own feeling of grandiosity and omnipotence. They think they will be able, by their love and caring and wisdom, to make this person happy, especially one who has frustrated several previous therapists in their efforts to accomplish this. Of course, the therapists feel very noble and generous and altruistic in this endeavor.
>
> But their satisfactions are hardly only altruistic. They start off having tremendous adulation and admiration from their "sick" mates. They begin in an unchallenged position of superiority and control. They are always "right" or "healthy" and their mate is always "wrong" or "sick." In addition to all of the narcissistic gratification this provides, it also gives a perfect assurance of acceptability and a near-guarantee against being abandoned.

Ultimately, this sort of relationship is not very profitable for either person involved. The therapist may eventually outgrow his spouse and come to resent the dependence that originally brought them together. "I used to complain that I saw outpatients all week long, and then had an inpatient on my hands every weekend," Robertiello says. But growth on the part of the spouse can pose a threat to the therapist. The couple may end up in a stale relationship, where even the gratification of adoration and dependence wears thin. Meanwhile, the whole household revolves around the initial narcissistic demands of the therapist, and the subordinate spouse may come to function more as a part of this pattern than as an autonomous entity. "My father was very shy and insecure," says one woman, a lawyer and the daughter of an analyst, "and he insisted that the family provide him with a lot of reassurance all the time. He stayed very close to home in every way—his office was in the house—and there was this ritual that my mother had to tell him how wonderful he was, even though he wasn't, and how great the things he did were even when they weren't. That seems to be why he needed her."

Close friendships are the other curative, but psychotherapists, as it happens, tend to have very few friends. Therapists explain this away as a result of the tremendous demands of their professional lives—long hours, teaching, society meetings—but such rationalizations seem forced. Statistics show that psychiatrists have more free time than almost any other medical specialists and that compared with many lawyers and businessmen—people not noted for a paucity of friends—psychotherapists do not have demanding schedules. Moreover, having little time does not automatically mean that one cannot make friends.

The real reason for the lack of friendships often appears to be a much more unpleasant, unconscious one. Many therapists do not need friends, because they live vicariously through their patients, just as clergymen seek love and self-worth vicariously through devotion to a congregation. For people who are uncomfortable with others and with themselves, the therapeutic situation offers an unparalleled opportunity for asymmetrical intimacy. The rules of therapy demand that the patient tell the therapist everything, while the therapist is under no obligation to reveal anything at all and thus can minimize the risk of pain incurred in normal human relationships. Life in the office can be exciting. One therapist told me the story of an analyst who retired and looked forward to the joy of reading novels but was dreadfully bored after a few months, because fiction did not possess the immediacy and veracity of clinical cases. And therapists who are allowed entry into their patients' lives are repaid for this privilege by the patients' grateful adoration. "My father had an inability to relate with his family or other people," says an analyst and the son of an analyst, "and his way of being close was through his patients. It was a way for him to have an interaction, but there was always a wall, or a desk, or a couch to protect him."

The Swiss psychotherapist Adolf Guggenbühl-Craig describes the tragic consequences to the therapist of this kind of vicarious living.

His own private life takes a back seat to the problems and difficulties of his patients. But a point may be reached where the patients might actually live for the analyst, so to speak, where they are expected to fill the gap left by the analyst's own loss of contact with warm, dynamic life. The analyst no longer has his own friends; his patients' friendships and enmities are as his own. The analyst's sex life may be stunted; his patients' sexual problems provide a substitute. . . . His own psychic development comes to a standstill. Even in his non-professional life he can talk of nothing but his patients and their problems. He is no longer able to love and hate, to invest himself in life, to struggle, to win and lose. His own affective life becomes a surrogate. Acting thus as a quack who draws his sustenance from the lives of his patients, the analyst may seem momentarily to flourish psychically. But in reality he loses his own vitality and creative originality. The advantage of such vicarious living, of course, is that the analyst is also spared any genuine suffering. In a sense this function too is exercised for him by others.

The particular danger for the patient, against which therapists must be vigilant but often are not, is that the therapy begins to settle in as part of the patient's life rather than remaining an active process through which he can reintegrate himself into living. The patient may begin to look forward to sessions excessively and to live his life for the unacknowledged purpose of interesting and pleasing the therapist. Problems may apparently be resolved and changes made because the patient feels that this is what the therapist wants; such changes have no profound or permanent effect, because they are performed more for dramatic value or the therapist's approval than from a sense of inner need. Patients do not want to leave the idealized therapist; nor, in the pathological relationship described above, is the therapist motivated to help the patient leave. In the worst case, the entire therapy is poisoned, because ultimately, unconsciously, the therapist cannot bear to cure the patient, for then he would lose him. He therefore perpetuates a curious relationship of a kind that he may have had with his parents and that he may inflict not only on his patients but also on his children.

I have heard such stories again and again. One of the first and most dramatic accounts came from a respected psychoanalyst who had always admired and sought to emulate his analyst father, had gone to the same medical school and analytic institute, and had set up his practice in the same city. He dated the beginning of his most significant personal growth from the time his father, during a period of illness, asked him to take over some of his cases.

"I agreed. I wasn't that busy. I was in analytic training and was getting some supervision analyzing, and I thought this would be more grist for the mill. Besides, I figured I could do it as well as anybody else, and I never thought about the possible consequences of this kind of involvement with him. But in the course of doing this two or three times, I began to realize that my father had a number of patients who were very dependent on him. He charged them low fees, for one thing. That should have been a clue. But then, more important, with a number of his patients I realized that he had no good idea of the difference between maintenance, support, and cure. With some of them he had developed a kind of *collusion*; they needed him, and he needed them."

What both alarmed and helped this man most of all was his realization that the same process was at work in the relationship between his father and himself. He idolized his father, and his father depended on this idolization, much as he did in his relationships with his patients. Though his father was willing to help him grow to a certain degree, and though the son benefited in many ways from his closeness to his father, at some point his independence worked against his father's interests—both the father's selfish interests and his inappropriate wishes for his son. I saw the contrast in the relationships between my psychoanalyst and me and my father and me. My analyst was providing me with an opportunity to grow up, while my father, apparently, didn't want me to go through the same sort of pain he had experienced growing up." Gradually the son established his own independence: he divorced his wife, having married in part to please his father, moved to another state, and eventually abandoned full-time psychoanalysis in favor of a psychiatric practice whose orientation was altogether removed from that of his father's.

Several teaching analysts and psychotherapists agree that what poses as professional dedication is often at heart a morbid addiction. A training analyst in New York has discussed with me the unwillingness of analysts to leave their practice even when they reach retirement age. "They may say that they can't give up the income, or offer some other explanation, but what they really miss is feeling needed. Personally, I think that it is unethical and immoral for analysts to practice beyond a certain time in life. You can say a word for experience, but how much experience is experience? You can't really say that a seventy-year-old's experience is better than that of someone who is fifty-five. There comes a time when you are simply repeating the same experiences. Yet analysts will not retire. They won't. Myself, I don't take on new patients anymore. I do consultations or see an occasional ex-patient, and mostly do teaching or supervising. But someone who is now in his eighties, a New York analyst whom everyone knows, said to me the other day, 'I have time,' meaning that he wanted some referrals. I told a friend, and she said I should have replied, 'Not much.' What is someone like that doing for his patients? He can't see as well, he can't remember as well, he can't hear as well, but he's still in there, and nobody's going to tell him what to do, and since there are no rules or laws or need for operating-room privileges, nobody can stop him, and he'll just keep doing it. And, transferential feelings being what they are, the patient doesn't have enough sense to move on or move up. Sometimes patients actually stay because they feel sorry for the therapist. I've known cases like that."

For most patients the problems of the wounded healer are irrelevant. Most people who seek therapeutic help need the benefit or knowledge, experience, and objectivity, and the opportunity to devote a specific amount of time to the careful scrutiny of whatever is wrong with their lives. The narcissistic therapist's sealed-off wound and secret self-centered agenda may have no discernible effect on this simple program. But in cases that demand more from the therapist, or tread close to his own problems, or issue challenges that his therapeutic persona cannot easily handle, serious harm may be done.

SOURCES OF STRAIN BETWEEN PHYSICIANS AND SOCIAL WORKERS: IMPLICATIONS FOR SOCIAL WORKERS IN HEALTH CARE SETTINGS

TERRY MIZRAHI, Ph.D., JULIE ABRAMSON, Ph.D.

INTRODUCTION

This article analyzes the sources of the strains that have characterized the physician/social worker interaction since the inception of medical social work in 1905 at Massachusetts General Hospital. The authors believe that the disparate perspectives of the two professions result from very different socialization experiences provided by social worker and physician training. Contrasting factors in the training process and orientation of each profession will be identified in order to locate those that impede the collaborative process.

While medical socialization differs by specialties, we have focused on internal medicine as representative of medical culture. It is the largest and one of the most prestigious medical specialties and gives leadership to mainstream American medicine.

Internal medicine addresses itself to the total adult patient (American Board of Internal Medicine, 1979) and therefore incorporates or interfaces with many social work functions. Yet social work literature focuses more on collaborative experience with pediatricians, psychiatrists and family practitioners than internal medicine physicians (Guy, 1977; Stine, 1976; Tanner and Carmichael, 1970). It appears that collaboration with these specialties is less difficult than with internists. A true "state of the art" view of professional strains between social workers and physicians must take into account that in number and status, these specialties have limited impact on the overall direction of medical practice.

Our emphasis will be on house staff physicians (interns and residents). These physicians-in-training provide a major proportion of health care for adult Americans in in-patient and out-patient settings. Social work interaction with them is significant.

Well-known structural differences exist with respect to age, sex, status, size, class and income. Huntington (1981) describes social work and medicine as existing in distinct symbolic worlds. This paper addresses additional factors: (1) contrasting professional socialization experiences; (2) major ideological differences with respect to content of patient care and role of practitioner; (3) conceptualization and use of knowledge; (4) role and rights of patients; (5) valuation of teamwork; and (6) perception of function of social work. For organizational purposes, each will be treated separately although they are interrelated. Documentation is drawn heavily from the clinical experience of one of the authors (Abramson) and the field research of the other author (Mizrahi) supplemented by the work of others through review of relevant literature.

While our purpose is to explore systematically sources of stress between the two professions, this is done in the context of an awareness that many individual physicians and social workers collaborate successfully on a daily basis.

SOCIALIZATION DIFFERENCES IN MEDICINE AND SOCIAL WORK

This discussion focuses on distinctions in the socialization processes with respect to self-awareness, learning opportunities and supervision and mentorship.

Self-Awareness

While it has been well established that the nature of the professional/patient relationship affects treatment outcomes (Rhodes, 1979), most housestaff physicians have little opportunity to acquire skill to effectively utilize that relationship.

> The doctor's general lack of preparation for relationship aspects results in his backing off from involvement. Because he has not been taught to focus on feelings, his own and those of others, it may be difficult for him to maintain any clarity about who "owns" the powerful feelings of anger, anxiety and despair. (Huntington, 1981)

Novice physicians have no place in training to "process" their own intense feelings about their life and work and the identity crisis (Huntington, 1981). They are expected to view others sympathetically; yet no provision is made for them to articulate their awareness of their own disgruntlement, frustration and tension (Mizrahi, 1983; Pfifferling, 1983; Tokarz, Bremer and Peters, 1979). Research has identified the sometimes dysfunctional results of maladaptive coping mechanisms used by physicians-in-training and in practice (Fox, 1957; McCue, 1982; Nadelson and Notman, 1978). Housestaff believed and acted on the premise that no one during their training is paying attention to their needs and "suffering." They resented the demand that they should treat others humanistically since they felt this lacking for themselves (Mizrahi, 1983).

In contrast, social work training emphasizes the importance of "self" and "relationship," concepts of transference and countertransference, viewing these as integral to its technology of helping (Kadushin, 1972; Perlman, 1979; Shulman, 1979). Social workers are expected to be aware of their reactions to any given individual or situation and to recognize that professionals have an impact on others. Their professional mentors nurture and require the development of self-awareness and the conscious use of self in transactions with others. Huntington (1981:132) notes:

> The use of *self* in a therapeutic *relationship* implies profound affective as well as cognitive involvement in the work. It is not that the social worker becomes personally or emotionally involved with the client, but that she deliberately makes available to herself as a worker, her whole range of feelings as a person, in a controlled and disciplined manner.

Structure of Learning Opportunities

Clinical medical education takes place in a rotational system deliberately designed with overlap, movement and change, at varying time intervals. Physicians-in-training experience a series of different medical services, relate to a variety of mentors and colleagues and interact with different types of patients—in order to be exposed to a wide spectrum of pathology and practice conditions. Time frame limitations inhibit efforts to establish quality physician-patient relationships. At the end of their monthly rotations, housestaff transfer cases routinely with little attention to transition issues for patients, themselves, or other staff.

In contrast, social work training structures the practicum to ensure the development of stable, sustained and intensive relationship with clients and supervisor. Basic clinical training in social work emphasizes the significance of "beginnings" and "endings" with a consciousness about the effect of case transfer and the treatment hazards related to status of student-worker. Impact of transitions on patient, student and system are explicitly delineated as part of the educational socialization to professional behavior (Golden, 1976; Rubin, 1968).

Patient/worker continuity is valued both to develop the necessary therapeutic relationship and to ensure an adequate learning experience for the student. Continuity of relationship is seen as a major professional tool. The common practice of following patients from one medical service to another is based on the view of relationship as essential to the accomplishment of treatment goals.

Supervision and Mentorship

Medical students are supervised in a formal multi-tiered hierarchy by a series of interns and residents who are concurrently going through their own training and responsible for patient management. Hence, developing physicians are socialized primarily by a pressured group of young housestaff one and two years ahead of them.

Bucher and Stelling (1977) found that the most salient reference group for student physicians is colleagues rather than faculty. Faculty involvement is limited and faculty criticism is discounted because they are less involved in the day-to-day management of patients. Due to a strong sense of solidarity and camaraderie, the peer group becomes the most important source of support and validation for the housestaff.

A teaching medical attending's time is usually two months during the academic year, or squeezed into a busy community practice. Social work designs its practicum so that supervision is with full time agency-based social workers who do supervision and teaching as an integral part of work responsibilities.

The social work supervisor has administrative, supportive and educational functions, while the medical attending is mainly expected to teach an area of specialization. Although the social work profession has been criticized for an infantilizing structure of supervision, social workers often do turn to their supervisors for assistance with cases and for help with the further development of skills. Peer learning also takes place, but it is not formally built in to the degree it is in the medical educational structure. The supervisor's contribution is not easily discounted. Where supervisors are perceived by staff as rigid or unskilled, their input is barely tolerated, but this is not the norm due perhaps to the supportive aspect of supervision and agency-based model of practice.

Pathology, Cure and Well-Being

The medical model framework for the teaching of patient care to the novice physician

> emphasizes the individual over the social environment, the treatment of rare and interesting over common and uninteresting disorders, the cure rather than the prevention of illness, and preventive medicine rather than what might be called "preventive welfare." (Friedson, 1970a:148)

While the medical focus on pathology and disease has facilitated the development of technological improvements in available care, the disease orientation does not foster the broader definition of health as a state of the mental, emotional, and social well-being of people (Beauchamp, 1979; Engel, 1977). To social workers the medical model seems to utilize a mechanistic process of thinking which reduces the complexity of human life to simple causal agents (Miller, 1980). It puts an episodic perspective on all illness emphasizing "parts" rather than the "whole" patient.

Despite common utilization of some aspects of the medical model, social work tends to takes a comprehensive view of the individual in his/her environmental context (Coulton, 1979; Germain and Gitterman, 1980). Persons are inherently viewed as social beings, and social work has attempted to focus simultaneously on the individual and on society (Falck, 1978). Social workers are taught to comprehend the relationship between private troubles and social ills and to analyze, and attempt to change where possible, structural and systemic conditions affecting individual problems (Schwartz, 1969). Hence, the thread of social mission always appears (Vigilante, 1974).

Impact of Social Values on Training Demands

While the idealization of the competent internist includes both the ability to establish a rapport with patients and a primary responsibility for dealing with the social aspects of illness (American Board of Internal Medicine, 1979), during the years of formal medical training, internal medicine housestaff are not provided sustained opportunities for understanding and relating to patients and their social environments (Engel, 1973). In everyday discussion and practice most housestaff view such dimensions as irrelevant, not a physician's responsibility, or as simply a matter of intuition or common sense. They also learn quickly that attention paid to those factors is not generally rewarded. Some housestaff acknowledge the importance of those values in patient care but give them low priority because of heavy training demands.

The social values underlying social work practice are heavily stressed in its education (Constable, 1978; Levy, 1982). In the triad of knowledge, skills and values, the third is not something to be eschewed or taken for granted. It is inextricably linked to the question: "knowledge for what?" (Lynd, 1939).

The extent to which professionals influence the lives of clients is receiving growing emphasis in the literature about health care (Conrad and Schneider, 1980; Zola, 1972). The "social control" effect, sometimes unintended, is included in social policy discussions within social work curricula. It is almost entirely absent in housestaff training curricula.

Views of the Patient

Most social workers and physicians, especially those in specialty training, have different views of what constitutes total patient care.

Housestaff routinely employ objectification techniques such as the separation of the patient from the disease, the denial of pain and suffering and dismissal of commonplace or uncomplicated illnesses. Through slang terms for certain categories of socially undesirable patients (Becker, Geer, Hughes and Strauss, 1961; Mizrahi, 1985; Mumford, 1970), and utilization of black humor which portrays the patient as the object of derision (Shem, 1978), a "blame the patient" perspective is often projected (Ryan, 1970; Scully, 1980; Sudnow, 1970).

Projective mechanisms tend to be less pronounced with social workers, because their socialization emphasizes self-awareness (Hollis and Woods, 1980; Gottesfeld and Lieberman, 1979; Lieberman and Gottesfeld, 1973) and the acceptance of patient's personal limitations. Also their focus on planning in conjunction with the patient rather than curing makes them less identified with outcome of treatment. While social workers may dislike certain types of patients, patient disparagement is not tolerated in the training or practice milieu. They are conditioned to the avoidance of labelling as undesirable even patients who were actively and consciously disparaged by the house staff—self-abusers, system abusers and housestaff abusers. Not having the "right" disease, coming from the wrong strata or being in the hospital for the wrong reason has negative implications for physicians responsible for medical treatment, but were less stressful for social workers.

Views of Patient Management

The intellectual challenge of making a diagnosis is important to internal medicine specialization. Since most patients have easily diagnosed diseases, many of which are also chronic or incurable, disconnection and frustration exists between the needs and interests of many housestaff physicians and large groups of patients (Zola and Miller, 1971). If physicians can neither diagnose nor "cure" in the traditional sense, the perspective that they can do little or nothing for most patients is constantly reinforced in their culture. Alternative models of patient care are rarely discussed, nor are broader definitions of professional service.

Social workers experience a different frustration. Since they see what they can do for patients more broadly, the perspective of the social worker in training extends beyond the hospitalization and beyond the patient's illness to the person in his/her social context. Hence, more arenas for intervention are perceived. Thus a patient for whom a physician feels little can be done is to the social worker a prime target for help. Social work encounters the frustration that patient needs exceed the available resources and response capacity (Kerson, 1980; Miller and Rehr, 1983).

DIFFERENCES IN PERCEPTIONS ABOUT KNOWLEDGE AND CERTAINTY

Social work historically has felt insecure about its knowledge base, often undervaluing its own knowledge and skill and overvaluing that of medicine (Kane, 1982). The examination of the similarities and differences within the two professions in relation to the state of their knowledge bases and attitudes toward this therefore becomes important.

Application of Knowledge in Medical Practice

The knowledge explosion in medicine in recent years is a well-known phenomenon. However, the existence of a body of knowledge in the basic sciences, particularly patho-physiology, does not automatically or always directly guide clinical medical practice. Medical students and practitioners, alike, identify the huge disparity which exists between basic theoretical science and experiential clinical years of physician training. The former is devalued and denigrated as largely irrelevant to their professional education.

The scientific mode of inquiry—empiricism, reducible units, analytical reviews (Kane, 1982)—is indeed characteristic of the scientific (bio-medical) research method. However, it has also been demonstrated that experiential learning takes precedent over the research or experimental mode. The "clinical mentality" prevails in everyday physician practice (Friedson, 1970b; Miller, 1970). Since physicians are reluctant to second-guess what they have not experienced or witnessed, housestaff mistakes are excused under the rubrics of "medicine as an art," "judgment calls," "gray areas," and human fallibility (Mizrahi, 1984; Stelling and Bucher, 1973).

Many critics share the view that in the interest of professional control patients and public are left ignorant of the uncertainties in medicine (Waitzkin and Waterman, 1974).

> Indeed much of what is called "medical management" is not truly scientific. The best part of such management is composed of occupational customs, no more codified and no more put to systematic empirical test than most social customs. This is part of what is called the "art" of medicine. It does not rest on a body of scientific knowledge; at best it rests on common occupational usages rather than individual habits. (Friedson, 1970a: 343)

Process Versus Outcome

Social work has been said to operate from a base of "soft" or impressionistic knowledge, to emphasize process rather than outcome, and values rather than facts.

As physicians are beginning to codify *the process as distinguished from the outcome* of their interventions, the social work and medical models may be closer than has been thought. Nevertheless, at this point in time, physicians and social workers come to the educational practicum with differing perceptions of their scientific data root systems and their commitment to process versus outcome.

Attitudes Toward Data—"Hard" Versus "Soft"

In spite of the limitations in medical knowledge and certainty, there are differences between physicians' and social workers' utilization of data that adversely affect the mutual recognition of social work competence. In communication with a social worker, a physician explains a patient's medical condition citing a reasonably defined body of data that led to a certain conclusion. Social workers intersperse facts with a value orientation and what appears to be subjective assessment of these facts.

The "hard" facts orientation of physicians predisposes toward immediate interventive and instrumental solutions. Housestaff often communicate urgency. Social workers often counter with wanting more time and information. Huntington (1981) characterizes these as differences between a "holding" versus an "action" orientation. This can put housestaff physicians in conflict with social workers who present the psychosocial factors which complicate simple straightforward decision-making. Social work knowledge and value base requires attention to process, caution, non-directedness and patient readiness. Social work devotes much energy to examining the dynamic process of relationship among the parts.

Social workers are frequently pressured to abandon their "holding" orientation, to put a given "prescription" into effect. The tendency to adopt the interests of the dominant profession holds the danger of reducing social work function to a matter of mechanics. When this occurs, the social worker simply reinforces the physician's misunderstanding of the social work function.

The concept of indeterminacy which is getting greater attention in medicine exists in all professional disciplines (Illich, 1976; Dubos, 1959). Awareness of this should strengthen the sense of commonality among disciplines and reduce educationally derived alienation.

DIFFERING PERSPECTIVES ON THE ROLE AND RIGHTS OF PATIENTS

Medicine and social work seem to operate from two distinct approaches to the role and rights of patients, the benefit and the autonomy principle, respectively (Gadow, 1981). The first approach, evident in the traditional physician perspective, aims to benefit the patient by disclosing or withholding information according to the anticipated effect upon the patient's well-being. The second approach, closer to the social work perspective, aims to facilitate patient autonomy in health matters.

Views of the Provider-Patient Relationship

The physician role as a decision-maker, moral authority and knowledgeable expert is integral to traditional medical practice. Inequality in the doctor-patient relationship is conceptualized as both necessary and valuable (Cassell, 1975; Parsons, 1949). Yet, the sense of ultimate responsibility for a patient seems to create an inordinate burden on a physician when problems are encountered that are beyond medical solution. For example, a physician can supply the full range of medical technology to an alcohol-ravaged body and yet recognize the futility of such intervention if the alcoholism remains active. Rather than questioning the adequacy of training, the physician is likely to project his/her sense of failure onto the patient. This mechanism appears as early as medical school (Fox, 1957; Martin, 1957; Becker, Geer, Hughes and Strauss, 1961; Coombs, 1978) and continues through training (Moser, 1978) and into practice (Groves, 1978). Since social workers are open to working with these individuals, housestaff may identify them with these "undesirable" patients, rejecting them by association and labeling them "bleeding hearts."

Social work and medicine also hold different perspectives on the concept of patient compliance. Within the ideology which emphasizes the passive patient and the omnipotent physician, patient compliance is usually defined by physicians as a change in patient behavior to correspond with physician-dictated medical regimens. Patient compliance is usually defined by the physician rather concretely, e.g., did the patient comply with specific medical orders, life-style changes, appointments? It is based upon certain assumptions about the asymmetry inherent in the doctor-patient relationship; namely, that recovery is aided by patient obedience and further enhanced by faith in the physician (Pratt, 1978; Cassell, 1975). In the eyes of most housestaff physicians, non-compliance represents a failing in the patient without taking into account the social circumstances that may be relevant to a patient's capacity to comply. The doctor-patient relationship is usually viewed as one to bring the patient "into line" with MD expectations. When it is used consciously, those expectations are often permeated with values that often have more to do with the individual physician's personal normative structure or with the collective norms of the housestaff subculture than with any specific consequences for the health of the patient (Davis, 1972; Roth, 1974). While there is some acknowledgement in the literature that non-compliance may be the result of patient misunderstanding, there is almost no recognition that it may sometimes be based upon a realistic understanding of the limits and even harm of following medical intervention. At times, "non-compliance" can reflect a healthy attitude or adaptive mechanism on the part of the patient (Pratt, 1978; Glogow, 1974).

The social work notion of client self-determination is likely to affect the social worker's definition of compliance. Intervention to encourage patient autonomy may be viewed as undermining the physician's authority to treat the patient. Since physicians may not understand patient resistance and the long range value of "working through" of negatives (Bartlett, 1940), they may misunderstand or disapprove of social work intervention.

Alternative views of patient compliance and provider-consumer interaction, physician-patient partnership and even patient dominance are options clearer to social workers than to physicians. That it can be normative and preferable for the patient to comply selectively with physician mandates is an idea whose time has come for more social workers than physicians.

Views of Patient Rights

Notwithstanding the codification of patients' bill of rights, it has been observed by many that significant involvement of patients in medical decision-making seems to be largely absent in the training setting (Annas and Healy, 1974). Mizrahi (1984) found housestaff to be: (a) perfunctory and superficial in this understanding of the principles of patients' rights or (b) flippant and cynical to the whole concept. Implementation was usually limited to the issue of informed consent.

Social work (along with nursing) has been in the forefront of advocating formally and informally for the rights of clients and patients (Madison, 1975; Miller and Rehr, 1982; NASW Health Policy Statement, 1979; Quinn and Somers, 1974). The concept of self-determination in social work is utilized in the transaction with clients to involve and empower them (Solomon, 1980). However, the advocacy model has the potential for complicating the collaborative interprofessional model (Mailick and Ashley, 1981).

DIFFERING PERSPECTIVES ON TEAMWORK

Training for Autonomy Versus Teamwork

Physicians have been schooled to take charge even when plagued with uncertainty (Bucher and Stelling, 1977). Such a stance, essential in many life and death situations, can impede interdisciplinary teamwork, where skills such as consensus building, negotiation, and equal participation are highly valued.

Major medical journals reflect little evidence of concern for the "why" and "how" of teamwork. While articles appear occasionally supporting the need for physicians to acquire better communication skills, this need is focused on relating to patients. Findings from limited numbers of studies of attempts at teaching medical students teamwork roles report resistance and little long term impact (Howard and Bye, 1971; Peeples and Francis, 1968).

Social work's linkage, resource and coordination function is dependent on skills in transmitting information from one professional source to another. Effective relationships are essential to these activities, and social work has long recognized the need to build these competencies systematically (Weiner, 1959). Social workers have been schooled to the value of collaboration and have begun to articulate the knowledge and skill components of collaboration (Brill, 1976; Mailick and Jordan, 1977).

The professional norms of medicine perpetuate medical autonomy and self-reliance (Crane, 1976; Mizrahi, 1983) while those of social work emphasize support, problem-solving, listening, understanding of complex organizations, group dynamics, systems analysis and group theory.

Attitudes Toward Other Staff

Emphasis on self-reliance in housestaff training promotes reluctance to depend on non-physician staff and a discounting of others' potential contribution to their learning. Housestaff tend to complain about other staff to their peer group and devote less energy to improving working relationships with others. In spite of the myriad social problems of patients, referrals to social workers do not occur in numbers commensurate with expected need (Mizrahi, 1983; Stoeckle, 1966). The data seem to indicate "collegial teamwork" exists primarily within the internal medicine peer group.

While physicians can and sometimes do ignore social workers, it is unlikely that the converse will occur since social work functions are dependent on communications with physicians and others. Receiving and coordinating information is crucial to social work patient assessment and planning. Communication tasks are accepted as essential.

Perspectives on the Work Setting

Whereas to the physician, the hospital bureaucracy has traditionally been viewed as an imposition on the professional domain (Friedson, 1970a), the social work agency model has been an integral part of the development of the social work profession (Epstein and Conrad, 1978; Kurzman, 1976).

Social work practice has emphasized a system of accountability to clients, peers, supervisors and board members. Because medicine has successfully claimed professional autonomy, its practice has been largely free from scrutiny by the lay public, patients and other professionals. This has minimized the necessity to cooperate with other groups.

Currently, there is greater potential for the development of team work among colleagues of different professional disciplines. The nature of technology and the complexity of disease management make physicians more dependent upon institutions and, within the institutions, more dependent on other workers (Ehrenreich and Ehrenreich, 1970; Starr, 1982). This, along with organized consumer pressure, reported abuses of physician power, and rising costs have involved all health professionals with government-mandated accountability mechanisms. Physician control over patient management is no longer absolute.

DIFFERING PERCEPTIONS OF THE ROLE AND FUNCTION OF SOCIAL WORK

Any attempt to review the function of social work in medical settings must take into account that it is, to a degree, the product of the setting in which it has developed. Dana, Banta and Deuschle (1974:81) spell out this impact:

> There can be little doubt in making its accommodation to the hospital setting . . . social work has taken on many of the behavioral and organizational characteristics associated with hospital-based medical care: (1) the acceptance of the physician's ultimate control of patient care; (2) the dominance of the medical model of patient care; (3) the concentration of intellectual and material resources on crisis-oriented intervention directed principally to the sick patient in the hospital bed; and (4) the specialty orientation.

Historical Sources of Present Tensions

The origin of medical social work as physician-initiated has created a significant legacy which actively affects current practice.

From the beginning, Richard Cabot, the founder of medical social work, himself a physician, conceived of the social work role as supplementary to the efforts of the physicians and nurses. In adopting the professional role of augmenter of physician derived treatment, social workers established themselves in an ancillary relationship to the profession of medicine (Caputi, 1978; Kerson, 1980). Both early and present hospital social work departments have organized their structures and functions almost exclusively to coincide with the needs and goals of the medical staff (Segal, 1970). That the physician would be seen as the appropriate, and early on, the only source of referral, is a natural concomitant. Early practitioners saw this as a fundamental of sound practice (Cannon, 1952). Such a referral structure has at times hampered social work's capacity for self-definition and autonomy of function. Despite the recent development of independent case-finding mechanisms (Berkman and Rehr, 1970), there are still hospitals where the physician is the only source of referral, especially of private patients.

Social Work's Perspective on Itself

Social work's efforts at defining its function have tended to dichotomize services into concrete and counseling components. Skewed by greater status generally accorded to the counseling function in social work and psychiatric circles, those activities involving efforts to mobilize crucial environmental resources on behalf of the patient have been given inferior status.

Discharge-planning activities have been particularly vulnerable to such separation. Yet, effective discharge-planning clearly requires an approach in which the provision of services is based on and integrated with sound diagnostic assessment and clinical skills (Davidson, 1978; Fields, 1978). Unfortunately, this crucial area of intervention gets poorly articulated by social work. Line social workers may feel that social work administrators, in their efforts to meet external mandates, do not provide adequate support for the professional component of discharge planning. This further dichotomizes practice. The principle is that the integration of clinical skill with the effective delivery of concrete services is the essence of effective social work practice. Actually, the articulation of the social component in clinical intervention distinguishes social work from other forms of individual counseling within the institution.

Physician and Social Work Expectations in Conflict

Studies have consistently shown that physicians expect more of social workers in the area of concrete service provision and less in the areas of professional liaison and counseling than social workers expect of themselves (Lister, 1980; Olsen and Olsen, 1967; Hess, 1982). Difficulties have emerged whenever social workers have attempted to add functions that were not doctor-defined. Primary among these are social work efforts to assist patients and families in coping with emotional reactions to illness and disability. Both physicians and social workers agree that discharge-planning is an essential social work function. However, by challenging adjustment to illness as an arena for social work intervention, physicians appear to have a more concrete view of discharge-planning than is compatible with the social work perception. It is illustrative of other areas where differing perceptions of role and function may be problematic.

Typical interactions between physicians-in-training and social work staff illustrated on a daily basis that housestaff viewed social work and its role only in terms of relevance to their daily work to "get rid of patients." The housestaff assessment of the value of social work was inextricably linked to the efficiency of the social workers in "clearing the beds." Kudos were offered when the social worker could arrange an expeditious discharge. The flip side of this was that social workers were constantly blamed when patients remained on a service longer than was deemed appropriate by housestaff. Only occasionally did housestaff acknowledge the serious structural problems involved in "disposition," especially when residential placement was needed; and rarely was note taken of the professional skill involved in making complex social, psychological, physical and financial arrangement among patients, families and institutions (Mizrahi, 1983).

Feeling blame for many factors beyond their control, social workers often react defensively. Some individuals counter-attack with pointed comments about the physician's lack of humanity or awareness of the complexity of social problems, or they succumb to the physician's perception of their job and gripe about the menial level of the work. None of these responses addresses housestaff confusion about social work, and may instead exacerbate the problem.

CONCLUSION

We have attempted to demonstrate that much of the strain between physicians and social workers is the result of countervailing perspectives on many fundamental components of professional practice. These basic concepts are projected, and presumably take root, during the professional training of both disciplines and are reinforced in practice settings. Disjunctures are evident in: perceptions of patient care, attitudes toward knowledge and certainty in medicine and social work, perspectives on patient's rights, perspectives on teamwork, and the perception of social work by social workers and physicians.

To identify these endemic strains is not to suggest the futility of attempting to create more successful collaborative models. Rather it is to sensitize social workers to the inherent complexities involved in establishing collegially based collaborative relationships. It is also to acknowledge that difficulties encountered on the worker or department level are likely to be structural/systemic rather than idiosyncratic/personal. Finally, by better understanding the professional culture and structure of medicine, social workers may be able to make more realistic demands upon physicians and to more appropriately evaluate their own responses.

REFERENCES

American Board of Internal Medicine. Clinical Competence in Internal Medicine. *Annals of Internal Medicine*, 90 (1979):402–411

Annas, G. J. and Healey, J. M., Jr. The Patient Rights Advocate: Redefining the Doctor-Patient Relationship in the Hospital Context. *Vanderbilt Law Review*, 27 (1974):243–269.

Bartlett, H. M. *Some Aspects of Social Casework in a Medical Setting*. Committee on

Functions. AAMSW, Chicago (1940).

Beauchamp, D. Public Health as Social Justice. In E. Gartley Jaco (Ed.), *Patients, Physicians and Illness.* The Free Press, New York (1979):443–57.

Becker, H.; Geer, B.; Hughes, E. C.; and Strauss, A. L. *Boys in White.* University of Chicago Press, Chicago (1961).

Berkman, B. and Rehr, H. Unanticipated Consequences of the Case-Finding System in Hospital Social Service. *Social Work,* 15 (1970):63–68.

Brill, N. *Teamwork: Working Together in the Human Services.* Lippincott, Philadelphia (1976).

Bucher, R. and Stelling, J. *Becoming Professional.* Sage Publications, Beverly Hills, California (1977).

Cannon, I. *On the Social Frontier of Medicine.* Harvard University Press, Cambridge (1952).

Caputi, M. Social Work In Health Care: Past and Future. *Health and Social Work,* 3 (1978):8–29

Cassell, E. *The Healer's Art.* Lippincott and Co., Philadelphia (1975).

Conrad, P. and Schneider, J. W. *Deviance and Medicalization: From Badness to Sickness.* St. Louis: Mosby (1980).

Constable, R. Toward an Ethical System for Social Work. In O. Dalkhe, T. Carlton, I. Mizrahi (Eds.), *A Foundation for Social Policy Analysis.* Xerox Individualized Publishing (1978):361–374.

Coombs, R. N. *Mastering Medicine.* The Free Press, New York (1978).

Coulton, C. J. A Study of Person-Environment Fit Among the Chronically Ill. *Social Work in Health Care,* 5 (1979):5–17.

Crane, D. *The Sanctity of Social Life: Physicians' Treatment of Critically Ill Patients.* Russell Sage Foundation, New York (1975).

Dana, B., Banta, H. D., and Deuschle, K. W. An Agenda for the Future of Interprofessionalism. In H. Rehr (Ed.), *Medicine and Social Work.* Prodist, New York (1974):77–88.

Davidson, K. W. Evolving Social Work Roles in Health Care: The Case of Discharge Planning. *Social Work in Health Care,* 4 (1978):43–52.

Davis, F. Uncertainty in Medical Prognosis: Clinical and Functional. In E. Friedson and J. Lorber (Eds.), *Medicine Men and Their Work.* Aldine-Atherton, Chicago (1972):239–248.

Dubos, R. *The Mirage of Health.* Harper and Row, New York (1959).

Ehrenreich, B. and Ehrenreich, J. *The American Health Empire.* Vintage Books, New York (1970).

Engel, G. E. The Best and the Brightest: The Missing Dimension in Medical Education. *Phanos,* 36 (1973):129–133.

Engel, G. E. The Need for a New Medical Model. *Science,* 196 (1977):129–136.

Epstein, I. and Conrad, K. Limits of Social Work Professionalization. In R. Sarri and Y. Hasenfeld (Eds.), *The Management of Human Services.* Columbia University Press, New York (1978):163–183.

Falck, H. Social Work in Health Care Settings. *Social Work in Health Care,* 3 (1978):395–403.

Fields, G. Editorial—The Anatomy of Discharge Planning. *Social Work in Health Care,* 4 (1978):5–6.

Fox, R. C. Training for Uncertainty. In R. Merton, Reader, G. G. and Kendall, P. L. (Eds.), *The Student Physician.* Harvard University Press, Cambridge (1957):207–243.

Freidson, E. *The Profession of Medicine.* Dodd, Mead and Co., New York (1970a).

Freidson, E. *Professional Dominance: The Structure of Medical Care.* Aldine-Atherton Press, New York (1970b).

Gadow, S. Truth: Treatment of Choice, Scarce Resource or Patient's Right? *Journal of Family Practice,* 13 (1981):857–860.

Germain, C. and Gitterman, A. *The Life Model of Social Work Practice.* Columbia University Press, New York (1980).

Glogow, E. The Problem Patient Gets Better Quicker. *Social Policy,* 4 (1974):72–76.

Golden, K. Client Transfer and Student Social Workers. *Social Work,* 21 (1976):65–66.

Gottesfeld, M. L. and Lieberman, F. The Pathological Therapist. *Social Casework,* 60 (1979):387–393.

Groves, J. E. Taking Care of the Hateful Patient. *New England Journal of Medicine,* 298 (1978):883–887.

Guy, L. The Social Work Component of a University-Based Family Residency. *Journal of Family Practice,* (1977) 5:463–464.

Hess, H. Clinical Practice Variation of Social Workers in Family Practice Centers. Paper delivered to APM of CSWE, 1981.

Hollis, F. and Woods, M.J. *Casework: A Psychosocial Therapy,* Second Edition. Random House, New York (1980).

Howard, J. and Bye, N. Pitfalls in Interdisciplinary Teaching. *Journal of Medical Education,* 46 (1971): 772–781.

Huntington, J. *Social Work and General Medical Practice: Collaboration or Conflict.* George Allen University, London (1981).

Illich, I. *Medical Nemesis.* Bantam Books, New York (1976).

Kadushin, A. *The Social Work Interview.* New York: Columbia University School of Social Work (1972).

Kane, R. Lessons for Social Work from the Medical Model: A Viewpoint from Practice.

Social Work, 27 (1982):315–321.

Kerson, T. Medical Social Work: The PreProfessional Paradox. Irvington, New York (1980).

Kurzman, P. A. Private Practice As a Social Work Function. *Social Work* (1976):363–68.

Levy, C. S. *Guide to Ethical Decisions and Actions for Social Service Administrators*. The Haworth Press, New York (1982).

Lieberman, F. and Gottesfeld, M. L. The Repulsive Client. *Clinical Social Work Journal*, 1 (1973):22–31.

Lister, L. Role Expectations for Social Workers and Other Health Professionals. *Health and Social Work*, 5 (1980):41–49.

Lynd, R. *Knowledge for What: The Place of Social Science in American Culture*. Princeton University Press, Princeton, N.J. (1939).

Madison, T. M. They Speak Up. *Mental Hygiene*, (MH) 59 (1975):28–31.

Mailick, M. and Jordan, P. A Multi-Model Approach to Collaborative Practice in Health Settings. *Social Work and Health Care*, 2 (1977):445–454.

Mailick, M. and Ashley, A. Politics of Interprofessional Collaboration: Change to Advocacy. *Social Casework*, 62 (1981):131–137.

Martin, W. Preference for Types of Patients. In R. Merton, G. G. Reader, and P.L. Kendall (Eds.), *The Student Physician*. Harvard University Press, Cambridge (1957):189–206.

McCue, J. D. The Effects of Stress on Physicians and Their Medical Practice. *New England Journal of Medicine*, 306 (1982):458–463.

Miller, R. S. and Rehr, H. *Social Work Practice in Health Care*. Prentice Hall, Englewood Cliffs, N.J. (1983).

Miller, S. *Prescription for Leadership*. Aldine Press, Chicago (1970).

Miller, W. L. Casework and The Medical Metaphor. *Social Work* (1980):281–285.

Mizrahi, T. The Impact of Graduate Medical Training of Internists on the Doctor-Patient Relationship. Unpublished Ph.D. Dissertation, University of Virginia, 1983.

Mizrahi, T. Managing Medical Mistakes: Ideology, Insularity and Accountability Among Internists-In-Training. Social Science and Medicine 19 (1984):135–146.

Mizrahi, T. Coping with Patients: Defense Techniques of Avoidance, Objectification, Intimidation, Fantasized Destruction, and Omission Among Interns and Residents. *Social Problems* (1985, forthcoming).

Moser, S. Housestaff and the Indigent Black Patient. *Forum on Medicine*, 1 (1978):21–27.

Mumford, E. *Interns: From Students to Physicians*. Harvard University Press, Cambridge, Mass. (1970).

Nadelson, C. and Notman, M. T. Adaptation to Stress in Physicians. In E. Shapiro and L. Lowenstein (Eds.), *Becoming Physicians*. Ballinger, Cambridge, Mass. (1979):201–215.

National Association of Social Workers. *Health Policy Statement* (1978).

Olsen, K. and Olsen, M. Role Expectations and Perceptions for Social Workers in Medical Settings. *Social Work*, 12 (1967):70–78.

Parsons, T. *The Professions and Social Structure. Essays in Sociological Theory: Pure and Applied*. The Free Press, Glencoe, Illinois (1949):198–199.

Peeples, E. and Frances, G. Social Psychological Obstacles to Effective Health Team Practice. *Nursing Forum*, 7 (1968):28–37.

Perlman, H. H. *Relationship: The Heart of Helping People*. University of Chicago Press, Chicago (1979).

Pfifferling, J. H. *The Impaired Physician: An Overview*. Durham, N.C.: Center for Professional Well-Being, 1983.

Pratt, L. Reshaping the Consumer's Posture in Health Care. In E. B. Gallagher (Ed.), *The Doctor-Patient Relationship in the Changing Health Scene*. Department of Health, Education and Welfare, Washington, D.C. (1978):197–214.

Quinn, N. and Somers, A. The Patient's Bill of Rights: A Significant Aspect of the Consumer Revolution. *Nursing Outlook*, 22 (1974):240–244.

Rehr, H. (Ed.). *Medicine and Social Work: An Exploration in Inter-professionalism*. Prodist, N.Y. (1974).

Rhodes, S. The Personality of the Worker: An Unexplored Dimension in Treatment. *Social Casework*, 60 (1979):259–264.

Roth, J. Some Contingencies of the Moral Evaluation and Control of Clientele—The Cases of the Hospital Emergency Service. *American Journal of Sociology*, 77 (1974):839–856.

Rubin, G. Termination of Casework: The Student, Client and Field Instructor. *Journal of Education for Social Work*, 4 (1968):65–69.

Ryan, W. *Blaming the Victim*. New York: Vintage Books (1970).

Schwartz, W. Private Troubles and Public Issues: One Social Work Job or Two? In the Social Welfare Forum 1969 Official Proceedings, 96th Annual Forum, National Conference on Social Welfare, N.Y.C., May 25–29, 1969. Columbia University Press, New York (1969).

Scully, D. *Men Who Control Women's Health*. Houghton Mifflin Co., Boston, (1980).

Segal, B. Planning and Power in Hospital Social Service. *Social Casework*, 51 (1970):399–405.

Shem, S. *The House of God*. Richard Marek Press, New York (1978).

Shulman, L. *The Skills of Helping Individuals and Groups*. Peacock, Itasca, Illinois (1979).

Solomon, B. *Black Empowerment—Social Work in Oppressed Communities*. Columbia University Press, New York (1980).

Starr, P. *The Social Transformation of American Medicine*. Basic Books, New York (1982).

Stelling, J. and Bucher, R. Vocabularies of Realism in Professional Socialization. *Social Science and Medicine*, 7 (1973):661–675.

Stine, B. Social Work and Liaison Psychiatry. *Social Work in Health Care*, 1 (1976):183–489.

Stoeckle, J. D., et al. Social Work in a Medical Clinic: The Nature and Course of Referrals to the Social Work Department. *American Journal of Public Health*, 56 (1966):157–179.

Sudnow, D. Dead on Arrival. In A. Strauss (Ed.), *Where Medicine Fails*. Transaction Books, New Brunswick, N.J. (1970):111-130.

Tanner, L. A. and Carmichael, L. P. The Role of the Social Worker in Family Medicine Training. *Journal of Medical Education*, 45 (1970):859–863.

Tokarz, W. Bremer and Peters, K. *Beyond Survival*. Americal Medical Association, Chicago (1979).

Vigilante, J. L. Between Values and Science: Education for the Profession During a Moral Crisis or Is Proof Truth? *Journal of Education for Social Work*, 10 (1974):107–116.

Waitzkin, H. and Waterman, B. *The Exploitation of Illness in a Capitalist Society*. The Bobbs-Merrill Co., Indianapolis (1974).

Weiner, H. The Hospital the Ward and the Patient as Client: Use of the Group Method. *Social Work*, 4 (1959):64–69.

Zola, I. Medicine as an Institution of Social Control. *Sociological Review*, 20 (1972):487–504.

Zola, I. and Miller, S. Erosion of Medicine from Within. In E. Freidson (Ed.), *Professions and Their Prospects*. Sage Publications, Beverly Hills, CA (1971):153–172.

AUTONOMY AND MANAGED CARE
IN CLINICAL SOCIAL WORK PRACTICE

CARLTON E. MUNSON, PH.D.

ABSTRACT

The decrease of autonomy in social work practice is the result of societal trends that include the rise of technology and massive restructuring of organizations. These trends are reflected in the emergence of managed care as an efficiency movement that has not been monitored. Social work's contribution to intervention is reviewed in relation to the emergence of managed care. Ethical issues, professional practice relationships, fee setting, privacy and confidentiality, supervision issues, professional language, professional status, and professional organizations are explored in the context of increasing control of clinical social work practice dictated by managed care.

We live in a world that constantly threatens our individual autonomy. In our personal lives we are threatened by big government that everyone resents, but no one seems to know how to manage. There seems to be a surrender by most individuals to the forces of control. This is reflected in the constant chant that "change is coming whether you like it or not, so you better get used to it, or get out of the way." It conveys a clear message that both senders and receivers must accommodate all forms of change whether they are good or bad. Advocates of managed care use variations on this quotation in giving advice to mental health professionals, and this theme serves as the background for this article.

Government continually passes laws to protect "our freedoms," and people then discover that these laws severely restrict their rights. People feel threatened and victimized by large, multi-national corporations that reorganize to maximize prices and profits, regardless of the cost to employees and customers. People are increasingly at the mercy of the media and computers, even while we are constantly bombarded by the illusion of "more options." Lasch (1979) has argued historically and Sullivan (1995) currently illustrates that loss of personal control is the result of a complex mixture of modern economic conditions, shifting family interaction and structures, and individual cognitive responses.

The loss of individual control that is taking place in professional life as well as in the larger community has been well documented by Sullivan (1995). As government and private industry downsize and reorganize to "cut costs," mental health practitioners and their clients are faced with large-scale loss of autonomy. Health care and mental health care reflect the large-scale societal loss of autonomy that is taking place. The management, cost, and delivery of health/mental health care has become chaotic, but no one seems able to do anything to make the system even slightly more rational. A mental health client illustrated this by describing that his employer, a large state agency, altered the health care plan to make it more cost-effective by inviting several companies to offer competing plans. In the following three years the cost to him went up 300%, and he is still not sure what coverage he has. He went to a "health fair" sponsored by the employer, where nine competing companies had "information booths." He described the scene as "bedlam," which is an interesting term for the client to use since it is derived from one of the earliest mental institutions, St. Mary of Bethlehem, in England. Over 150 people were shouting at the lone representative at each booth. Everyone was grabbing the information packets, and supplies were soon exhausted. People were panicked because the employer had given them a dead-line for enrollment. If they didn't enroll in a specific plan by the deadline, they would have no health/mental health insurance for a year, until enrollment was reopened. At the health fair this partici-pant realized he had completely lost control of his health/mental health care destiny. Most would agree this is not a rational way for people to make major decisions about health care for themselves and their families. On an individual basis, it illustrates the generally agreed-upon larger view that the United States health/mental health care system is in serious crisis (Goodman, Brown & Deitz, 1992).

Background

For the last decade society has been undergoing a major restructur-ing. Remarkably, this restructuring has gone unnoticed by most professional groups, even though it is having significant impact on professional relationships with clients. The revolutions in informa-tion technology and communication methods have affected power relationships in the private, employment, and social spheres, and are redefining the rules of social life, as well as concepts of freedom and justice (Altheide, 1995). Advances in technology have made these changes possible. Massive mainframe computers and small personal computers have made it possible to manage, control, manipulate, and predict in ways that present new challenges. Computers and other information technologies have led large corporations to eliminate jobs and centralize functions that increase profits at the expense of employee and consumer satisfaction. Technological change has speeded up the pace of institutional activity, thus increasing stress for employees and consumers. Employees are expected to accomplish more in less time for less money, and consumers find many products obsolete soon after they are purchased.

This restructuring is also occurring in the social service and clinical social work sectors. In many states, public social and mental health services are being privatized and/or contracted to managed care companies (Feldman & Fitzpatrick, 1992). There are no reliable data indicating that privatization cuts costs, but there is compelling evidence that it results in inadequate services for clients, and hard-ship for professionals who work in the privatized environment (Motenko, Allen, Angelos, Block, DeVito, Duffy, Holton, Lambert,

Parker, Ryan, Schraft, & Swindell, 1995; Munson, 1993a).

At the organizational level, change and technology will continue to produce even larger entities. Corporate mergers and agency consolidations are producing ever larger bureaucracies. Larger hospitals, chains of nursing homes, and large-group psychotherapy practices can be cost-efficient without being efficient in their social functioning. While large organizations try to assure us of their "entrepreneurial compassion" in dealing with clients and consumers, we have observed that when financial strain occurs, profit becomes the ultimate criterion. In this climate, clients, practitioners, and supervisors receive little or no support, and few resources. As this environment develops and expands, government programs and private insurance provide little protection for people. The combination of technology and privatization has transformed mental health services from a humanitarian commitment to a private industry. Some argue that mental health has always been an industry, but this has not been true historically, especially in social work. The heritage in social work has been that work in mental health, as in other areas of social work practice, reflects "a calling" rather than an industrial endeavor, i.e., manufacturing product units to insure profitability. It is commonplace for managed care officials to refer to the mental health services they provide as "product lines" and to clients as "bodies or lives covered." In the coming years, the social work profession will have to confront a market orientation to mental health services that challenges the basic social commitments of our profession.

Social Work's Unique Contribution

Historically, social work has made many contributions within the constellation of the primary mental health professions, but three contributions stand out: social reform, social work's focus on client advocacy, and the social work model of supervision. In regard to social reform, social work's emphasis on reform was short-lived. It peaked in the 1920s (Lundblad, 1995; Reeser & Epstein, 1990) and has been declining since, to the point that, currently, advocacy is not usually a part of individual practice or professional organizational emphasis. In regard to client advocacy, the decline in emphasis on social reform has coincided with a loss of concern about client advocacy. Both trends have paralleled the development of the managed care model for social work practice. Ironically, social work first evolved the short-term therapy models of treatment that are hallmarks of managed care. Short-term treatment can be traced from the works of Mary Richmond (1917), to Helen Harris Perlman's problem-solving approach (1957), to Reid and Epstein's task-centered model (1972). In regard to the third major contribution, social work supervision, the effects of managed care will be discussed later in the paper.

Effects on Social Work

In many ways, clinical social work reflects society in microcosm. The "speeding up" of society is mirrored in the emphasis on brief therapy, and applications of technology to clinical practice. Among the most important technological innovations clinical social workers must increasingly contend with is the use of machines to support and supplement psychotherapeutic practice. Computers generate social assessments and diagnostic reports. Telephone answering machines, pagers, and word processors are used for accounting and record-keeping. Machines play an increasing role in clinical and supervisory practice. The use of audio and video machines to record sessions for subsequent use in treatment and supervision is becoming ever more common. In clinical interviews, video and audiotape machines are often third parties to treatment. In some settings where videotaping is considered a valuable therapeutic agent, there are few, if any, guidelines for its use. When used properly, videotaping can enhance treatment, but its improper application can produce desultory and destructive intrusions into the treatment relationship (Munson, 1993b).

Other types of technology increasingly used by clinicians are communication devices, such as paging instruments. These devices have come into common use in hospital and public welfare settings, and among private practitioners. All of these technologies have implications for psychotherapy-related "high-tech/high-touch" (Naisbitt, 1982) practice. No studies have been done regarding the effects of these devices on practitioner functioning. In some cases they are used voluntarily, and in others, involuntarily. In addition, there have been no studies as to whether these instruments actually improve practitioner response time or effectiveness. Supervisors need to be more cognizant of how widely such devices are utilized, as well as their effect on the therapeutic process. Over time, the increased use of machines for communication is likely to result in procedures that minimize or eliminate direct contact between client and therapist, and between therapist and supervisor (Handy, 1995).

Advances in technology necessitate greater emphasis on values and ethics in graduate education programs. Increased use of machines in practice brings practitioners into closer contact with machine operators, designers, and analysts who have a "machine mentality." In such contacts, practitioners may find that their own values have been compromised. This is especially the case in large agencies and medical settings where machines increasingly are being used on a grand scale. Technology has also increased electronic transmission of sensitive client information over telephone lines, and has facilitated long-term archiving of client information in computer storage systems. These changes challenge practitioner values regarding confidentiality and privileged information. Practitioners are losing control of information they generate about clients, and often fail to inform clients adequately about the use entities such as managed care companies and employers may make of confidential information. Many of these technological changes are forced on social workers by managed care companies. One managed care company, in its efforts to increase the use of electronic claims submissions, found the "lack of automation" by therapists a major hinderance to its automation plans. The company discovered that small and solo practices were the most resistant to technology, and that 70% of such providers had nothing more sophisticated than a telephone in their offices. As a result of these findings, the company embarked on a strategy to increase the use of technology by providers *(Psychotherapy Finances,* 1995c).

Managed Care

In the social work profession, restructuring of practice has been connected to the growth of managed care. Over the last five years, managed care has grown rapidly. In 1990, approximately 29% of people with health insurance were covered by managed care contracts. In 1995, 51% were covered (Randal, 1995). Managed care is directly connected to corporate restructuring in the sense that health programs are usually incorporated into overall benefit packages which employers negotiate with one or a number of managed care companies. Managed care is also increasingly employed to cover services to clients insured by public social service systems, many of which are being privatized. In these contexts, managed care plays an increasingly significant role in the delivery of mental health services (Munson, 1995a).

The increased use of managed care models parallels the increased philosophical and practical importance of technology in this society. This is not a new phenomenon. Beliefs about mental functioning and intervention strategies have always been closely connected to scientific theories about how the universe functions. For example, in the nineteenth century, new knowledge about electricity and magnetism generated the belief that mental illness was caused by an unbalanced distribution of magnetic currents in the body. As a result, Mesmer developed a procedure in which magnets were waved over the body to redistribute magnetic energy (Davison & Neale, 1990). The modern equivalent to this outdated theory can be seen in our obsession with technology, especially the ability to complete and repeat tasks with ever increasing speed, and efficiency. This has led to a mental health delivery system based on delivering specific prepackaged procedures rapidly and without variation to large numbers of clients. The demand for rapid service delivery has resulted in a decrease in the number of sessions allocated to accomplish specific therapeutic goals. Moreover, the common practice of forcing practitioners to join large group practices reflects the speeding process, in this instance, under the guise of increased efficiency. There is no documented research that any of these actions result in more efficient treatment, or greater productivity. Clinicians should always look for more effective and efficient ways of delivering care, but the managed care efficiency movement has produced a shift away from clinical process, to therapeutic procedures that are fragmented, and of short duration. The problem is compounded by the fact that schools of social work continue to teach process and relationship models of intervention, whereas managed care companies only approve mechanistic, task-oriented, linear models. As a result, master's degree graduates in social work enter a practice world in which they have not been trained to function effectively.

Change and Autonomy

Managed care companies and other payors control major aspects of mental health practice in the public and private sector. Payors routinely state that benefit programs and intervention strategies are "fluid." They remind practitioners that mental health care is changing or will change every six months. Constant change and threats of change concentrate control in the hands of those parties who are capable of producing change. This strategy keeps clients and practitioners off balance, and renders them incapable of planning treatment or treatment programs rationally. The unbalancing effect of restructuring can be seen when managed care companies force solo practitioners to join group practices so it is easier to control what they do in treatment. In some instances, managed care companies are even willing to buy out group practices. The rationale for this policy is that group practices are more effective and cost-efficient. There is no documented research or statistics to justify this claim. Unfortunately, practitioners and professional organizations cannot counter these claims either because they have no research studies that address effectiveness, efficiency and outcome issues, or they fail to use the outcome research that does exist. Managed care companies have no such difficulty, since they have accumulated significantly more outcome data on professional practitioners than any of the major mental health professional organizations. In fact, independent studies by *Consumer Reports* (1995), and the National Advisory Mental Health Council (1993) provide compelling statistics on the positive outcomes of longer-term mental health intervention, as reported by clients treated in traditional models of practice. The shortage of professionally-sponsored outcome studies, and the failure to marshall even readily available research data are key indicators of the degree to which the professions have surrendered authority and control to external entrepreneurs.

Professional Relationships and Autonomy

Client-practitioner relationships are being altered significantly by managed care policies. Increasingly, practitioners receive fewer client referrals because payors are closing provider lists to cut costs. Such policies also affect clients. "Payors," rather than clients, determine which therapist the client will see. By depriving clients of control over who they choose to work with in treatment, and over how long they wish to be treated, "payors" violate the social work ethic of right to self-determination. In some sense, these routine procedure go to the heart of the problem managed care presents: corporate control replaces client and therapist control in almost every instance.

Initial Intervention

Selecting a therapist can be a complex process (Amada, 1995), and the ultimate selection decision should remain with the client. There is an old rule in mental health treatment that if a client starts treatment and does not develop a positive relationship with the therapist, the client should find another therapist. Clients are advised to repeat this process until they find a therapist with whom they feel comfortable working. This choice is no longer available, except for the very wealthy who pay for treatment "out of pocket."

Many managed care companies implement procedures that reverse the traditional process of a client initiating contact with a therapist. New procedures require clients to contact the insurance company first. In many instances, the company then chooses a therapist from its provider pool and "authorizes" that therapist to meet with the client for a limited, pre-established number of sessions, typically, one diagnostic and two treatment sessions. Upon receiving authorization, the practitioner contacts the client to initiate treatment. This procedure puts therapists in the position of pursuing clients at the beginning of treatment. After the initial "authorization" has expired, the therapist must then contact the company for a second "authorization," which typically results in approval for three to six additional sessions. Decisions about additional sessions are often made by non-professional technicians, and the number of sessions allocated is based on a standardized protocol, rather than on client needs as individually articulated. This results in a course of treatment based on financial parameters rather than on a diagnostic assessment of the severity of functional impairment. No research has been done on how this allocation system affects either the therapeutic relationship or treatment outcome.

Fees

The loss of control of billing by therapists and the use of electronic billing usurps another therapeutic function. A long-standing therapeutic principle affirms that negotiating fees and discussing regular payment are essential parts of the therapeutic process. Under current procedures, fees are not negotiated as part of the treatment process, but are instead determined by the managed care company. In addition, the therapist is often placed at risk for non-payment when payors "authorize" sessions before therapy begins, but deny payment on the basis of some minor technicality when the first claim is submitted. The increased use of electronic billing takes control of the process and mechanics of billing out of the therapist's hands, and places it totally in the control of the payor.

Privacy and Confidentiality

Clients and therapists lose control over the right to privacy and confidentiality within managed care systems. In addition, record-keeping required by government agencies and mandated by recent court decisions severely limits the control of privacy. Increasingly, therapists are required to tell clients that there is *no* confidentiality when the legal system or managed care are involved. Some managed care companies have radically altered the conditions of confidentiality. They justify "no confidentiality" policies by requiring therapists to inform clients of the policy as part of provider agreements. One legal interpretation of no confidentiality policies is "... that the patient has to be told either to give up the right to confidentiality or forego treatment" (Mathias, 1995). Informal surveys have found that, when a client's care is handled by a managed care company, at least 17 people have varying degrees of knowledge about the person's treatment; this is a conservative estimate according to some experts. In some settings clients must sign confidentiality statements that are three pages in length (Zuckerman & Guyett, 1992).

Supervision

The role of supervision has changed as the locus of control has shifted from practitioners to managed care companies. Historically, supervisory practices have reflected the degree of autonomous practice endorsed by each of the mental health professions. Historically, the decreased emphasis on practice supervision has paralleled social work's quest for professional status through autonomous practice. In many states, supervision has been replaced by multiple-choice licensing examinations which constitute the basic method of establishing professional competence. As a result, the monitoring function of supervision has been severely downgraded. Managed care companies do not require supervision because their model of accountability is not based on supervisory oversight. Face-to-face individual and group supervision provided by a seasoned clinician has been replaced by telephone and written contacts with managed care case managers, many of whom have no clinical background. In this process, clinicians not only lose control of the treatment process, but also, in many instances, of reasonable access to case managers who make crucial decisions regarding the availability, outcome, and duration of care.

The only times clinicians regain a measure of control is when something goes wrong, or there is litigation. The majority of managed care companies require clinicians to sign contracts stating they will hold the managed care company harmless. This means that still another institution, the courts, becomes involved in controlling what clinicians do. The courts have ruled that, under certain conditions, "hold harmless" clauses are invalid. In the process of making these rulings however, courts have defined specific steps therapists must take to avoid being liable when care, or termination of care, is dictated by a managed care company. Court rulings directly impact on what therapists can and cannot do in treatment. Decisions in the Tarasoff case (Munson, 1993b), the Ramona case, the Diane Franklin case (Terr, 1994), and other pending legal actions, have direct impact not only on therapist activity, but also on the monitoring function that supervisors traditionally perform. While the implications of these decisions are slow to affect the average practitioner, in coming years these decisions will change practice in fundamental ways.

Ironically, the historical complaint that supervision stifled professional responsibility and creativity has not re-emerged, even though managed care practices have eroded professional autonomy far beyond the control functions supervisors previously exercised. In the past, if supervisors had tried to enforce even a small measure of the control managed care companies now exercise routinely, professional organizations would have initiated massive negative sanctions against the offenders. It is not clear why, at this point in time, professional organizations are not resisting managed care intrusions on decision-making that directly affects client care.

Professional Language

Some clinicians (Corpt & Reison, 1994) advocate that practitioners "behaviorize" the language they use in record-keeping to please managed care companies. These authors identify a list of professional words that should be replaced with managed care "preferred language." For example, they recommend that "dealing with depression" be replaced with "affect management." Ironically, the suggested language is less descriptive than the original. Such changes involve micro-management at a level that, historically, most professions would not and have not, until recently, tolerated. It is difficult to imagine a situation in which a supervisor would dictate the language a practitioner could use in record-keeping. And, if a supervisor did suggest different wording, it would be to clarify, not obscure. The "prescribed language" of managed care goes to the essence of our professional identity as social workers, since language is the most fundamental connection between individuals and society, as well as the "ultimate social tool" (Allman, 1994). If a profession is stripped of its own language, not much core of professional humanness or individuality remains. The postmodernists' view of language is relevant here. They hold that in its essence, language is neither innate nor about communication. From their perspective, language involves a series of word games (Flax, 1990), and, in this case, the game is about control.

Corpt and Reison's (1994) recommendations about "behaviorizing" professional language can be viewed as a kind of supervision guide, with managed care companies functioning as the supervisor, and practitioners as the supervisees. Corpt and Reison (1994) also recommend that practitioners "conduct ... evaluation interviews with managed care in mind" (p. 3), remembering "... that you are being rated by them on a continual basis" (p. 3). There is an old adage in supervision that the supervisor's role is to be symbolically present, looking over the shoulder of the practitioner as treatment occurs (Munson, 1979, 1993b). Moreover, in contrast to the established practices that guide traditional social work supervision, managed care companies never share the results of their evaluations with practitioners, even though the practitioners are constantly being rated on their "ability to take new patients, the thoroughness of ... assessment and the length and efficacy of the treatment" (Corpt & Reison, 1994, p. 3). Corpt and Reison (1994) continue by saying that the changes managed care companies require can be accomplished "... without changing your theoretical perspective or without making major alterations in your clinical practice" (p. 4). In their view, the degree of control payors exercise has little or no effect on what the practitioner does or says, and no substantial effect on the outcome of treatment. These assertions are not supported by any substantial body of intervention outcome research.

A research study (Munson, in press) of externally determined length of treatment illustrates some of the problems involved in predetermining the length of treatment. Practitioners were given a written case to analyze and were asked to establish a diagnosis and a treatment plan. The subjects were randomly assigned six, twelve, or an unlimited number of sessions in which to accomplish their treatment goals. The findings showed statistically significant differences in diagnosis, treatment techniques, and treatment plan formulation, based on the number of sessions "authorized." It thus appears that predetermining the length of treatment has a very significant effect on various aspects of the treatment process, including anticipated outcome. Moreover, the largest mental health treatment outcome survey ever done, consisting of voluntary reports from 4,000 people *(Consumer Reports,* 1995), found that positive outcome was directly linked to length of treatment. The study found that people who were in therapy for six months or longer, reported the most improvement. This finding directly contradicts the managed care philosophy that brief therapy is equally or more effective. It also suggests that the managed care strategy of limiting duration of treatment may increase rather than reduce long-term costs. Since managed care companies rarely authorize anything close to six months of treatment, poor outcomes which cause people to re-enter treatment repeatedly, may significantly increase costs over time.

Ethical Issues

The actions of managed care companies have produced direct ethical conflicts for social work practitioners that are not being addressed by the profession. It is not surprising that the dramatic increase in professional concern about risk management and legal liability has paralleled the rise of managed care. The National Association of Social Workers (NASW) *Code of Ethics* has many contradictory statements that limit its usefulness, but it is the only professional guide the profession has, and it does state that social workers who subscribe to it, including the members of NASW, are required to abide by it. A number of the guiding principles included in the NASW *Code of Ethics* (National Association of Social Workers, 1990) create conflict for clinicians involved with managed care companies either as employees or as contract providers. The most important of these are outlined below:

- The social worker should regard as primary the service obligation of the social work profession.
- The social worker's primary responsibility is to clients.
- The social worker should:
  - act in accordance with highest standards of professional integrity;
  - make every effort to foster maximum self-determination ... of clients;
  - should respect privacy of clients and hold in confidence information obtained in the course of professional service;
  - adhere to commitments made to employing organizations;
  - uphold and advance the values, ethics, knowledge, and mission of the profession;
  - assist the profession in making social services available to the general public;
  - retain ultimate responsibility for quality and extent of service that individual assumes, assigns, or performs;
  - act to prevent practices that are inhumane or discriminatory against any person or group of persons;
  - be alert to and resist influences that interfere with exercise of professional discretion and impartial judgement required for performance of professional functions;
  - provide clients with accurate and complete information regarding extent and nature of services available to them;
  - apprise clients of risks, rights, opportunities, and obligations associated with social service to them;
  - share with others confidences revealed by clients, without their consent, only for compelling professional reasons;
  - withdraw services precipitously only under unusual circumstances, giving careful consideration to factors in the situation and taking care to minimize possible adverse effects;
  - work to improve employing agencies' policies and procedures, and efficiency and effectiveness of its services;
  - take action through appropriate channels against unethical conduct by any other member of the profession; and
  - advocate changes in policy and legislation to improve social conditions and to promote social justice.

It has been argued that, since professional ethics codes are outdated, they should be altered to conform with managed care policies and procedures (Phillips, 1995; Wolf, 1994). The NASW *Code of Ethics* is currently being revised, and the draft document (National Association of Social Workers, 1995) appears to have been modified in ways that reflect aspects of the managed care view of ethics. A profession that reshapes its ethical principles to comply with corporate, managed care guidelines has lost its moral compass. In order for ethics codes to be effective, they must be clear, consistent, and enduring (Munson, 1995b). Changing the profession's ethics codes to address supervisor and clinician dilemmas in regard to managed care policies violates the rules of consistency and endurance. This point can be illustrated by asking which of the NASW code items listed above would we want to change to accommodate managed care? Would we change our responsibilities to clients? The right to privacy? The right to self-determination? The requirement that we work toward changing policies that harm clients? The expectation that practitioners take responsibility for services delivered?

Instead of changing ethical principles, the social work profession should develop a model of clinical advocacy that assists clients in obtaining competent, fair, just, and understandable intervention in the managed care environment. There is much resistance to this kind of advocacy because many managed care companies have explicit policies that punish providers who advocate for clients. In some cases they do so by removing offending practitioners from their provider lists.

Process and Task

Managed care has forced practitioners to shift from a focus on relationship to a focus on tasks and outcomes. This shift has ethical implications. When practice is based on tasks related to outcomes, ethics do not play a role. Managed care has no stake in how practitioners conduct the task or how the outcome is achieved. The task or outcome is the only judgement of value. In a relationship model, ethics are central to the process because, in relationships, people always have expectations about how one person should behave toward the other, regardless of the expected outcome. This is a basic and crucial point that clinicians and supervisors who work for managed care companies must constantly keep in mind.

Ethical Practice Guides

Psychiatry has taken initial steps to identify what is considered ethical practice in relation to managed care (Macbeth, Wheeler, Sither & Onek, 1995), and many of the items they identify are relevant to clinical social work. To practice ethically in connection with managed care, the clinician should determine that:

- clients can make informed treatment decisions based on knowledge of:
    - their options;
    - benefit limitations;
    - the authorization process;
    - their rights to appeal utilization decisions;
    - the limits on choice and copay requirements;
    - the potential invasion of privacy by the review process;
- no exaggerated claims of excellence or quality are made by the managed care company;
- treatment is competent and meets client needs within benefit limits;
- the utilization review process is not invasive of the therapeutic relationship; and
- reviewers are not financially rewarded for denying treatment or claims. (Macbeth et al., 1995)

Professional Organizations

Professional organizations also undermine practitioner autonomy by establishing licensing standards, devising multiple layers of credentialing, and requiring continuing education credits. Licensing is directly linked to managed care policies since companies use licensing to establish provider eligibility. Professional organizations currently compete with one another to control practitioner functions and activities. The National Association of Social Workers is vying for practice "turf" with the National Federation of Societies of Clinical Social Work, which is vying with the American Association of Marriage and Family Therapists, which is vying with the American Association of Guidance Counsellors, which is vying with the National Registry of Certified Group Therapists, which is vying with the American Psychiatric Association, which is vying with the American Psychological Association. The list could go on and on as overwhelmed supervisors, practitioners and clients respond with confusion and frustration. Competition between disciplines constantly shifts and reshifts the balance between the different professional organizations, and allows managed care companies to maintain and extend their control of mental health practice.

In spite of widespread practitioner dissatisfaction with managed care practices, professional organizations have not taken steps to confront the problem (*Psychotherapy Finances,* 1995d). A survey by the National Federation of Societies for Clinical Social Work *(Psychotherapy Finances,* 1995a) found that 90% of 428 respondents reported an overall negative response to managed care.

Professional Status

Current trends threaten our status as a profession. Sullivan (1995) has reaffirmed the time-honored criteria necessary to establish professional status: 1) specialized training based on 2) codified knowledge used to 3) live out a commitment to public service that is 4) carried out with a certain degree of autonomy as perceived and accepted by the public. Given much of the activity surrounding managed care and social work practice, the only tenet of professionalism that does not appear to be eroding is specialized training. In regard to the second criterion, there is compelling research (Randall & Thyer, 1994; Thyer & Vodde, 1994) that the theory base of social work is not sufficiently codified. For example, their research shows that graduate students can achieve high scores on licensing examinations by randomly selecting answers on the scoring sheets, even when they have not read the examination questions. In regard to the third criterion, it seems clear that social workers who practice through managed care are not performing a public service, as defined by Courtney and Specht (1994). And finally, in regard to the fourth criterion, the previous section of this paper documents the profession's growing loss of autonomy. These threats to professional status present the social work profession with a dilemma similar to the ethical dilemmas discussed early. Given the erosion of professional values and prerogatives, our failure to address these issues proactively is significant. Social work has devoted decades to convincing the public that it is an autonomous profession (Munson, 1979), but managed care could seriously damage the profession's public autonomous image if present trends continue.

Social Work Education

Up to this point in time, social work education does not appear to view the managed care movement and privatization as topics of sufficient importance to warrant inclusion in social work curricula. Most of the theory of social work intervention taught in schools of social work is outdated, having been generated long before modern managed care was initiated. A national survey (McNutt, 1995) of the social work macro/administration practice curriculum in graduate schools produced no mention either of managed care or privatization. An informal survey, by the author of this article, of practice texts most frequently used in schools of social work revealed that the majority were first published more than twenty years ago, and none have been published during the last twelve years. These books have undergone minimal revisions and none cover managed care aspects of practice. The most frequently used texts are Hollis' (1964) *Casework,* Turner's (1974) *Social Work Treatment,* and Compton and Galaway's (1975) *Social Work Processes.*

Conclusion

What direction the control trend will take is unclear. It is most likely to continue (Patterson & Sharfstein, 1992), and to get worse. It is possible that our 100-year quest for professional autonomy will be significantly altered if there is no professional response to these trends. Ironically, the emerging role of social workers in the managed care environment is strikingly similar to the role of social workers who were paid agents in the charity organization societies.

There is hope that comes from an unsuspected source: Nietzsche. He states that tyranny of any kind leads to servitude, but the danger of tyranny "... acquaints us with our own resources, our virtues, our armor and weapons, our spirit, and forces us to be strong" (Kaufman, 1954, p. 542). There are increasing indications that society has begun to view certain aspects of managed care practice as unfair and worthy of negative sanctions. The fact that the State of Rhode Island recently fined a managed care company $100,000 and placed it on probation for one year because of "unfair practices" *(Psychotherapy Finances,* 1995b) is, perhaps, a harbinger of change. Historically, social work has been a profession concerned with social justice and the well-being of oppressed clients. This is our "hallmark" and it has distinguished us from psychiatry, psychology, and counseling (Reamer, 1992). Many of the oppressive trends in mental health care have been fostered by managed care and other social institutions that have a disproportional impact on the lives of relatively disempowered people. It remains to be seen whether the social work profession will recover its historical role and its unique strength as advocate for disempowered clients, or whether it will continue its slide into the role of willing slave to managed care company philosophies and practices. The words of Kenneth Pray in his 1946 presidential address to the National Conference of Social Work can serve as an enduring guide for addressing the challenges that now face our profession:

> If American social work can stand true to its own faith, in its daily practice and in its broader relations with the whole society .... it can reach in our time an achievement of incalculable value to mankind, by bravely and competently helping at least some parts of this sorely troubled world, caught in the turmoil of a social revolution, to discover and to fulfill their own permanent, positive values and their own truly creative purpose. (Fink, 1949)

REFERENCES

Allman, W. F. (1994). *The stone age present: How evolution has shaped modern life — from sex, violence, and language to emotions, morals, and communities.* New York: Simon & Schuster.

Altheide, D. L. (1995). *An ecology of communication: Cultural formats of control.* New York: Aldine de Gruyter.

Amada, G. (1995). *A guide to psychotherapy.* New York: Ballantine.

Compton, B. R., & Galaway, B. (1975). *Social work processes.* Homewood, IL: The Dorsey Press.

Consumer Reports. (1995, November). Mental health: Does therapy help? 734-739.

Corpt, E. A., & Reison, M. (1994). Behaviorizing your clinical language. *Managed Care News,* 1-4.

Courtney, M., & Specht, H. (1994). *Unfaithful angels: How social work has abandoned its mission.* New York: The Free Press.

Davison, G. C., & Neale, J. M. (1990). *Abnormal psychology.* New York: John Wiley & Sons.

Feldman, J. L., & Fitzpatrick, R. J. (Eds.). (1992). *Managed mental health care: Administrative and clinical issues.* Washington, DC: American Psychiatric Press.

Fink, A. E. (1949). *The field of social work.* New York: Columbia University Press.

Flax, J. (1990). *Thinking fragments: Psychoanalysis, feminism, and postmodernism in the contemporary west.* Berkeley, CA: The University of California Press.

Goodman, M., Brown, J., & Deitz, P. (1992). *Managing managed care.* Washington, DC: American Psychiatric Press.

Handy, C. (1995, May/June). Trust and the virtual organization. *Harvard Business Review,* 40-50.

Hollis, F. (1964). *Casework: A psychosocial therapy.* New York: Random House.

Kaufmann, W. (Ed.). (1954). *The portable Nietzsche.* New York: Penguin.

Lasch, C. (1979). *The culture of narcissism: American life in an age of diminishing expectations.* New York: Norton.

Lundblad, K. S. (1995). Jane Addams and social reform: A role model for the 1990s. *Social Work, 40*(5), 661-669.

Macbeth, J. E., Wheeler, A. M., Sither, J. W., & Onek, J. N. (1995). *Legal and risk management issues in the practice of psychiatry.* Washington, DC: Psychiatrists' Purchasing Group.

Mathias, W. N. (1995, May 16). Personal communication.

McNutt, J. G. (1995). The macro practice curriculum in graduate social work education: Results of a national survey. *Administration in Social Work, 19*(3), 59-74.

Motenko, A. K., Allen, E. A., Angelos, P., Block, L., DeVito, J., Duffy, A., Holton, L., Lambert, K., Parker, C., Ryan, J., Schraft, D., & Swindell, J. (1995). Privatization and cutbacks: Social work and client impressions of service delivery in Massachusetts. *Social Work, 40*(4), 456-463.

Munson, C. E. (in press). Length of treatment, diagnosis, and treatment planning. *The clinical supervisor.*

Munson, C. E. (1995a). Control and authority in mental health services. *Managed Care News,* March/May, 2-4.

Munson, C. E. (1995b). *Foundation concepts for survival of ethical social work practice in the health care environment.* Paper presented at National Institutes of Health, Bethesda, MD.

Munson, C. E. (1993a). The "P" word and mental health services. *The Clinical Supervisor, 11*(2), 1-5.

Munson, C. E. (1993b). *Clinical social work supervision* (2nd ed.). New York: The Haworth Press.

Munson, C. E. (Ed.). (1979). *Social work supervision: Classic statements and critical issues.* New York: The Free Press.

Naisbitt, J. (1982). *Megatrends: Ten new directions transforming our lives.* New York: Warner Books.

National Advisory Mental Health Council. (1993). Health care reform for Americans with severe mental illness: Report of the National Advisory Mental Health Council. *American Journal of Psychiatry, 150*(10), 1447-1465.

National Association of Social Workers. (1995). *Draft code of ethics.* Washington, DC: National Association of Social Workers.

National Association of Social Workers. (1990). *Code of ethics.* Washington, DC: National Association of Social Workers.

Patterson, D. Y., & Sharfstein, S. S. (1992). The future of mental health care. In J. L. Feldman & R. J. Fitzpatrick (Eds.), *Managed mental health care* (pp. 335-343). Washington, DC: American Psychiatric Press.

Perlman, H. H. (1957). *Social casework: A problem-solving process.* Chicago, IL: University of Chicago Press.

Phillips, D. (1995). Professional standards and managed care. *National Federation of Societies for Clinical Social Work Progress Report, 13*(1), 11.

Psychotherapy Finances, 21(10), 5. (1995a). Managed care notes.

Psychotherapy Finances, 21(9), 1. (1995b). Managed care: Consumer complaints lead to sanctions against a company.

Psychotherapy Finances, 21(8), 5. (1995c). Survey results: A snapshot of managed care company policies.

Psychotherapy Finances, 21(7), 6. (1995d). Special report: What is your professional organization doing for your practice?

Randal, J. (1995). Managed care reshapes health care delivery, U.S. Department of Health and Human Service. *SAMHSA News, 3*(3), 10-14.

Randall, E. J., & Thyer, B. A. (1994). A preliminary test of the validity of the LCSW examination. *Clinical Social Work Journal, 22*(2), 223-227.

Reamer, F. G. (1992). From the editor: The wheels of change in social work education. *Journal of Social Work Education, 28*(10), 3-5.

Reeser, J. C., & Epstein, I. (1990). *Professionalization and activism in social work: The sixties, the eighties, and the future.* New York: Columbia University Press.

Reid, W. J., & Epstein, L. (1972). *Task-centered practice.* New York: Columbia University Press.

Richmond, M. (1917). *Social diagnosis.* New York: Russell Sage Foundation.

Sullivan, W. M. (1995). *Work and integrity: The crisis and promise of professionalism in America.* New York: Harper Business.

Terr, L. (1994). *Unchained memories: True stories of traumatic memories, lost and found.* New York: Basic Books.

Thyer, B. A., & Vodde, R. (1994). Is the ACSW examination valid? *Clinical Social Work Journal, 22*(1), 105-111.

Turner, F. J. (1974). *Social work treatment.* New York: The Free Press.

Wolf, S. (1994). Health care reform and the future of physician ethics. *Hastings Center Report, 24*(2), 28-41.

Zuckerman, E. I., & Guyett, I. P. R. (1992). *The paper office 1.* Pittsburgh: The Clinician's ToolBox.

RESIDENT GUESTS: SOCIAL WORKERS IN HOST SETTINGS

BARBARA OBERHOFER DANE, BARBARA L. SIMON

SINCE their profession was formalized, social workers have been working guests in "host settings," or organizations whose mission and decision making are defined and dominated by people who are not social workers. Like guests in any circumstance, social workers in host organizations must make their stay of continuing interest to their employers by providing evidence on a regular basis of their indispensability to either the mission or overall welfare of the host.

Hospitals, schools, psychiatric clinics, and juvenile courts constituted the first wave of host organizations that invested in or at least tolerated social workers during the heyday of progressivism and the settlement movement (Allen-Meares, Washington, & Welsh, 1986; Radin, 1989; Roberts, 1983; Shevlin, 1983). As urbanization, industrialization, and immigration accelerated the urgency of interconnecting the resources of families, informal support networks, and community institutions, social workers carved out roles and responsibilities in diverse arenas, many under the aegis of other professions. This centrifugal tendency intensified following World War I, when industrial and military organizations began employing social workers in a systematic fashion (Akabas & Kurzman, 1982; Maas, 1951).

During the New Deal, federal and state governments became host settings for thousands of social workers (Fisher, 1980). Still later, leaders of labor unions, juvenile correctional facilities, prisons, jails, probation and parole programs, police departments, and legal aid societies invited social workers into their midst (Roberts, 1983; Weiner, Akabas,

& Sommer, 1973). More recently, new niches for social work have emerged within nursing homes, health maintenance organizations, and hospices (Proffitt, 1987; Rossen, 1987). In addition, corporations, long-standing employers of social workers, have found additional roles for them in employee assistance programs and philanthropic units.

The status of resident guest has carried with it a number of problems and opportunities that merit periodic reexamination as social work and host organizations evolve. Some of these challenges are idiosyncratic, found only in host organizations of a particular category such as hospitals. Others are generic to most if not all host settings, regardless of occupational domain. This article addresses generic challenges, drawing on a century of professional experience that can guide contemporary students and experienced practitioners working in a variety of host organizations.

Social workers have repeatedly been confronted with predictable forms of professional challenge during the many decades of residence in host settings. These challenges appear to be associated unavoidably with guest status. Regardless of the kind of host setting, social workers have repeatedly encountered four types of problem: (1) discrepancies between professional mission and values and those of dominant individuals in the employing institution; (2) marginality of token status within workplaces employing few social workers; (3) the devaluing of social work as women's work in settings that are predominantly male in inspiration and composition; and (4) role ambiguity and role strain.

Predictable Issues Encountered in Host Organizations

Discrepancies between Professional Mission and Value Differences

One does not have to work long in a hospital, corporation, or school before recognizing the discrepancy between the mission and values of the organization and those of the social work unit, team, or lone practitioner. Social workers in host agencies face numerous stresses and pressures if they serve with integrity and maintain their commitment to client self-determination. Although the social work profession traditionally has recognized the value of the individual practitioner as one of the constituent components of practice, organizational leaders in host settings necessarily focus more on accountability to boards of directors and funding sources that focus on cost containment and profit incentives; in these instances, organizational goals are placed ahead of client well-being (Balgopal, 1989). A host environment with multiple and often conflicting expectations poses predictable difficulties for social workers, including stress, accountability, and shrinking resources.

Stress is inherent in host agencies in which multidisciplinary teams invoke values that may be at variance with the values to which the social worker owes allegiance. The social worker collaborates with legal, education, penal, corporate, and health professionals who see clients through heterogeneous, distinctive disciplinary lenses.

For example, school administrators and teachers may stress the primacy of cognitive development, whereas social workers may emphasize multidimensional student growth. Yet student development remains the common ground that both educators and social workers share. In other circumstances, the variance may be of major import, perhaps even threatening the integrity of the social work conducted. For instance, a school administrator or board of education may decide that a school should devote itself primarily to the success of children who have demonstrated the best verbal and mathematical talent, relegating to secondary status the development of students who have evidenced less intellectual promise. Collaborating with this stated or unstated mission would pose a fundamental difficulty for school social workers, who are charged by their profession with serving clients in an equitable manner.

Although social workers in host agencies often have values akin to those of the organization, tacit value differences usually abound. In the prison system, a social worker faces value conflicts with guards who view prisoners with contempt, hostility, or rejection based on the premise that the prisoner deserves punishment rather than rehabilitation. Contradictions are often present between legal requirements and child welfare policies and procedures. For example, working in the best interests of the child may be at odds with court-ordered mandates and directives (Jayaratne & Chess, 1984).

A second source of strain for social workers is the intensification of bureaucratic control over service delivery. Numerous regulations and monitoring bodies, compounded by an espousal of business principles and bottom-line values as the panacea for salvaging social service delivery, constrain social work professionals who are serving clients in host organizations. Administrative decisions that reflect the priorities of boards of directors and of funding sources who reconfigure the allocation of agency resources and profits sometimes pose a dilemma for social workers, whose central mission is maximizing the resources and choices of clients.

Social workers are required in host agencies to be both diplomatic and assertive in defending actions reflecting professional values. As a result, social workers are caught in a number of disempowering organizational binds that grow out of inherent differences between the priorities of agency executives and line workers. For example, in hospital settings, administrators must emphasize efficiency and cost containment, whereas clinicians necessarily focus on patient problems and services. Timely assessment and discharge planning appear to be the central tasks for social workers. If the physician or hospital administrator wants to discharge the patient before community resources are in place, ethical problems arise for the social worker who is asked to implement this decision.

Other examples of conflict between agency priorities and workers' values can be found in unions and schools. In one union, a social worker proposed day care for employees' children or elderly parents suffering from Alzheimer's disease. The agency administrator, however, was more interested in work performance and increased productivity and believed resources should be allocated to treat substance abuse problems. In school, administrators focused on student absenteeism and reorganized the school accordingly, sometimes eliminating social workers and replacing them with field workers who contributed to the school's mission of filling classroom seats, rather than treating students and their families.

Unable or unwilling to deal with the double binds and value conflicts in host agencies, some social workers leave the system. Others incorporate and identify with the values of the host organization. To diminish their value conflicts, they screen out the double-bind messages of the agency. Sherman and Wenocur (1983) reported that these social workers stop acting as effective advocates for clients, shut down their empathic responses, and often resort to complex paper shuffling. Kadushin (1985) suggested that social workers should acknowledge the stress these actions induce and accommodate and articulate different points of view regarding a problematic situation, keeping in mind their own conception of the best interests of the population served. Social workers should foster an open climate in which different points of view can be heard, even when their views differ from those of others.

Marginality of Token Status

Tokens are members of an organization who belong to a subgroup that constitutes 15 percent or fewer of the members of a work force in which another subgroup predominates (Kanter, 1977). In host settings in which 85 percent or more of the employees share a profession or occupation other than social work, social workers are tokens. Prisons, corporations, schools, hospitals, and military organizations are all institutional contexts in which social workers are a tiny minority.

As Kanter discovered in her path-breaking studies of women within male-dominated corporations, token workers encounter many barriers and discriminatory practices caused by perceptual distortions of the predominant majority within an organization (Kanter, 1977). Token workers' unusual visibility within a workplace results in extreme performance pressures and allows them little margin for error and few opportunities for trial-and-error learning. Majority group members tend to view token workers as different from themselves in every respect and overestimate the homogeneity among tokens. These misperceptions lead majority group members to avoid token workers and to prejudge them as inadequate to perform their assigned tasks. Token workers are isolated on the job and deprived of important informal opportunities to learn from and work side by side with majority group members (Kanter, 1977).

Social workers within host institutions are subject to the same hazards of tokenism that Kanter's corporate women encountered. Because there are relatively few social workers in corporations, schools, prisons, hospitals, and military organizations, their every decision and action can be scrutinized for deviation from overall organizational norms, routines, and ideology. Lone social workers on psychiatric units of hospitals, for example, have reported experiencing extreme pressures in team meetings and case conferences to perform and conform (Hubscham, 1983). The small number of social workers in host settings makes it possible for other professionals and staff members to work for months or even years without direct face-to-face exchanges with the social workers which permits biases to remain unexposed to experiential verification and challenge. Testimony from social workers employed at jails and prisons suggests that correctional officers and wardens tend to view the work of social service personnel with the presupposition that social workers, unlike themselves, are "soft" on criminals and easily taken in by the manipulations of the inmates (Grodd & Simon, 1990). Veteran and beginning social workers alike fight a continual battle to reduce misperceptions of themselves in host settings.

Devaluing of Social Work as Women's Work

Social work has largely been a profession peopled by women (Leiby, 1978; Lubove, 1975). Consequently, it bears the attributes and stigmas historically found attached to such professions. Like teaching, nursing, and librarianship, social work was founded to attend in the public domain to the same functions that women were assigned under industrial capitalism and its family ethic (Abramovitz, 1988; Kessler-Harris, 1982). These functions included caring for dependents and ensuring intergenerational continuity by nurturing people and transmitting traditional values.

Caretaking, child-raising, and social maintenance generally have been conducted during the 20th century by women from the lower professional rungs of large public or not-for-profit bureaucracies such as hospitals, schools, and welfare offices (Ehrenreich, 1985). In most circumstances, these large bureaucracies are headed and managed by men (National Association of Social Workers [NASW], 1987). For social workers in host settings, this predictable gender distinction between line workers and executive-level leaders compounds the differences between hosts and guests. One consequence of this gender distinction is that, even in the same agency, social workers are paid less than other line-level members of male-dominated professions, such as physicians, correctional officers, and accountants (Kessler-Harris, 1982; U.S. Bureau of the Census, 1989).

The legacy of the family wage remains embedded in the salary structures of women's work and women's profes-

sions. The family wage—the wage paid to male breadwinners that was supposed to be sufficient to maintain an entire family, including their wife and children—hinged on the dual assumptions that all women are married and that women workers, therefore, do not need to support themselves or their families. The correlative concept to the family wage was that of "pin money," or wages allotted to women workers who, it was presumed, worked only to afford extra treats because basic necessities were covered by their husbands' earnings. As outmoded as these two notions are in a world of two-earner households, their potency throughout at least eight decades of professional life, from 1890 to 1970, has a lasting effect on the wages of female professionals and of male professionals in women's professions (NASW, 1987).

Another consequence of the gender difference between most social workers and most managers in host agencies is the reduced likelihood that social workers will be promoted into top decision-making positions within those agencies. The homosociality that Kanter (1977) documented in corporations—the preference for surrounding oneself at work with people as much like oneself as possible—appears to work directly against such promotions. Social workers in host settings are "other" in two senses: they bring an alien professional tradition with them, and they are typically female. Regrettably, pay and formal promotions are not the only casualties of this gender difference. The informal influence that social workers can bring to bear on host environments is less than it would be if managers were women or if the majority of social workers were men (Gummer & Edwards, 1985; Holloway & Brager, 1985; Karlins & Abelson, 1970; Reardon, 1981).

Female social workers in host organizations run by men of other professions encounter a work universe of male-defined behaviors and assumptions. Distinctions between men's and women's ways of talking, interacting, making ethical judgments, knowing, leading, and making decisions reflect behavioral and attitudinal patterns that women's studies scholars have elaborated on and documented in detail (Belenky, Clinchy, Goldberger, & Tarule, 1986; Gilligan, 1982; Henley & Thorne, 1976;

Jaggar & Rothenberg, 1984; Wood & Karten, 1986). Women or men in male-dominated organizations who conduct themselves in a "female mode" risk invisibility and inaudibility. A female mode is an interactional and problem-solving style in which open-ended statements and questions are used more frequently than closed-ended statements. This mode relies more on direct references to experience, intuition, and logic than does the "male mode" of communication (Belenky et al., 1986; Henley & Thorne, 1976; Wood & Karten, 1986). The risks of operating in a mode other than the dominant one are accentuated by the generic role ambiguity and role strain experienced by resident professional guests in host settings.

Role Ambiguity and Role Strain

Role ambiguity and role strain engender stress for social workers in a host agency (Jayaratne & Chess, 1984). Although much of the research has been in the child welfare arena, role strain and ambiguity can be found regardless of occupational domain. The intensity of the stress experienced may change from one host setting to another.

Depending on the social, economic, and political conditions of the organization, the social worker is asked to assume both a helper and controller role. In the helper role, direct services to clients on both an emotional and a concrete level are paramount. The allocation and management of resources, the drive for efficiency, and the engagement in routine tasks to meet the demands of regulatory agencies and fiscal constraints invoke the role of control.

The political and cultural upheavals of the late 1960s and 1970s inspired social workers to organize client groups to advocate for services and civil rights. In contrast, present regulatory policies, budget constraints, public scrutiny, and civil liability (Besharov, 1984) have reshaped social work's role and the delivery of services. Larger numbers of elderly people, social and political upheavals in the Caribbean and Central and South America, and changing immigration policies in the Soviet Union have shifted the composition of the population and presented new problems and client populations for social workers.

Increasingly, professional roles in

large host service agencies focus on outcomes and the processing of a maximum number of people in the shortest period of time (Fabricant, 1985). This shift toward short-term interventions, rapid assessment, and brief treatment requires social workers to modify their practice orientation to meet organizational needs while continuing to protect the quality and continuity of care.

Operating, as social workers often do, from a low-ranking position in host agencies, they must exert deliberate efforts to influence organizational life. This society socializes many of its members to fit into prescribed organizational roles rather than to create or expand them. Creative and innovative social workers in host agencies have exploited ambiguities of function to extend the scope and character of the profession's function (Gitterman & Miller, 1989). For example, hospital social workers can engineer a new work role by redefining their tasks as discharge planners. Instead of being bombarded with referrals from all personnel on their assigned floors, they can coordinate the discharge planning process by initiating weekly rounds with team members. This process allows them to gain more control over the content and context of the work assignment (Murdach, 1983) and provides an opportunity to exercise judgment and to refine skills. Social workers in employee assistance programs in corporations initially provided only alcoholism counseling, but they have broadened their role to include labor and community relations, case management, retirement planning, and work with retirees.

Some social workers undervalue concrete services because they sometimes require less clinical skill than other tasks. Social workers who have relinquished task responsibilities to other professions in host agencies have suffered a significant loss of power (Fabricant, 1985). Ironically, the mundane details of discharge planning (for example, the provision of wheelchairs or homemaker services) have become a priority in the current fiscal climate in health care, and recognition for the performance of this important function has gone to other disciplines.

Questions of professional turf and autonomy arise because many professionals in host agencies are concerned with similar activities and interventions related to clients' welfare. Although these problems are not new in host agencies, there is growing concern and discussion about the increased role blurring in work with psychosocial aspects of the client's life. Environmental demands and current trends cause some social work roles to be relinquished to other professions in the organization. Confusion over the role of other disciplines occurs most often when a task seems to belong to more than one discipline (Lister, 1980). Toseland, Ganeles-Palmer, and Chapman (1986) studied teams in psychiatric hospitals and found that role confusion emerged around the question of who was responsible for supervising the work of team members. For example, some social workers reported that nurses were performing traditional social work roles. Such role confusion, according to Burt (1979), is not something to be avoided. It is not a sign of weakness but rather is an accurate reflection of the nature of interpersonal and power relationships in host agencies.

In the criminal justice system, the collaborative role of social work has complemented the orientation of parole officers to achieve a treatment goal with a client. The officers' more directive approach can help greatly when tempered with social workers' understanding of the client's needs.

Social work practitioners in host agencies can provide leadership and still maintain their traditional concern with clients and their environment. While tending to clients' needs, social workers can respond to both changing agency environments and organizational structures.

Social Work's Strengths

In spite of the complexity of guest status in host settings, social workers are in an advantageous position because of their holistic perspective and their specialized knowledge and ability to transfer skills across disparate settings. Siporin (1980) stated that from the beginning, the social work profession has been concerned with people and their environments. Social workers' educational training and knowledge, modeled on an ecosystem framework (Germain & Gitterman, 1980; Meyer, 1983), support this view.

Social workers in host settings are often viewed by staff as possessing special expertise in the areas of human services, community resources, community organization, and assistance in obtaining financial benefits. These perceptions have given social workers a base from which to exercise influence. As one of the leading professions for advocacy for the rights of clients, social work historically has focused on prevention. When social workers have worked together with parents, union members, or health professionals to advocate for change or to safeguard existing legislation, a forceful and effective alliance has resulted. Social workers' advocacy strategies have focused on providing support, information, and organization for the exertion of political pressure to obtain expanded resources. The advocacy role is one of many discrete roles used by practitioners to balance the needs of their clients with the demands of the social environment (Compton & Galaway, 1989). Constructive parental involvement has a multiplier effect among school personnel. When the worker initiates purposeful, professional interchange with parents, it may well be the parents' first positive contact with school personnel, and as a result parents may become advocates for the school. A number of special interest groups such as Concerned Citizens for Handicapped Children have emerged because of social work (Dane, 1985). The school social worker can further advocate for students by reaching out to varied constituencies in the district.

The process of collaboration is pervasive in host settings. All forms of collaboration require particular knowledge, skills, and attitudes in working with others to meet clients' needs, to solve problems, and to carry out clinical tasks. The social worker views the strengths and disabilities of clients within the context of the environment in which they need to function. This perspective can be shared with other staff members and is helpful to each discipline involved in the client's life.

One area open to collaboration between social work and medicine is health care delivery to special populations. Social workers and doctors can influence the design of clinics and programs aimed at low-income, immigrant, aged, and handicapped populations. Physicians are knowledgeable about disease, disability, and treatment. Social workers understand social characteristics and their effects on patient access, communication, compliance, and comfort (Schilling & Schilling, 1987).

School social workers can encourage pregnant adolescents to comply with both their school work and medical regimes by collaborating with both teachers and doctors. Social workers employed by a public defender's office can advocate for clients in the legal system and perform valuable services for clients and attorneys (Ashford, Macht, & Mylym, 1987).

The use of interdisciplinary teams to plan and deliver human services has become increasingly common in host settings. Most social workers are members or leaders of an interdisciplinary team (Toseland et al., 1986). Team members lay claims to areas of competence and particular associated tasks. Effective teamwork is particularly important for social workers in a host agency because it gives them an opportunity to cultivate support and alliances. For example, in a psychiatric setting, social workers can help each other reduce isolation; share the joys, tensions, and frustrations of clients; and become valued team members by providing a comprehensive and coordinated treatment plan for discharge. As the social work profession matures and validates its particular areas of expertise, it will have the capacity to gain power, influence, and respect in host settings.

Recommendations

Like any group in the minority, social workers in host agencies are frequently vulnerable and under scrutiny. Stereotypical behavior may be attributed to the social worker, who has yet to be viewed as an equal partner in the host agency. Social workers will only take their rightful place in host agencies when they can demonstrate their value to the organization and articulate their contribution to the setting and when they are represented in sufficient numbers and strength to make evident their support of the central mission of the agency.

Imprecise delineation by social workers of their responsibilities and inadequate performance by social workers may be responsible for the chipping away of many traditional social work roles by other practitioners in the help-ing professions. Social workers must not weaken their power by carelessly abdicating professional territory to other individuals or groups. This does not mean that social workers should hesitate to share their responsibilities; in fact, they need to share them willingly with others. They must, however, always maintain the right of final review and approval for any shared task.

Social workers should establish realistic expectations about what they can and cannot do. This stance requires social workers to maintain a willingness and capacity to continually negotiate the conditions of their work. They must become aware of the many sources of power available to them in their role and become comfortable with taking and using power (Patti & Resnick, 1972). Social workers in host settings must decide on their role and then make it viable and essential; the knowledge they bring and the values they espouse add a positive dimension to client services.

By managing tension and being aware of value differences, social workers can create a work environment that is sensitive to both clients' needs and agency diversity. Wax (1971) explained that such tensions need not be detrimental and can be healthy if managed creatively. He noted that practitioners and team members in host agencies draw on the same principles and values in their respective practices. Both subscribe to behaviors that enhance dignity and self-esteem in the individual, maximize their capacities, and foster self-determination.

Token workers in many settings have found support groups to be invaluable aids for surviving and thriving. These groups can consist of social workers from the same workplace or from several different workplaces (Toseland et al., 1986). Supportive mentors on the job or from other arenas are another recommended and less costly source of assistance for token social workers. Informal or formal caucuses of token workers at worksites also assist them in drawing strength from each other and making suggestions to or demands on the organization in a collective fashion.

Similarly, female social workers in male-run organizations can help themselves with support groups, mentors, and caucuses. In addition, if study groups of female social workers explored the litera-ture on male and female patterns of behavior in complex organizations, they would be better equipped to navigate the water of host bureaucracies.

In the 1990s the social work profession is entering new areas of practice in host settings, such as employee assistance programs and outplacement agencies. New kinds of client problems, new reference groups, and new organizational settings will challenge the social work profession to expand its eclectic and ecological orientation, to remain open to new perspectives on practice, and, simultaneously, to function flexibly in multiple host settings.

References

Abramovitz, M. (1988). *Regulating the lives of women.* Boston: South End Press.

Akabas, S. H., & Kurzman, P. (1982). *Work, workers, and work organizations: A view from social work.* Englewood Cliffs, NJ: Prentice Hall.

Allen-Meares, P., Washington, R. O., & Welsh, B. L. (1986). *Social work services in schools.* Englewood Cliffs, NJ: Prentice Hall.

Ashford, J., Macht, M., & Mylym, M. (1987). Advocacy by social workers in the public defender's office. *Social Work, 32,* 199–203.

Balgopal, P. (1989). Occupational social work: An expanded clinical perspective. *Social Work, 34*(5), 437–444.

Belenky, M. F., Clinchy, B. M., Goldberger, N. R., & Tarule, J. M. (1986). *Women's ways of knowing: The development of self, voice, and mind.* New York: Basic Books.

Besharov, D. J. (1984). Liability in child welfare. *Public Welfare, 7,* 28–49.

Burt, R. (1979). *Taking care of strangers: The rule of law in doctor-patient relationships.* New York: Free Press.

Compton, B., & Galaway, B. (1989). *Social work process* (4th ed.). Belmont, CA: Wadsworth.

Dane, E. (1985). Professional and lay advocacy in the education of handicapped children. *Social Work, 30,* 505–510.

Ehrenreich, J. (1985). *The altruistic imagination.* Ithaca, NY: Cornell University Press.

Fabricant, M. (1985). The industrialization of social work practice. *Social Work, 30*(5), 389–395.

Fisher, J. (1980). *The response of social work to the depression.* Cambridge, MA: Schenkman.

Germain, C., & Gitterman, A. (1980). *The life model of social work practice.* New York: Columbia University Press.

Gilligan, C. (1982). *In a different voice.* Cambridge, MA: Harvard University Press.

Gitterman, A., & Miller, I. (1989). The influence of the organization on clinical practice. *Clinical Social Work Journal, 17*(2), 151–164.

Grodd, B., & Simon, B. (1990). Imprisonment. In A. Gitterman (Ed.), *Handbook on social work with vulnerable populations* (pp. 647–676). New York: Columbia University Press.

Gummer, B., & Edwards, R. L. (1985). A social worker's guide to organizational politics. *Administration in Social Work, 9*(1), 13–21.

Henley, N., & Thorne, B. (1976). *She said—he said.* Pittsburgh: Know, Inc.

Holloway, S., & Brager, G. (1985). Implicit negotiations and organizational practice. *Administration in Social Work, 9*(2), 15–24.

Hubscham, L. (Ed.). (1983). *Hospital social work practice.* New York: Praeger.

Jaggar, A. M., & Rothenberg, P. S. (1984). *Feminist frameworks.* New York: McGraw-Hill.

Jayaratne, S., & Chess, W. (1984). Job satisfaction, burnout, and turnover: A national study. *Social Work, 29,* 448–453.

Kadushin, A. (1985). *Supervision in social work* (2nd ed.). New York: Columbia University Press.

Kanter, R. M. (1977). *Men and women of the corporation.* New York: Basic Books.

Kàrlins, M., & Abelson, H. (1970). *Persuasion* (2nd ed.). New York: Springer.

Kessler-Harris, A. (1982). *Out of work.* New York: Oxford University Press.

Leiby, J. (1978). *A history of social welfare and social work in the United States.* New York: Columbia University Press.

Lister, L. (1980). Role expectations of social work and other health professionals. *Health and Social Work, 5,* 41–49.

Lubove, R. (1975). *The professional altruist.* New York: Atheneum.

Maas, H. S. (Ed.). (1951). *Adventure in mental health: Psychiatric social work with the armed forces in World War II.* New York: Columbia University Press.

Meyer, C. (1983). *Clinical social work: Ecosystems perspective.* New York: Columbia University Press.

Murdach, A. D. (1983). Skills and tactics in hospital practice. *Social Work, 28,* 279–284.

National Association of Social Workers. (1987). *Salaries in social work.* Silver Spring, MD: Author.

Patti, R., & Resnick, H. (1972). Changing the agency from within. *Social Work, 17,* 48–57.

Proffitt, L. J. (1987). Hospice. In A. Minahan, et al. (Eds.), *Encyclopedia of social work* (18th ed., Vol. 1, pp. 812–816). Silver Spring, MD: National Association of Social Workers.

Radin, N. (1989). School social work practice: Past, present, and future trends. *Social Work in Education, 11,* 213–225.

Reardon, K. K. (1981). *Persuasion: Theory and conflict.* Beverly Hills, CA: Sage.

Roberts, A. R. (1983). The history and role of social work in law enforcement. In A. R. Roberts (Ed.), *Social work in juvenile and criminal justice settings* (pp. 91–103). Springfield, IL: Charles C Thomas.

Rossen, S. (1987). Hospital social work. In A. Minahan, et al. (Eds.), *Encyclopedia of social work* (18th ed., Vol. 1, pp. 816–821). Silver Spring, MD: National Association of Social Workers.

Schilling, R., & Schilling, R. (1987). Social work and medicine: Shared interests. *Social Work, 32,* 231–235.

Sherman, W., & Wenocur, S. (1983). Empowering public welfare workers through mutual support. *Social Work, 28,* 375–379.

Shevlin, K. M. (1983). Why a social service department in a hospital? In L. Hubscham (Ed.), *Hospital social work practice* (pp. 1–14). New York: Praeger.

Siporin, M. (1980). Ecological systems theory in social work. *Journal of Sociology and Social Welfare, 7,* 507–532.

Toseland, R., Ganeles-Palmer, J., & Chapman, D. (1986). Teamwork in psychiatric settings. *Social Work, 31,* 46–52.

U.S. Bureau of the Census. (1989). *Statistical abstract of the United States: 1988* (109th ed.). Washington, DC: U.S. Government Printing Office.

Wax, J. (1971). Power theory and institutional change. *Social Service Review, 45,* 277–280.

Weiner, H. J., Akabas, S. H., & Sommer, J. J. (1973). *Mental health care in the world of work.* New York: Association Press.

Wood, W., & Karten, S. J. (1986). Sex differences in interaction style as a product of perceived sex differences in competence. *Journal of Personality and Social Psychology, 50,* 341–347.

Barbara Oberhofer Dane, DSW, is Associate Professor, New York University School of Social Work, 2 Washington Square North, New York, NY 10003. Barbara L. Simon, PhD, is Associate Professor, Columbia University School of Social Work, New York, NY 10025.

CASEWORK AND CONGRESS: A LOBBYING STRATEGY

ELLIOT PAGLIACCIO, BURTON GUMMER

THE GROWING POLITICAL CONSERVATISM in the United States and the resulting attacks on social spending have increased the need for social workers to develop effective political lobbying skills.[1] The nonprofit sector, particularly, is experiencing heightened concern over political threats to its tax-exempt status on the federal and state levels. For the first time in decades, the issue of "related" political activity by tax-exempt nonprofit agencies is being reviewed by Congress. Nonprofit organizations must protect themselves by informing federal and state legislators about their purposes and contributions to the community. Although the politicization of social welfare issues has created a greater awareness in the social work community of the importance of political advocacy, the profession's efforts in this respect have been limited, by and large, to "part-time, single-issue advocates who make occasional forays into the legislative arena to promote a bill of immediate interest to their agency or a client constituency."[2] Moreover, these efforts have been almost exclusively confined to the nation's capital where social workers, competing with professional lobbyists with considerable power and influence, are relegated to a minor role in shaping social policies.

The present article offers an alternative strategy for influencing legislators based on lobbying at the local district level. These activities capitalize on social workers' expertise and skills. In addition, such activities may be less expensive to conduct, may enable participation by a greater number of social workers and consumers, and may provide workers with the opportunity to exercise more control over the process. Although the discussion is confined to lobbying national legislators, the issues and tactics presented are also relevant to state legislators.

Lobbying

Lobbying is an effort to "influence" others to act in ways different from what might be predicted on the basis of knowledge of the individual prior to taking those actions.[3] A critical factor in the exercise of influence is deciding what actions will lead to the desired result. This decision, in turn, depends largely on the extent to which the goals of the influencer (the "actor") are shared by the person being influenced (the "target").[4] When the actor and target hold common goals, the actor may persuasively communicate with the target to make him or her aware of the degree to which they share common goals in an effort to influence the target to take cooperative actions to attain these goals.

When the actor and target do not have similar goals, which is often the case when social workers try to influence legislators, the actor must enter into an *exchange* relationship with the target wherein the target agrees to support the actor's goals in return for resources that the actor can provide the target. Before this can occur, the actor must identify the resources that the target deems valuable, whether these resources are available to the actor, and, if not, whether they can be acquired by the actor.

Legislators need resources that enable them to perform their jobs more effectively. Therefore lobbyists must first understand the nature of the legislator's job, so they can determine whether they control or have access to resources that legislators want and would be willing to negotiate for.

Understanding the Legislator's Job

Federal legislators, as well as their state and local counterparts, have two different yet closely related roles: *legislator* and *representative*. Although the present article concentrates on the role of representative, a review of the legislative role will help the lobbyist keep the congressperson's overall responsibilities in perspective. As a legislator, a congressperson's work is dictated in large part by committee assignments acquired through a combination of seniority and procedural and political infighting. Although the majority party in the House of Representatives and Senate controls the key committees through committee majorities, members must often compete with representatives of their own party for positions of authority — primarily chairs of committees.

Committees do the work of the Congress. Since the voting choices of a member of Congress are limited to in favor, opposed, or absent, the intricacies and complexities of the legislative process result from the endless amendments, compromises, rules, procedural debates, and steps through which a bill must progress before it is considered by the House of Representatives or Senate. Legislators, consequently, must not only produce bills that have substantive merit, but bills that have political appeal to a majority of their colleagues.

Congresspersons assume the role of representative when they are in their local districts. When removed from the aura and trappings of Congress, they become, in practice, local politicians who are highly conscious of with whom they are interacting and of the issues important to their constituents.[5] The representative or senator *wants* to interact with his or her constituents. A typical weekend trip to a congressperson's district is measured by the degree of contact with constituents, the amount of local media exposure, and the amount of contact with key local leaders. The trip is further assessed in terms of the impression the congressperson will make on his or her audiences. Congresspersons may talk about monies they have secured for district-based projects and explain how legislation that they are co-sponsoring may affect a local problem while downplaying the national issues that they will face when they return to Washington, D.C.

Congresspersons must be briefed about the concerns of local groups with whom they meet. Whenever possible, meetings with local groups are arranged when significant updates can be provided, good news shared, or blame cast on opponents who do not share the congressperson's or audience's opinions and positions. These visits also measure the shifting needs and attitudes of constituents and indicate how well the representative is received by specific interest groups and subpopulations within the district.[6]

The skills that a congressperson needs to move legislation in Congress are not necessarily the same as those that are effective in the district. As representatives of their districts in states, these officials must respond quickly to requests from constituents and must convey interest in the issues. They must have public-speaking abilities that allow them to present themselves well at various public functions and be able to repackage their speeches to accommodate a group's particular interests.

The District Office

The organization of the district office reflects the special requirements of the representative function. District offices provide local visibility for elected officials and serve as the vehicle for structuring interactions with the representative's constituents. Office locations are chosen to allow both geographic accessibility and political visibility. This latter objective is typically based upon the congressperson's assessment of voter trends and, more importantly, the potential for increased voter support from a given area. If representatives rely heavily on particular areas within their districts for support, or if an area is designated a "swing" district with potential for increased support through greater local activity and visibility, an office or satellite unit may be warranted.

Much can be inferred from an office's location and appearance. Storefront offices convey accessibility and an active, constituency-serving image. Professional buildings, shared federal or state office space, or more reserved, traditional settings convey stability, professionalism, and a business-like approach. Representatives may, in fact, not wish to stimulate greater walk-in business because, like other service agencies, they must weigh the amount of assistance they can provide against their resources. When a constituent makes a request, a response must be generated. For a member who enjoys a healthy margin of voter support, it may not be politically beneficial to encourage more intakes through the district office, because additional district workers translate into fewer legislative aides in Washington.

Conversely, members who receive marginal support (less than 55 percent of the vote in the last election) are likely to concentrate staff in the district. If the voters do not share the congressperson's views regarding national issues, the congressperson's reputation as an effective district advocate and constituency service broker is that much more critical. Elections are won or lost in the district. Although legislative initiatives are important accomplishments upon which legislators build their reputations, the degree to which they are known and how they are perceived locally dictate their elective longevity.

Regular and positive coverage by the local newspapers and other media sources is critical for congresspersons. Since few congresspersons can generate enough legislative accomplishments to maintain continuous positive press coverage, they must rely on their district staff to fill the gaps. The district workers are responsible for turning appearances at events, successful case interventions, grant announcements, and positions on local issues into positive press coverage. As David Mayhew points out,

Whether they are safe or marginal, cautious or audacious, Congressmen must constantly engage in activities related to reelection. There will be a difference in emphasis, but all members share the root need to do things — indeed, to do things day in and day out during their terms.[7]

The District Staff

Congresspersons differentiate between their Washington and district office staffs. Congressional offices are staffed by young legislative aides who are supervised typically by veterans of the legislative process. The vast majority of these workers operate primarily behind the scenes and have little constituent and public contact beyond their specific functional areas. They usually perform research and advise the congressperson on one or more legislative categories.

Whereas Washington staff serve as advisors and as interpreters of information, district staff share these duties while functioning as the congressperson's surrogates by doing outreach work and public presentations and by representing the congressperson within the district. Unlike the legislative aide, they often have extensive public contact and are usually hired for their skills in this area. They state the congressperson's position on issues based upon their assessment of how the congressperson has dealt with similar issues in the past or upon consultation with the congressperson or a legislative aide.

Thus the district office has a life of its own with which the congressperson usually has little direct contact. Typical district office service functions include constituent (case) advocacy and assistance with federal agencies; screening and recommending applicants to military academies; obtaining information from the federal government; providing grant research assistance; information and referral; and collecting, recording, and referring constituent opinions and questions to the Washington office for written responses.

Key staff persons in the district office direct the office, respond to human-service issues and cases, handle the representative's schedule, and serve as office manager and press liaison. In some offices these tasks may be performed by one person, whereas larger district offices may have four or five people performing different functions. In addition to serving as the district chief of staff, the administrative assistant (or district director) is usually the congressperson's political operative at the local level and is entrusted with considerable discretion and authority.

Relationship between District Office And Washington Staff

Relationships between the district and Washington offices typically reflect organizational rivalry not unlike component programs within human service agencies. District staff often perceive Washington legislative assistants as indifferent and slow to respond to district-generated constituent requests. Moreover, they often feel that the Washington office is insensitive to the public complaints they receive when responses are inadequate. Washington staff often perceive work on the district level as less prestigious and important than their duties and as only indirectly related to the development of legislative recommendations, which they view as their exclusive domain.

Because of the pressure of deadlines for public and press responses to an ever-changing agenda of community issues and legislative initiatives, the two offices compete for the attention and availability of the congressperson. In addition, all three parties are simultaneously in contact with diverse people and information, which even in fully computerized offices presents information-management problems.

District staff may have little legislative experience and may lack the time to remain current on minor legislation. Similarly, few legislative staff, other than those who have prior professional experience, bring to Washington an established network of contacts upon which they can obtain information, ideas, and recommendations. At this level, the lobbyist can facilitate the work of both Washington and district aides.

A general rule for the lobbyist is to view the district as one's advocate. The lobbyist can nurture this relationship by establishing his or her credibility as well as the agency's and by communicating the importance of the issue and how its resolution will serve the needs of the people in the district. By communicating effectively with the district office, the lobbyist enables the district office to provide Washington staff with accurate information that supports legislative recommendations. The Washington staff, in turn, are then able to act as "conduits of influence by utilizing information made available to them and seeing that it receives consideration by the legislator."[8] Washington aides require highly focused and immediate input. Washington staff are more likely to seek this information from a lobbyist when the district reinforces the lobbyist's credibility.

Exercising Influence At the District Level

In a relationship based on influence, both parties must derive benefits that reinforce their interest and commitment to the relationship. Social workers must emphasize mutual benefit when relating to elected officials. Relating to members of Congress only once or twice a year to request funding or legislative support contributes to the view that social workers request help without offering help in return. However, before a worker initiates contact with a legislator, he or she should be able to answer the following questions: (1) What specifically do you want? (2) What secondary items do you want if your initial request is not met? (3) What do you have or what can you do that the legislator might want? (4) What is the best way to approach the legislator? (5) Where do you want the relationship to proceed from this first contact?

What Do You Want?

Typically, workers ask legislators to vote for or against legislation or to support increased funding for programs. However, the legislative process allows legislators to display leadership and support for social programs beyond their actual vote. For example, a legislator may speak in favor of a bill in an effort to influence undecided colleagues, offer and advance amendments, hold district-based hearings on legislation, promote legislation through newsletters and other publications, enable testimony to be heard to support a bill, and sponsor or co-sponsor legislation.[9]

In addition to legislative matters, workers can request grant research assistance, federal information documents, and, most important, case advocacy on behalf of clients. In addition, legislators can be asked to announce grant awards, recognize volunteers and board members from social work programs through award ceremonies, and add credibility to events by their participation and attendance. These activities add to the congressperson's public visibility as well as benefit social programs and services.

What Do You Have to Offer?

Consistent with the National Association of Social Workers' recommendations, social workers should establish themselves as *resources* for public officials.[10] Social workers can help elected officials by providing the following: (1) direct services to the congressperson's constituents, (2) information and referral of constituents to other services, (3) access to diverse community groups, subpopulations, or other key informers, (4) case summaries and information on social problems and need areas, (5) advice and recommendations on social policy issues and legislation, and (6) training and technical assistance to legislative staff on services and programs as well as casework procedures.

Credibility is best achieved by simply doing what the worker knows best, that is, providing services to people in need. An active congressional district office that receives various constituent requests and hears numerous problems may welcome the opportunity to utilize social workers on a referral basis. For example, the

district office in which one author of the present article worked dealt with numerous cases involving suicidal telephone callers, requests for admission to nursing homes, Viet Nam veterans with physical and mental disorders, missing persons, neighborhood disputes, abused spouses and children, delinquent child-support payments, emergency housing requests, and social security and public assistance problems. Clearly, in these and other situations, social service agencies can play a vital role.

Workers can also provide educational and informational forums that address human service needs and that describe and offer social services under the public sponsorship of a legislator. For example, while serving as District Director for Representative Mrazek, the senior author organized conferences and forums in cooperation with district-based human service agencies, including a conference on aging parents and forums on child abuse and youth issues.

These examples do not mean that all politicians are open to and interested in the involvement of social workers. Members of Congress interact primarily with constituents who support and share their views. A representative serves a geographic area, the congressional district; this area defines whom he or she represents and who is eligible to vote for candidates to a particular congressional seat. Whereas social workers focus on demographic and need areas, congresspersons focus on voter concentrations, political affiliations of constituents, and voter patterns.

Therefore, if workers are to influence these officials, they must frame "appeals in terms of the specific effects of a proposed measure upon their own district."[11] Legislators who are philosophically undecided about a bill may respond strictly according to the impact and benefits of the bill to their districts. Needs assessments and descriptions of service gaps along district boundaries are more likely to increase a legislator's understanding of social service issues and to be included in the legislator's public presentations. Packaging information about services or resources in ways that congresspersons and their staffs can quickly comprehend makes it easier for them to call and ask for help or advice. In other words, workers should orient congressional offices to what they do in an effort to initiate a working relationship.

How Do You Approach the Legislator?

As noted earlier, district directors usually have considerable authority and power in their respective offices. Even if they are only remotely involved with the issues that concern the worker, they should be given the courtesy of an initial call or meeting, because they will likely influence the amount of attention that the district staff gives to a particular issue. An agenda of clearly stated and reasonable goals should be developed in advance and shared with the legislator's staff. In addition, written information should describe the agency and the problem areas that the worker wishes to address. These issues should always be made relevant to the congressional district. Moreover, the worker should let the legislator know that he or she is available and would like to be called upon as an ongoing source of information and technical advice.

Unlike meetings in the Washington office, meetings in the district allow the worker to structure the meeting. The worker can arrange to meet with the legislator in the worker's environment and can create the atmosphere and the message that is important to the worker. In so doing, the worker is able to impress and gain the appreciation of officials by creating a context in which they are presented in a favorable light to constituents, local leaders, and the media. Workers can also use these occasions to convey the strength of local support and effectiveness of social programs.

Luncheons with legislators and members of agency boards, open houses, legislative breakfast-briefings, award ceremonies, and similar functions provide opportunities for both the worker and the legislator to achieve mutual objectives. In arranging such an event, it is important that the worker work closely with the district staff in preparing the meeting and clearly state the congressperson's role at the event. Staff people who are responsible for scheduling and press liaison should be given directions to events, briefings on the issues and concerns that will be addressed, and be informed whether a photographer is needed and whether events will be co-ordinated with print and electronic media deadlines. Attention to these details will contribute to the district staff's positive impression of the worker and agency.

Where Do You Go from Here?

This question is important if the initial contact has been positive and critical if it has not met the worker's expectations. By knowing in advance how one would like to structure the relationship, the worker lets the congressperson know that he or she wishes to build an ongoing relationship. The worker should be ready to offer options such as a designated liaison person from the social service organization or another meeting with the congressperson in a few months to review items discussed. The worker should know with whom on the district and Washington staffs he or she will interact and when a response to the worker's request can be expected. If the worker concludes the meeting without defining these procedures, he or she may get lost in the shuffle of petitioners, organizations, and meetings that these officials must attend and respond to.

Regardless of the particular techniques used, it is important to maintain sight of the overall goal of establishing a series of progressively important exchanges. In so doing, familiarity and credibility are established that support the worker when he or she must ask the legislator for critical support for funding or legislation.

Can Social Workers Really Have an Impact?

Social workers often rationalize their hesitance to engage elected officials by presuming that elected officials cannot be influenced because they are either ideologues who are fixed in their opinions or opportunists who are willing to sell out their principles for political advantage. However, workers must ask themselves how rooted they are in their own opinions and positions on various issues. Although a person's experiences, background, and attitudes predispose him or her to take stands on certain issues, individuals often change when forced by circumstances or when presented with reasonable, informed, and convincing arguments. When a person is unsure, he or she seeks direction and advice from *trusted* others.

Although legislators may have fixed views on certain gut-level issues such as capital punishment, abortion, or nuclear disarmament, many legislators go through several political metamorphoses during the course of their political career. A critical element in understanding elected officials is to hone in on the particular areas of agreement and disagreement on a given legislative initiative. The extent of social workers' impact is based on how well they are able to provide information, arguments, and compromises that relate to their professional expertise. The congressional district is a familiar environment where workers can and should seek opportunities. Such activities complement the more focused legislative lobbying in Washington. The local lobbyist may be the only voice heard on certain less publicized pieces of legislation; his or her efforts may lessen opposition and point out the relevance of a particular issue to the district.

Thus the worker who wishes to influence legislation must be a person of consequence, credible and consistent in his or her arguments, rich in information resources, and capable of earning legislators' attention and respect by mobilizing and organizing people and events. Although the worker must ensure the legislator that public recognition of his or her achievements will occur, the worker must also clearly state his or her expectations on behalf of people in need.

1. Maryann Mahaffey, "Lobbying and Social Work," *Social Work* 17 (January 1972): 3–11; Virginia W. Smith,

"How Interest Groups Influence Legislators." *Social Work* 24 (May 1979): 234–39; Rino J. Patti and Ronald B. Dear, "Legislative Advocacy: A Path to Social Change," *Social Work* 20 (March 1975): 108–14; Cecilia Kleinkauf, "A Guide to Giving Legislative Testimony," *Social Work* 26 (July 1981): 297–305; James L. Wolk. "Are Social Workers Politically Active?" *Social Work* 26 (July 1981): 283–88; Maryann Mahaffey and John W. Hanks. eds., *Practical Politics: Social Work and Political Responsibility* (Silver Spring. Md.: National Association of Social Workers, 1982).

2. Ronald B. Dear and Rino J. Patti, "Legislative Advocacy: Seven Effective Tactics," *Social Work* 26 (July 1981): 289.

3. James G. March. "An Introduction to the Theory and Measurement of Influence." *American Political Science Review* 49 (June 1955): 431–51.

4. James S. Coleman. "Comment on 'On the Concept of Influence,'" *Public Opinion Quarterly* 27 (Spring 1963): 63–82.

5. David Mayhew. *Congress: The Electoral Connection* (New Haven. Conn.: Yale University Press. 1974). p. 69.

6. Aage R. Clausen. *How Congressmen Decide: A Policy Focus* (New York: St. Martin's Press, 1974). p. 69.

7. Mayhew, *Congress: The Electoral Connection*, p. 49.

8. Patti and Dear. "Legislative Advocacy: One Path to Social Change." p. 112.

9. Louis A. Froman. Jr., *The Congressional Process: Strategies. Rules and Procedures* (Boston: Little. Brown, 1967). pp. 16–27.

10. National Association of Social Workers. "Lobbying for Social Programs." *NASW 1983 Legislative Agenda*. prepared by NASW Legislative Program Staff. April 1983.

11. Kay L. Scholzman and John T. Tierney. "More of the Same: Washington Pressure Activity in a Decade of Change." *The Journal of Politics* 45 (May 1983): 364.

SPONTANEOUS SELF-DISCLOSURES IN PSYCHOTHERAPY

JOSEPH PALOMBO

ABSTRACT: The closeness and intensity of feeling that develops between therapist and patient raises complex issues related to the therapist's neutrality, the transference, the countertransference, the therapeutic alliance, and the very essence of the curative aspects of the relationship. The issue of the relationship of self disclosure and the evolving transference, countertransference complex is discussed. It is suggested that on some occasions, the pressure a therapist feels to spontaneously disclose something intimately personal is an indication that the therapeutic role has become reversed and the therapist is using the process to heal a vulnerability in himself or herself. The patient unconsciously participates in the interest of safeguarding the treatment process. In such instances the self disclosure need not interfere with the evolving transference. It may lead to great spontaneity in the process and to opening areas of affect previously unreachable. Self disclosures cannot be viewed as technical innovations to avoid stalemates in clinical practice. Rather, they are facts of our clinical life, facts that must be explained and understood rather than judged and condemned.

It is a dictum of psychoanalytic therapy that an inverse relationship exists between a patient's knowledge of the personal life or thoughts and feelings of the therapist and the patient's capacity to develop a transference to the therapist (Freud, 1912a, 1912b). Under this rule, self disclosure subverts the process and is technically unacceptable. It represents a countertransference response in the sense that it is derived from the therapist's own psychopathology or technical ineptness.

In this paper, I would like to question the extent to which this dictum is applicable and propose an explanation for some deviations from that stance. The validity of the stance that the therapist's anonymity is essential to the process is not questioned; only its universal applicability is being disputed.

My thesis is a restricted one: self disclosure, *when it occurs spontaneously,* may constitute an attempt by the therapist at self-healing and at working through a previously unresolved issue, and that such divulging can also serve to enhance the therapeutic alliance and to further the therapeutic process. The self disclosure then represents a healthy attempt at becoming more effective and helpful to the patient. While the therapeutic role, under those circumstances, may be said to have become reversed (Searles, 1975), the therapist uses the process to heal a vulnerability and the patient unconsciously participates in the interest of safeguarding his or her treatment. On the other hand, the self disclosure can also represent an attempt on the part of the therapist at responding to a patient's self object needs. The response may confound the patient's transference anticipations and may be seen as a gratification which provides the patient with a "corrective experience." However, it may also have the effect of breaching the patient's defenses against getting in touch with emotionally laden material. The self disclosure then becomes a manifestation of the level of closeness achieved in the therapeutic relationship, and demonstrates to the patient the therapist's readiness to be open to a deepening of the relationship. The patient is brought into touch with an area of affect that had been previously walled off, an aspect of the past which can then be relived with fuller intensity. The development of the transference is facilitated, rather than impeded.

In what follows I shall first present a brief review of the literature on self disclosure. The issues of countertransference and neutrality will be taken up as they bear on the topic. This will be followed by a discussion of the concept of closeness or "intimacy" in the therapeutic process. A case illustration will be given to focus the discussion of the place of self disclosure in the therapeutic process.

BRIEF REVIEW OF THE LITERATURE ON SELF DISCLOSURE

The contents of self disclosures vary enormously. They range from information that must realistically be given to a patient in order to transact the mechanics of the therapy, to highly personal information regarding the therapist's private life, information which under no circumstances would be available to the patient. A distinction also must be made between disclosures that are made *spontaneously* and those that are made *intentionally and consciously* as part of a treatment strategy. In this paper the emphasis is on the first of these. In the literature this distinction is not generally made. No references could be found that dealt with the issue of spontaneous self disclosures.

The literature on the topic is sparse. What references have been uncovered may be divided into the following three categories:

Authors who consider self disclosure acceptable. In certain modalities self disclosure is considered to be part of the therapeutic process. For example, therapists who work with groups of substance abusers, or severe delinquents, often feel that mutual sharing of past experiences is necessary to achieve the therapeutic goal. The similarities in background and experience are felt to facilitate the healing process. The rationale given is that the therapeutic process involves an identification with the therapist which is furthered by the self disclosures.

A few authors encourage divulging personal information in individual treatment (Weiner, 1972); they argue that it provides a corrective emotional experience in a supportive relationship. In those cases, the therapist is less a transference figure and more a real object. The intent is to facilitate an identification with the therapist, rather than to provide insight. Whether this technique achieves its hoped for result is controversial. Some theorists believe that internal changes that come about through this technique cannot be permanent.

Authors who consider self disclosure as, at times, necessary though undesirable. In individual psychotherapy, most authors consider it generally acceptable to disclose to patients the fact that one is going away on vacation and perhaps the location of one's vacation. Some limited data is often shared regarding illnesses when these occur and when patients request information about them. Furthermore, women therapists generally announce the fact of a pregnancy in on-going treatment rather than letting the patient wonder about the therapist's weight gain. These authors generally also consider acceptable announcing to patients major life changes, such as divorces, marriages, or deaths, when these affect the therapist in some deep fashion (Chernin, 1976; Flaherty, 1979; Jourard & Laskow, 1958; Lax, 1969; Little, 1967; Leider, 1984). It is generally felt that the patient is aware of the emotional change in the therapist and is left wondering as to the source of that change. While the patient's fantasies may be useful, the negation of the reality that an actual change has occurred would be detrimental. The stance generally taken is that when such disclosures are made then the therapist is to wait and watch for the impact the revelation has on the process, and to anticipate possible disruptions. The expectation is that these parameters will eventually be discussed and their meaning worked through (Dewald, 1982; Abend, 1982).

Another set of issues arises out of the fact that therapists periodically commit errors which patients soon identify. Greenson (1967) recommends that in those circumstances the therapist acknowledge to the patient the fact of the error but not dwell too much on the motives behind what may have produced it.

A further set of issues is raised in the treatment of very difficult patients. Searles (1959) and Giovacchini (1978), following Winnicott's example, recommend the direct expression of intense feelings of patients. Winnicott (1949) in his famous paper on "Hate in the Countertransference" considers the disclosure of the intensity of the feelings as therapeutic and beneficial to the process. The literature on the difficult patient is generally sympathetic to the therapist who shares intense feelings that arise towards patients (Groves, 1978; Martin, 1975). The rationale appears to be that the direct expression of such feelings is beneficial to both the therapist and the patient and furthers the treatment. However, much controversy exists regarding this stance and many writers take the position that when such intense feelings exist, they are clearly indicative of serious countertransference problems and need to be addressed rather than played out in the relationship with the patient.

Authors who consider self disclosure as clearly untherapeutic. Most of these authors tend to feel that therapists ought not to share countertransference feelings, nor volunteer personal information under any circumstances (Langs, 1973), although differentiations are sometimes made between the type of therapy and the stance therapists ought to take regarding such disclosures. In the more supportive therapies where identificatory processes are expected to occur, the injunctions against self disclosure are much less stringent. However, in insight oriented, as in analytic therapy, these are clearly considered to be breaches of therapeutic etiquette, and represent gross interferences with the development of the transference (Dewald, 1964).

It would appear then that three sets of issues emerge from this review: first, those related to the role of the transference/countertransference configuration; second, those related to the therapist's neutrality in the therapeutic process; third, those related to the appropriate level of closeness or distance between therapist and patient, especially when intense feelings are evoked in the therapist.

The next three sections are devoted to discussing each of these issues, and the effects of each on the unfolding transference.

COUNTERTRANSFERENCE

Self disclosures may be conceptualized as occurring at a number of different junctures within the treatment. The context within which they occur will be determined by the forces at play within the transference countertransference configuration.

In previous publications (Kraft et. al., 1986; Palombo, 1985) counter-transference was redefined to include all of the therapist's responses to the patient. Its role in the process was conceptualized as occurring at three different levels: the concordant, the complementary, and the disjunctive. Each of these levels will be discussed briefly.

Concordant Positions and Responses

Concordant positions are those attitudes which stem from the therapist's attempt to remain in empathic contact with the patient and to understand the patient's psychic reality.

In this context self disclosures may take one of two forms. Within the therapeutic alliance the therapist may reveal data that is public but may not be known to the patient. This may be done in the service of avoiding embarassment, or as an acknowledgement of the patient as an independent center of initiative who has a life outside the transference context. These disclosures are generally significant only to the extent that they might later affect the course of treatment.

A different type of disclosure is the revelation by the therapist of a personal experience that parallels the patient's current or past experience which is evoked by the therapist's identification with the patient. When done intentionally the purpose of such a disclosure might be to foster an identification with the therapist to convey to the patient that the therapist understands how the patient feels. This strategy may be hazardous, and is subject to debate. When, however, the revelation occurs involuntarily, i.e., spontaneously, its effect on the process is less predictable but can at times be quite dramatic.

Example:

A young woman therapist, whose father had recently died, was seeing a 17 year old young woman who had lost her father some years previously. The patient had been unable to discuss the loss of her father, and the therapist felt blocked in her attempts at broaching the subject. In one session the therapist found herself bursting into tears and commenting on how sad it must have felt to have lost a father, since she herself was so grief stricken by the loss of hers. The patient spontaneously joined the therapist in a tearful exchange, and proceeded to reminisce about her beloved father. In this case, the disclosure not only furthered the therapist's mourning process, but it also enabled the patient to experience feelings that had previously been repressed.

Complementary Positions and Responses

By its very nature, the therapeutic process calls for the patient to relive earlier relationships in the transference. The therapist's experience parallels the patient's. The intensity of the transference leads the therapist to feel either as the patient's parents may have felt toward the patient as a child, or to respond as the patient may have wished the parents to respond.

The therapist's complementary positions reflect the childhood milieu which the patient regressively recreates. By refraining from acting on the feelings, the therapist is guided to a benign response and the process is moved along. But, at times, the transference pressures tend to intensify the feelings of vulnerability in the therapist. Either unresolved issues are stirred up, or intense yearnings are aroused that reverberate with the patient's experience. The pressure to share an experience becomes irresistible and a "confession" is made to the patient, who in turn may become reassuring to the therapist. The patient appears then able to move to deeper levels of experiencing and understanding.

Example:

While treating a young woman who was the victim of incest a woman therapist found herself reliving intensely an espisode of sexual abuse by a babysitter in her own childhood. As the therapist struggled with her feelings she found herself distancing from the patient and unable to respond. Suddenly she found herself sharing the episode with the patient and began to weep quietly. The patient, who during her childhood had felt isolated because she could not turn to her depressed mother for support, found herself once more burdened and needing to help the person from whom she expected to receive help and protection. This repetition within the transference/countertransference was not experienced as traumatic, however; rather, it brought home to the patient the extent of her childhood deprivation and the disavowal of the intense feelings she experienced then.

Disjunctive Attitudes and Responses

Disjunctive responses have traditionally been called countertransferences which stem from the therapist's own psychopathology, insensitivity or technical ineptness (Brandchaft & Stolorow, 1984). Such breaches in the process are different from those which occur in the concordant or complementary positions. Their only therapeutic value may be to demonstrate to the patient the therapist's imperfection and humanity.

To summarize then, countertransference, if defined as the totality of the therapist's reactions to the patient during the ongoing therapeutic process, enables us to conceptualize the role of self disclosure less stereotypically than in the past. Whereas a self disclosure may represent a disjunctive response which is detrimental to the process, it may at times represent a concordant or a complementary response which, in the long run, may have a benign or even beneficial effect.

NEUTRALITY IN THE THERAPEUTIC PROCESS

Freud integrated the concept of methodological neutrality (i.e. objectivity) into his metapsychology and his clinical theory (Shapiro, 1984; Poland, 1984; Leider, 1983; Wolf, 1983; Basch, 1983). The transference, of course, arises in an atmosphere of neutral expectancy on the part of the analyst. The absence of interference leads to the patient's displacements and projections. Abstinence is defined as the forebearance from any activity that may be "gratifying." Gratification in this context refers to the satisfaction of conscious or unconscious wishes. It represents taking sides with or against the libidinal or aggressive impulses and would be equivalent to guiding the patient to acting out or to repression.

If transference is redefined, however, as representing the expression of unsatisfied longings for selfobject needs (Kohut, 1971; 1977), then the issue of what constitutes abstinence and gratification must also be reconsidered. Withholding a selfobject function from a patient who is fragmenting would represent cruelty rather than neutrality or therapeutic abstinence. Self disclosures may then be understood on a variety of levels. It would be too simplistic to interpret every instance of a self disclosure as a gratification of the patient's selfobject needs that is untherapeutic. Rather the self disclosure could be understood either as reflective of the therapist's attempt to convey understanding for the patient's experience or a complementary response within the countertransference to the unexpressed longings the patient conveys.

If the concept of therapeutic neutrality is translated into a technique that places a strong prohibition on self disclosure, then the constraints placed on the therapist will preclude spontaneous responses which may be of beneficial effect. If, on the other hand, neutrality is viewed not as avoidance of contaminating the therapeutic process, but as an expression of a desire for openness in the interaction, then it may be maintained that to allow spontaneous exchanges would ultimately further the therapeutic goal of restoring health to the patient.

ON CLOSENESS OR INTIMACY IN THE THERAPEUTIC PROCESS

The difficulty with discussing the concepts of "closeness" and "intimacy" is that these are not metapsychological concepts. (Interestingly, these are concepts to which no reference is made in the index of Freud's work.) Generally, these concepts denote the subjective experiences of the therapist and/or patient and relate to an affective state created in the process, a state usually carrying a positive valence. Ordinarily, value overtones are attached to these concepts, and it is suggested that the optimal stance on the part of the therapist is to be neither too close to nor too distant from the patient.

Concepts that may be related to the concept of closeness are those of "symbiotic unions" or of "mergers." For Mahler (1968), symbiotic unions represent a regressive infantile need state in which a person becomes fused with the object. Such fusions are judged to be pathological. Mergers, on the other hand, although conceptualized differently by different authors, seem to denote either a voluntary or an involuntary loss of "self-boundaries" which may occur in the course of treatment. When, as with empathy, such loss of boundaries is in the service of understanding another person the result is seen as positive.

Phenomenologically it is possible to define closeness or intimacy as "an experience-near" phenomenon (Kohut, 1959). It denotes a level of affective expression by the patient to which the therapist responds with empathic resonance without defending against the feelings nor acting upon them. Self disclosures, whether made intentionally or unintentionally, often have the effect of engendering greater closeness. These place the therapist in the position of opening the door to a level of intimacy that may take the process into totally unchartered regions. The exploration of these regions may often yield important data in areas of the transference which have remained untouched previously.

The patient's wish for closeness while depending on his or her developmental level is replicated in the transference. Those needs may also be defended against, in which case the therapist experiences the feeling of distance. If the transference evokes feelings in the therapist which are too intense to tolerate, then defensive distancing by the therapist may be instituted or at times a self disclosure may occur. The distancing may lead to a disjunction with the patient, while the disclosure becomes an opportunity for self healing on the therapist's part, and for a resumption of the therapeutic process.

To the extent that therapy goes beyond understanding the patient and interpreting the patient's dynamics, it involves the meaningful re-experiencing of aspects of the past. Such re-experiencing can occur only in an atmosphere that permits the expression of feelings at great depth. The establishment of an atmosphere of rigidity within the therapy or by attitudes which prohibit such expressions will be untherapeutic.

Case Illustration

Approximately 20 years ago, when I was still somewhat of a novice in the practice of psychotherapy, I was fortunate to have had as a patient a person who taught me much about how to be a good therapist. The patient was a woman in her early thirties who was married and had two young children. She had been referred because of problems rearing her children. Although she generally felt she was a good mother, she would periodically lose her patience with them, and would become terribly distressed at the thought that she would damage them in the way she had felt damaged by her own mother. She would then get very anxious and depressed, would berate herself and would withdraw into what she described as an abyss of darkness.

This patient was unusual in the demands she made of the relationship with me, demands which were quite different from those made by most patients. From the very beginning she insisted that I not "act" the role of the therapist with her, that I in no way use the fact of my position as a helper to make her feel inferior. She berated me if I used language that made her feel that I was displaying my superior understanding to the detriment of her sense of self esteem. She chided me if I postured and used my knowledge to make comments or intrepretations that were stereotypic.

I should make it clear that these injunctions were not made by this patient as a set of demands that were conditional to her remaining in treatment, but rather these arose out of specific interactions we had with each other. Whenever she sensed some unnaturalness in my voice, whenever she felt that I was doing something which she felt was at her expense, she would call me to task and request that I mend my ways. Since I could always see what she was getting at, I did not feel injured or defensive but, indeed, strove to modify my approach to help her feel comfortable in what was evidently an extremely painful situation for her. I did not feel manipulated by her, but rather, felt that she was trying to help me be a better helper to her.

Matters did not rest there, however, but went much further, for, in addition, she had become so sensitive to the nuances of my facial expression and to my moods that she could always tell when I drifted off from listening to her or when I was preoccupied or distracted. She would interrupt herself at such moments to ask where I had gone and what I was thinking about. While at first I would be discomforted by such requests and hesitate to share the flow of my own associations, I soon learned that if indeed I could capture my reveries sufficiently to articulate them and share them with her then invariably these would turn out to be connected to feelings she was having or was about to express. At times when my own thoughts drifted too far from our dialogue or when I was distracted by preoccupations of my own, I would then confess to her that I was indeed thinking of something that had little to do with her and had been interrupted in my being with her. She would accept my statement implicitly trusting me to be honest with her and would continue with her own associations.

As can be imagined, this patient came to know me very well. I was, of course, well aware at the time of the injunctions against self disclosure and the possible dangers to an unfolding transference. But I felt that I had no choice but to follow this patient's lead if she were to be helped at all. The problems I often confronted were not whether to share what I thought but rather how much to share of my personal life with her. For often, the flow of my associations would lead me to memories of my childhood, experiences in my personal life, and at times intensely personal and private matters that I would share with no one except perhaps my analyst. On the whole, however, with much tact, I managed to keep her knowledge of my very private life to a minimum. But, obviously, she came to know much about me that casual acquaintances and personal friends knew.

The intensity of the closeness that developed is best exemplified by the following statement which she brought to a session in the third year of her treatment:

Thursday Night

Tremendous anxiety—began to build up during movie—maybe anxiety has to do with people's caring about one another. Couldn't sleep. Began to think about dependency and recalled your comment about me expecting you to sense my feelings even though they are not outwardly manifested.

Began to reflect on my never having cried in therapy. Crying is a revelation of vulnerability—a sharing of vulnerability—a letting up of the repression of wishes and unmet needs. Alone, it's a release of feelings, a mechanism to reduce pressure. With another person, it's more than that. In order to feel safe in revealing vulnerability and letting deeply felt needs and the pain that surrounds them become conscious and shared, you must feel that the other person can be trusted to care about you. (Comfort you?)

If I were to cry here—to uncap those feelings and let them become fully conscious, I would have no way to deal with your response. You would respond in one of two ways, and I couldn't manage either of them. Your response would either be empathic, but maintaining "therapeutic distance," or actively comforting, which would include physical contact. The first I would experience as rejecting, as lacking in caring (and as an expression of your need to maintain a particular stance at my expense). The second would also be impossible. The physical comforting, the reaching out and touching, would be so profoundly moving and painful that it would uncork all those years of unmet needs and wishes and I'd be flooded by those feelings.

I think this is a re-creation of the "thing" with my mother. (Also the fantasy of being held and comforted and protected by mother.) There are the deeply felt needs to be valued, cared for, and comforted. And there is my mother—who can't fulfill any of them. (She needs to maintain a particular stance at my expense.) The needs grow as they remain unmet. I make accomodations—I repress them, I deny them, I give up the expectation they'll ever be met, I meet my own needs. But they're still there, and the excruciating pain that surrounds them is still there. The comforting would be a trigger for those old needs and wishes, and the feelings that surround them.

You are either the rejecting mother, or the trigger for feelings that I've never been able to deal with, and have spent my whole life avoiding.

The specific self disclosure on which I wish to focus is the following: Throughout the time of her treatment, I had been in analysis, a fact which she had come to know by inference rather than by my telling her directly. One day in the midst of a session, she stopped herself and looked at me and said she had been wondering about something, as she had noticed a recent change in me that was qualitatively different from any other she had noticed before. She began to wonder aloud and said that the only way she could understand what was going on was that it had little to do with my relationship to her and she thought that perhaps what was on my mind may be the fact that I either had terminated or was about to terminate my analysis. I was momentarily startled by her comments but did not respond. Then she asked me either to confirm or deny it. Indeed, she was quite correct. Two weeks before my analyst and I had agreed on a termination date, a fact which I had shared with no one except my wife. I felt somewhat embarrassed that she could have read my feelings so accurately but felt also, once more, on familiar grounds with her. The dilemma I confronted was that to refuse to answer would have embarrassed or humiliated her. I would create a rupture between us which would have been damaging but probably not irreparable. Yet, to answer her would have been to reveal something intimately personal. Whether it was correct or not I did answer her and with this the work together went on.

DISCUSSION

A number of issues are raised by this case which touch on the topics discussed so far. First, it may be that the level of self disclosure was related to my inexperience as a therapist. Professional maturity and the greater self-discipline that comes with it might have led to a different stance on my part, without affecting the course of the therapy. This suggests a developmental line for each therapist in which the discretion used in, and the forebearance from self-disclosure are related to one's level of experience.[1] However. this alone cannot explain all that occurred.

Second, the nature of the transference/countertransference configuration could be understood as one in which an archaic merger was sought by the patient, the therapist became the longed for selfobject. The intense need for mirroring was such that any hint of a barrier to the merger was experienced by the patient as distancing. When she thought that I was not in absolute synchrony with what she experienced. then she would correct me. and lead me back into the merger. Those times when I was unable to be attentive and could acknowledge that fact confirmed for her that the breaches she experienced were of my doing. and not hers. My complying with her requests to share what I was thinking permitted an openness in the process which she experienced as reassuring. She was then able to continue the exploration of her feelings rather than feel restrained by my inhibitions.

As to her speculations regarding the termination of my analysis, I confronted the dilemma as to whether to honor the request, or risk a breach by not responding. On the one hand, she touched a vulnerability in me regarding an event toward which I had numerous complex feelings. I was still working through the wisdom of the decision that had been made. On the other hand, my concern to preserve the ambience that had been created was also urgent. To not answer may have threatened that aura, and may have led to irreparable damage. To answer, meant a further confrontation, on my part, with the impending loss of my analyst, and also to face the joy and sorrow associated with the successful completion of a major life task. It also meant my sharing, implicitly, feelings with her which were intensely personal. My decision affirmed my belief that the preservation of the ambience was more important than the risk of self-exposure, and my commitment to allowing the patient to experience the requisite closeness in the hope that it would lead her to some eventual working through of her deficits.

The suggested reconceptualization of countertransference can make a significant contribution to understanding this aspect of the therapeutic process. When feelings of such startling intensity are stirred within the therapist that the very limits of his or her capacities for a concordant response are reached, then the bounds of what is usually considered technically appropriate may be overstepped. It is as though the therapist leaves the safe confines of traditional technique and of habitual responses and jumps into the turbulant reality of the patient's life. The compulsion to share some fact or event with the patient comes as an unanticipated and surprising revelation to both the therapist and the patient.

It is possible to conceive of the interaction at such moments as representing the dramatic unfolding and convergence of the flaws of the personalities of both patient and therapist. From such a perspective, the inevitability of a clash was present from the day of the first encounter. Such collisions can neither be predicted nor avoided. The demand implicitly made of the therapist is that personal limitations or vulnerabilities be transcended in the service of assisting the patient. The therapist must heal himself or herself in order to heal the patient. The encounter then becomes one in which growth and healing can occur in both patient and therapist. The self disclosure not only does not interfere with the developing transference but rather sets the stage for the possibility of its deepening.

The optimal distance or closeness to be maintained between therapist and patient become. therefore, a function of the therapeutic need for the patient to re-experience the past in all of its fullness (Gitelson. 1952; Greenacre. 1966; Greenson, 1960; Gunther. 1976; Schamess. 1981). Clearly, self disclosure is not to be elevated to the position of a technique. Neither is it, however, to be condemned out of hand as invariably destructive. Refraining from a disclosure can be motivated by defenses against the wish for, or fear of, closeness, just as self disclosure can hide the wish for merger with a patient. Closeness is not necessarily achieved through disclosures on the therapist's part, but rather through the intimacy that develops from the experience of two people coming to share deeply in the unfolding drama of a person's life.

Self disclosures when they occur spontaneously must therefore be seen as part of the context in which an intense interactive process gives rise to a particular type of response. The response is reflective of an intense wish for closeness initiated either by the patient or the therapist. The therapist's capacity to cope with that level of closeness is then tested. If not overwhelmed by that request, the work with the patient can continue. Self disclosure from this perspective goes beyond a position of sharing a reality or an experience with the patient to one of becoming an intervention. While, in part, the intervention is on behalf of the therapist, it must also be seen as an overture to the patient to continue to allow the process to deepen and to allow for the full immersion into the experiences of the past.

CONCLUSION

Psychoanalysis began in an ideological atmosphere in which the methods of the physical sciences were considered to be the most reliable avenues for leading us to an understanding of the universe. In that context, countertransference was seen as an impediment to the treatment process. and as an interference to the uncontaminated observation of the processes within the patient. The related concept of neutrality was, in part. shaped by that ideology and by the social context in which Freud lived.

It has been necessary for us to reformulate the concepts of countertransference and of neutrality in order to take into account elements of the process which have come into creative focus as our knowledge has increased. The nature of the therapeutic process itself is now conceptualized as an interactional one in which therapist and patient mutually influence and shape one another's responses. Such a view of the process necessitates the inclusion of a conceptualization of what, in lay terms, has been called "closeness and intimacy."

The need for closeness to patients and the disclosure of personal information were previously interpreted as stemming from countertransference, and as interfering with the developing transference. However, the closeness we achieve with our patients in the clinical setting is not that of scientists peering through a microscope to examine specimens. Neither is it equivalent to the social interactions of everyday life. It is of a different order. It is closeness engendered by the regard for others, by being touched and moved by the lives of those whom we seek to help. When we allow ourselves to experience the full measure of those feelings and can acknowledge that we are being privileged to participate in another person's revelation of their inner being, and if we respond within the limits of our humanity, then we can admit that we too come to benefit from the encounter. Such a stance does not hinder, but, rather, furthers the therapeutic process.

REFERENCES

Abend, S. M. (1982). Serious illness in the analyst: Countertransference considerations. *Journal of the American Psychoanalytic Association, 30*, 365–380.

Basch, M.F. (1983). Affect and the analyst. *Psychoanalytic Inquiry, 3*(1), 691–704.

Brandchaft, B., & Stolorow (1984). A current perspective on difficult patients. In P.E. Stepansky & A. Goldberg, (Eds.). *Kohut's Legacy.* (pp. 93–116) The Analytic Press.

Chernin, P. (1976). Illness in a therapist-loss of omnipotence. *Archives Gen. Psychiatry, 33,* 1327–1328.

Dewald, P. (1964). *Psychotherapy—a dynamic approach.* New York: Basic Books.

Dewald, P. (1982). Serious illness in the analyst: Transference, countertransference, and reality responses. *Journal of the American Psychoanalytic Association, 30*, 347–364.

Flaherty, J. A. (1979). Self-Disclosure in therapy: Marriage of the therapist. *American Journal of Psychotherapy, 33*(3), 442–452.

Freud, S. (1912a, 1962). *Recommendations to physicians practising psycho-analysis. (Standard Editors).* 12:111–120.

Freud, S. (1912b, 1962). *The dynamics of the transference. (Standard Edition).* 12:97–109.

Giovacchini, P.L. (1978). The psycholanalytic treatment of the alienated patient. In J.F. Masterson (Ed.), *New perspectives on psychotherapy of the borderline adult.* (pp. 1–19) New York: Brunner/Mazel.

Gitelson, M. (1952). The emotional position of the analyst in the psychoanalytic situation. In: *Psychoanalysis, science and profession.* New York: International Universities Press.

Greenacre, P. (1966). Problems of overidealization of the analyst and of analysis: Their manifestation in the transference countertransference relationship. In: *Emotional Growth.* (pp. 743–761) New York: International Universities Press.

Greenson, R. R. (1960). Empathy and its vicissitudes. *International Journal Psycho-Analysis, 41*:418–424.

Greenson, R. R. (1967). *The technique & practice of psychoanalysis.* (Vol. 1.) New York: International Universities Press.

Groves, J. E. (1978). Taking care of the hateful patient. *The New England Journal of Medicine, 4*, 576–681.

Gunther, M.S. (1976). The endangered self: A contribution to the understanding of narcissistic determinants of countertransference. *The Annual of Psychoanalysis, 4*, 201–224.

Jourard, S. M., & Lasakow, P. (1958). Some factors in self-disclosure. *Journal of Abnormal Psychology, 51*, 91–103.

Kohut, H. (1959). Introspection, empathy and psychoanalysis. *Journal of the American Psychoanalytic Association, 7*, 459–507.

Kohut, H. (1971). *The analysis of the self.* New York: International Universities Press.

Kohut, H. (1977). *The restoration of the self.* New York: International Universities Press.

Kraft, A. D., Palombo, J., Mitchell, D. L., Woods, P. K., Schmidt, A. W. & Tucker, N. G. (1986). Some theoretical considerations on confidential adoption part IV: Countertransference. *Child & Adolescent Social Work Journal.*

Langs, R. (1973). *The technique of psychoanalytic psychotherapy* (Vols. I & II.). New York: Mason Aronson, Inc.

Lax, R. F. (1969). Some considerations about transference & countertransference manifestations evoked by the analyst's pregnancy. *International Journal of Psycho-analysis, 50,* 363–371.

Leider, R. J., (1983). Analytic neutrality—a historical review, *Psychoanalytic Inquiry, 3,* 665–674.

Leider, R. J., (1984). The neutrality of the analyst in the analytic situation, *Journal American Psychoanalytic Association, 32,* 573–586.

Little, R. B. (1967). Transference, countertransference & survival reactions following an analyst's heart attack. *Psychoanalytic Forum, 2,* 107–126.

Mahler, M. S. (1968). *On human symbiosis and the vicissitudes of individuals.* New York: International Universities Press.

Martin, P. A. (1975). The obnoxious patient. In P. L. Giovacchini, (Ed.). *Tactics & techniques in psychoanalytic therapy, Vol. 2: Countertransference.* (pp. 96–204). New York: Jason Aronson.

Palombo, J. (1985). Selfpsychology and countertransference in the treatment of children. *Child and Adolescent Social Work Journal, 2,* 36–48.

Poland, W. S. (1984). On the analyst's neutrality, *Journal of the American Psychoanalytic Association, 32,* 283–300.

Schamess, G. (1981). Boundary issues in countertransference: A developmental perspective. *Clinical Social Work Journal, 9,* 244–257.

Searles, H. (1975). The Patient as therapist to his analyst. In P. Giovancchini, (Ed.) *Tactics & techniques in psychoanalytic therapy, Vol. II: Countertransference.* New York: Jason Aronson.

Searles, H. (1959). Oedipal love in the countertransference. In *Collected papers on schizophrenia and other subjects* New York: International Universities Press 1965.

Shapiro, T. (1984). On neutrality. *Journal of the American Psychoanalytic Association, 32,* 269–383.

Weiner, M. F. (1972). Self-exposure by the therapist as a therapeutic technique. *American Journal of Psychotherapy, 26*, 42–56.

Winnicott, D. W. (1949). Hate in the countertransference. *International Journal of Psych-Analaysis, 30*, 69–74.

Wolf, E. S. (1983). Aspects of neutrality. *Psychoanalytic Inquiry, 3*, 675–690.

PUBLISH OR PRACTICE: WHY NOT BOTH?
JANICE M. PROCHASKA

Publishing Practitioners

Over the past five years, the social work field has aggressively urged practitioners to publish. Editorial boards have asked that social workers improve journals and advance the profession by analyzing practices and social problems and by writing and submitting articles.[1] Editors have given workshops at professional meetings to educate practitioners on the publishing process.[2] Schools of social work have added classes that help clinical students define empirically based practice and enable them to evaluate and write papers on their interventions.[3] Agencies have begun to encourage staff to publish new programs and services that are being developed as a response to their communities' changing needs.

In spite of such encouragement, practitioners have been slow to respond. Traditionally, social work faculty members are more likely than any other type of social workers to publish articles. Although they constitute no more than 2 or 3 percent of all social workers, social work faculty members account for 44 percent of the articles published in social work journals.[4] Of course, faculty value publishing highly, in part, because of career pressures. They also have flexible time, training in research, the help of a mentor, and supportive staff to help them.

Not only do practitioners lack many of the above resources, they typically believe that only reports on empirical research are being sought by the journals. A recent study on research publications, however, showed that between 1974 and 1980 only 19.1 percent of the 1,033 articles published in general social work journals were based on empirical research.[5] The present article is designed to help practitioners increase their chances of being published.

Benefits and Costs

Practitioners have implicit knowledge; writing can help make that knowledge explicit. Writing as an aid to thinking is not often appreciated. Practitioners who write not only order their thoughts, but also the very act of writing can help them clarify their thinking and conceptualize their work, since writing completes the communication process. Publishing also allows practitioners to take on a new challenge, establish areas of expertise, bring visibility to themselves and to their agencies, contribute to the field, and serve as role models to their students and colleagues. The more one writes, the easier it becomes. Ease in writing, in turn, helps practitioners write better contracts and grant proposals. More personally, publishing can make practitioners proud, enhance their self-esteem, and allow them to leave something after they are gone. The reinforcements from writing are often delayed, however, as the result of publishing lags. But reinforcements can be long lasting—from continued requests for reprints and speaking engagements to new contacts. The costs of time, the hurt on rejection, an additional responsibility, the patience to revise and revise need to be considered. Indeed, it is often painful to get started—to overcome the anxiety—and then to cope with the preoccupation with the writing that needs to be done.

Getting Started

To be successful, practitioners first need to select a topic that (1) they know and care a lot about and (2) at least one editor believes is of current interest to a large number of subscribers. To find the right topic, it is important to focus on strengths. Practitioners need to look at their specific skills and then expand on them to apply them to a broader market. For example, if one of their strengths is sexual abuse treatment in an agency, practitioners might consider pursuing this one step further by writing about how to develop a sexual abuse treatment program in a nonprofit organization. The practitioner should also be enthusiastic about the topic selected.

Enthusiasm is more likely to generate the effort required to commit the topic to ink and to inspire the writer to be creative about the topic.[6] Finally, information gaps should be sought. It is important to keep up with what topics are in the journals, to do a computer search through a university library, and to send letters of inquiry to editors on the topic being considered.

Tips on Writing

The well-written paper has two essential ingredients: organization and appropriate language within that organization. Editors repeatedly advise authors to write simply and clearly and to organize their articles by following an outline. Definitive aids are Strunk and White's book, *The Elements of Style*[7] and Robert Day's article and book on writing scientific papers.[8] Articles should describe and analyze the practice situation, review the literature, discuss the theories or frame of reference useful for assessment and intervention, evaluate the interventions, and indicate the relevance of the experience in other situations.

To get the writing done, authors find it helpful to set aside a minimum of two hours at a time in a writing environment to which they can regularly return. A weekly appointed writing time gives structure and tempo to the work. Breaking down the work into short sections gives writers achievable goals. For practitioners to obtain uninterrupted time, the major part of their writing may have to be done at home, provided they have the support of their families and quiet and freedom from interruptions.

Targeting the Journal

Many manuscripts are rejected because authors have written the manuscripts with no particular audience or journal in mind. To avoid rejections, practitioners can use specific criteria to select a target journal before writing the manuscript. The audience, format, acceptance rate, and referee status are four important criteria to consider.[9] An invaluable resource is *An Author's Guide to Social Work Journals*,[10] which provides information on over sixty social work journals. Reading the masthead statement, "Instructions to Authors," and the table of contents in current issues of suitable journals will aid authors in finding the right journal for their articles.

Because every journal has a slightly different target audience, the authors should carefully identify their intended readership—medical social workers, administrators, family therapists, or whatever. Some journals focus more on scientific for-

mat and topics; others publish more how-to clinical application articles. For example, the journals *Family Relations* and *Journal of Marriage and the Family* have the same affiliation, but the former is practice oriented and the latter is research oriented. Specialty and new journals, such as *Administration in Social Work* and *Journal of Divorce*, have more favorable acceptance rates (25 and 35 percent) than general journals like *Social Work* (16 percent).

Journals are refereed or nonrefereed. A refereed journal is one that usually uses three experts to review the manuscript. Here the major advantage is that each manuscript is reviewed by more than one person, but this is a slower review and decision process. Refereed journals usually have higher status and therefore lower acceptance rates. The editor of a nonrefereed journal usually makes the decision to accept or reject. Here, the editor is better able to help an author with the further development of a topic because there is not the need to anticipate reviewers' viewpoints. This can be important to a beginning practitioner-author.

The Review Process

A paper is typically judged on the following criteria: style and readability; relevance to social work practice; evidence of originality; scholarship and expertise in social work theory and practice; and objectivity.[11] Steven Kerr, James Tolliver, and Doretta Petree found several manuscript characteristics to be important determinants of reviewer rejection. Foremost among these were (1) results that were not statistically significant, (2) studies that replicated other studies, (3) manuscripts that lacked new data, (4) articles on the same topic as other recent articles in the journal, and (5) articles that were not within the mainstream of the discipline.[12] Michael J. Mahoney, Alan E. Kazdin, and Martin Kenigsberg found that positive data were much better received than negative, that a low tolerance for ambiguity of outcome existed, and that there was a very low degree of consensus among journal reviewers.[13]

This last point is important to keep in mind. Editors or referees, on the one hand, may reject the paper because it is weak, because they are imposing inappropriately stringent standards, because they are not sufficiently familiar with the field to appreciate the significance of the work, because they have not studied the paper closely, or because the paper contradicts one of their pet theories. On the other hand, editors or referees may accept the paper because it is genuinely good, because they are relatively lenient, because their own work is favorably cited in the paper, because they have not devoted enough attention to the paper to discover its fatal flaws, or because the paper supports one of their pet theories.[14]

A fascinating study that further confirms the low degree of consensus among journal reviewers was that of Douglas P. Peters and Stephen J. Ceci.[15] Twelve previously published articles from twelve journals with high rejection rates (80 percent) were resubmitted to the journals that had originally refereed and published them eighteen to thirty-two months earlier. Fictitious names and institutions were substituted for the originals, and the articles' titles were changed. Only three journals detected the resubmissions—eight of the other nine articles were rejected. The grounds for rejection in several cases were described as "serious methodological flaws"—this from the same journals that had published the articles earlier. Because of all the variables involved, it is important to take acceptance and rejection somewhat philosophically.

Acceptance and Rejection

Four basic categories are typically used by the editor or referee in making recommendations on articles submitted for publication in a journal. These categories are (1) accept without question; (2) accept with minor revisions indicated; (3) reject, but request major revisions and resubmission; and (4) reject. Only about 5 percent of manuscripts are accepted as submitted, yet such acceptance tends to be the expectation, especially by new authors. When their expectations are not met, some new authors give up. Their ego investment may be too high; the risk of exposing one's thoughts in writing to others is seen as being met with "failure." The result is to retreat behind the clinician's closed door. Handling rejection includes developing a thick skin, having a support system to help with revision and resubmission, and being persistent. Rejection of an article is first of all a statement about the reviewer—not a rejection of the author. An author would be wise to submit work to at least three journals before setting the manuscript aside.

The vast majority of authors will receive either a reject with major revisions and resubmit or a plain reject statement. When authors receive a revision and resubmit letter, they should carefully examine it and the accompanying reviewers' comments. One of several things is likely to happen. One, the reviewers are right and the author should follow their directions and rewrite the manuscript accordingly. Two, the reviewers are correct on some points, but some of their criticisms are invalid. In this case, authors should incorporate all the acceptable suggested changes and then when resubmitting send a cover letter with a point by point disposition of the reviewers' other comments. Three, it is possible that one or both reviewers and the editor seriously misread or misunderstood the manuscript and their criticisms are not valid. The first option is to point out the error; the second is to submit the manuscript to another journal and hope that it will be judged more fairly by its reviewers. Revision and resubmission take time and work but are usually worth the effort.

Agency Support

Because practitioners need special support to begin publishing, it is vital that agencies provide some backup. For example, typing and copying services could be made available to staff. Costs of a library computer search could be paid for, and time could be allowed for training in publishing or for peers to work together on a manuscript. Working with an experienced colleague is one of the best ways to get started writing. Forming a study support group would be another helpful method.

A Sharing Experience

The author has attempted to shatter stereotypes by providing new information and encouraging and inspiring more practitioners to take up a pen, so that the field of social work can continue to advance. Practitioners, as well as faculty, need to share their practice experiences and clinical insights through published works.

1. Anne Minahan, "Reaching and Writing to Improve Practice," *Social Work* 25 (January 1980): 3–8.

2. Jacqueline Marx Atkins, "Publishing in Professional Journals" (Workshop given at Family Service America and National Association of Social Workers Conferences, 1979 and 1983).

3. Deborah H. Siegel, "Defining Empirically Based Practice," *Social Work* 29 (July–August 1984): 325–31.

4. Stuart A. Kirk and Aaron Rosenblat, "The Contribution of Women Faculty to Social Work Journals," *Social Work* 29 (January–February 1984): 68.

5. Tony Tripodi, "Trends in Research Publication: A Study of Social Work Journals from 1956 to 1980," *Social Work* 29 (July–August 1984): 353–59.

6. Roger Neuglbauer, "To Burn Out or to Churn Out: How to Experience Stimulation Through Writing," *Child Care Information Exchange* (January 1982): 5–12.

7. William Strunk, Jr., and E.B. White, *The Elements of Style*, 3rd Ed. (New York: Macmillan, 1979).

8. Robert A. Day, "How to Write a Scientific Paper," *American Society for Microbiology* 41 (July 1975): 486–94

194

and *How to Write and Publish a Scientific Paper* (Philadelphia: Institute for Scientific Information, 1979).

9. Suzanne Hall Johnson, "Selecting a Journal for Your Manuscript, *Nursing and Health Care* 3 (May 1982): 258–63.

10. Henry N. Mendelsohn, *An Author's Guide to Social Work Journals* (Silver Spring. Md.: National Association of Social Workers, 1983).

11. Evaluation guidelines for reviewers of *Social Casework* manuscripts (Milwaukee: Family Service America).

12. Steven Kerr, James Tolliver, and Doretta Petree, "Manuscript Characteristics Which Influence Acceptance for Management and Social Science Journals," *Academy of Management Journal* 20 (March 1977): 132–41.

13. Michael J. Mahoney, Alan E. Kazdin, and Martin Kenigsberg, "Getting Published," *Cognitive Therapy and Research* 2 (January 1978): 69–70.

14. Andrew M. Colman, "Editorial Role in Author-Referee Disagreements," *Bulletin of the British Psychological Society* 32 (October 1979): 390–91.

15. Douglas P. Peters and Stephen J. Ceci, "Peer-Review Practices of Psychological Journals: The Fate of Published Articles, Submitted Again," *The Behavioral and Brain Sciences* 5 (June 1982): 187–255.

INFORMED CONSENT IN SOCIAL WORK
FREDRIC G. REAMER

THE EMERGENCE OF widespread concern recently about client rights has had a marked effect on contemporary social work practice. Discussions concerning client rights to confidentiality, self-determination, and privileged communication, for example, are commonplace in part because of the increased sensitivity of social workers to the general subject of professional ethics, and in part because of the concern of practitioners about their own liability. The noteworthy growth of social work literature since the mid-1970s on the subjects of professional ethics and client rights is evidence of this phenomenon.[1]

A central theme in discussions of client rights is the obligation of practitioners continually to inform clients about plans to intervene in their lives, and to obtain client consent to intervention. Consistent with the longstanding commitment of the social work profession to the value of self-determination, social workers traditionally have respected the right of clients to participate fully in efforts to assist the clients.[2]

Despite social worker commitment to and discussion of the general concept of self-determination, social workers through the literature have provided little examination of the manner in which client consent is obtained in practice, of circumstances when consent is required, and of permissible exceptions to client consent.[3] In this article, the historical and legal background of the concept of informed consent is described, informed consent standards are outlined, and exceptions to informed consent are detailed. The protection of client rights through informed consent and avoidance of liability for malpractice and negligence are discussed, as are the implications of informed consent for social work practice.

HISTORICAL AND LEGAL BACKGROUND

How much information should clients have about their circumstances, prognoses, and prospective treatment? Do social workers have the right to withhold information from certain clients? If so, under what circumstances? Who should be authorized to consent for clients who are unable to make their own informed decisions? Professionals, principally those in the health care field, have debated these and other issues for decades. The historical roots of informed consent have been traced to Plato, who in *The Laws* compared the Greek slave-physician who gave orders "in the brusque fashion of a dictator" with the free physician who "takes the patient and his family into confidence ... [and] does not give prescriptions until he has won the patient's support."[4] The medieval French surgeon, Henri de Mondeville, also stressed the importance of obtaining patient consent and confidence, although he also urged his colleagues to "compel the obedience of his patients" by selectively slanting information provided to them.[5]

By the late eighteenth century, European and American physicians and scientists, such as Condorcet, Mirabeau, Cabanis, Volney, Chaussier, Virey, Rush, Gregory, and Young, had begun to develop a tradition that encouraged professionals to share information and decision making with their clients.[6] The first major legal ruling in the United States on informed consent is found in the 1914 landmark case of *Schloendorff v. Society of New York Hospital*, in which Justice Cardozo set forth his oft-cited opinion concerning an individual's right to self-determination: "Every human being of adult years and sound mind has a right to determine what shall be done with his own body."[7] To do otherwise, Cardozo argued, is to commit an assault upon the person. Revelations following World War II of medical experiments performed without consent of the subjects and following the civil rights movements of the 1960s helped form the foundation for current informed consent legislation and guidelines.[8] The red-letter event during this era was the 1957 case of *Salgo v. Leland Stanford Jr. University Board of Trustees*, in which the phrase *informed consent* was introduced. The plaintiff in this case, who became a paraplegic following a diagnostic procedure for a circulatory disturbance, alleged that his physician failed to disclose properly ahead of time pertinent information regarding risks associated with the treatment.[9]

Although the concept of informed consent has its origin in medicine and health care, recently it has been applied legislatively, judicially, and administratively to a wide range of other client groups. Social workers regularly provide services to these client groups and social workers often must serve as advocates for the mentally ill and retarded, minors, medical patients, prisoners, and research subjects. In agencies that provide mental health services, for example, social workers must be familiar with consent requirements related to voluntary and involuntary commitment and the rights of institutionalized and outpatient clients regarding the use of psychotropic drugs, restraints, aversive treatment measures, isolation, sterilization, and psychosurgery. What do local statutes require for an individual to be committed to a psychiatric facility against his or her wishes? To what extent does a facility's client bill of rights require that clients be consulted about treatment decisions?[10]

Social workers in agencies that serve minors must keep pace with rapidly changing standards regarding consent of minors. For example, consent issues arise related to abortion counseling, contraception, treatment of sexually transmitted diseases, mental health services, treatment for substance abuse, and services for children in foster care. Traditionally, minors have not been considered capable of giving consent or entering into contracts; the consent of parents or someone standing in loco parentis typically has been required in other than genuine emergencies.[11] Especially since the 1970s, however, a number of states have begun to recognize the concepts of "mature" or "emancipated" minors, which imply that certain minors in fact are capable of providing their own consent in their relationships with professionals. Mature minors are those who are

"judicially recognized as possessing sufficient understanding and appreciation of the
nature and consequences of treatment despite their chronological age."[12] Emancipated minors, on the other hand, are
those who have obtained the legal capacity
of an adult because they are self-support-
ing, living on their own, married, or in the
armed forces.[13]

States vary considerably in the extent
to which they grant minors autonomy and
the right to consent. For example, with respect to abortion services, substance abuse
treatment, dispensing contraceptives, and
treatment of sexually transmitted diseases,
some states permit professionals to treat
minors without obtaining parental consent;
some require that parents be notified, that
their consent be obtained, or both; and
some merely permit agency staff to notify
parents, obtain their consent, or both.[14]
States also differ in the extent to which
parental consent is required to place a child
in an inpatient or outpatient mental health
program. Missouri and Oregon, for example,
require parental consent for commitment of
a minor, while California and Montana permit minors who meet certain conditions to
provide their own consent.[15]

Consent issues related to the care of
medical patients have received considerable
attention recently, especially regarding the
care of hospital patients and their right to be
informed, refuse treatment on religious
grounds, consent to experimental treatment, participate in research, and donate
organs. Once again, states vary considerably in the amount of autonomy they grant
patients and the procedures health care staff
are expected to follow when patients fail to
provide consent or request controversial
treatment. For instance, in the well-known
Quinlan case, the Supreme Court of New
Jersey required hospital staff to consult with
a hospital ethics committee, rather than
a court of law, concerning the decision to
remove extraordinary treatment. However,
in *Superintendent of Belchertown v.
Saikewicz*, the Massachusetts Supreme
Judicial Court rejected the New Jersey approach, with its reliance on administrative
procedures, in favor of court approval of
decisions concerning life-prolonging care of
incompetent patients.[16]

Debate concerning client consent to participate in research also has received much attention. Discussion has been especially
vigorous with respect to clients whose competence to consent is considered questionable, or who are considered especially
vulnerable. Particular attention has been
paid to the right of the mentally ill, elderly,
minors, and prisoners to consent to participate in research related to drugs, treat-

ment techniques, and program evaluation.[17]

OBTAINING VALID CONSENT

Although states and local jurisdictions
differ in their interpretation and application
of informed consent standards, there is
general consensus about what constitutes
valid consent by clients, in light of prevailing legislation and case law. In general, for
consent to be considered valid, six standards must be met: (1) an absence of coercion and undue influence must exist, (2)
clients must be capable of providing consent, (3) clients must consent to specific
procedures, (4) the forms of consent must
be valid, (5) clients must have the right to
refuse or withdraw consent, and (6) client
decisions must be based on adequate information.[18]

Absence of Coercion and Undue Influence

Social workers frequently maintain some
degree of control over the lives of their
clients. Access to services, money, time,
and attention are but a few of the resources
social workers control. It is especially important that social workers not take advantage of their positions of authority to coerce
a client's consent, subtly or otherwise.[19]
Practitioners who want clients to agree to
enter or terminate a program, release information to third parties, or take medication,
for example, need to be sensitive to the fact
that clients may be particularly susceptible
to influence, thus jeopardizing the validity
of their consent.

The inappropriate use of coercion is illustrated in the case of *Reif v. Weinberger*,
in which a judge in the District of Columbia ruled that the expenditure of federal
funds should be enjoined in some sterilization cases because of the use of coercion.
The evidence in this case indicated that
a number of public aid clients had been
coerced into agreeing to sterilization procedures; they had been told that a portion
of their welfare benefits would be withheld
unless they agreed to the proposed procedures.[20]

Capacity to Give Consent

Although there is widespread agreement
among professionals that only competent
clients are capable of giving informed consent, there is much less consensus about
the determination of competence. According to Applebaum and Roth, practitioners
must consider the ability of the client to
make choices, comprehend factual issues,
manipulate information rationally, and ap-

preciate his or her current circumstances.[21]
Olin and Olin argue for a single standard,
the ability to retain information, whereas
Owens emphasizes one's ability to "test
reality."[22] In contrast, the President's Commission for the Study of Ethical Problems
in Medicine and Biomedical and Behavioral
Research stated in its 1982 report that competency is determined by client possession
of a set of values and goals, the ability to
communicate and understand information,
and the ability to reason and deliberate.[23]

Despite the unsettled debate about determining competence, practitioners seem to
agree that incompetence should not be
presumed absolutely for any particular
client group, such as children, the mentally ill, or mentally retarded, except for those
who are unconscious. Rather, some client
categories should be considered to have
a greater probability of incapacity—perhaps
children or profoundly retarded adults.
Assessments of client capacity should at
least consist of measures such as a mental
status exam (accounting for one's orientation to person, place, time, situation, mood
and affect, content of thought and perception); ability to comprehend abstract ideas
and make reasoned judgments; history of
mental illness that might affect current
judgment; and the client's recent and remote memory.[24] In instances when clients
are judged incompetent, practitioners
should be guided by the principle of "substituted" or "proxy" judgment, in which
a surrogate attempts to "replicate faithful-
ly the decision that the incapacitated person would make if he or she were able to
make a choice."[25] An important point for
social workers to consider is that clients
whose competence fluctuates may be capable of giving or withdrawing consent during a lucid phase.[26]

Consent to Specific Procedures

It is not uncommon for social service
agencies to have clients sign general consent forms at the first appointment or at the
time of admission to a program. In a number of cases, however, clients have challenged in court such blanket consent forms,
claiming that they lacked specificity and
failed to authorize intervention introduced
subsequently.[27] Professionals thus are advised not to assume that general consent
forms are valid. Rather, consent forms
should include specific details that refer to
specific activities or interventions. As
Rozovsky has observed, "Reliance on a general consent form may be of questionable
merit. Courts have been known to examine
the circumstances of a specific case to
determine whether the general consent was

broad enough to permit the treatment in question."[26]

Agency staff especially should be advised to refrain from having clients sign blank consent forms; this is a practice used occasionally to avoid having to contact clients in person for their signatures at a later date. If challenged in court, consent forms might not be considered valid, given the absence of information related to treatment by the agency or intervention at the time client signatures were obtained. In addition, the language and terminology that appear on consent forms must be understandable to clients, and clients should be given ample opportunity to ask questions. Practitioners should avoid as much as possible the use of complex and technical jargon. Particular care must be taken with clients who do not have good command of the English language; social workers should be aware that some clients who are able to speak English reasonably well may not be equally capable of understanding the language. Having access to an interpreter in such instances is important.

Valid Forms of Consent

Many states authorize several forms of consent. Consent may be written or verbal, although some states require written authorization. In general, consent obtained verbally is considered valid, providing that all other criteria for valid consent have been met. In addition, consent may be expressed or implied. Expressed consent entails explicit authorization by a client of a specific intervention or activity such as admission to a residential facility or the release of specific information to a third party. Implied consent, on the other hand, occurs when consent is inferred from the facts and circumstances surrounding a client. An example is when a client visits a community mental health center and voluntarily requests a regular dose of her psychotropic medication. A reasonable assumption is that the client has consented to the treatment.

Right to Refuse or Withdraw Consent

While it is important for social service staffs to develop sound procedures for obtaining valid consent from clients, it also behooves practitioners to plan for the possibility that clients will refuse or withdraw consent. Of course, such clients also should be considered legally and mentally capable of such a decision, and their decisions need to be informed by details shared by practitioners concerning the risks associated with refusing or withdrawing consent. The fact that clients may be taking psychotropic medication or may be disabled to some degree by mental illness does not by itself provide grounds for denying them the right to refuse or withdraw consent. Rather, client capacity should be judged based on the ability of the clients to think clearly, grasp details relevant to their conditions, understand the extent to which their psychiatric history is likely to affect their current judgment, and understand the extent to which they pose a public health risk. Ordinarily, it is in the best interests of an agency to have a client sign a release form, absolving staff members of responsibility for any adverse consequences stemming from a decision not to give consent. If a client refuses to sign such a form, detailed notes describing the client's decision and the negotiation should be placed in his or her record.

Client Decisions Based on Adequate Information

Professionals generally agree about the topics that should be covered in discussions with clients before obtaining consent. Commonly cited "elements of disclosure" include the nature and purpose of the recommended service, treatment, or activity; the advantages and disadvantages of the intervention; substantial, probable, or significant risks to the clients, if any; possible effects on clients' families, jobs, social activities, and other aspects of their lives; possible alternatives to the prospective intervention; and anticipated costs to be borne by clients and their relatives. This information must be presented to clients in understandable language, without coercion or undue influence, and in a manner that encourages clients to ask questions.[29]

EXCEPTIONS TO INFORMED CONSENT

A variety of circumstances exist under which professionals may not be required to obtain informed consent before intervention. In genuine emergencies, for example, professionals may be authorized to act without client consent. According to many state statutes and case law, to qualify as an emergency, a client must be incapacitated and unable to exercise his or her mental ability to make an informed decision. Interference with decision-making ability must be a result of injury or illness, alcohol or drug use, or any other disability. In addition, a need for immediate treatment to preserve a life or health must exist. As Rozovsky has noted, it is important for practitioners not to assume "that a person who has consumed a moderate amount of alcohol or drugs or who has a history of psychiatric problems is automatically incapable of giving consent; the facts and circumstances of individual cases are essential to such determinations."[30] Further, many statutes authorize practitioners to treat clients without their consent to protect them or the community from harm. Cases involving substance abusers, prisoners, and people with venereal disease are examples.[31]

As social workers have come to learn, they may be obligated to disclose information to third parties, even lacking client consent, if there is evidence that serious injury to others or to the state might otherwise result. The well-known case of *Tarasoff v. Regents of the University of California* is cited frequently as an example of circumstances when a mental health worker, because of the danger that a client poses, is expected to share information with third parties that ordinarily would be considered confidential.[32] Cases involving abuse and neglect, and where minors request social services, also are relevant.

Both statutes and case law have recognized the right of clients to request that they not be informed about the nature of or risks associated with impending treatment or services.[33] In these instances, clients may decide that they are better off not knowing what the services or treatment will entail, and thus waive their right to give informed consent. Professionals generally are advised to document such a waiver and to consider having clients sign a waiver form.

The most controversial exception to informed consent concerns the concept of therapeutic privilege. In several statutes involving the physician–patient relationship, states have permitted practitioners to withhold information if they believe that disclosure would have "a substantially adverse effect" on the welfare of a patient.[34] These statutes allow considerable discretion by professionals and, thus, have led to extensive debate about possible misuse of the privilege by physicians and other health and mental health professionals. In general, practitioners are cautioned to exercise the exception of therapeutic privilege only in extreme circumstances that can be documented thoroughly.[35]

PROTECTION OF CLIENTS

The concept of informed consent has done much to protect the rights of clients who are served by professionals. Protection especially is important for social work clients who are vulnerable by virtue of their age, mental or physical capacity, lack of resources, or other forms of dependency. The infamous Tuskegee and Willowbrook cases demonstrate the shocking abuses to which vulnerable clients can be subjected. The Tuskegee experiment, begun in Alabama in the 1930s and concluded in the 1970s, monitored the effects of untreated syphilis in 400 black men, ending only when an account in the *Washington Star* in 1972 sparked tremendous outrage. At Willowbrook, an institution for the mentally retarded on Staten Island, New York, a research team systematically infected groups of new residents with hepatitis viruses. In both instances, vulnerable clients were exposed to extraordinary risks in medical research, without adequate protection of their right to consent.[36]

In addition to protecting client rights, it is important to acknowledge other benefits to clients that the process of informed consent can effect. For example, several studies provide evidence that disclosure of detailed information to clients about the nature of impending treatment actually can enhance therapeutic progress.[37] As the President's Commission for the Study of Ethical Problems in Medicine and Biomedical and Behavioral Research concluded in its final report: "Not only is there no evidence of significant negative psychological consequences of receiving information, but on the contrary some strong evidence indicates that disclosure is beneficial."[38] The commission also found that the process of informed consent can provide a useful mechanism for involving family members in the care of a client when a client requests such involvement.

Social workers also must consider that obtaining informed consent entails more than having clients merely sign a form. Consent is a process that includes the systematic disclosure of information to a client over time, along with an opportunity to engage in dialogue with the client about forthcoming treatment and service. As part of this process, practitioners must be sensitive especially to cultural and ethnic differences among clients related to the meaning of concepts such as self-determination, autonomy, and consent. Hahn observes that "the individualism central to the doctrine of informed consent is absent in the tradition of Vietnamese thought. Self is not cultivated, but subjugated to cosmic orders. Information, direct communication, and decision may be regarded as arrogant."[39] In contrast, Harwood suggests that mainland Puerto Rican Hispanics expect to be engaged in the therapeutic process and have a strong desire for information and for information given without condescension.[40] It is essential for social workers to be cognizant of such cultural beliefs and preferences if they are to engage in the process of informed consent effectively and sensitively.

The process of informed consent is a key ingredient in the efforts of social workers in attending the rights of clients. As practitioners increase their understanding of this concept, they simultaneously advance the profession's pursuit of its ethical obligations and engage clients as genuine partners in the helping relationship. As with other ethical issues in social work, such as those related to the limits of confidentiality or self-determination, guidelines regarding informed consent leave considerable room for professional discretion, and it is important that such discretion be exercised responsibly. In the end, it is the proper exercise of such judgment that characterizes truly professional practice.

Notes and References

1. *See* M. W. Elliott, comp., *Ethical Issues in Social Work: An Annotated Bibliography* (New York: Council on Social Work Education, 1984); F. G. Reamer and M. Abramson, *The Teaching of Social Work Ethics* (Hastings-on-Hudson, N.Y.: The Hastings Center, 1982); and D. J. Besharov, *The Vulnerable Social Worker* (Silver Spring, Md.: National Association of Social Workers, Inc., 1985).

2. S. Bernstein, "Self-determination: King or Citizen in the Realm of Values," *Social Work*, 5 (January–February 1960), pp. 3–8; A. Keith-Lucas, "A Critique of the Principle of Client Self-determination," *Social Work*, 8 (July–August 1963), pp. 66–71; H. H. Perlman, "Self-determination: Reality or Illusion?" *Social Service Review*, 39 (1965), pp. 410–421; and F. E. McDermott, ed., *Self-determination in Social Work* (London, England: Routledge & Kegan Paul, 1975).

3. A review of the social work literature dating back to 1960 produced few references on the subject of informed consent. *See* J. K. Perry, "Informed Consent: For Whose Benefit?" *Social Casework*, 62 (1981), pp. 537–542; R. Macklin, "Ethical Issues in Treatment of Patients with End-Stage Renal Disease," *Social Work in Health Care*, 9 (Summer 1984), pp. 11–20; S. J. Wilson, *Confidentiality in Social Work* (New York: Free Press, 1978), pp. 56–67; F. Loewenberg and R. Dolgoff, *Ethical Decisions for Social Work Practice* (Itasca, Ill.: F. E. Peacock Publishers, 1982), pp. 41–48; and F. G. Reamer, *Ethical Dilemmas in Social Service* (New York: Columbia University Press, 1982), pp. 92–97.

4. M. S. Pernick, "The Patient's Role in Medical Decisionmaking: A Social History of Informed Consent in Medical Therapy," in President's Commission for the Study of Ethical Problems in Medicine and Biomedical and Behavioral Research, *Making Health Care Decisions: The Ethical and Legal Implications of Informed Consent in the Patient-Practitioner Relationship* (Vol. 3; Washington, D.C.: U.S. Government Printing Office, 1982), p. 5. *See also*, M. Siegler, "Searching for Moral Certainty in Medicine:

A Proposal for a New Model of the Doctor-Patient Encounter," *Bulletin of the New York Academy of Medicine*, 57 (January–February 1981), p. 68; and F. A. Rozovsky, *Consent to Treatment: A Practical Guide* (Boston: Little, Brown & Co., 1984), pp. xxxi–xxxii.

5. Pernick, "The Patient's Role in Medical Decisionmaking," pp. 4–5.

6. Ibid.

7. Ibid., pp. 28–29.

8. President's Commission for the Study of Ethical Problems in Medicine and Biomedical and Behavioral Research, *Making Health Care Decisions* (Vol. 1), p. 20.

9. Ibid., pp. 20–21.

10. Rozovsky, *Consent to Treatment*, pp. 337–412; and D. Wikler, "Paternalism and the Mildly Retarded," *Philosophy and Public Affairs*, 8 (1979), pp. 377–392.

11. Rozovsky, *Consent to Treatment*, pp. 235–336; and J. Cowles, *Informed Consent* (New York: Coward, McCann & Geoghegan, 1976).

12. Rozovsky, *Consent to Treatment*, p. 240.

13. Ibid., pp. 242–243.

14. *See, for example*, CONN. GEN. STAT., sec. 19-89A (1977); NEB. REV. STAT., sec. 71-1121 (1972); OKLA. STAT. ANN. tit. 63, sec. 2602 (West 1976); GA. CODE, sec. 74-104.3 (1971); ILL. ANN. STAT. ch. 111, sec. 4505 (Smith-Hurd 1980); LA. REV. STAT. ANN., sec. 1065.1 (West 1970); ME. REV. STAT. ANN. tit. 32, sec. 2595 (1979); OR. REV. STAT., sec. 109.650 (1977); and VT. STAT. ANN. tit. 18, sec. 4226 (1975).

15. *See* MO. ANN. STAT., sec. 632.110 (Vernon 1980); OR. REV. STAT., sec. 426.220 (1975); CAL. CIV. CODE, sec. 25.9 (West 1979); and MONT. CODE ANN., sec. 41-1-406 (1977).

16. *See* Matter of Quinlan, 70 N.J. 10, 355 A.2d 647 (1976); and Superintendent of Belchertown State School v. Saikewicz, 373 Mass. 728, 370 N.E. 2d 417 (1977).

17. Rozovsky, *Consent to Treatment*, pp. 195–234 and pp. 489–578. *See also*, G. J. Annas, L. H. Glanz, and B. F. Katz, *Informed Consent to Human Experimentation: The Subject's Dilemma* (Cambridge, Mass.: Ballinger Publishing Co., 1977).

18. Rozovsky, *Consent to Treatment*, pp. 8–41.

19. F. G. Reamer, "Protecting Research Subjects and Unintended Consequences: The Effect of Guarantees of Confidentiality," *Public Opinion Quarterly*, 43 (1979), pp. 497–506; and P. C. Giordano, "The Client's Perspective in Agency Evaluation," *Social Work*, 22 (January–February 1977), pp. 34–39.

20. Relf v. Weinberger, 372 F. Supp. 1196 (D.D.C. 1974).

21. P. S. Applebaum and L. H. Roth, "Competency to Consent to Research," *Archives of General Psychiatry*, 39 (1982), pp. 951–958.

22. G. A. Olin and H. S. Olin, "Informed Consent in Voluntary Mental Hospital Admission," *American Journal of Psychiatry*, 132 (1975), pp. 938–941.

23. President's Commission for the Study

of Ethical Problems in Medicine and Biomedical and Behavioral Research. *Making Health Care Decisions* (Vol. 1). p. 57.

24. Ibid., pp. 177–188.

25. Ibid., p. 178; and J. F. Drane, "The Many Faces of Competency." *Hastings Center Report.* 15 (April 1985). pp. 17–21.

26. Rozovsky. *Consent to Treatment.* p. 18.

27. In Winfrey v. Citizens Southern Natl. Bank. 149 Ga. App. 488, 254 S.E.2d 725 (1979). a female patient challenged her physician's authority to perform a complete hysterectomy, based on her consent to an exploratory operation. In Darrah v. Kite, 32 A.D. 2d 208, 301 N.Y.S.2d 286 (1969). the father of a young child challenged a neurosurgeon's authority to conduct a ventriculogram on the child when the consent form referred only to "routine brain tests" and a "workup."

28. Rozovsky. *Consent to Treatment.* p. 26.

29. President's Commission for the Study of Ethical Problems in Medicine and Biomedical and Behavioral Research. *Making Health Care Decisions.* Vol. 1. p. 195; and ibid., pp. 41–51.

30. Rozovsky. *Consent to Treatment.* p. 89.

31. Ibid., pp. 103–106.

32. Tarasoff v. Regents of the University of California. 17 Cal.3d 425, 551 P.2d 334, 131 Cal. Rptr. 14 (1976).

33. Holt v. Nelson. 11 Wash. App. 230, 523 P.2d 211 (1974); ALASKA STAT.. sec. 09.55.556 (1976); DEL. CODE ANN. tit. 18. sec. 6852 (1976); N.Y. Pub. Health Law sec. 2805-d (McKinney 1975); UTAH CODE ANN.. sec. 78-14-5 (1976); and VT. STAT. ANN. tit. 12, sec. 1909 (1976). *See also.* Ferrara v. Galluchio. 5 N.Y.2d 16, 176 N.Y.S.2d 996, 152 N.E.2d 249 (1958).

34. ALASKA STAT.. sec. 09.55.556 (1976); N.Y. Public Health Law. sec. 2805-d (McKinney 1975); PA. STAT. ANN. tit. 40. sec. 1301.103 (Purdon 1976); and UTAH CODE ANN.. sec. 78-14-5 (1976). *See also.* F. G. Reamer. "The Concept of Paternalism in Social Work." *Social Service Review.* 57 (June 1983). pp. 254–271.

35. *For additional discussion of exceptions to informed consent. see* Rozovsky. *Consent to Treatment.* pp. 114–123.

36. D. J. Rothman. "Were Tuskegee and Willowbrook 'Studies in Nature'?" *Hastings Center Report.* 12 (April 1982). pp. 5–7; and J. Jones. *Bad Blood* (New York: Free Press. 1981).

37. President's Commission for the Study of Ethical Problems in Medicine and Biomedical and Behavioral Research. *Making Health Care Decisions* (Vol. 1). p. 100.

38. Ibid.

39. R. A. Hahn. "Culture and Informed Consent: An Anthropological Perspective." in President's Commission for the Study of Ethical Problems in Medicine and Biomedical and Behavioral Research, *Making Health Care Decisions* (Vol. 3). pp. 55–56.

40. Ibid., p. 56; and A. Harwood, ed., *Ethnicity and Health Care* (Cambridge. Mass.: Harvard University Press. 1981).

PRACTICE EFFECTIVENESS: MORE GROUNDS FOR OPTIMISM

ALLEN RUBIN

SINCE 1973, three comprehensive reviews of research have evaluted the effectiveness of direct social work practice in the United States. The first two reviews (Fischer, 1973; Wood, 1978) summarized experiments that consistently reported findings suggesting that direct social work practice methods are ineffective. These reviews covered studies published prior to 1973. Fischer covered 11 studies; Wood covered 22. The third review (Reid and Hanrahan, 1982) sought to discover whether experiments conducted subsequent to the first two offered a different answer, in terms of particular programs with particular types of clients, to the question of effectiveness. Reid and Hanrahan's review covered 22 controlled experimental studies of direct social work intervention published from 1973 to 1979. Reid and Hanrahan reported that

> all but two or three of the twenty-two studies yielded findings that could on balance be regarded as positive. . . . no recent study that involved a comparison between treated and untreated groups failed to yield at least some evidence of the positive effects of social work intervention. [P. 331.]

Citing recent reviews of research with positive findings regarding psychotherapy outcomes (Bergin and Lambert, 1978; Smith, Glass, and Miller, 1980), Reid and Hanrahan concluded that "the helping professions seem to have resolved the question of 'Are we effective?' " (P. 338.) Not everyone, however, accepted Reid and Hanrahan's conclusion. Questions were raised about the internal and external validity of some experiments they reviewed. Chief among these concerns were the appropriateness of the data analysis procedures, the amount of reactivity and obtrusiveness in measurement, and the failure to separate out the nonspecific practitioner effects from the effects of their interventions (Fischer, 1983; Epstein, 1983).

NEW FINDINGS

In light of the limitations of the literature on practice effectiveness, there is a continued need for experimentation on the effectiveness of particular interventions with particular types of clients. There is also a need to update the field with findings and methodologies of experiments conducted subsequent to the earlier reviews.

The author was asked by the Division of Human Resources of the National Institute of Mental Health to assess the state of social work research by reviewing studies that appeared in journals from July 1, 1978, through June 30, 1983. A previous review article, on community-based care for the mentally ill, was reported by Rubin in 1984. Among the several hundred articles covered in that review were 12 controlled experiments on the effectiveness of direct social work practice that were not among the 22 studies reviewed by Reid and Hanrahan. (Two of the 12 studies were cited by Reid and Hanrahan as being among the six that appeared too late for them to review thoroughly, but that seemed to support their conclusions [Reid et al., 1980; Velasquez and McCubbin, 1980]).

The 12 experiments reviewed in this article do not constitute all experimental studies on direct social work practice effectiveness reported during the time period. The larger review was concerned only with research conducted in the United States and published in journals, in which at least one of the authors had a social work degree or worked in a social work school or agency. Studies reported only in media other than journals were not included, nor were studies not written by members of the social work profession. Sixty-seven journals were identified that appeared likely to contain research studies authored by social workers, and every issue of the journals during the five-year period was examined. Many more than 12 studies attempting to evaluate the effectiveness of direct practice interventions were published, but only the 12 reviewed here met Reid and Hanrahan's criterion of random assignment "to service or control groups or to groups receiving alternative forms of service" (p. 329).

As was done in the previous reviews, this one summarizes each study with respect to the nature of the interventions evaluated, type of clients served, problems targeted, research methods, and findings. The summaries include more methodological detail than did those in the previous reviews to enable readers to judge the internal and external validity of the findings. Each summary also identifies methodological strengths and weaknesses that, in this author's judgment, strongly influence the study's credibility. Each summary is headed by a brief label identifying the intervention evaluated and the type of clients served or problems addressed.

POSITIVE OUTCOMES AND SOUND METHODS

Social Skills Training for Mentally Retarded Adults. Two studies verified the effectiveness of social skills training in improving the interpersonal functioning of mentally retarded adults. The first study (Matson and Senatore, 1981) selected mildly to moderately retarded clients in sheltered workshops. Staff reports indicated that these clients had deficits in interpersonal functioning. The clients were randomly assigned to one of three conditions: no-treatment control, traditional psychotherapy, or social skills training. The psychotherapy treatment consisted of group discussions of workshop activities, client-centered interpersonal conditions (empathy and so forth), and various dynamics of Yalom's approach to group therapy (1975). The social skills training emphasized role play, modeling, and praise—all in relation to the target behaviors of acknowledging others and making positive statements about them.

Pretest, posttest, and follow-up assessments of outcome were made using the following two measures: (1) Ratings of the two target behaviors during videotaped group meetings and role-play scenes. (The raters of the videotapes and the role play were two trained independent observers whose interrater reliability was high.) (2) Two standardized rating scales of the clients' performance completed by workshop staff (who were not informed about experimental conditions and the study's purpose). An analysis of covariance found that clients with social skills training had significantly better outcomes on three of the four measures of the dependent variable. These results were sustained in a three-month follow-up assessment.

The second study (Senatore, Matson, and Kazdin, 1982) built on the previous one by comparing the standard social skills training to an en-

riched social skills training that added active rehearsal, props, and fading of the therapist's control. The adults in this study, outpatients at a mental health and mental retardation clinic, were in the borderline-to-severe range of mental retardation. They were randomly assigned to one of the two treatment groups or to a no-treatment control group. Outcome was measured with a behavioral rating scale of social skills completed by trained raters who were not informed about experimental conditions and whose interrater reliability was high. Different raters completed this scale based on their observations in interviews with clients, in hearing audiotaped role plays, or in unobtrusively observing client behaviors in a natural setting (at a party). An analysis of covariance found that for the interview and role-play measures, treatment conditions were significantly and strongly associated with outcome ratings, accounting for 77 percent and 41 percent of the variance in outcome, respectively. An analysis of variance was used to analyze the unobtrusive observations, which were collected only in a posttest. It yielded the same significant results, with 67 percent of variance in outcome accounted for by treatment conditions. In all three analyses, the enriched social skills training group did significantly better than the other two groups, and the standard social skills training group did better than the control group. These results were sustained in a six-month follow-up assessment.

Social Therapy in the Aftercare of Schizophrenic Patients. For more than a decade, Hogarty and his associates have been conducting rigorous longitudinal experiments in various settings on the effects of drug and social therapy in the aftercare of schizophrenic patients discharged after institutionalization. Reid and Hanrahan, in their review of studies up to 1979, summarized the earlier experiments conducted by Hogarty and his collaborators. Those studies found that drug therapy, alone, could forestall relapse, but that drugs by themselves had no effect on community adjustment. Social therapy decreased relapse after the sixth month of treatment for the subgroups of patients who did not relapse during the first six months. As to community adjustment, patients treated with the combination of drug and social therapy

adjusted the best. However, social therapy appeared to be harmful when combined with a placebo (Hogarty, Goldberg, and Schooler, 1974; Goldberg et al., 1977).

In a subsequent study not covered by the Reid and Hanrahan review, Hogarty et al. (1979) noted that one possible explanation for the effects of social therapy in the earlier experiments was that it may have increased the patients' compliance with chemotherapy. That is, the social therapy may have had no direct therapeutic benefits; rather, it may have enhanced adjustment only insofar as it promoted the taking of medication. As a test of this alternative hypothesis, 105 previously hospitalized schizophrenic patients were randomly assigned to four groups: (1) oral medication alone, (2) oral medication plus social therapy, (3) injection of medication alone, and (4) injection of medication plus social therapy. (Injection of medication assured drug compliance.) Throughout two years of study, no significant differences in relapse were found between patients receiving the two forms of chemotherapy. As in the earlier studies, however, social therapy had a significant effect in forestalling relapse in the second year.

The social therapy assessed in these studies was termed "Major Role Therapy"; it was administered by experienced MSWs and involved "a problem-solving method designed to respond to the interpersonal, personal, social, and rehabilitative needs of patients and their families (Hogarty et al., 1979, p. 1286). It focused on the patient's major role performance as a homemaker or potential wage earner. It also attempted to improve the quality of interpersonal interactions and relationships, ameliorate social isolation, and provide for self-care, financial assistance, housing, and compliance with medications. "Principles of practice included acceptance, clarification, material and emotional support, and appropriate assurance" (p. 1286).

Outcome in the Hogarty et al. studies was assessed according to length of time patients were able to remain in the community and by the use of a variety of standardized inventories with demonstrated validity that were completed by psychiatrists, social workers, patients, and families. In the 1979 study, data were analyzed by various bivariate and multivariate procedures, including discriminant function analysis.

Day Treatment in the Aftercare of Schizophrenic Patients. This study (Linn et al., 1979) was concerned with day treatment, another approach to the aftercare of schizophrenic patients. Like the studies by Hogarty et al., this one looked at the combined effects of the tested social treatment and chemotherapy. The day treatment programs attempted to enhance social interaction skills, provide a place to socialize and engage in productive activities, and provide a sheltered environment outside an institution. Chronic schizophrenic patients discharged from Veterans Administration (VA) hospitals were randomly assigned to chemotherapy alone or to chemotherapy plus day treatment at ten VA centers throughout the country. Treatment outcome was measured according to length of time patients were able to remain in the community and by scores on standardized scales of social functioning, symptoms, and attitudes. Ratings on the criterion measures were taken prior to treatment and every six months thereafter, up to the twenty-fourth month of treatment. Data were analyzed in a multivariate analysis of covariance and by means of curve-fitting with orthogonal polynomials.

No significant differences between the two groups were found in regard to the length of time patients were able to remain in the community; however, significant differences favoring the day treatment group were found on all other measures by the end of the twenty-fourth month. A retrospective analysis compared the attributes of the six centers that had good results with the four centers that had poor results. Centers with poor results were found to provide significantly more group psychotherapy and family counseling, whereas centers with good results offered significantly more occupational therapy. Therefore, it was postulated that treatment environments stimulating high levels of cognitive arousal may be harmful when indiscriminately applied to chronic schizophrenic patients— particularly those patients with symptoms of motor retardation, emotional withdrawal, and anxiety.

Environmental Intervention for the Chronically Mentally Disabled. This study (Stein and Test, 1980) assessed the effectiveness of another community-based treatment approach geared to chronically mentally disabled patients. The treatment package emphasized helping patients secure material resources; training patients in basic living skills such as those needed to use public transportation, budget money, and prepare simple meals; developing support systems to motivate and encourage patients; freeing patients from pathological dependence on families or institutions; supporting and educating community members involved with patients; and training staff to persevere and use assertive outreach with patients who fail to keep appointments or drop out of treatment. The treatment was labeled "Training in Community Living" (TCL). Subjects seeking institutional care were randomly assigned to (1) a control group that received hospitalization for as long as necessary and then linkage with appropriate community agencies, or (2) the TCL approach for 14 months before integration into existing community programs. Subjects were assessed at the time of admission and every four months thereafter for 28 months by an independent research staff using face-to-face interviews and standardized scales to measure symptomatology, community adjustment, and self-esteem.

During the 14 months of the TCL treatment, significant results favoring the TCL subjects were found on measures of time patients spent in independent living situations, time spent unemployed, amount of interpersonal contact, satisfaction with life situations, and symptomatology. Data were analyzed using *t*-tests and analyses of covariance. When patients were weaned from the TCL program and integrated into traditional community programs, most of the beneficial differences disappeared. This further supported the efficacy of the TCL approach "as an ongoing rather than time-limited endeavor" (p. 396) and indicated, as well, the inadequacy of traditional community programming for these patients.

Residential Milieu Therapy for Mentally Ill Young Adults. This experiment (Velasquez and McCubbin, 1980) tested the effectiveness of a community-based treatment program for a population of young adults who were diagnosed as functionally psychotic, severely neurotic, or having a personality disorder and who were less disabled than those previously mentioned. Ninety-four subjects were randomly assigned to an experimental group receiving milieu therapy in a community-based residence or to a comparison group that was merely encouraged to seek other forms of care (such as inpatient hospitalization, day treatment, or custodial boarding homes). The milieu therapy stressed improved role performance, a problem-solving model, gradual escalation of task or problem difficulty, extensive social interaction, supportive interaction, and reward for task completion or problem resolution. Outcome was measured by pretests and posttests on six standardized rating scales and two self-report measures. The experimental group outcome was significantly better than the comparison group outcome on measures of responsibility for self, capacity to live in independent settings, social participation, degree of psychiatric impairment, employment, number of hospitalizations, self-concept, and problem-solving capacity. Data were analyzed by separate tests of significance of change on each measure. However, this was not a serious flaw, because every test yielded statistically significant findings.

Stress Management Training for Women on Public Assistance. This study (Tableman et al., 1982) assessed the effectiveness of a training package for life-coping skills designed to enhance self-esteem and teach life planning and stress management to women on public assistance. Small-group sessions included discussion of self-esteem, identification of tasks to work on, explanation of feelings and the effect of negative feedback, practice in accepting and providing positive feedback, values clarification, interpersonal strategies, review of signs and sources of stress, role-play practice, and other exercises on stress awareness and resolution. Women receiving Aid to Families with Dependent Children who were not receiving community mental health services and who agreed to participate were randomly assigned to experimental and control groups. Pretest and posttest data were collected on standardized scales, including a checklist of psychiatric symptomatology; a self-report scale on anxiety; and a standardized test of ego strength, submissiveness versus dominance, self-confidence, and tension. Multiple *t*-tests compared mean group change scores individually for each measure.

Differences were significant on six of the eight measures, and the changes on all eight measures were in the predicted direction.

POSITIVE OUTCOMES BUT QUESTIONABLE METHODS

Task-Centered Treatment with Elementary School Children. This study (Reid et al., 1980) assessed the effectiveness of task-centered methods in helping elementary school pupils overcome academic, behavioral, and interpersonal problems. The sample consisted of 21 lower-income children (aged 7 to 13) who were willing to participate and who were

> able to form a contract with the practitioners to work on at least two problems that were sufficiently distinct so that treatment of one would not necessarily affect the other. [P. 11.]

The intervention followed the task-centered model, which has been described in depth in various sources (for example, Reid, 1978; Reid and Epstein, 1977). The intervention was implemented with the 21 cases by 21 first-year MSW students as part of their field training in a task-centered sequence. After a contract was formed between the practitioner and child to work on two target problems, the problems were randomly assigned to an A or B condition. The intervention was applied to problem A for three weeks, during which time the intervention for problem B was delayed. At the end of this period, the intervention was withdrawn from problem A and applied to problem B for three weeks. Change was measured by collecting data at three points: prior to random assignment, immediately after the first three weeks, and immediately following the second three weeks. All data were reported retrospectively on the frequency of the target behaviors during the seven-day period immediately following the treatment phase. At each point, the data were reported by the client and a collateral (usually a teacher or parent) in brief interviews conducted by the practitioner assigned to the case. (Reid et al. acknowledged that this method of data collection was vulnerable to measurement bias.) Analyzing their data by means of one-tailed t-tests of paired means, Reid et al. (1980) found significantly

$(p < .05)$ more improvement on the problems being treated during each phase than on those not being treated.

Case Management with Disability Claimants. This study (Akabas, Fine, and Yasser, 1982) assessed the effectiveness of case-management services provided to disabled workers at the onset of their disability. Outcome was assessed in terms of insurance-carrier costs, likelihood of returning to work, physical self-perceptions, services received, and perceptions of those services. The subjects included disability claimants employed as municipal workers of New York City who expected to be returned to work in less than three weeks, had a home phone, and suffered from one of the following disabilities: "circulatory disorder; digestive disorder; musculoskeletal disorder; malignant neoplasm; or multiples of any of the above" (p. 172). Matched pairs of claimants were randomly assigned to an intervention condition or a comparison condition. The latter provided only the routine procedures of medical evaluations to determine eligibility for financial benefits. The intervention condition assigned a case manager who assessed the claimant's problems and needs, developed problem-solving strategies with the claimant, delivered services to and brokered referrals for the claimant, and provided follow-up to ensure planned services were being sought by and delivered to the claimant.

Although insurance-carrier costs were lower for the intervention group, the efficacy of the intervention was not supported in regard to their returning to work, because 83 percent of those in the comparison group did so, as compared to 56 percent of those in the intervention group. As to self-perceptions of physical state, 42 percent of the intervention group—as compared to only 9 percent of the comparison group—said they felt better than before their disability. Likewise, 7 percent of the intervention group and 29 percent of the comparison group said they felt worse. Intervention group claimants also received more than twice as many services as did control group claimants and were much more satisfied with the services than were the controls. No inferential statistical analysis was reported on the significance of the percentage differences. How the perceptions of physical state or of ser-

vices received were measured also was not reported.

Early Discharge Planning for Orthopedic Inpatients. This study (Boone, Coulton, and Keller, 1981), also assessed the impact of social services in reducing the costs of caring for the physically ill. The subjects were orthopedic patients, and the goal was to reduce their length of stay in the hospital. The main focus of the intervention was to provide early and comprehensive social work services to resolve social and psychological barriers that prevent patients from being discharged as soon as their physical condition permits. The intervention included the formulation of an early assessment and discharge plan, linkage to community agencies, and collaboration with medical and nursing staff. Patients were randomly assigned to intervention or control conditions. The control patients received routine hospital services, in which only a few received social work services, usually late in their stay, after being referred by physicians. A two-way analysis of covariance found that when age and diagnosis were controlled, experimental group patients had a signficiantly shorter mean length of stay than did control patients. Overall, experimental patients averaged 1.25 fewer days of hospitalization than did controls.

Aside from questions as to whether earlier discharge was in the best interests of all patients, one major methodological issue bearing on the internal validity of this study is that the social work, medical, and nursing staff knew which patients were in the experimental group. Consequently, the shorter mean stay of the experimental patients may have had less to do with social work services they received than with bias among social work staff wanting to advocate more vigorously for their earlier discharge and the effect of this bias in predisposing medical staff toward earlier discharge of experimental clients. In short, it is plausible that the intervention was effective; however, it seems equally plausible that the difference of 1.25 days in length of stay may have been due to the practitioners' awareness of experimental conditions.

EQUIVOCAL OUTCOMES

Mutual Support Groups among the Elderly. This study (Toseland,

Sherman, and Bliven, 1981) compared the effectiveness of two group work approaches for developing mutual support among community-based elderly. The first approach used a less structured and less directive discussion-group format (for explication of the format, see, for example, Drum and Knott, 1977; Rose, 1977). The other approach used a more structured and task-oriented format based on behavioral methods designed to enhance social skills (for explication of the format, see, for example, Klein, 1970; Roberts and Northen, 1976). The first approach focused on process: Group autonomy was emphasized, members defined the group's structure and purpose, and the leader's role was to facilitate and provide insight into group process. The second approach emphasized learning social skills through role-playing and using those skills to provide mutual support to group members. The leader was highly directive and defined the group's purpose and processes. Forty members of two senior service centers were randomly assigned at their respective centers to one of three groups: (1) an experimental group using the first approach, (2) an experimental group using the second approach, or (3) a no-treatment control condition. Pretests and posttests used standardized instruments to measure the dependent variables of locus of control, self-esteem, and life satisfaction. A brief global scale of happiness, the fourth dependent variable, was also administered.

The behavioral (second) approach ceased in each center during the intervention period due to lack of attendance or open rebellion against the format. Toseland, Sherman, and Bliven therefore concluded that the directive, behavioral role-play approach is not preferred when the purpose of the group is to develop mutual support. As to the effectiveness of the process-oriented approach, t-tests were used to compare pretest and posttest change scores of the participants in the group using that approach with that of control group participants. Of the four separate bivariate t-tests reported (one for each dependent variable), only the one on locus of control was significant. Although the researchers did not mention it, the one significant t-test result may have been due to chance, because conducting several separate analyses instead

of a single multivariate statistic increases the probability of Type I error (Glisson and Fischer, 1982).

Cognitive-Affective Group Work to Enhance Coping with Life Changes. This study (Roskin, 1982) tested the effectiveness of a group work approach designed to improve the emotional health of adults who had incurred two or more specified life changes in the previous six weeks to one year. The specified life changes included death of a family member or close friend, divorce, separation, loss of work, incapacitating illness of or accident to self or close family member, imprisonment, and retirement. Subjects who met at least two criteria and who had not received any formal treatment since experiencing the life changes were identified in a mailed survey and were invited to participate in the intervention. Proportionate stratified sampling procedures were used to compose two groups: A semi-crossover design was used, which involved two phases. In the first phase, one group received the intervention. In the second phase, the intervention was withdrawn from the first group and introduced to the other. The intervention consisted of six seminars involving lectures and group discussions aimed at providing clients with knowledge and a frame of reference to help them place critical life changes in proper perspective. It also attempted to foster mutual aid and supportive interactions among members and used problem-solving and behavioral techniques to identify tasks and practice skills relevant to achieving those tasks.

Outcome was measured by means of a previously validated self-rated symptom checklist covering somatization, obsessive compulsiveness, interpersonal sensitivity, depression, and anxiety. The checklist was administered to each group before and after each of the two crossover phases. In the first phase, the treated group showed significantly greater improvement than the untreated group on only one of the five separate t-tests—that on the symptom of interpersonal

sensitivity. In the second phase, the treated group did significantly better than the control group on two of the five t-tests—those for depression and anxiety. Participants improved most who had experienced more life changes or the death of a family member or close friend. As in the study by Toseland, Sherman, and Bliven (1981), the use of multiple t-tests instead of a multivariate statistic changes the meaning of the significant findings, which were found in only three of the ten separate comparisons.

Cognitive-Behavioral Intervention for Self-Criticism among Women. This study (Berlin, 1980) evaluated the effectiveness of a cognitive-behavioral treatment package consisting of the following components for reducing self-criticism: explanation; self-monitoring; rational evaluation of self-expectations; modeling, substitution, rehearsal, and relaxation; and performance assignments with self-evaluation, group support, and reinforcement. Fifty adult women who responded to advertisements and were judged to have a major problem with self-criticism, but not any serious psychopathology, were randomly assigned to the intervention, a waiting-list control, or an attention-placebo condition. Outcome measures assessed frequency of self-critical statements, depression, self-esteem, and fear of negative evaluation from others. The latter three measures were done on self-report scales; however, frequency of self-criticism was assessed in two ways—via hourly self-monitoring (for the experimental and attention-placebo groups, only) and a self-criticism analogue test in which subjects discussed on an audiotape their feelings about their social functioning. Multiple but separate significance tests were conducted for each of the measures. A significant between-group difference in improvement favoring the experimental group over the attention-placebo group was found only on the self-monitoring measure of self-critical statements. But that difference, which was significant on a t-test of change scores, was no longer significant when an analysis of covariance controlled for regression toward the mean (which was necessary because of the dramatic pretest differences between the two groups). A significant difference in between-group change favoring both the experimental and attention-placebo groups over the waiting-list control group was found for the measure of fear of negative evaluation. (Berlin also reported various other significant findings of more debatable importance. For example, in several instances she described paired comparisons between the experimental group and the waiting-list control group that were significantly different at posttest or at follow-up, but in which the overall F-ratio for change over time across all three groups was not significant. Likewise, she reported that the within-group changes on four measures were significant for the experimental and attention-placebo groups but not for the waiting-list control group.)

COMMON THREADS

Because the reviewed studies assessed different interventions with different target populations and because there may be unpublished studies of these interventions that had negative outcomes, any attempt to extract general practice principles from this review must be done with extreme caution. Yet there is value in exploring commonalities among the studies for heuristic purposes—that is, to stimulate the generation of and future testing of hypotheses about what interventive procedures and core principles may enhance practice effectiveness.

A prominent commonality among the studies was the use of highly structured forms of practice that were well-explicated and specific about the problems the social workers sought to resolve, the goals they sought to accomplish, and the procedures they used to achieve those ends. This observation agrees with a commonality cited by Reid and Hanrahan in their review (1982). A related commonality was that the studies carefully and narrowly defined the types of clients for whom the tested interventions were targeted.

The importance of particularizing practice components and target populations was illustrated in several studies of cognitive and behavioral methods. For example, the studies by Roskin (1982) and Berlin (1980) partially supported the effectiveness of cognitive interventions in helping people without serious psychopathology to cope with life changes or alleviate self-criticism. Yet the studies by Hogarty and associates (Hogarty, Goldberg, and Schooler, 1974; Goldberg et al., 1977; and Hogarty et al., 1979) and by Linn et al. (1979) suggested that high levels of cognitive arousal may be harmful in the aftercare of chronic schizophrenics. Likewise, most studies supported the efficacy of behavioral methods to enhance social skills. However, Toseland, Sherman, and Bliven's study (1981) found that community-based elderly may not tolerate this approach when it is applied for the purpose of providing mutual support to group members.

This suggests that in considering the application of an interventive approach whose effectiveness has been empirically supported, the practitioner must understand that the same outcome may not be attained—indeed an undesirable outcome may ensue—if the approach is applied to cases, situations, or problems unlike those for which it was tested. This caveat applies to researchers, too, who should not simply ask, What interventions are effective? Rather, they should ask, What interventions are effective or harmful with what types of clients? With this warning in mind, we can proceed to examine interventive commonalities that the reviewed studies tended to support.

In keeping with Reid and Hanrahan's findings (1982), most of the studies with unequivocally positive outcomes tested forms of practice that relied heavily on problem-solving and task-centered methods, usually in conjunction with behavioral methods such as social skills training. These forms of practice were found to be successful with such diverse groups as mildly to moderately retarded adults; chronic schizophrenics in aftercare; young, nonchronic psychiatric inpatients; women on public assistance; and low-income children experiencing school problems. Practitioners considering the application of these interventions will require more specificity about the detailed components of these forms of practice and the target populations. They are referred to the studies themselves, as well as to basic texts on these

approaches (see, for example, Reid, 1978; Schinke, 1981).

A common thread among the studies dealing with the physically disabled or the chronically mentally disabled was the support found for the effectiveness of case management principles. For example, in their (effective) treatment package for the chronically mentally disabled, Stein and Test (1980) included support and education for community members involved with patients and assertive perseverance and outreach with patients who failed to keep appointments. Akabas, Fine, and Yasser's study (1982) assigned case managers to disability claimants. The case managers brokered referrals for claimants and provided follow-up to ensure that planned services were being sought by and delivered to claimants. Boone, Coulton, and Keller's study (1981) did not use the term "case management," but focused on early discharge planning, linkage to community agencies, and collaboration with medical and nursing staff, which are fundamental components of case management. Elsewhere the present author noted the conceptual similarity between case management and emerging frameworks for social work practice (Johnson and Rubin, 1983). The key issue in the studies reviewed is not the semantics of the term "case management" but whether such principles or procedures as early discharge planning, mobilization of community support systems, assertive perseverance in outreach, brokerage and linkage with community agencies, and follow-up and advocacy to ensure that services are delivered and used as planned are effective with the target groups.

A related common thread involves the experiments in the aftercare of chronic schizophrenics. These studies emphasized a comprehensive treatment package distinguished by an emphasis on restoration of major role performance, instruction in basic living and social skills, drug therapy, support system development, family education, and provision of material resources. Also distinctive to these studies was a practice orientation emphasizing support (material and emotional), linkage, education, rehabilitation, and an avoidance of psychodynamic, cognitively arousing approaches. These studies sought to facilitate role performance and living conditions, not to "cure" psychopathology (thus evoking Morris's recommendation [1977] that the profession be more attentive to "caring for" disabled individuals and be less concerned with "curing").

One implication of these common threads is that additional research is needed to isolate the effects of particular components of treatment packages. For example, in the aftercare of chronic schizophrenics, how much of the effectiveness of the overall treatment package is attributable, respectively, to such separate components as training in social and living skills, support system development, material support, and emotional support? The necessity of drug therapy with this target population has been well established (Hogarty et al., 1979), but how much of the overall effectiveness is lost or gained when other specific components are deleted from or added to the treatment package? Likewise, with case management, how much of the effectiveness can be attributed simply to early discharge planning, to the case manager's supportive relationship with the client, and so on? To what extent, in any of these broad practice approaches, is the entire package necessary to attain a successful outcome?

LIMITATIONS

Although this review provides further grounds for optimism about the existence of effective forms of practice, it certainly does not warrant euphoria. This review covered published studies only. Perhaps during the same period there were unpublished controlled experiments with negative outcomes. Also, the profession can hardly take pride in the fact that the author found only 12 experiments meeting the inclusion criteria of this review during the five-year period studied. The need for many more such studies is obvious. This does not necessarily mean that we need much more research evaluating the effectiveness of direct practice; it means that we need much more *methodologically credible experimental* research evaluating the effectiveness of direct practice. Readers are reminded that a great deal of research attempting to evaluate direct practice was found that did not qualify for inclusion in this review on methodological grounds. This condition may reflect in part the state of the profession's research enterprise, but it may have even more to do with the political and practical barriers in agencies blocking many researchers from conducting the rigorous experiments they would prefer. One such barrier is the belief that research experiments about practice effectiveness tend to find only negative results. (For a discussion of this and other barriers, see Bushnell and O'Brien, 1979). If social workers become more optimistic about the potential for experimental research to find positive outcomes about practice effectiveness, perhaps these barriers will diminish.

Bibliography

Readers will note that bibliographic style has been used for references in this article. This style is used only for reviews of the literature.

Akabas, H.; Fine, M.; and Yasser, R. "Putting Secondary Prevention to the Test: A Study of an Early Intervention Strategy with Disabled Workers." *Journal of Primary Prevention*, 2 (Spring 1982), pp. 165–187.

Bergin, E., and Lambert, M. J. "The Evaluation of Therapeutic Outcomes," in S. Garfield and Bergin, eds., *Handbook of Psychotherapy and Behavior Change: An Empirical Analysis*. 2d ed. New York: John Wiley & Sons, 1978.

Berlin, S. "Cognitive-Behavioral Intervention for Problems of Self-Criticism among Women," *Social Work Research and Abstracts*, 16 (Winter 1980), pp. 19–28.

Boone, R.; Coulton, C. J.; and Keller, S. M. "The Impact of Early and Comprehensive Social Work Services on Length of Stay," *Social Work in Health Care*, 7 (Fall 1981), pp. 1–9.

Bushnell, J. L., and O'Brien, G. M. St. L. "Strategies and Tactics for Increasing Research Production and Utilization in Social Work Education," in A. Rubin and A. Rosenblatt, eds., *Sourcebook on Research Utilization*. New York: Council on Social Work Education, 1979.

Drum, D. J., and Knott, J. E. *Structured Groups for Facilitating Development*. New York: Human Sciences Press, 1977.

Epstein, W. M. "Research Biases." Points and Viewpoints, *Social Work*, 28 (January–February 1983), pp. 77–78.

Fischer, J. "Evaluations of Social Work Effectiveness: Is Positive Evidence Always Good Evidence?" Points and Viewpoints, *Social Work*, 28 (January–February 1983), pp. 74–77.

——."Is Casework Effective: A Review." *Social Work*, 18 (January 1973).

Glisson, C., and Fischer, J. "Use and Nonuse of Multivariate Statistics." Research Notes, *Social Work Research and Abstracts*, 18 (Spring 1982), pp. 42–44.

Goldberg, S. C.; Schooler, N. R.; Hogarty, G. E.; and Roper, M. "Prediction of Relapse in Schizophrenic Outpatients Treated by Drug and Sociotherapy." *Archives of General Psychiatry*, 34 (February 1977), pp. 171–184.

Hogarty, G. E.; Goldberg, S. C.; and Schooler, N. R. "Drug and Sociotherapy in the Aftercare of Schizophrenic Patients." *Archives of General Psychiatry*, 31 (November 1974), pp. 603–618.

Hogarty, G. E.; Schooler, N. R.; Ulrich, R.; Mussare, F.; Ferro, P.; and Herron, E. "Fluphenazine and Social Therapy in the Aftercare of Schizophrenic Patients." *Archives of General Psychiatry*, 36 (November 1979), pp. 1283–1294.

Johnson, J., and Rubin, A. "Case Management in Mental Health: A Social Work Domain?" *Social Work*, 28 (January–February 1983), pp. 49–55.

Klein, A. F. *Social Work through Group Process*. Albany: State University of New York at Albany, 1970.

Linn, M. W.; Caffey, E. M.; Klett, C. J.; Hogarty, G. E.; and Lamb, R. "Day Treatment and Psychotropic Drugs in the Aftercare of Schizophrenic Patients." *Archives of General Psychiatry*, 36 (October 1979), pp. 1055–1066.

Matson, J. L., and Senatore, V. "A Comparison of Traditional Psychotherapy and Social Skills Training for Improving Interpersonal Functioning of Mentally Retarded Adults." *Behavior Therapy*, 12 (1981), pp. 369–382.

Morris, R. "Caring for vs. Caring about People." *Social Work*, 22 (September 1977), pp. 353–359.

Reid, W. J. *The Task-Centered System*. New York: Columbia University Press, 1978.

Reid, W. J., and Epstein, L. *Task-Centered*

Practice. New York: Columbia University Press, 1977.

Reid, W. J.; Epstein, L.; Brown, L. B.; Tolson, E.; and Rooney, R. H. "Task-Centered School Social Work," *Social Work in Education,* 2 (January 1980), pp. 7–24.

Reid, W. J., and Hanrahan, P. "Recent Evaluations of Social Work: Grounds for Optimism," *Social Work,* 27 (July 1982), pp. 328–340.

Roberts, R. W., and Northen, H. *Theories of Social Work with Groups.* New York: Columbia University Press, 1976.

Rose, S. D. *Group Therapy: A Behavioral Approach.* Englewood Cliffs, N.J.: Prentice-Hall, 1977.

Roskin, M. "Coping with Life Changes—A Preventive Social Work Approach," *American Journal of Community Psychology,* 10 (Fall 1982), pp. 331–339.

Rubin, A. "Community-Based Care of the Mentally Ill: A Research Review," *Health and Social Work,* 9 (Summer 1984), pp. 165–177.

Schinke, S. P. (ed.). *Behavioral Methods in Social Welfare: Helping Children, Adults and Families in Community Settings.* New York: Aldine Publishing Co., 1981.

Senatore, V.; Matson, J. L.; and Kazdin, A. E. "A Comparison of Behavioral Methods to Train Social Skills to Mentally Retarded Adults," *Behavior Therapy,* 13 (1982), pp. 313–324.

Smith, M. L.; Glass, G. V.; and Miller, T. I. *The Benefits of Psychotherapy.* Baltimore, Md.: Johns Hopkins University Press, 1980.

Stein, L. I., and Test, M. A. "Alternative to Mental Hospital Treatment," *Archives of General Psychiatry,* 37 (April 1980), pp. 392–412.

Tableman, B.; Marciniak, D.; Johnson, D.; and Rodgers, R., "Stress Management Training for Women on Public Assistance," *American Journal of Community Psychology,* 10 (Fall 1982), pp. 357–367.

Toseland, R.; Sherman, E.; and Bliven, S. "The Comparative Effectiveness of Two Group Work Approaches for the Development of Mutual Support Groups among the Elderly," *Social Work with Groups,* 4 (Spring–Summer 1981), pp. 137–153.

Velasquez, J. S., and McCubbin, H. I. "Towards Establishing the Effectiveness of Community-Based Residential Treatment: Program Evaluation by Experimental Research," *Journal of Social Service Research,* 3 (Summer 1980), pp. 337–359.

Wood, K. M. "Casework Effectiveness: A New Look at the Research Evidence," *Social Work,* 23 (November 1978), pp. 437–458.

Yalom, I. D. *The Theory and Practice of Group Psychotherapy.* 2d ed. New York: Basic Books, 1975.

Accepted August 20, 1984

BOUNDARY ISSUES IN COUNTERTRANSFERENCE: A DEVELOPMENTAL PERSPECTIVE

GERALD SCHAMESS

ABSTRACT: In treatment, characterologically disturbed patients evoke affective and behavioral responses that are frequently antitherapeutic. Such responses reflect the therapist's involvement in a reciprocal relationship in which the patient attempts to communicate very early pathogenic experiences. In this process the therapist is induced to act in ways that replicate significant aspects of the patient's first reciprocal relationship. Problematic replications may be recognized and modified when therapists carefully monitor their own boundaries between thought, affect, and action. This developmental paradigm is particularly useful in resolving therapeutic impasses that result from the patient's need to use the therapist as a "real" rather than a symbolic object.

Affectively Charged Countertransference Reactions

Patients with severe characterological problems, particularly those who are diagnosed as schizoid characters, borderline personalities, and impulse-ridden character disorders, typically evoke intense feelings of unpleasure in the therapist. Common affective reactions include frustration, confusion, hostility, helplessness, hopelessness, and revulsion. Therapists frequently experience these affects on an unconscious level and therefore attempt to defend against them. The use of such mechanisms as denial, projection, projective and introjective identification, dissociation, and reaction formation is common. In addition, therapists tend to develop a range of interpersonal stratagems that supplement their intrapsychic defenses and protect them from the patient's wish to draw them into a "real" relationship. Emotional withdrawal, premature termination, changes in the "frame" of treatment (Langs, 1976), and such creative mechanisms as flight into interpretation and rejection through confrontation, all reflect the therapist's need to preserve the interpersonal boundaries of the relationship.

Characterologically disturbed patients may also evoke pleasureable reactions in their therapists for limited periods of time. Feelings of intense empathy, the wish to nurture, rescue phantasies, and states of therapeutic grandeur or omnipotence are likely to be experienced at different stages of treatment. Ordinarily therapists tend to experience gratification at precisely those times when the patient has satisfied some instinctual wish or achieved a state of symbiotic-like union in the relationship. Because a process has developed in which the therapist's feelings of self-esteem have become linked to the ebb and flow of the patient's affective and instinctual life, the therapist's positive feelings tend to evaporate when the patient begins to feel frustrated or disappointed. Under conditions of frustration, the patient is likely to act in ways that "make" the therapist feel inadequate and/or guilty, thereby evoking or reviving feelings of unpleasure. The patient's ability to stimulate intense affective states that are experienced on an unconscious or preconscious level, makes it extremely difficult, if not impossible for the therapist to consistently maintain a posture of neutrality and objectivity.

The concept that the therapist's affective response may be induced by the patient has been discussed by a number of authors including Adler (1972), Briggs (1979), Flescher (1953), Litner (1969), Searles (1965), Spotnitz (1969), and Winnicott (1958). The literature differentiates between those countertransference reactions that constitute an objective response to the patient's pathology and those that reflect the therapist's unresolved intrapsychic conflicts and/or problematic character traits. Well trained and well analyzed therapists regularly experience a range of affective reactions that are evoked by the patient's use of splitting, projective identification (Kernberg, 1975), denial, and acting out as primary defenses against primitive hostile impulses. In this model of countertransference, the therapist's affective reaction constitutes a nonverbal response to the patient's nonverbal communication about object experiences that occurred during the first three years of life. These affective interchanges develop at the level of coenesthetic receptivity (Spitz, 1965), thereby undercutting the higher level cognitive and expressive processes that ordinarily structure communication between the patient and the therapist.

Behavioral Responses to the Patient's Character Pathology

Although a good deal has been written about the affective aspects of induced countertransference, less attention has been paid to the behavioral responses that characterologically disturbed patients routinely evoke from their therapists. Because such responses are frequently viewed as indications that the therapist is either inadequately trained or psychologically troubled, clinicians are understandably reluctant to discuss their behavioral responses in any detail. While there is a critical distinction between a therapist's affective reaction to a patient and the behavioral response that such a reaction may engender, behavioral responses seem to be unavoidable in the treatment of characterologically disturbed patients. For this reason they should be studied rather than repressed, concealed, or rationalized.

The process by which characterologically disturbed patients "persuade" their therapists to respond to them behaviorally has not been adequately investigated. It appears that their ability to do so is related to the fact that they are not willing or able, developmentally, to distinguish between real and symbolic relationships. Every relationship is real to them and, accordingly, they expect the therapist to behave in ways that will either gratify or frustrate their infantile impulses. Fixations at the oral and anal stages of development determine the type of gratification that they seek and whether it is predominantly libidinal or aggressive. Deviations in ego organization reflect arrests and failures in the maturational processes that normatively lead to the establishment of object constancy, secondary process thinking, and a stable sense of gender-linked self-identity. All of these factors contribute to their search for an external object who will help them maintain a fragile sense of homeostatic balance in the face of internal processes that leave them feeling divided, incomplete, desolate, and impulse-ridden.

This persistent need for external ego support leads to the development of adaptive interpersonal stratagems that allow the patient to attract the attention and control the behavior of potentially gratifying objects. In the therapeutic relationship these stratagems include: (1) enhancing the therapist's self-esteem through a combination of flattery and gratitude; (2) creating crisis situations that seem to demand some form of behavioral intervention and (3) threatening the therapist with self-destructive behavior, a poor therapeutic outcome, or termination of the treatment relationship. Given these unspoken pressures and demands, even therapists who are intellectually committed to maintaining clear boundaries between thought, affect, and action find themselves responding behaviorally to one aspect or another of the patient's need to replicate an early pathogenic object relationship.

Behavioral Reciprocity Both as a Defense and as a Form of Communication

Because the inductive process is based largely on coenesthetic receptivity, therapists frequently do not realize that they are responding behaviorally to a patient until there is a crisis in treatment. Exploration of the therapist's behavior when it has been recognized and acknowledged typically uncovers specific feelings of unpleasure, overinvolvement, or narcissistic gratification in regard to the patient. On this level, the therapist's behavioral response constitutes a defense and thus mirrors the patient's defensive use of acting-out as a way of avoiding intolerable affects, particularly anxiety and depression.

In addition to its defensive significance, however, the therapist's behavior constitutes a specific response to the patient's pathological needs and expectations. It completes a pattern of reciprocal interaction in which the patient plays out one aspect of an earlier dyadic relationship while the therapist plays out the other, complementary aspect. This unconscious replication of a pathogenic "reciprocal relationship" with a primary caretaker (Spitz, 1965), reflects the patient's effort to master problematic experiences by repeating them behaviorally within the therapeutic relationship. The therapist's behavioral reaction thus represents an unconscious or preconscious response to an interactional initiative coming from the patient. Over the course of a lifetime, this initiative has been carefully developed so as to induce and release a specific behavioral response (Stern, 1977) that makes it possible for the patient to re-experience some aspect of the original pathogenic relationship.

As the reciprocal interaction develops, the therapist is affected by one side or the other of the patient's incompletely fused loving or hateful feelings toward a primary object. The patient wishes the therapist to respond behaviorally in order to achieve a desired state of symbiotic-like fusion with the object, or conversely to maintain a posture of premature differentiation (Mahler, 1975) and pseudo independence. Because characterologically disturbed patients have not achieved the capacity for emotionally meaningful speech, or for self-observation in regard to egosyntonic behavior, replications of earlier relationships provide the only available avenue through which they can convey affectively charged information about the significant aspects of their life history. In the reciprocal interplay, the patient may relive, for example, experiences as a rejected and deprived child, while the therapist uncharacteristically behaves like the depriving and rejecting parent (Lieberman & Gottesfeld, 1973). Conversely, the therapist may begin to feel and act in much the way the patient did as a young child, while the patient assumes the parental role with uncanny fidelity and more than a touch of sadism.

Therapeutic Actions as Part of a Reciprocal Interchange

For the purposes of this discussion, a wide range of therapeutic activities will be viewed as behavioral responses to the patient's character pathology. It is neither necessary nor possible to list all of the problematic behaviors that therapists engage in while attempting to treat characterologically disturbed patients. However, a brief sample is in order.

Many such patients present themselves in treatment as being deprived, rejected, and vicitimized. They yearn for an external "part-object" who will "make" them feel complete and want the therapist to demonstrate interest and concern through actions that will "make" them feel loved and secure. At such times they are quite adept at evoking behavioral responses that temporarily promise safety, relief from painful affects, and emotional nurturance. In responding to these "needs" the therapist may: (1) offer unrealistic praise, encouragement, and/or sympathy with the aim of "improving the patient's self-image"; (2) take over life tasks that the patient had previously managed, albeit with difficulty; (3) agree with and encourage actions on the patient's part that undermine relationships with significant objects whom the patient perceives as frustrating and hostile; (4) alter the framework of treatment to lower the realistic "demands" on the patient, as in reducing the fee or changing appointment times without sufficient exploration of the realistic or emotional need for such changes; and (5) promise the patient companionship, friendship, and/or love outside of the treatment relationship.

At the other polar extreme, when such patients have begun to experience mistrust, disappointment, and hostility toward the therapist, they become increasingly anxious about the extent and implications of their hostile feelings. Under these circumstances they feel more secure if they can create a fight or flight situation that will allow them to leave treatment feeling that the therapist has misunderstood and rejected them. By evoking behavioral responses that they can interpret as hostile, they focus on the injustices they have suffered, and thereby avoid any recognition that they unconsciously view themselves as defective and hateful (Redl, 1957; Slavson, 1965). The therapeutic behaviors that are typically evoked by this constellation of self and object representations include: (1) confronting the patient or making interpretations that are critical and/or demeaning; (2) acting in an impatient, forgetful, bored, or restless way during sessions; (3) avoiding supervision or consultation even when treatment is not progressing well; (4) referring the patient to another therapist of lower status or to an agency that deals with more seriously disturbed people; and (5) changing the framework of treatment in ways that are excessively frustrating, as in shortening the treatment hour, raising the fee before the patient is emotionally ready to assume financial responsibility at a more mature level, or capriciously changing the appointment time to suit the therapist's convenience.

Particularly during the middle stages of treatment, when a pattern of reciprocal interaction has already been established, it is very difficult for therapists to distinguish between those affects and behaviors that have arisen internally and those that are being induced by the patient. For this reason, therapists should be prepared to discover, frequently after the fact, that they are behaving in ways that are both uncharacteristic and antitherapeutic. The therapist's ability to recognize such responses, to interrupt them when they are already in process, and to understand their meaning as part of a reciprocal communication process, is an essential component in effective therapeutic work with characterologically disturbed patients.

The Developmental Paradigm: Reciprocity in the Earliest Relationship

The American Heritage Dictionary defines "reciprocal" as "concerning two or more people...performed, experienced or felt by both sides, interchangeable, complementary." *The Oxford Dictionary of English Etymology* uses the definition "...done in return." Both dictionaries thus emphasize an interchange in which each person or subgroup of people in an interaction share similar or complementary feelings, so that the behavior of one develops in response to the behavior of the other. This description aptly describes the behavioral interchanges outlined above and is also congruent with Spitz's discussion of the earliest mother/child relationship.

In describing the interchange of emotions between mother and child, Spitz states: "Consciously or unconsciously each partner in the mother/child couple perceives the affect, a continuing reciprocal affective exchange....It is of special interest—that the unfolding of affective perception and affective changes precedes all other psychic functions; the latter will subsequently develop on the foundations provided by affective exchange. The affects appear to maintain this lead over the rest of development at least until the end of the first year of life. It is my personal opinion that they maintain it a good deal longer" (Spitz, 1965, pp. 139-140).

Spitz also discusses action and reaction as vital components in the early relationship between infant and primary caretaker. He describes communication within the mother/child dyad as "...a circular, reverberating process" (1965, p. 132). At another point he paraphrases Freud, stating that the earliest nonspecific discharge mechanisms in the newborn are carefully designed to evoke action in the caretaker. Only a "specific intervention" from "outside" can bring relief to the infant who is hungry or in pain. "Outside help is necessary and that is obtained by arousing the attention of an individual in the surround through the nonspecific random discharge mechanism of screaming, diffuse muscular action, etc." These mechanisms bring about "...an understanding with other people; and the original helplessness of human beings is thus the prime source of all moral motives" (Spitz, 1965, pp. 128-129).

Stern in his studies of infant behavior (3 to 12 months) emphasizes the infant's ability to evoke, modulate, and terminate specific activities in the mother. His films indicate that facial expressions, the position of the infant's head and face in relation to the mother's face, the direction and duration of the "gaze," and certain affectively evocative sounds such gurgling and fussing, effectively stimulate or turn off playful and communicative initiatives from the mother. "These integrated motor patterns are for the mother...the crucial stimulus which, once viewed and processed, lead her to *act in a specific way* [emphasis added]....Very clearly then, by 3 months at the latest, the infant is well equipped with a large repertoire of behaviors to engage and disengage his caretakers" (Stern, 1977, p. 48).

This formulation is particularly useful in thinking about adult behavior. We ordinarily assume that engagement and disengagement in psychotherapy takes place verbally through the interplay of symbolic and secondary process communication. However, in face to face treatment one can easily observe the manner in which, for example, a full-face gaze accompanied by a widening of the patient's eyes rivets the therapist's attention and thereby commands a response indicating either a willingness or refusal to interact. Evocative behaviors of this sort typically evoke a behavioral reaction from the therapist even before the process of understanding and evaluating the patient's motivation has consciously begun.

A Clinical Example of Reciprocity

In discussing the heroic aspects of psychotherapy with schizophrenics, Schwartz (1978, p. 201) presents the following vignette concerning Stephen Fleck. The scene is Yale Psychiatric Institute. "He knows all the patients, their development, family structure, and so on, in meticulous detail...We entered the room of a young woman who had been in the hospital for a considerable period of time. The patient greeted us with a barrage of disorganized comments—half word-salad, it seemed—about the window, her teddy bear, the bureau, the floor, dirt, the clouds in the sky, and more. Fleck listened, fixed her with a firm stare and said, 'Young lady, you need to find out who you are!' The patient suddenly began to speak English. She described in clear sentences how she confused herself with the bed, her teddy bear, the clouds. As we walked out of her room Fleck turned to me and said, 'You know, it was the damndest thing—for a time I couldn't remember her name.' "

On one level, Fleck's inability to remember the patient's name reflects his defensive use of repression in response to the patient's overwhelming anxiety and confusion. On another level, it constitutes part of a reciprocal interchange in which the patient succeeds in communicating some crucial information about her early object relations. There is the striking image of patient and therapist together, each privately facing the realization that neither one knows who she is! Given her level of ego development, she has no other way of making him understand that her mother did not recognize her as a separate person and, accordingly, could not help her establish a firm sense of personal identity. She had no other way of conveying what it felt like to be her mother. She unwittingly invites Fleck to replicate her mother's behavior by failing to recognize who she is and how deeply she is suffering. Because he does not minimize or rationalize the implications of his having forgotten, he is able to provide a corrective experience. He says, I want you to know who you are and I want to know also. It is this implicit understanding of the reciprocal nature of their interaction that makes his response both impressive and emblematic of the psychotherapeutic process with seriously disturbed patients.

This example is particularly instructive because it demonstrates that fragmentary and poorly organized communications can be understood as replications of pathological object relations from the past, if and when they are correlated with the complimentary affective and behavioral responses that they evoke in the object. The phenomenon is noteworthy because traditional views about transference and countertransference do not describe it adequately. One must turn to some of the more recent theoretical reformulations to gain any perspective on what is happening between the patient and therapist in such interactions. Gertrude and Rubin Blanck take the position that patients who have not achieved the "...degree of separation of self and object images that make transference possible...," enter treatment as part of an ongoing search for "...replication of primary object experience(s)" (Blanck & Blanck, 1979, pp. 13 and 197). This concept makes it possible to consider how the preoedipal patient's feelings and actions may lead to replication of early object relations without becoming hopelessly enmeshed in the historical argument about narcissistic versus object-oriented transferences.

Spotnitz (1976) makes a distinction between "objective" and "subjective" countertransference reactions to distinguish between those situations in which therapists are reacting realistically to the patient's pathology and those in which their responses are engendered by their own unresolved problems. This reformulation reduces the likelihood that a therapist who openly discusses countertransference reactions will be stigmatized, and also makes it possible to study those responses as a function of the patient's pathology.

While these changes in the theoretical framework are helpful, it is useful to emphasize that the characterologically disturbed patient's early pathogenic experience cannot be adequately understood as long as we attempt to view what is happening in the patient's mind and what is happening in the therapist's mind as separate and distinct phenomena. The two fields of experience are complementary and interconnected to a degree that makes it impossible to understand one without reference to the other. Accordingly it seems fitting to characterize this aspect of the patient/therapist relationship as a reciprocal one in which there is a reverberating mutual exchange of affect and behavior based on a series of projective and introjective identifications in which both parties actively engage. The distinction between patient and therapist emerges from the fact that the patient engages in these identifications on an unconscious level and has no choice about doing so, while the therapist is able to achieve conscious awareness of them by studying the affective and behavioral responses that the patient induces.

Over the past decade there have been a small number of articles about dyadic relationships between patient and therapist that illuminate some central aspect of the patient's pathology. These include descriptions of the patient who actively invites rejection and the therapist who experiences the patient as "repulsive" (Lieberman & Gottesfeld, 1973); the embittered, critical, demeaning patient and the "helpless" therapist (Adler, 1972); the "help-rejecting complainer" and the frustrated therapist and/or therapeutic group (Berger & Rosenbaum, 1967); and finally the "excitement-craving group" and the therapist who is either excluded or invited to become an accomplice in the group's acting out (Rosenthal, 1971). All of these reports constitute important advances in our understanding of particular types of pathological reciprocal relationships and, it may be hoped, will serve to promote further study of the phenomena.

Applications to Group Treatment

Although the idea may seem rather startling, there is substantial evidence to indicate that reciprocal relationships occur regularly in group as well as in individual treatment. Since groups are frequently recommended when a therapist wishes to dilute the intensity of an individual relationship, or limit the opportunities for regression, there is considerable justification in asking how the group arena can become a setting for the type of intensely dyadic relationship described above.

The dyadic possibilities in group treatment are somewhat more complex than those in individual treatment and for that reason may be more difficult for the therapist to follow. They include possible reciprocal relationships between two patients, between the therapist and a patient, between two subgroups of patients, and between the entire group as one half of the dyad and the therapist as the other half. It is also possible for one patient to play out a reciprocal relationship against an alliance comprised of all the other group members plus the therapist. This last configuration usually occurs when a group member is being scapegoated, a process that has dynamics of its own and should be considered separately. Because this paper is focused on transference-countertransference dyads, the following illustration will involve a situation in which the therapist is involved reciprocally with a single patient.

A Group for Mothers

This group was comprised of six characterologically disturbed women, all of whom were single parents. Their male children (ages 2 to 4 years) had serious developmental problems as a result of neglect and/or abuse. The group had met for one year, during which time several of the women had shown marked improvement in their parenting ability.

Mrs. J. had been an enthusiastic group member and had seemed to make progress until shortly after her mother's death, at which time she began to attack the female therapist and criticize the group. She complained that the therapist was ineffectual and critical, that the other group members looked down on her and that her son, L., was not making progress. Her rage was so intense that she had started to call the other group members at home, inviting them to join her in leaving the group.

The therapist recognized that Mrs. J. was reacting to her mother's death and investigated the history of their relationship. Mrs. J. reported that she had always hated her mother, who had developed a degenerative neurological illness when Mrs. J. was 17 years old. In spite of her hateful feelings, Mrs. J. had visited her mother daily to give her medication and attend to her physical needs. She reported that her mother had never been satisfied with her care and had complained that Mrs. J. did not love her and did not do enough for her. Mrs. J.'s younger sister who visited rarely and took no responsibility for the mother's care was praised and held up to Mrs. J. as an example of a "good daughter." Mrs. J.'s father was alcoholic and had deserted the family when she was 15. As a result Mrs. J. had primary responsibility for her mother after the illness was diagnosed.

When the therapist attempted to explore Mrs. J's feelings about her mother's death, Mrs. J. insisted that she was relieved to be rid of her mother who had always been a burden. In the group she denied having any feelings of loss or guilt, but began to abuse her son in a way that she had given up some months previously. When the therapist confronted her about this and tried to help her understand some of L.'s developmental needs, her abusive treatment increased. The therapist then commented on how desperate she seemed to be feeling and attempted to point out the connection between her mother's death and the feelings of anger she was experiencing toward her son, the group, and the therapist. These interventions were met with hostile denial followed by an even more vehement attack on the therapist. Following this attack the therapist decided that, because the group was in jeopardy, she had little choice except to drop Mrs. J. from the group and make a referral to protective services.

At this point in treatment, the therapist was aware of feeling angry, helpless, and inadequate. Mrs. J. seemed determined to annihilate her and destroy the group. By behaving toward the therapist with the same implacable hostility that she felt her mother had directed toward her, Mrs. J. created a situation in which the therapist felt obligated to act in order to preserve L. and the group. Initially, the therapist had anticipated that her interventions would be helpful to Mrs. J. When Mrs. J. disqualified those interventions through a mixture of denial and projection, she "made" the therapist experience what she had experienced throughout her childhood; feelings of frustration, overwhelming anxiety, isolation, and impotent rage.

As the treatment process developed, the reciprocal aspects of the interaction became quite apparent. When Mrs. J. began to act-out the role of the critical and dissatisfied mother, the therapist responded by acting-out the role of the rejected child who attempts to soothe and protect her mother because she is afraid to lose her. In technical terms, a reciprocal process of projective and introjective identification had taken place, leading to a reversal of roles within the transference. As the therapist allowed herself to experience the induced feelings, she became aware of her impulse to expel Mrs. J. from the group and refer her to an angency that would evaluate her "fitness" as a mother. This impulse had developed out of the therapist's wish to regain her therapeutic role and out of her anger at feeling herself in the position of a demeaned and helpless child. She then realized that if she were to act on her impulse, she would confirm Mrs. J.'s feelings of worthlessness and self-hatred, thereby replicating the maternal relationship in the transference. As the therapist continued to study the introjected impulse to expell Mrs. J. from the group, she gradually came to understand that Mrs. J. unconsciously viewed herself as a "bad" child who was unworthy of her mother's love and who deserved to be punished because of her murderous impulses toward her mother.

Since Mrs. J. was unable to tolerate any conscious awareness of these feelings, the technical problem in treatment involved working out a corrective emotional experience for her that would neither threaten her precarious sense of self-esteem, nor further endanger L. or the group. The therapist and consultant devised an approach in which she would respond to Mrs. J.'s next attack by saying: "It is clear that I am not helping you and that I don't understand your feelings. I would appreciate your telling me what I am doing or not doing to make you so angry with me. It seems likely that I am at fault in some way that I am not aware of, and would like to correct any mistakes I have made in working with you." This technique was used consistently for the next six months. While Mrs. J. did not respond specificaly to the therapist's invitation to be critical, and never talked directly about her ambivalent feelings toward her mother, her behavior changed markedly. She stopped trying to destroy the group, and began to take better care of L. She arranged for him to have an audiological examination and discovered that recurrent ear infections had interfered with his hearing and contributed to his speech difficulty. When she told the group about the examination she initially attacked the physician's competence. As the group listened attentively, she began to weep. Subsequently she talked about how guilty she felt for having neglected L.'s physical and emotional care. This incident confirmed that Mrs. J. was identifying with the therapist's attitude of thoughtful self-examination. Her willingness to accept responsibility for having neglected L. suggests that her hostility toward him had diminished and that she was beginning to differentiate him from her sister who, having been favored by her mother, had always been the object of her hatred.

As this reciprocal relationship developed between Mrs. J. and the therapist, the other group members acted in much the way that siblings act when one child in a family (Kadis, 1956) is being scapegoated and the others seek safety by becoming invisible. When Mrs. J. criticized the therapist and tried to disrupt the group, the other members attempted to placate her, while looking silently toward the therapist to see if she would survive Mrs. J.'s attacks. Clearly they were anxious about whether the group would survive, but were even more anxious about taking sides or commenting on the struggle between Mrs. J. and the therapist. When Mrs. J.'s hostility began to diminish and her feelings toward the therapist became somewhat more positive, the other group members talked associatively about their own problems with their mothers, about their tendency to look to men for support and gratification and about how the men in their lives had failed them.*

Therapeutic Intervention

While this article has not focused primarily on treatment approaches, it is useful to note that in both of the clinical examples the therapeutic impasse was resolved through the use of an intervention in which the therapist interrupted the established pattern of reciprocal interaction, thereby making it necessary for the patient to internalize the therapist in a new and different way. Such interventions seem to have a positive effect on characterologically disturbed patients because they do not threaten defenses or lower self-esteem. Particularly in situations where the reciprocal interaction replicates a primary relationship in which the patient felt rejected and demeaned, genetic interpretations or confrontations tend to perpetuate a pathological response because they

---

*I am grateful to Carol Brevera, MSW for her permission to use this material. Her willingness to explore her own feelings and her devotion to the welfare of the women in this group deserve high praise.

are experienced as proof that the therapist views the patient as inherently inadequate and worthless.

Summary and Conclusions

This article attempts to expand the concept of countertransference by using a developmental paradigm to account for the responses that characterologically disturbed patients normatively evoke in their therapists. When the process of treatment is carefully studied, it becomes apparent that a reciprocal pattern of interaction often exists between the therapist and the patient, even when the therapist intends to maintain a neutral, objective, and semidetached professional role. For this reason it may be extremely difficult for the therapist to distinguish between instances in which the patient's reaction to a therapeutic intervention is unrealistic and "transferential," and instances in which it is responsive to attitudes and actions that the therapist has actually adopted and acted out as a result of the patient's need to replicate early object experiences. The clinical evidence indicates that in the treatment of characterologically disturbed patients, transference and countertransference do not develop as separate and distinct entities, but rather, as a series of intertwined and reverberating exchanges that mutually influence one another across interpersonal boundaries. In these exchanges, the patient's need to achieve a state of defensive equilibrium is satisfied when the therapist assumes a role that replicates some specific aspect of the patient's original reciprocal relationship with the primary caretaker. Since the patient and the therapist may each have well established tendencies to identify with the aggressor or the victim, situations develop in which either party may assume the role of child or parent in relation to the other.

Typically, therapists become aware of induced countertransference reactions when they realize they have been acting in ways that are uncharacteristic and antitherapeutic (Giovacchini, 1979; Spotnitz, 1979). For this reason, the capacity to re-establish clear boundaries between thought, affect, and action is crucial in the treatment of seriously disturbed patients. After a reciprocal pattern of interaction has been identified, it is necessary to understand its repetitive aspects as well as its typical outcome for the patient. To accomplish this, it is helpful for the therapist to study the interrelationship between the patient's early developmental history, the patient's characteristic difficulties in object relations, and the reciprocal role the therapist has been induced to act out.

When the underlying dynamic and interpersonal elements have been clarified, the therapist is then in a position to modify the pathological aspects of the replication, sometimes by interpreting the pattern, but more frequently by assuming an interpersonal posture that confounds the patient's expectations. If the intervention is correctly formulated, the therapist implicitly conveys a message that the impulses and affects that were threatening to the parent in the "first edition" of the reciprocal relationship, are not threatening to the therapist in the "new (transferential) edition," and therefore do not endanger either the therapist or the treatment relationship. As the patient's hostility is accepted and to some degree, neutralized, it becomes possible for the patient to experience feelings of inadequacy, shame, and self-hatred, without being overwhelmed by anxiety. The inter-personal intervention thus addresses itself to both internal and extrernal object relations, as well as to the patient's defensive organization; particularly the primitive defenses of denial, projection, splitting, and acting-out. The concept that the treatment relationship is shaped by reciprocal interactions that replicate early object experiences is particularly useful as a therapeutic paradigm because it allows the therapist to understand and unravel the negative therapeutic reactions that occur as a result of the patient's unspoken demand that the therapist act as a real rather than a symbolic object.

REFERENCES

Alder, G. Helplessness in the helpers. *British Journal of Medical Psychology*, 1972, *45*, 315.

American heritage dictionary. Boston: Hougton Mifflin Company, 1976.

Berger, M., & Rosenbaum, M. Notes on help-rejecting complainers. *International Journal of Group Psychotherapy*, 1967, *17*, 357.

Blanck, G., & Blanck, R. *Ego psychology II*. New York: Columbia University Press, 1979.

Briggs, D. The trainee and the borderline client: Countertransference pitfalls. *Clinical Social Work Journal* 1979, *7*, 133.

Flescher, J. On different types of countertranseference. *International Journal of Group Psychotherapy*, 1953, *3*, 357.

Giovacchini, P. Countertransference in primitive mental states. In L. Epstein and A. H. Feiner (Eds.), *Countertransference: The therapist's contribution to the therapeutic situation*. New York: Jason Aronson, Inc., 1979.

Kadis, A. Re-experiencing the family constellation in group psychotherapy. *Journal of Individual Psychology*, 1956, *10*, 63.

Kernberg, O. *Borderline conditions and pathological narcissism*. New York: Jason Aronson, Inc., 1975.

Langs, R. *The bipersonal field*. New York: Jason Aronson, Inc., 1976.

Lieberman, F., & Gottesfeld, M. The repulsive client. *Clinical Social Work Journal*, 1973, *1*, 21.

Litner, N. The caseworker's self-observation and the child's interpersonal defenses. *Smith College Studies in Social Work*, 1969, *39*, 95.

Mahler, M. *The psychological birth of the human infant*. New York: Basic Books, Inc., 1975.

Oxford dictionary of American etymology. London: Oxford University Press, 1966.

Redl, F. *The Aggressive child*. New York: Free Press, 1957.

Rosenthal, L. Some dynamics of resistance and therapeutic management in adolescent group therapy. *Psychoanalytic Review*, 1971, *58*, 354.

Schwartz, D. Psychotherapy. In J.C. Shershow (Ed.), *Schizophrenia science and practice*. Cambridge, MA: Harvard University Press, 1978.

Searles, H. Oedipal love in the countertransference. In *Collected papers on schizophrenia and related subjects*. New York: International Universities Press, 1965.

Slavson, S. *Reclaiming the delinquent through para-analytic group psychotherapy and the inversion technique*. New York: Free Press, 1965.

Spitz, R. *The first year of life*. New York: International Universities Press, 1965.

Spotnitz, H. *Modern psychoanalysis of the schizophrenic patient*. New York: Grune and Stratton, 1969.

Spotnitz, H. *Psychotherapy of preoedipal conditions*. New York: Jason Aronson, Inc., 1976.

Spotnitz, H. Narcissistic countertransference. In L. Epstein and A. H. Feiner (Eds.), *Countertransference: The therapist's contribution to the therapeutic situation*. New York: Jason Aronson, Inc., 1979.

Stern, D. *The First Relationship*. Cambridge, MA: Havard University Press, 1977.

Winnicott, D. W. Hate in the countertransference. In *The collected papers: Through paediatrics to psycho-analysis*. London: Tavistock Publication, 1958.

INTRODUCTION AND EDITORIAL
Gerald Schamess

INTRODUCTION

Who Profits and Who Benefits from Managed Mental Health Care?

For social service/mental health facilities and for practitioners, managed behavioral health care has produced changes of astonishing magnitude within a decade or less. Mental health delivery systems and practitioner roles have been substantially transformed, and graduate schools in all the mental health disciplines are discovering that traditional curricula are no longer adequate to prepare students for practice. Presumably, these changes are the result of upwardly spiralling health and mental health costs which, during the last decade, have increased health insurance premiums to a level that is or seems to be insupportable over time. Accordingly, containment of health care costs has become a national priority if not a new gospel. In a concerted effort to reduce health and mental health care costs, both private and public institutions have encouraged and, in some instances, forced employees to join managed health care plans.

While some non-profit managed health care plans still operate (notably, Kaiser and subsidiaries of Blue Cross/Blue Shield), for-profit plans have come to dominate the "industry" by competing aggressively to control a greater proportion of the available market. Their basic strategy is to lower premiums whenever there is competitive advantage in doing so, and to enroll as few seriously ill or high risk subscribers as possible. They achieve market control by driving competitors out of business or buying them out. This is, of course, a fundamental business strategy throughout corporate America. For-profit HMOs are experts at creating an environment in which non-profit insurers find it necessary either to offer benefit packages and premiums comparable to the for-profit packages, or accept a significant loss of market share and thereby endanger their continued existence. These and other similar strategies allow for-profit plans to control both benefit packages and premiums throughout the health/mental health "industry."

Because these developments have had such a profound effect on practice this special issue of the *Studies* focuses on practitioner views of how profit, as a primary motivation for service delivery, affects organizational systems, education for practice, and face-to-face interactions between clinicians and patients/clients. (Parenthetically, it seems that historians will have to determine how much of the current financial "crisis" in health care results from changing demography and other realistic factors, and how much has been manufactured [in post-industrial terminology, "constructed"] to provide insurers with unprecedented opportunities for-profit.)

Among the few things that proponents and critics of managed care can usually agree about are changes that have already been implemented. For better or worse, the network of public and private social, human service, and mental health agencies built up, piece by piece, over the last 60 years has been largely dismantled. In the process, social agencies, psychiatric hospitals, mental health clinics, community mental health centers, and family service agencies have either become profit centers for insurers or disappeared as distinct entities. As for-profit managed care companies expand their reach, well-established institutions and mental health care networks merge, merge again, are bought, and are sold with amazing frequency, as competing insurers jockey for competitive advantage. Over time, the control of mental health care has been concentrated in the hands of fewer and fewer large insurers.

In order to limit the utilization of the most costly services, inpatient psychiatric care has been reduced to a minimum, typically ranging from three to twenty-one days. Most managed plans work actively to limit longer-term inpatient stays, preferring to authorize repeated brief rehospitalizations when patients relapse. Solo mental health practice is rapidly disappearing, and most clinicians who wish to support themselves in private practice find it necessary to apply for places on managed mental health care panels. Practitioners who apply may or may not be accepted, depending on how full the panels are, and how well the individual's practice "profile" conforms to the insurer's established treatment policies. When accepted, practitioners explicitly agree to allow case managers employed by, and responsible to the insurer, control how and who they treat. Typically, case managers determine the length and nature of care on the basis of pre-established treatment protocols derived from diagnostically-related groupings. Most insurers endorse biological and cognitive-behavioral interventions, and authorize or deny treatment after evaluating the patient's/client's level of functional impairment. Basically, this procedure reflects a behavioral approach to assessing psychological difficulties.

These changes have profound implications for institutions, practitioners, and recipients of care. Proponents of managed care contend that they are unavoidable, and ultimately beneficial. While the immediate consequences are sometimes unpleasant, new systems and new policies are necessary to control the upwardly spiralling cost of mental health care. Whatever disruption and/or personal hardship they cause is necessary to make a bloated, inefficient system of service delivery more responsive to the healthy discipline of free market forces. Proponents argue that managed care benefits society by creating delivery systems which provide larger numbers of consumers (formerly, patients/clients) with less restrictive, less stigmatizing, more cost-effective behavioral health care. Programs of care are developed and implemented on the basis of "best practice" protocols, as determined by insurer-constructed outcome research. Within newly developing systems of care, surveys of consumer satisfaction inform administrators and providers about the kind of services consumers want. Whenever possible, administrators are expected to seek guidance from panels of consumer consultants in developing new, cost-effective programs that better address consumer needs and concerns. Insurers and health network managers assert that the research they sponsor confirms the efficacy of managed, for-profit, behavioral care systems.

Managed care critics paint a dramatically different picture. They contend that for-profit managed care has replaced well-tested, well-established professional standards, treatment procedures, and guiding ethical principles with new principles and procedures that rationalize the pursuit of profit above all other goals. As a result, the quality of patient/client care has suffered, and practitioners have been disempowered professionally. Critics assert that professional judgements about patient/client problems and needs are regularly overruled by poorly trained, therapeutically inexperienced case managers who are well-paid by insurers to limit, and where possible, deny appropriate care. They also argue that the dissolution of existing, in many instances venerable, social service/mental health agencies has seriously undermined treatment for the poor, for racial and ethnic minorities, and for the seriously disturbed, while simultaneously diminishing the quality and availability of care for working and middle class patients/clients who assume they have adequate insurance coverage until they attempt to utilize it.

Critics also contend that because insurers typically refuse to pay for any services except face-to-face treatment contacts, children, the aged, the poor, and people with serious and persistent emotional difficulties are routinely denied necessary collateral interventions (school visits, ancillary contacts with family members, help in arranging for concrete services such as housing, legal representation, and public assistance). Moreover, professional training opportunities both in graduate school programs and within mental health provider systems have been seriously undermined by insurer productivity/profit expectations. One consequence of increased productivity requirements (more face-to-face interviews) is that in most settings, post-professional in-service clinical education for practitioners has been eliminated or significantly reduced. Ironically, critics say, mental health care rationing has become the norm for all but the very affluent as practice judgements increasingly come under the control of corporate insurers whose concern for cost containment (i.e., profits) takes priority over any interest they may have in helping people.

Topics and Contents

The sharply conflicting viewpoints outlined above frame a debate that is frequently acrimonious. Up to this point in time, important philosophical and ethical controversies coupled with the extraordinarily rapid pace of change have made it impossible to reach anything approaching consensus about current controversies. Very little middle ground has yet been established. This collection of papers provides an up-to-date cross-section of opinion about the principles which inform managed mental health care programs, and the ways in which those principles are implemented in day-to-day practice.

Both implicitly and explicitly, the contributors emphasize the degree to which policy decisions and corporate initiatives at a national level determine the nature of clinical practice and practice education. The volume includes several papers which analyze the reasons public policy has changed so rapidly, others which examine ethical and professional issues, others which review the impact of change on professional education, and still others which look closely at how philosophical and management principles are implemented at the level of service delivery. The volume is unique in presenting case examples which illustrate how new service delivery systems and policies affect specific patients/clients. Needless to say, a central subtext in all of the papers is the effect that very rapid change is having on people located at different points within the mental health system.

All the contributors are practitioners currently working in mental health. They include system managers, a psychologist/accounts manager, educators in social work and psychiatry, and social work clinicians. Some are ardent proponents of managed care and some are equally ardent critics. A third subgroup is committed to developing new initiatives that preserve humane and effective treatment interventions and educational programs within managed, for-profit behavioral care systems; i.e., in accord with current reality as we have come to know it. Although the authors did not read one another's papers while preparing their own, the works selected emphasize sharply different points of view. The point-counterpoint format is designed to inform readers about significant dilemmas and opportunities inherent in managed mental health care, and to encourage both discussion and debate. The editorial board of the Studies will welcome reader reactions to individual papers and to the issue as a whole; as well as opinions, questions and personal/professional experiences with managed mental health care systems. We hope to publish a selection of letters and brief articles commenting on this volume in the March 1997 issue of the *Studies*.

EDITORIAL

Profits and Caregiving: Are They Compatible?

In editing this volume, every effort has been made to insure that its contents are balanced and different points of view are fully and fairly represented. As a therapist and social work educator, however, I have learned a great deal about managed mental health care from clients, colleagues and especially, in terms of change at a national level, from faculty fieldwork advisors at the School for Social Work. While I try be open-minded and to consider a range of different opinions, I am not, by any means, neutral. Accordingly, I will use this space to supplement some viewpoints to be presented later by commenting on the effect unregulated pursuit of profit has on patients/clients, clinical practitioners, and treatment institutions.

I will begin with a disclaimer. My personal experience in the 1950s with the Health Insurance Plan of New York City, an early *non-*profit health maintenance organization, convinced me that it is possible for managed medical groups to offer effective, appropriate mental health care to a wide range of clients if clearly defined standards of care are established and if the organization providing care is regulated by an independent government agency. This view, however, does not correspond well with current political opinion. As the conservative members of Congress inform us daily, government regulation is anathema to them, and presumably to the public at large. Without doubt, it is anathema to for-profit, behavioral health care companies. For this reason, if for no others (and there are others), I have grave misgivings about the ability and willingness of corporate America, in the 1990s, to provide effective and appropriate treatment for people with serious emotional disturbances. The problem lies in corporate values and in the policies corporations implement to insure their profitability. During the last five years, wave after wave of layoffs during a period of upwardly spiraling, record-breaking corporate profits leave little doubt that, when opportunities present themselves, contemporary corporations consistently choose profit over people; at least to the degree outside forces (e.g., unions, government regulators) do not prevent them from doing so.

The New York Times, in its March 3, 1996 issue (Uchitelle & Kleinfield, 1996, p. 26) listed fifteen major companies that had, between them, publicly announced their intention to eliminate 662,900 jobs between 1992 and 1996. By 1996, these companies had laid off or planned to lay off between thirteen and thirty-five percent of their workforces, mostly relatively well-paid, white collar, middle level managers. *Newsweek* magazine (Sloan, 1996) commented on these layoffs in an article titled "Corporate Killers."

> You lose your job, your ex-employer's stock price rises, the CEO gets a fat raise. Something is just plain wrong when stock prices keep rising on Wall Street while Main Street is littered with the bodies of workers discarded by big companies like AT&T and Chase Manhattan and Scott Paper. Once upon a time, it was a mark of shame to fire your workers *en masse.* It meant you had messed up your business. Today, the more people a company fires, the more Wall Street loves it, and the higher its stock price goes. (p. 44)

Apparently, both this article and *The New York Times series* "On the Battlefronts of Business" (Uchitelle & Kleinfield, March 3, 1996, p. 1) were generated by Pat Buchanan's early success in the Republican party presidential primaries. Before the widespread positive response to Buchanan's challenge to established business practices (especially "downsizing" and its relationship to free trade) the litany of layoffs was reported routinely and factually. With few exceptions, no one in the media seemed to think the layoffs and the underlying business philosophy they reflect were worthy of editorial comment or serious investigative reporting. No one in public life except union leaders and a few liberal legislators expressed public outrage.

In the human service field, it is impossible to ignore the devastating economic and psychological effects that "downsizing" in pursuit of profit has had for millions of individuals and their families. In this context, it seems incomprehensible (perhaps, downright immoral) to turn health and mental health care into an industry and entrust its administration to yet another group of corporate directors and CEOs whose value systems predispose them to sacrifice patient/client well-being on the altar of profit.

Of all the many possible motivations for providing care to people who suffer from serious emotional problems, the pursuit of profit is among the most dismal. Practitioners have known for decades that it is extremely difficult to maintain a reasonable balance between self-interest and patient/client need in treating people who are mentally ill or emotionally disturbed. When practitioners minimize the importance of self-interest and self-care they become vulnerable to despair, helplessness, and what is commonly called "burn-out." When they become too invested in personal self-interest, they exploit and/or abuse their patients/clients. Over the last thirty years we have taken note of the many excesses built into the solo practitioner/teaching hospital model of mental health care; e.g., inflated incomes for those in positions of power and authority, inpatient stays of inordinate length, training at the expense of patient care. Did that model of care need to be reformed? Indeed! Can it be reformed by corporate executives for whom profit is, increasingly, the major criterion of success? I doubt it. Are there large profits to be made from privatizing health and mental health care? You bet there are!

On April 11, 1995 (Section D, pages 1 and 5), *The New York Times* published the 1994 salaries and stock awards to the CEOs of the seven largest for-profit HMOs. The highest remuneration was $15.5 million, paid to the president and chief executive of Healthsource of Hooksett, NH. The second highest was $13.7 million paid to the CEO of Foundation Health Corporation. The *average* remuneration package for all seven CEOs was $7 million, and the lower end of the scale was $2.8 million. When we compare these remuneration packages with the salaries of some Fortune 500 company CEOs who have laid off large numbers of employees (Sloan, 1996, p. 44-45), there is a startling discrepancy. The two highest 1996 salaries listed in Sloan's report are $3.36 million (AT&T) and $3.075 million (Sears & Roebuck), not including bonuses. While I cannot estimate the extent to which bonuses and stock options will eventually inflate these salaries, it is still noteworthy that the total remuneration packages for the health maintenance organization CEOs are so high. Moreover, it does not seem likely that bonuses and stock options, however generous, will raise the remuneration packages for the AT&T and Sears & Roebuck CEOs by 450%, the amount necessary if their packages are to equal the 1994 high end packages granted to for-profit health maintenance organization CEOs.

What have managed care CEOs done to warrant these generous rewards? Not surprisingly, they have produced huge profits for their companies. According to the brokerage house Smith Barney Inc., Healthsource's 1995 net income rose no less than 44%, while its earnings per share rose by 29% in the fourth quarter alone. Foundation Health's profits were somewhat disappointing given Smith Barney's prior estimates, rising by only 22% per share in 1995. Overall, the Standard and Poor Health Care Composite Index rose 57.8% in 1995, exceeding the very large 45.9% rise in the Standard and Poor 500 stock average by a very healthy (for the corporations if not for their patients) twenty-five percent. Without doubt, there is money to be made in the for-profit managed care industry, a great deal of money. And, right now, while organizational systems are being reorganized from top to bottom, the time to profit is ripe.

High profits and high CEO salaries, in and of themselves, do not negate the possibility that private corporations can provide inclusive, appropriate, quality mental health care. Corporate greed does negate that possibility, as does opportunistic profiteering at the expense of people in distress, unwillingness to recognize the depth and complexity of psychological dysfunction, and reliance on quick, simple, technological fixes for problems that involve human suffering. Problematic as these attitudes are, the factor that most disqualifies corporations from providing care to people in emotional distress is the underlying assumption that both the recipients of care and the workers who provide it are "human resources," to be used and/or exploited, however necessary, in pursuit of profit. It is a profoundly exploitative assumption which implies that people do not have value in and of themselves simply as human beings, but only acquire value when they become "resources"; i.e., when they advance corporate objectives. Unfortunately, recent corporate behavior suggests that most if not all of their major policy decisions are shaped by this very assumption. It might even be said, without significant disagreement from the business community, that, for American corporations, money talks and profit rules. The current rationale for this attitude, repeated daily in the business news, is that American stockholders demand that corporations be profitable.

In this context, it is instructive to ask how HMOs generate their profits. Careful observation of their strategies suggests that they profit from the misapplication of standard business practices; i.e., they apply business practices to tasks and problems that are not amenable to business solutions. Some of the strategies currently in use include:

- denying insurance coverage to people with pre-existing conditions, or those who seem likely to use services extensively;

- limiting and/or denying treatment to people whose difficulties do not respond to interventions prescribed by standardized treatment protocols;

- replacing professional clinical judgement with multiple levels of bureaucratic decision-making;

- increasing requirements for record-keeping and report writing so clinicians spend enormous amounts of time doing work appropriate to insurance clerks, and institutions find it necessary to expand their bookkeeping and billing offices exponentially;

- removing case managers responsible for utilization review from direct contact with both patients/clients and practitioners, and by providing access to them only through overloaded telephone lines (a busy signal is the *leitmotif* of behavioral managed care);

- requiring that clinicians (now called contract workers, vendors, or stakeholders) comply with insurer policies and protocols, or find employment elsewhere (if they can);

- instituting appeal procedures that are difficult to access, impersonal, time-consuming, and inherently frustrating;

- using economic power to drive down unit of service payment rates to treatment institutions and practitioners alike;

- purposefully and systematically magnifying public and legislative alarm about the rising cost of health and mental health care;

- purposefully and systematically using the media to promote managed care as the most efficient, if not the only approach to cost containment, while suppressing and/or disqualifying dissenting viewpoints.

There is nothing surprising or innovative about any of these policies. All of them are congruent with principles and practices utilized routinely throughout corporate America. They are equally applicable to making cars, running airlines, managing banks, and flipping hamburgers in fast food restaurants. They make it possible to sell minimally acceptable goods and services to consumers, while increasing production pressure on employees whose salaries have been more or less frozen (for at least a decade), whose fringe benefits (especially health insurance) have been systematically reduced, and who have less and less job security. All in all, its not a pretty picture either for consumers or employees. Certainly, it should not be viewed as an acceptable blueprint for providing mental health care. Health and mental health care are not commodities that can be packaged and distributed in handy recyclable containers. When care is provided on these terms, many too many patients/clients simply become disposable, since there is no way to profit from them.

From my perspective, the implications of these observations are clear. Mental health care needed reform before for-profit, managed care took over the field. It now needs reform again. Since established systems rarely if ever change willingly or easily, it is reasonable (albeit distressing) to argue that the chaos and human suffering managed care has thus far created for many people, were necessary to modify dysfunctional aspects of the pre-existing system. At this point in time, however, the constructive changes which corporate policy and technological innovation can affect have, for the most part, been incorporated into systems of care. Time-limited psychodynamic and cognitive-behavioral forms of psychotherapy are widely accepted and utilized, brief hospitalization has become the norm, home- and community-based care programs are expanding, biological treatment has become more sophisticated, medication is prescribed routinely, and the cost paid for "units of care" in different settings has been significantly reduced. Given these changes, it is time (perhaps past time) to regulate the managed care companies, or to introduce a single payer system. A recent research report (Beinecke & Perlman, 1996, p. 16) states that in Massachusetts the managed care organization which took over the Medicaid system in 1992, spent "... about *six* times (emphasis added) what Medicaid spent for administration before managed care." That 600% increase represents a great deal of money not being used on behalf of people who seek and need mental health care. Moreover, it is quite a remarkable commentary on the relative cost-effectiveness of "bloated, inefficient" government bureaucracies, as compared to "lean, mean, fiscally responsible" corporate systems. Do I dare talk about bloated corporate bureaucracies that are purposefully designed to be inefficient?

People who are mentally ill and/or who suffer from serious emotional disturbances should not be subjected to exploitation or profiteering either from the private or the public sectors. Because they are vulnerable, they need relationships that are compassionate, and thoughtfully attuned to painful memories and feeling states. Even though patients/clients use services, they are not, in essence, consumers. Moreover, their problems cannot be effectively addressed by providing them with behavioral health "products." Since role functions are, in large measure, defined by the names assigned to them, it is important to think of psychotherapists, psychopharmacologists, case managers, community aides, and peer counselors as healers or helpers, not as contract workers, vendors, or stakeholders.

The specific terminology corporations and practitioners use reflects theoretical models which define the nature and causes of problems, and the remedies likely to ameliorate them. According to the *Random House College Dictionary* (1988, p. 609) healers "make whole or sound; restore to health, free from ailment." Vendors are "people or agencies that sell" (1988, p. 1459). Stakeholders "hold the stakes of a wager" (1988, p. 1279). The different terminologies suggest that, as a society, we are currently being forced to choose between vastly different philosophies and views of humankind. The one emphasizes the importance of trying to make people with emotional problems whole, while the other views emotional problems in terms of functional impairments which can be repaired through the use of well-designed, technologically up-to-date, aggressively marketed products. Consume, incidentally, according to the *Random House College Dictionary* (1988, p. 289) means "to destroy or expend by use ... to devour." A consumer, of course, is "a person or thing that consumes."

We need reforms that better address patient/client needs, and better support practitioners in providing effective help through healing relationships, symptom-reducing medications and constructed, supportive communities of peers. The time has come for patients/ clients, mental health practitioners, legal advocates, legislators, and community representatives to join together in creating a new mental health system that can integrate these and other needed reforms. If it is true, as many reports say, that between 20% and 30% of every HMO premium dollar actually goes toward administrative costs or profits, it should be possible to create a new system that not only provides universal care at lower cost, but also preserves a reasonable level of profitability for private insurers.

REFERENCES

Beinecke, R. H., & Perlman, S. B. (1996, March/April). Managed Medicaid: The Massachusetts experience. *Behavioral Health Management, 16*(2), 14-16.

The New York Times. (1995, April 11). Nation's big for-profit health maintenance organizations had banner year in 1994. Section D, pp. 1, 5.

The Random House College Dictionary (Rev. ed.). (1988). New York: Random House.

Sloan, A. (1996, February 26). Corporate killers: The hit men. *Newsweek,* 44-48.

Uchitelle, L., & Kleinfield, N. R. (1996, March 3). On the battlefields of business, millions of casualties. *The New York Times,* p. 1.

MANAGING PROFESSIONAL INTERPERSONAL INTERACTIONS
HARRY SPECHT

A LARGE SEGMENT of professional education and the literature of social work is devoted to the study of, development of knowledge about, and skill in understanding and managing relationships between social workers and clients. These interpersonal relationships, after all, provide the acceptance, empathy, warmth, understanding, and knowledge that enable clients to make the choices and the decisions that are in their best interests.[1]

However, most social workers also have significant professional interpersonal interaction with "others" who are not clients: some spend all their time in work that is not clinical. Thus, social workers interact with collateral others (people who have close relationships with clients, such as family, friends, and neighbors), collegial others (such as trainees, consultants, and consultees), and sociopolitical others (such as employers, people who control funds or community resources, and policymakers). Although clear guidelines and considerable knowledge exist about the management of professional-client relationships, little attention has been given in the practice literature to the management of interaction with these three types of others. Yet the norms, expectations, and ethics of interactions, as well as the rules of exchange and the resources exchanged, vary considerably with each type of relationship.

Moreover, most complaints about violations of ethics are concerned not with client-professional interaction but with interactions between professionals and their collegial and sociopolitical others. For example, in a study of complaints filed with the National Association of Social Workers (NASW), McCann and Cutler report that only 13 percent involved clinical interactions. Nineteen percent dealt with collegial interactions, and the majority of cases (65 percent) involved sociopolitical interactions (i.e., managers and employees).[2] How many collegial and sociopolitical complaints involved clinical issues is unknown. Also unknown is the number of violations of ethics in clinical interactions for which complaints are not filed.

The purpose of this article is to present a theoretical framework for dealing with a variety of professional interpersonal interactions, a larger task than may be apparent at first. Following the presentation of a framework for analyzing such interactions, the author describes the types of others with whom professionals interact. The concluding section deals with the implications of the theoretical framework for the development of knowledge about practice.

FRAMEWORK

Expert Helper and Others

The expert helper might be a caseworker, group worker, teacher, supervisor, consultant, planner, or whoever else performs direct and indirect services. The other with whom the helper interacts could be a client, a relative of a client, a student, a supervisor, a consultee, a person who controls community resources, or an agency administrator. Although interactions may be primarily clinical, collateral, collegial, or sociopolitical in nature, some might be a mix; for example, interaction between a social worker and his or her supervisor might contain both collegial and sociopolitical elements. As the order of these interactions descends from *clinical*, to *collateral*, to *sociopolitical*, the professional worker exercises a decreasing degree of power and autonomy and is able to maintain less control over the purpose of the interaction and the context in which it takes place. (See Fig. 1.)

The view of professional interaction that is supported here is similar to that of Gergen who believes that it is not possible in considering social interaction to establish predictive principles that are truly independent of time, place, and circumstance.[3] With this view in mind, the best that one can hope for in developing a "science" for social work intervention is to develop a set of sensitizing theories that one has to update periodically.

Professional interaction takes place in contexts that can be more or less defined to correspond to the professional's objective.[4] Thus, at one extreme, in clinical interaction, time, place, entrances, exits, and so forth can be controlled largely by the professional. At the other extreme, in sociopolitical interaction, these elements can be controlled by the professional to a lesser degree, and thus, their management is more likely to be a problem.[5] Sociopolitical interaction can take place in boardrooms, bars, and bedrooms; at all times of day and night; and in social contexts that range from office interviews and formal meetings to dinners, parties, and "meeting for a drink." The social etiquette of these interactions frequently is not clear; friendly and evocative talk, touching, and other kinds of intimate interaction may not be proscribed for the participants. In fact, higher degrees of social intimacy may be appropriate during sociopolitical interaction than in other types of professional interaction because of the places, times, and contexts in which these interactions take place.

Qualities of Interaction

Interactions with all types of others vary in duration, degree of intensity, and disposition, as well as in the amount of skill required to manage the situation. These qualities are defined as follows:

• *Duration* is the amount of time spent in interaction. The smallest unit of interaction is an *encounter*, in which two or more people come into contact and exchange some resource. Encounters may be brief or extensive. An *intervention episode* consists of one or more encounters. What binds the professional and another in an intervention episode is the intentionality or problem orientation of the participants.[6] That is, the interaction has intentionality or a problem orientation if the professional and the other have a contractual understanding, arrived at formally or informally, about the purpose of the interaction.

• *Intensity* concerns the strength or depth of an interaction. Professional interaction varies from light and superficial to intense and consuming. Brief encounters are likely to be light and superficial. Extensive encounters, especially those that occur in intervention episodes, are most likely to be more intense. Professional *relationships* with others, as distinct from encounters, are likely to develop during intervention episodes.

• *Disposition* refers to the feeling that characterizes an interaction, which may range from extremely positive, to neutral, to extremely negative. Professionals may interact intentionally with others in ways that are warm and supportive or challenging, adversarial, commanding, and rejecting.

• *Skill* is the knowledge and expertise that is required to complete a task. Some professional tasks require more skill than others. For example, providing someone with a list of agencies that serve particular categories of clients requires less skill than helping clients assess their problems and then referring them to appropriate agencies.

Professionals' Needs

Professionals perform their roles for a variety of reasons. Bolan notes that the professional engaged in action has several needs, including a striving for enhanced self-esteem and self-fulfillment, mastery of the professional domain, consistency between one's perceptions and values, and significant impact on the world of contemporaries.[7] These needs can be satisfied to varying degrees through inter-

Figure 1.
The Interpersonal Interactions of Professionals

When the "Other" Is a:	The nature of the Interaction is Primarily:	Relative to the "Other" the Power and Autonomy of the Professional is:
• Client	Clinical	High
• Intimate of the client	Collateral	
• Trainee		
• Supervisee		
• Consultee		
• Consultant		
• Colleague	Collegial	Equal
• Cognate-colleague		
• Community resource controller		
• Employer		
• Policymaker-funder	Sociopolitical	Low

action with each of the previously mentioned types of others. For example, the need to experience mastery of the professional domain is more likely to be met in work with clinical others, whereas the chance to have a significant impact on the world of contemporaries is greater in interaction with collegial and sociopolitical others.

Resources Exchanged

All interpersonal interaction involves an exchange of resources, which can be concrete or symbolic: a wink, a welfare payment, a food basket, or a punch in the nose. According to Foa and Foa, all resources fall into six classes: (1) love—verbal or physical expressions of regard, empathy, warmth, or comfort, (2) status—expressions that convey esteem, regard, or prestige, (3) information—advice, opinions, instruction, (4) money, (5) goods—tangible objects and materials, and (6) services.[8] These resources are concrete or symbolic to different degrees. For example, goods and services are the most concrete resources; status and information the most symbolic. Love and money are in between because they can be exchanged in both symbolic and concrete terms.

In addition, the value of some resources may be more universal than others. For example, the person from whom one receives love matters a great deal, but the value of money remains the same regardless of the relationship between the giver and receiver. Thus, a client is likely to accept reassurance and emotional support only from his or her particular therapist, whereas the person who seeks money, goods, or information is not as particular about the person who provides it.

Of course, interpersonal encounters are likely to involve a combination of resources. For example, one interaction between a client and a professional may involve the exchange of warmth and support, money, and information.[9]

Thus, interaction with different types of others requires different behaviors and satisfies different needs of the professional. A good part of the interaction of professionals cannot be characterized as management of clinical relationships or as intervention episodes but as encounters of varying intensity, in which a variety of resources may be exchanged. The fluid nature of encounters injects a high degree of ambiguity into the interpersonal interactions of the professional. But, as Bolan states, the attempt to minimize or eliminate ambiguity "may not only be unrealistic, it may also impede effective action."[10]

KINDS OF INTERACTION AND 'OTHERS'

Clinical Interactions

Clinical interactions are those in which a professional engages in "study or practice based on actual treatment and observation of a client."[11] The professional's salient need in these interactions is "mastery of the professional domain."[12] In social work practice, this domain includes such activities as direct provision of information and practical helps, referrals, counseling, advice, advocacy, and a variety of other services for persons in need.

Professional interaction with clients differs from other kinds of interaction in two ways: It is guided by value and knowledge more than by emotion, sentiment, or a desire for status or financial profit; and its sole purpose is to provide the expert help sought by the client. However, although the NASW Code of Ethics describes with relative clarity desirable professional behavior with regard to clinical interaction,[13] there are still gray areas in the management of clinical interaction, such as: How much self-determination is realistically possible for young, dependent, disabled, and mentally ill clients? And how can a clinical relationship develop in coercive circumstances (for example, if the clinical other is a probationer or parolee)? Furthermore, the management of professional interaction with a client may be complicated by transference and countertransference; professionals have the same complement of hungers, fears, and loathings as clients; and there is, too, the necessity to integrate knowledge about interpersonal behavior with knowledge about policies and programs.

As already mentioned, the duration and intensity of clinical encounters and the skill required to manage them vary. Providing a concrete resource such as food stamps requires less professional skill than does counseling a client. And the latter clinical interaction is more likely to be extensive and intense. In addition, the professional's disposition in clinical encounters varies from warm and accepting to challenging and contentious, depending on the circumstances.

Furthermore, the identity of the clinical other is not always obvious.

Professionals work with and for individuals, families, groups, organizations, and communities; it is sometimes difficult to determine in whose interest the professional is working and to whom the professional has ultimate accountability. Although terms such as "recipients," "clients," "consumers," and "constituents" presumably have different meanings that should provide some direction to the professional managing various kinds of clinical interaction, in actual practice they seem highly interchangeable. However, even though sometimes it is difficult to manage clinical interaction and to follow the strictures of NASW's Code of Ethics, there is considerable clarity about what is *expected* of the professional in clinical interaction.

Collateral Interaction

Collateral interaction involves people who are part of clients' social environments, such as relatives, friends, and neighbors. It does not include clients' significant others who are engaged in clinical interaction (for example, two or more persons in family therapy).

Professionals fulfill their needs for mastery of the professional domain in management of collateral interaction, but, because their commitments to, and concerns about, clients differ somewhat from their commitments to and concerns about collateral others, professionals are confronted with the need for cognitive and value consistency in these interactions. A client's collateral others are sometimes referred to as a "natural helping network." Such people often provide emotional, social, financial, and physical supports that can enable the client to continue to live independently and healthfully. Or they may be significant persons in the clients' environments who *prevent* them from living independently and healthfully.[14] Professional interaction with these others is among the least understood in social work practice, especially with respect to the professional's and the agency's authority and the legal, ethical, and affectional conditions of exchange of resources among the parties involved. The social work literature on social support networks is shallow.[15]

Clients' support networks tend to be perceived as consisting only of collateral others—people similar or re-

lated to the client by lineage, life experience, or propinquity. Thus, the roles of collegial and sociopolitical others in providing social supports tend to be excluded, although the reality is that collegial and sociopolitical others are frequently of great significance in the client's social support network. Moreover, social support networks are frequently confused with voluntary organizations and self-help groups. But the concept of "network" in social science theory refers to the individual "interacting with others, some of whom interact with each other and yet others."[16] The whole network of such relations is much more fluid than the relatively stable units referred to as voluntary associations and self-help groups. Thus, the social support network of a particular client is unique to that client, not a fixed entity that relates to many clients in the same way.

Parker, in a cogent discussion of "tending" (that is, caretaking of dependent persons), indicates there is a critical need to develop practice and policy aimed at using the services of intimate caretakers to best advantage.[17] He poses such questions as the following: How long can one person be counted on to look after another? How does the intensity of the care required affect the tending relationship? How is the relationship affected when special skills are required to give the care? And how is the relationship affected by the prognosis regarding whether the need for care will increase or decrease?

Interaction with collateral others—an important aspect of social work practice—might be enriched by the application of different kinds of social science theory. Social network analysis provides many useful concepts for understanding these interactions, such as "size," "degree," "density," "clustering," "maintenance costs," "boundaries," and "content."[18] It is curious that a profession defined as "the art of helping the person in his situation" has developed so little knowledge concerning the management of interaction with collateral others.

Collegial Interactions

Collegial interactions are exchanges among professional peers. In his book on social work ethics, Levy notes that the ethical principles applied to clients differ appreciably from those applied to colleagues. The latter, he says, are matters of etiquette, good manners, and tact.[19]

These qualities are important because the knowledge that professionals have of colleagues' flaws, foibles, and failings could threaten the profession's existence if some degree of control were not exercised over use of such knowledge. Colleagues, Goffman says,

> share a community of fate. In having to put on the same kind of performance, they come to know each other's difficulties and points of view; whatever their tongues, they come to speak the same social language. And while colleagues who compete for audiences may keep some strategic secrets from one another, they cannot very well hide from one another certain things that they hide from the audience. The front that is maintained before others need not be maintained among themselves.[20]

The collegial relationship is one in which the parties are essentially on equal footing, each respecting the other. However, some colleagues are "more equal" than others. For example, in interactions with trainees, supervisees, and consultees, the professional is more of the expert helper who introduces the other to the knowledge, skills, and values of the profession. And each of these three kinds of interaction involves respectively higher degrees of "equality" between colleagues.

Frequently, some aspects of clinical or sociopolitical interaction enter into these collegial interactions. If the interaction involves the sharing of delicate and confidential matters about the self, the colleague-other frequently needs or demands the disciplined use of knowledge and skill that the professional is expected to use with clients. Sociopolitical elements often enter into collegial interactions, as when professionals are competing for organizational resources (for instance, "Who gets the grant?"), authority ("Who gets the appointment as director?"), or power ("Who makes the decisions?"). In addition, professionals' interaction with colleagues in related fields—nurses, physicians, psychologists, and lawyers—increases the potential for conflict and disagreement because of the differences in values, knowledge, and objectives held by their respective professions.

Collegial interactions provide a way for professionals to fulfill their needs for significant impact on the world of contemporaries. Recognition from and acceptance by peers is a significant force that shapes the professional's behavior.

Although there is a body of literature on intervention with colleagues under the rubrics of "supervision," "consultation," and "teamwork," most of it is a confusion of elements of several different kinds of interaction. Clear distinctions are not drawn, for example, between the sociopolitical authority of administrative roles and the professional expertise used in the collegial roles of teacher and consultant.

Sociopolitical Interaction

Sociopolitical interaction involves decision making about the allocation and control of organizational resources—authority, status, power, and money. Frequently there are high personal stakes involved in the management of sociopolitical interactions among employees, employers, policymakers, and funders. Poor management of a clinical interaction rarely results in the kind of loss to a professional that can occur if the professional mishandles interaction with a sociopolitical other. Clinical interaction also involves allocating and exchanging resources that have universal value: the professional's expertise and skill are exchanged for a salary or fee. However, in ethical clinical practice the terms of this financial exchange are clarified and agreed on *before* the clinical work begins. Sociopolitical interaction, on the other hand, is based on a continuous concern with allocations and exchanges of organizational resources. The primary objectives of sociopolitical interaction are instrumental in that they develop around tasks concerned with the allocation of organizational resources such as assigning responsibilities, scheduling, hiring, firing, and budgeting.

In sociopolitical interactions, professionals struggle to meet all the needs described earlier: enhanced self-esteem and self-actualization, mastery of the professional domain, perceptual and value consistency, and impact on the world of contemporaries. Special difficulties arise in the management of this interaction because the professional's status vis-à-vis sociopolitical others is frequently more uncertain than in other types of interaction. The official and politically legitimate power and authority to allocate organizational resources lies with the sociopolitical other. The professional brings to the interaction only the vague and tenuous authority of expertise.

Interaction with sociopolitical others is, more frequently than other types of interaction, the source of a great deal of discomfort that professionals are reluctant to talk about. This is because this interaction can more often result in experiences that are painful, humiliating, ambiguous, and confusing. This interaction, more than any other, may demand the exchange of resources that are inappropriate and undesirable in the professional's view, such as money, status, prestige, and even love in return for organizational resources.

Some findings from research on social exchange theory about the differences in resources exchanged in clinical and sociopolitical encounters are thought-provoking. First, people tend to exchange love with love; but money is the resource that is most frequently exchanged for all other resources. The exchange of love tends to require the most time and may require many encounters; the exchange of money takes the least time and can be done in a single encounter. The exchange of love requires small social units—usually a dyad; the exchange of money can take place in larger groups, and as the size of the social unit increases, exchanges of money increase.[21] Though these findings from experimental research are somewhat speculative and perhaps overstated, they provide challenging insights into the nature of different types of social interaction.

Social work literature pays little attention to the management of professional sociopolitical interaction. For example, in the index of Rothman's encyclopedic work, *Planning and Organizing for Social Change*, which is a review of research and theory on practice in administration, planning, and community organization, there are no listings for such topics as interpersonal interaction, encounters, and relationships.[22] With the exception of Brager's "Advocacy and Political Behavior" and Brager and Specht's *Community Organizing*, research and writing has focused primarily on "strategies and tactics" in community organization, social planning, and social action.[23] This kind of work usually refers to the behaviors of organizations and groups. The professional's management of interpersonal interaction is discussed only incidentally, if at all. To be sure, Bolan provides a compendium of professional sociopolitical relationships and discusses the major organizational, political, and structural variables that bear on them.[24] But there has not been a systematic analysis of the dynamics and management of this kind of interaction.

The reasons for this lack of discussion of—and this discomfort about—sociopolitical interaction are complex. Many social workers consider the kinds of management of interpersonal relationships described by Brager to be "manipulation." This response is in part due to a failure to distinguish among the attributes of the clinical, collateral, collegial, and sociopolitical others with whom the professional interacts. The discomfort occurs also because theories based on situation, such as social network analysis and social exchange theory, suggest a rational, calculating motivation for human behavior that runs counter to the assumptions of ego-psychologically based theory. However, more recent work—for example that in social exchange theory—has integrated many of the concepts and principles of dynamic psychology. As Emerson observes, "rationality in the sense of action based upon prior calculation of expected returns forms only one part of the larger subject matter of social exchange."[25]

IMPLICATIONS

This article has only touched on the central elements that should be included in a theory to explicate professional interpersonal interaction. Each of the elements requires detailed development.

New theory is needed because the literature on social work practice deals primarily with clinical interaction. There has been little attempt to integrate social science theory to explicate professional collateral, collegial, and sociopolitical interaction. This deficiency has had significant consequences for social work practice. It is one of the reasons why both education for and the practice of profes-

sional interactional tasks focus primarily on therapeutic work. To state the matter simply: If there is not, at a minimum, a language to describe practice with nonclinical others, it is not possible to educate and train practitioners to carry out these kinds of interactions. Without a conceptual language, theory for these aspects of practice cannot be developed. With neither theory nor language available to describe and analyze these interactions, their management tends to be perceived as unimportant and insignificant. People working in the field possess much practice-based wisdom about these matters, but it has not been codified into theory.

Over the last 50 years, the ego-psychological literature has been the richest source of theory available for understanding professionals' interactions with clinical others. The introduction of small-groups theory into social work practice in the 1940s and 1950s and of behaviorism in the 1960s and 1970s stirred debate in the profession. This resulted in the absorption into social work practice of group dynamics and behavior modification techniques. But behaviorism provides part of the base of social learning theory and behavior modification is derived in large part from social learning theory.[26] Behavior modification's referent is the individual and, in this sense, it bears a closer relationship to ego-psychological theories than to situationally oriented theories. Small-groups theory and group dynamics, on the other hand, may be oriented either to the personality or to the situation. Through the 1950s, emphasis in social group work was on the situation, but since then the balance has shifted toward clinical concerns for personal change.

The foregoing are, of course, broad generalizations about practice. Exceptions can be found. For example, there is the substantial treatment of nonclinical interactions in Germain and Gitterman's *The Life Model of Social Work Practice*.[27] Using an "ecological perspective," they take account of interchanges between people and environmental elements to find solutions to problems of living. Although they use different terms to describe them, Germain and Gitterman discuss collegial others involved in service provision, collateral others related to the client, and sociopolitical others in the organizational con-

text of practice. However, they do not draw theoretical distinctions among these different types of professional interaction; the worker's behavior in dealing with nonclinical others is treated nearly the same as is professional behavior in a clinical interaction. Nonetheless, Germain and Gitterman expand considerably the purview of practitioners.

Acknowledging such occasional exceptions, it is not an exaggeration to say that the core theory used in social work practice is of the ego-psychological variety. Social work has been enriched considerably by the application of this kind of theory, especially in clinical work requiring the engagement of the client's self to bring about changes in perceptions, attitudes, behaviors, and ways of relating to others. However, the ego-psychological literature is not the most useful source of theory for management of professional interactions that are nonclinical. Situationally oriented theories are of greater use with collateral, collegial, and sociopolitical others. Theories of this kind include symbolic interactionism, impression management, social exchange theory, and social network analysis, along with other bodies of material from sociology, anthropology, and social psychology.[28] Such theories can enhance social work practice because they illuminate the social and environmental aspects of practice considerably. These kinds of theories are most useful in describing nonclinical practice, because the primary objective of the professional in nonclinical work is to change the other primarily with respect to improving the client's situation or to enhance the context of professional practice.

There are some clinicians who would go even further and reject the notion of ego psychology as the core theory of clinical work. Loewenstein, for example, asserts that

It would be best for caseworkers to accept situation and communication theories as the *major* conceptual frameworks for casework practice. . . . An interactional, situational approach provides a more hopeful philosophy than ego psychology.[29]

However, we tend to believe that ego psychology provides a sound basis for clinical practice, especially if the work requires the engagement of the client's self in the change effort.

The important point is, however, that a major task of the profession for the future should be to enlarge understanding of the other side of its practice mission—*the situation*. Greater attention must be given to the development of skills and knowledge for the management of nonclinical interaction, along with attention to the structural features of the situations in which social work is practiced.

This charge should not be construed as an attack on social work, whose achievements have enriched society in this century. No other profession has sought to embrace the task of linking persons to their social environments in the way that social work has. But now the profession must embrace the social environmental aspects of this task with vigor and imagination.

Notes and References

1. See, for example, Felix Biestek, *The Casework Relationship* (Chicago: Loyola University Press, 1957): Helen Harris Perlman, *Relationship: The Heart of Helping People* (Chicago: University of Chicago Press, 1979): and Howard Goldstein, *Social Work Practice: A Unitary Approach* (Columbia: University of South Carolina Press, 1973), p. 10.

2. Charles W. McCann and Jane Park Cutler, "Ethics and the Alleged Unethical," *Social Work*, 24 (January 1979), p. 7.

3. Kenneth J. Gergen, "Social Psychology as History," *Journal of Personality and Social Psychology*, 26 (1973), pp. 309–320.

4. Richard S. Bolan, "The Practitioner as Theorist," *Journal of the American Planning Association*, 46 (July 1980), p. 269.

5. Ibid.

6. Ibid., p. 264.

7. Ibid., p. 268.

8. Edna B. Foa and Uriel G. Foa, "Resource Theory: Interpersonal Behavior as Exchange," in Kenneth J. Gergen, Martin S. Greenberg, and Richard H. Willis, eds., *Social Exchange: Advances in Theory and Research* (New York: Plenum Press, 1980), pp. 77–94.

9. The possibilities of mixing these elements is what makes works such as Erving Goffman, *The Presentation of Self in Everyday Life* (New York: Doubleday & Co., 1959): and Goffman, *Behavior in Public Places* (New York: Free Press, 1963), such fascinating and absorbing reading.

10. Bolan, "The Practitioner as Theorist," p. 272.

11. Jean L. McKechnie, ed., *Webster's New Twentieth Century Dictionary of the English Language* (Cleveland, Ohio: Collins & World, 1975), p. 339.

12. Bolan, "The Practitioner as Theorist," p. 268.

13. *Code of Ethics of the National Association of Social Workers* (Silver Spring, Md.: NASW, 1980).

14. Robert D. Vinter and Maeda J. Galinsky, "Extra-group Relations and Approaches," in Paul Glasser, Rosemary Sam, and Robert D. Vinter, eds., *Individual and Change Through Small Groups* (New York: Free Press, 1974), pp. 281–294.

15. Alice H. Collins and Diane L. Pancoast, *Natural Helping Networks: A Strategy for Prevention* (Washington, D.C.: National Association of Social Workers, 1976): and Charles Froland et al., *Helping Networks and Human Services* (Beverly Hills, Calif.: Sage Publications, 1981).

16. Geert A. Banck, "Network Analysis and Social Theory: Some Remarks," in Jeremy Boissevain and J. Clyde Mitchell, eds., *Network Analysis: Studies in Human Interaction* (Mouton, Paris: Monographs Under the Auspices of the Afrika-Studiecentrum-Leiden, 1973), p. 4.

17. Roy Parker, "Tending and Social Policy," in E. Matilda Goldberg and Stephen Hatch, eds., *A New Look at the Personal Social Services* (London, England: Policy Studies Institute, 1980).

18. See Boissevain and Mitchell, *Network Analysis*.

19. Charles S. Levy, *Social Work Ethics* (New York: Human Sciences Press, 1976), p. 177.

20. Goffman, *The Presentation of Self in Everyday Life*, p. 160.

21. Uriel G. Foa and Edna B. Foa, *Societal Structures of the Mind* (Springfield, Ill.: Charles C Thomas, Publisher, 1974).

22. Jack Rothman, *Planning and Organizing for Social Change: Action Principles from Social Science Research* (New York: Columbia University Press, 1974).

23. George A. Brager, "Advocacy and Political Behavior," *Social Work*, 13 (April 1968), pp. 6–15: and Brager and Harry Specht, *Community Organizing* (New York: Columbia University Press, 1973).

24. Richard S. Bolan, "The Social Relations of the Planner," *Journal of the American Institute of Planners*, 37 (November 1971), pp. 387–396.

25. Richard M. Emerson, "Social Exchange Theory," in Alex Inkeles et al., eds., *Annual Review of Sociology*, Vol. 2 (Palo Alto, Calif.: Annual Reviews, 1976), p. 344.

26. Alan E. Kazdin, *History of Behavior Modification: Experimental Foundations of Contemporary Research* (Baltimore, Md.: University Park Press, 1978).

27. Carel B. Germain and Alex Gitterman, *The Life Model of Social Work Practice* (New York: Columbia University Press, 1980), especially chap. 4. See also Max Siporin's discussion of "situational interventions" in *Introduction to Social Work Practice* (New York: Macmillan Publishing Co., 1975), pp. 302–310.

28. B. N. Meltzer and J. W. Petras, *Symbolic Interaction* (Boston: Allyn & Bacon, 1972): Bill Horner, "Symbolic Interactionism and Social Assessment," *Journal of Sociology and Social Welfare*, 6 (January 1979), pp. 19–32: Barry R. Schlenker, *Impression Management* (Monterey, Calif.: Brooks/Cole Publishing Co., 1980): Gergen, Greenberg, and Willis, eds., *Social Exchange*: J. K. Chandwick-Jones, *Social Exchange Theory: Its Structure and Influence in Social Psychology* (San Francisco: Academic Press, 1976): B. F. Meeker, "Decisions and Exchange," *American Sociological Review*, 36 (June 1971), pp. 485–95: and Boissevain and Mitchell, *Network Analysis*.

29. Sophie Freud Loewenstein, "Inner and Outer Space in Social Casework," *Social Casework*, 60 (January 1979), p. 29.

FATE OF IDEALISM IN SOCIAL WORK: ALTERNATIVE EXPERIENCES OF PROFESSIONAL CAREERS

DAVID WAGNER

SOCIAL WORK PRACTICE historically has required not only professional skill and training, but a commitment to social idealism and social change. As long ago as 1929, social workers were urged to embrace both the cause of reform and the function of professional skill (Lee, 1929). However, the literature of recent decades has suggested that such a marriage was not easy and that many social workers abandoned their idealism as they advanced professionally. In the 1960s, research studies noted the prevalence of a "bureaucratic orientation" among many social workers, in which the primary loyalty of social workers was to the employing agency's rules and commands, rather than to professional ethics or ideals (Billingsley, 1964; Epstein, 1970a, 1970b, 1970c; Wilensky, 1964). Literature on burnout and job dissatisfaction among social workers also has revealed the decline of idealism and commitment among practitioners (Cherniss, 1980; Daley, 1979; Karger, 1981; Kermish & Kushin, 1969; Knapp, Harissis, & Missiakoulis, 1981; Maslach, 1976; Streepy, 1981; Zastrow, 1984). Some have criticized social work professionalism entirely and have maintained that social workers tend to abandon social action and social change as they become committed to professional self-interest and career advancement (Bailey & Brake, 1975; Cloward & Piven, 1977; Greenwood, 1957).

Few studies, however, have focused on social workers' subjective experience of their working lives, nor have many studies followed a cohort of social workers to explore how they maintain (or fail to maintain) their ideals over time. The author explores the fate of idealism in social work through a study of a group of social workers who have been committed at some time in their careers to radical change and traces the ability of these subjects to maintain their commitment over the course of their careers.

The Study

To understand how idealistic professionals balance occupational commitment with political ideology, the author studied a population of radical social workers (Wagner, 1988a, 1988b, 1989, in press). In 1986 and 1987, the author conducted in-depth interviews with past and present members of the *Catalyst*—a collective based in New York City. *Catalyst*, along with other activities, was the longest consecutively published radical journal in the social services. Many subjects also were former or current members of a variety of other radical organizations in the social services such as the Radical Alliance of Social Service Workers in New York, the Union of Radical Human Service Workers in Boston, and the Bertha Capen Reynolds Society. Those interviewed all held master of social work (MSW) degrees and ranged in age from 31 to 51 years. Although their involvement with *Catalyst* and other groups varied over time, the majority of subjects reported that they had been radicalized between 1966 and 1971 and were strongly influenced by the new left, the civil rights movement, the antiwar movement, and the women's movement.

Data were collected on all 43 individuals who had participated in *Catalyst* as of 1987. To secure a research population whose members had considered themselves to be radicals for a significant period, only the 24 individuals who held membership for 2 or more years were selected for in-depth interviews.

An ethnographic approach to this material was chosen for a variety of reasons. Some previous studies had been done on the political viewpoints of social workers (Epstein, 1970a, 1970b, 1970c; Ressner, 1986), but survey methods of these studies had several built-in weaknesses. The studies primarily used lists provided by professional associations, which left out many social workers, per

haps most importantly those who had departed from the profession. Second, the surveys relied on "objective" measures of professional identification such as journal readership or participation in professional activities, which are relatively shallow behaviors as compared with subjective identification with a profession. Finally, surveys cannot illuminate data about an individual's process of maintaining a professional or political identity or ideology; they only provide a measure of views held at a particular time.

The author's access to subjects' resumes, to written memos and articles by the subjects, as well as to other historical documents such as subjects' applications to graduate school, allowed subjects' reports in interviews to be confirmed, to some extent, by documentary material. With documentation of their past views on politics, social work, and professionalism, the author was able to confront subjects during interviews to elicit comments on the consistency or contrast between their current and past views.

Although the subjects' social work careers do not necessarily reflect the experience of all MSW social workers, the problem of how this group of politically committed social workers balanced their idealism with the demands of bureaucratic work underlines the problem of mission and function that affects the entire profession. The methodology is similar to that employed by Michels (1962) in his turn-of-the-century work, *Political Parties,* in which he tested his theory of the "iron law of oligarchy" by studying the German Social Democratic Party (SDP). Michels was interested in the inevitability of domination of organizations by the few. Rather than surveying numerous German organizations, he intensively studied the one German party clearly committed to democracy and suggested that SDP's difficulty in sustaining organizational democracy reflected the deeper struc tural problem of maintaining democracy in any major organization. Similarly, the author suggests that social workers who have committed themselves at some point to socialist, feminist, or other radical ideologies provide an ideal research base to test the compatibility of a career in social work with the maintenance of personal ideals and ethics.[1]

Because of the nature of qualitative data obtained from lengthy semistructured interviews and the lack of previous study of this subject, this study introduces a number of new measures and concepts based on a content analysis of the interview data. Such concepts are used to review briefly the subjects' retrospective accounts of their choice of social work as a career, their socialization to the profession in schools of social work, and their early to middle career (an average of 12 years of post-master's experience). A typology of work attachments explains how these social workers now interpret their careers and their attitudes toward professionalism and political radicalism.

"Missionary Zeal" and the Choice of Social Work

The social workers interviewed came to the profession with a strong idealism that can be described as "missionary zeal." The following quotes from subjects were typical:

I thought that if I wanted to change the world, which, of course, I wanted to do, that I would be a social worker.

One becomes a social worker to do good. It's a way of serving, it's a way of understanding the human condition and acting on it and changing it. . . . It goes back to when I was 9 years old, understanding that poverty was wrong. . . . I was going to be a good person when I grew up and I was going to help people.

Subjects were coded as expressing strong "missionary zeal" if they cited strong political, religious, or social change motivations to enter the profession, rather than references to career mobility, opportunities for promotion, or fortuitous circumstances. Eighteen of the 24 subjects had strong "missionary zeal" upon entry to the profession; however, only eight expressed this ideal-

ism as a political calling at the point they chose social work as a career. Those who stressed political objectives tended to enter social work between 1966 and 1975 and chose community organization as a method area. As one subject explained:

I thought there would be some way of combining my political beliefs with a job . . . figured I could do community organizing that I'd get paid for, instead of earning $25 a week like I was doing. I had this image of social work trying to meet people's needs and educate people too . . . like the Black Panther Party was doing.

Most subjects came to social work with a vague understanding of the field and of their particular goals within the field. Their idealism and zeal was high, but their initial interest in and commitment to social work professionalism was low.

Professional Socialization as Radicalizing

The question of how professional education affects students has been controversial in the social science literature. Sociologists such as Parsons (1964), Merton, Reader, and Kendall (1957), and Goode (1960) approached professional training as an acculturation process in which norms such as impartiality, social distance, and scientific inquiry are inculcated to students. Not only did the structural functionalists regard professional norms as system maintaining, but many radical critics in social work and other professions frequently have argued that professional training discourages the more radical impulses of initiates in favor of conservative professional norms (Cloward & Piven, 1977; Monchek, 1979; Pearson, 1975). On the other hand, social scientists such as Lipset (1976) explained the student unrest of the 1960s as resulting from the congregation of roleless youths, freed from occupational commitment, being exposed to liberal or radical faculty creating a breeding ground for radicalism.

In this study, social work graduate school proved to have been radicalizing: converting altruistic neophytes to more political theories of change and leading to increased activism among those who already identified themselves as radicals. Subjects cited particular professors, campus strikes, and field placements in

school in the 1960s said,

It was very exciting. Before I knew it, I was getting arrested, blocking the doors of a welfare center. I felt we were in the midst of a revolution with the welfare rights movement.

A subject in social work school in the late 1970s said,

All of a sudden there I was stopping trucks, writing the Teamsters union, working out strategies for mass arrest.

A subject in social work school in the early 1970s said,

My placement was a great experience! Here I was in this multi-ethnic community, doing housing organizing with a socialist-feminist as my supervisor.

Although only 11 of the 24 subjects identified themselves as being politically radical at the time they entered social work educational programs, 22 considered themselves leftists upon graduation from social work schools.

Content analysis revealed that as subjects were becoming committed to radical politics, their commitment to social work professionalism increased and they were influenced greatly by a tradition of idealism they had read about in social work texts or heard about from their professors. Nineteen of the 24 subjects interviewed described themselves as strongly committed to and enthusiastic about achieving political change through social work.

Graduation from social work school was the apex of subjects' attachment to social work as an idealistic, altruistic profession that could satisfy both their needs for income, security, and job autonomy and the idealistic principles of changing society. Professional and idealistic identification with social work were at their highest at graduation for all subjects, whether they had been trained for direct treatment, community organization, or other method areas and whether they received their education in the 1960s, 1970s, or 1980s.

Images of Success, Worlds of Pain

Although a complete review of the experience of the subjects with approximately 150 different jobs over the years is beyond the scope of this article, several interesting points emerged from a review of the subjects' careers.

The subjects interviewed had increased their income, status, and organizational positions considerably since graduate school. At the time of the study, the subjects were employed as business executives, union officials, faculty members, researchers, high-level social service administrators, social work supervisors, direct practitioners, and doctoral students. Many were well known in their fields through their published work, professional awards, or media coverage of their work.

As interviews proceeded, it appeared that a recitation of work achievements or a review of resumes tended to determine their careers. Professionals self-consciously developed written documents that sought to convince their employers, educational institutions, professional associations, and colleagues of a linear progression in their current status. Not only are job tensions, periods of unemployment, and the loss of jobs through quitting and firing naturally minimized, but the very sequence of jobs is presented as to appear rational and intentional. Subjects responded to the interviewer's questions about their resumes with comments such as "Now, let me tell you what I really did!" One subject's response to a question about career suggested that the entire concept of a career is a social construct:

I don't know. It's not like I feel I have this *career*. You know, like a career that's moving along. . . . I just ended up doing different things. . . .

Minimized in the concept of a career or in objective indices of mobility is the subjective experience of work life. Of 24 subjects, 19 had experienced high tension in their work lives (*high tension* is defined here as at least one extremely conflictual job situation that lasted 2 years).

Many subjects revealed, in addition, that despite their current success, they previously had experienced such severe problems at agencies or employing institutions that they had been forced to leave. Because many professionals technically are not fired but are asked to leave or resign under pressure, the author used the term "negative career

Table 1.
Typology of Work Orientations

Category	Strong Adherence to Idealism and Social Change	Strong Adherence to Social Work Professionalism
Mediated	+	+
Critical	+	−
Detached	−	−
Professionalist[a]	(−)	(+)

[a]Potential orientation; not found in this study.

events" to cover firings, forced resignations, and other job terminations. Thirteen subjects suffered from at least one major negative career event, with some experiencing more than one.

Another index of employment difficulties was that the subjects' turnover rate was high—they averaged five positions held in the past 10 years, and some had held as many as seven positions. Eleven subjects (45.8 percent) had left social work positions for at least 1 year and entered fields as diverse as union organizing, business, arts, and carpentry. Many of these subjects returned to social work, and at the time of the study, only six (25 percent) appeared to have left the profession permanently.

Alternative Interpretations of Work and Idealism

In contrast to the "missionary zeal" that subjects felt when they chose social work as a career and the strong link between their idealism and professional identification upon graduation from social work school, a considerable diminution in such idealism had occurred by the time of their interviews in 1986 and 1987. On the one hand, consistent with Epstein's research (1970a, 1970c), upward mobility and professionalization showed little relationship to political conservatism, and the majority of subjects distinguished themselves from those they disdainfully described as "yuppies." On the other hand, fewer subjects associated social change and idealism with social work (Table 1).

Four conceptual orientations to social work were identified relating idealism and social change and identification with professional social work (Table 1). Those

who remained strongly identified with social work professionalism and with radical ideologies strongly believed that social work is an instrument of social change. This category was labeled "mediated" because these individuals mediated their idealism successfully through their professional identification. Eight subjects fell into this category.

The largest number of subjects, however, fell into the category labeled "critical." Although these subjects continued to adhere strongly to idealistic principles, they no longer strongly identified with social work as a profession. Rather, they viewed social change as being linked to broader social movements in society that have little to do with the organized profession of social work.

The third group, labeled "detached," was neither strongly committed to social work professionalism nor to the idealistic principles that they initially espoused. Unlike the other two categories, which cut across occupational roles, the detached subjects all occupied high-level positions in social service administration or business. Like the mediated subjects, they associated social work with idealism or radicalism, but, in contrast, they dismissed both as "follies of youth."

A fourth conceptual category would be logical: individuals could have a diminished attachment to idealism and social change, but a strong commitment to social work professionalism. This orientation, labeled "professionalist," was not found in the study.

The author classified subjects into the appropriate groups after analyzing their responses to questions about their views on radical politics and social work professionalism (Table 2). Those most able to mediate social work professionalism with idealistic principles tended to be women trained in direct social work practice who were strong feminists.[2] At the time of the study, subjects classified as mediated were employed as counselors, program directors, or midlevel supervisors or administrators, but did not control large amounts of funds or staffs, as did those in the detached category. Although these subjects had work histories that appeared to represent upward movement on a resume, the majority also had considerable negative experiences, including being fired or forced to quit. Nevertheless, all of the members of this group had remained in social work and had secured positions that they regarded as meeting their career and political or idealistic needs.

Characteristically, these social workers identified their idealism and professional identities with a particular historic tradition in social work, particularly the settlement house movement and past leaders in social work such as Bertha Reynolds. Members of the mediated group saw good social work practice as subversive activity because empowering clients, whether through casework, group work, or community organization, means helping clients overcome personal barriers to political activity and social participation. The practice style most characteristic of this group can be called "prefigurative," for as Breines (1982) described the term, the practice attempts to create the preconditions for a new society on a micro-level through a series of personal transformations.

Believing that the "personal is political," the mediated group was able to see the process of change as critical and developmental progress as meaningful. A subject described how helping a client confront a welfare worker can be empowering:

I've been working with this woman and [welfare] is giving her a horrible time. She has this very controlling, awful caseworker there. [We] spent a lot of time talking about her family and how her sister constantly tried to control her. And as she is talking about Mr. B, who is the welfare caseworker, I thought this sounds so much like her sister and how she couldn't deal with this guy, how she was totally intimidated. I began to ask her if she saw similarities and she made the connection too. If we can keep helping her [stand up] to this sister of hers who dominates her, hopefully she can eventually confront Mr. B and the welfare bureaucrats. . . . This [is] an example of how I see therapy being radical.

One of the key distinctions between mediated social workers and the critical group is their perceptions of the efficacy of consciousness raising on a micro-level as a strategy of social change. For the mediated group, such consciousness raising is political and radical. They view good social work practice as a vehicle for social change even if it does not directly link clients to political action overtly:

There is radical potential in all social work practice. That's why the far right doesn't like us . . . they know good social work practice is inherently subversive.

But the critical subjects differed from this view:

People say that the process is radical, but this seems to me to be an extraordinary gutting of the term . . . . We used to think of "radical" as meaning significant changes in society, but now I don't even know how the term is used.

Critical subjects were somewhat more likely to be male than the mediated group; they were older; they more often came from professional families; and they had been influenced more profoundly over the years by Marxist or socialist ideas (Table 2). But the most outstanding differences between the groups were the critical subjects' attachment at some point in their careers to intellectual reading in a social science discipline such as sociology, anthropology, or psychology and critical subjects' tendency to believe they are in a marginal segment of the social work method area (such as community organization, research, or policy) or field of practice (such as settlement house work or probation and corrections).

Critical subjects moved toward academic pursuits, movement positions in leftist organizations or unions, or direct service positions. The latter two groups generally sacrificed upward career mobility to obtain job positions in which they believed they could more openly do political work. One subject worked for a union that allowed her to spend much of her time working in support of the Nicaraguan revolution and other political causes. Another subject, a social worker in a public corrections unit, suggested that she would forgo promotion to continue to be a union activist and remain free to pursue outside interests:

I took another job for a while—one most social workers grab right away. It was at a psychiatric outpatient clinic and it paid

Table 2.
Stances toward Professional Values and Social Ideals

Factor	Mediated	Critical	Detached
Gender	Majority female	Mixed	Majority male
Age	Youngest (median = 34)	—	Oldest (median = 40)
Religion	Mostly Roman Catholic	—	Mostly Jewish
Social class of origin	More working class than critical subjects	Most from families of professionals	Largely working class
Area of social work training	Direct treatment	Mixed, but included majority of those trained in community organization, planning, research, and social policy	Direct treatment
Theoretical paradigms	Systems theory, generalist social work practice	Social science knowledge base (sociology, anthropology, and so forth) or more ego psychology	Not applicable
Current occupational positions	Predominantly social work supervisors, low-level administrators, and counselors	Predominantly academics, counselors, "movement" organization or trade union workers	Predominantly workers in business or high-level management of public or nonprofit agencies
Work history	High job tension, many negative career events	Lowest degree of past job tension and "negative career events," often departed field, sacrificed mobility	Highest amount of past job tension and "negative career events," often departed field
Political ideology	Feminism, consciousness-raising, "empowerment" philosophy	Marxism, socialism, New Left, and feminist ideologies	Prior New Left history, little or no current attachment to past idealism
Orientation to social change	"Prefigurative": social change through social work	Movement related: social change not embedded in professional work	Personalistic: identified reform with own power
Descriptive label for work role	"Classical" professionals	"Organizational intellectuals"	"Technobureaucrats"

more and it had more status. But I hated it and came back here. For me the goal is to stay at the agency until I retire, to retain a progressive attitude, stay as a line worker and a union member. I don't like this moving up the organization stuff.

Mediated group members most closely resembled the classic definition of professionals in that they identified with the symbols of the profession and its dominant paradigms, usually were members of professional associations, and interpreted and judged their work in terms of colleague reference groups. Critical subjects more closely resembled Zald and McCarthy's (1975) label for some social service workers as "organizational intellectuals." Most of this group did not describe their work in terms of a commitment to a profession or an institution, but in terms of outside social forces and movements that linked their work with social change or knowledge production. Though they may have performed the same daily work as the mediated group, their reference point was not the social work field, but movements such as peace groups, left-wing parties, women's organizations, and religious groups.

Members of the detached group overwhelmingly were male, came from working-class backgrounds, and generally had moved over the years into business or high administrative positions in the social services. Few of these subjects had anticipated becoming managers, but as line workers they usually had suffered from extreme tension and negative career events. For example, one subject, who at the time of the study was an executive with a publishing company, described two extremely distressing experiences she had had as a social worker at a hospital and at a mental health clinic. She interpreted these experiences as resulting from overidealism and psychological burnout and found working in an efficiently organized company far preferable to working in a social service agency. Another subject, who began his social work career as an organizer and was involved in a major community battle that dominated the news in a major city in the mid-1970s, described himself as bitter about the lack of support he had received from his board, staff, and the community as the battle wore on. "Burned out," he moved from organizing to administration, where he found the work with professional ser-

vice providers to be "saner" than with "lay people."

Like the mediated group, the detached group at one time identified with social work values and idealism and even radicalism, but they now reject them. Some of the subjects were hostile to both social work and the poor:

I'd look at social work like a business, and let some of social work go out of business. In the old days, you could just say "give us the money and resources and we social workers and radicals and liberals could save the world." Well, nobody believes that anymore, and even with all the resources we wouldn't eliminate poverty. Maybe we should eliminate welfare...60 to 70 percent of the country agrees with [President Ronald] Reagan that welfare is a mess.

As the mediated group could be described as professionals and the critical group as organizational intellectuals, the "detached" were committed to a personal search for excellence removed from professional identification and any outside reference group. The detached group suggest what Larson (1977) and others have described as a "technobureaucratic" orientation. Their loyalty was bound to their particular organization only, rather than generalized to a collectivity, and their orientation to change was personalistic and bureaucratic.

The technobureaucratic orientation replaced detached subjects' previous idealism and quests for social reform or even revolution. In the study, such an orientation seemed to be linked to other negative career events in previous social work jobs and weak attachments to mediating ideologies such as feminism or socialism. In the absence of strong intellectual commitment to an ideology, detached subjects tended to view negative job experiences in the lower echelons of employment as repudiating the ideals of social work and social change, and they came to view upward mobility as an end in itself.

Finally, the logical fourth category of professionalist, in which the social worker becomes more strongly identified with the profession but less idealistic, was not found among subjects in this study. Several reasons exist to believe that this orientation is less likely to occur in social work than in other professions. Strong attachment to professional identification in this study, as in Ep-

stein's (1969) study, did not imply a detachment from idealism or social change strategies, including radical ideologies. The vague boundaries of the professional community and professional norms are broad enough to incorporate line social workers, organizers, and lower level supervisors who maintain idealistic views or even radical political ideologies.

On the other hand, high-level managerial positions often appear to conflict with the goals of social work staff or activist groups. It is suggested—though this requires more study—that administrative personnel in the social services are most likely to suffer detachment from idealism and from an identification with social work. Moreover, in a period of high turnover and mobility for social workers, one would anticipate that social workers disengaged from idealism and social change would often seek more lucrative positions than low-level social work jobs or might move to different fields.

Conclusions

If commitment to social work as a profession and to idealism are viewed in absolute terms, then the environment of social work school appears to be the high point for such commitment. The employment market fragments the ideal of the professionally and socially committed social worker as a result of the perceived blockage of social change strategies in hierarchical organizations, the availability of other careers and jobs for those committed to social change, and the presence of segments in the field that often have a weak identification with social work professionalism (such as research, policy, or community organization) because they feel less central to the dominant paradigms of social work in the 1980s. On the whole, political ideology remained more stable for the subjects of this study than professional identifications and loyalty. Professional commitments are argued to be more highly contingent than political ideology (although this issue would benefit from further research with different populations). However, the fact that only a small number of previously idealistic social workers had abandoned their ideals and that the majority of this group remained in the social work field is encouraging for the profession.

The study indicated that social workers, depending on their personal and political ethics and their fields of practice, may interpret their work life and professional roles quite differently. Literature in the profession may be somewhat restrictive in its definitions of professionalism or unrealistic in its expectations that social workers will uncritically subscribe to professional identity. For example, the ability of the critical subjects to maintain their idealism and, for many of them, continue careers in the social services, came from an intellectual perspective critical of the professions themselves, along with other social institutions in society. The subjective interpretations of social work careers require further study.

The diverse interpretations of social work practice support the argument made by Bucher and Strauss (1961) and others that social work and other professions comprise segments that do not compose a unified professional community (Epstein & Conrad, 1978; Wagner, 1986). Those closest to the core paradigm of social work (particularly social casework) most often identify strongly with the profession; other methods and some fields of practice are more marginal.

The departure of some social workers strongly committed to social idealism and social change from the traditional bounds of the field to work for activist organizations or labor unions also has implications for studies of job turnover and job satisfaction in social work. At a minimum, such studies in helping to explain why individuals leave social work should distinguish those who are "burned out" from those seeking a more political or alternative career route. Further, because many trained social workers work on the borders of social work but tend to have a weak identification with the profession, professional leaders and educators need to reassess the boundaries of the social work field.

Detachment from idealistic principles in social work appears to result from both negative job experiences in social work and mobility into powerful positions. Interestingly, those subjects who remained strongly committed to social change, whether strongly identified with social work or not, tended to limit their goals for upward mobility because of their idealistic principles. They often perceived high managerial positions and attainment of high status and high income as contradictory to their political and personal views.

This finding raises challenging questions for those who train social administrators and for leaders and educators who stress the upward mobility of social work to attract students and new practitioners. More detailed career studies of social workers with high administrative positions are necessary to explore further the problem of detachment from social work identification and political idealism, but serious conflicts may exist between the advocacy of unbounded mobility in the social services and retention of idealism.

[1] Although *Catalyst* was an explicitly socialist journal, interviews with subjects revealed classification of their ideologies to be far more complex. To the extent subjects were able to self-label at all, such labels ranged from "socialist" to "socialist-feminist" to "feminist" to "radical feminist" to "anarchist" to "Marxist" to "radical." For a fuller discussion, see Wagner (1988a).

[2] Descriptors of ideology are not mutually exclusive. Almost all subjects in the mediated group described themselves as feminists, but many also used labels such as socialist or Marxist. Some critics also described themselves as feminists, but the preponderance of ideological attachment of the critics was toward socialist or Marxist ideas.

References

Bailey, R., & Brake, M. (Eds.). (1975). *Radical social work*. New York: Pantheon.

Billingsley, A. (1964). Bureaucratic and professional role orientations in social casework. *Social Service Review, 38,* 400–407.

Breines, W. (1982). *Community and organization in the New Left, 1962-1968: The great refusal.* New York: Praeger.

Bucher, R., & Strauss, A. (1961). The professions in process. *American Journal of Sociology, 66,* 325–334.

Cherniss, G. (1980). *Staff burnout: Job stress in the human services.* Beverly Hills, CA: Sage.

Cloward, R., & Piven, F. F. (1977). The acquiescence of social work. *Society, 4,* 55–65.

Daley, M. (1979). Burnout in protective services. *Social Work, 24,* 375–380.

Epstein, I. (1969). *Professionalization and social work activism.* Unpublished doctoral dissertation, Columbia University, New York.

Epstein, I. (1970a). Organizational careers, professionalization, and social work radicalism. *Social Service Review, 41,* 123–131.

Epstein, I. (1970b). Professional role orientation and conflict strategies. *Social Work, 15,* 87–92.

Epstein, I. (1970c). Professionalization, professionalism, and social worker radicalism. *Journal of Health and Social Behavior, 11,* 67–77.

Epstein, I., & Conrad, K. (1978). The empirical limits of social work professionalism. In Y. Hasenfeld & R. Sarry (Eds.), *The management of human services,* (pp. 163–183). New York: Columbia University Press.

Goode, W. (1960). Encroachment, charlatanism, and the emerging professions. *American Sociological Review, 25,* 902–914.

Greenwood, E. (1957). The attributes of a profession. *Social Work, 2,* 45–55.

Karger, M. (1981). Burnout as alienation. *Social Service Review, 52,* 271–283.

Kermish, I., & Kushin, F. (1969). Why high turnover? Social work staff losses in a county welfare department. *Public Welfare, 27,* 134–139.

Knapp, M.R.J., Harissis, K., & Missiakoulis, S. (1981). Who leaves social work? A statistical analysis. *British Journal of Social Work, 11,* 421–444.

Larson, M.S. (1977). *The rise of professionalism.* Berkeley: University of California Press.

Lee, P. (1929). Social work: Cause and function. *Proceedings of the National Conference of Social Work, 1929.* Chicago.

Lipset, S. (1976). *Rebellion in the university.* Chicago: University of Chicago Press.

Maslach, C. (1976). Burnout. *Human Behavior, 5,* 16–18.

Merton, R., Reader, G., & Kendall, P. (1957). *The student physician.* Cambridge: Harvard University Press.

Michels, R. (1962). *Political parties.* New York: Free Press.

Monchek, M. (1979). Drawing the lines: My political education in social work school. *Catalyst, 1*(4), 19–34.

Parsons, T. (1964). *Essays in sociological theory.* New York: Free Press.

Pearson, G. (1975). Making social workers. In R. Bailey and M. Brake (Eds.), *Radical social work* (pp. 13–45). New York: Pantheon.

Ressner, L. (1986). *Professionalization and social activism.* Unpublished doctoral dissertation, Bryn Mawr College, Bryn Mawr, PA.

Streepy, J. (1981). Direct service providers and burnout. *Social Casework, 62,* 352–361.

Wagner, D. (1986). Collective mobility and fragmentation: A model of social work history. *Journal of Sociology and Social Welfare, 13,* 657–700.

Wagner, D. (1988a). *Political ideology and professional careers: A study of radical social service workers.* Unpublished doctoral dissertation, City University of New York, New York.

Wagner, D. (1988b). Whither the radicals in the professions? *Wisconsin Sociologist, 24,* 76–87.

Wagner, D. (1989). Radical movements in the social services: A theoretical framework. *Social Service Review, 63,* 264–284.

Wagner, D. (in press). *The quest for a radical profession: Social service careers and political ideology.* Lanham, MD: University Press of America.

Wilensky, H. (1964). The professionalization of everyone? *American Journal of Sociology, 70,* 137–158.

Zald, M., & McCarthy, J. (1975). Organizational intellectuals and the criticism of society. *Social Service Review, 46,* 344–362.

Zastrow, C. (1984). Understanding and preventing burnout. *British Journal of Social Work, 14,* 141–155.

David Wagner, PhD, is Assistant Professor, Department of Social Work, University of Southern Maine, 96 Falmouth Street, Portland, ME 04103.

FROM CLINICIAN TO SUPERVISOR: ESSENTIAL INGREDIENTS FOR TRAINING
JOSEPH A. WALSH

I N MANY SOCIAL SERVICE AGENCIES, the best clinicians are tapped to become supervisors. Although being a supervisor does not necessarily require abandonment of front-line clinical activities, it does demand that such duties be fused with the duty to guide and manage clinical work conducted by others.

However, the brief description of supervision noted above does not adequately describe the responsibilities of supervisors. Often, new supervisors are only vaguely aware of the more subtle aspects of being a supervisor. The need to discipline, evaluate, motivate, and orchestrate staff may be overlooked by potential or new supervisors.

Moreover, unless one is given the opportunity to apply principles and precepts of supervising, these concepts remain theoretical and platitudinous. Continuing education and in-service training for supervisors as they begin to immerse themselves in that role are the most effective methods of helping to inculcate supervisory skills, attitudes, and behaviors. To attempt to train supervisors outside this context is often a wasted effort.

The present article describes the reactions of supervisors to a training course and their evaluation of its helpfulness for them in their supervisory role. Participants were asked to respond anonymously to questions covering the following areas: (1) specific elements that should be retained in the course (ranging from number and length of sessions to topics discussed and style of presentation); (2) aspects of the course they would alter or refine; (3) what two or three ways the course helped them in their supervisory duties; and (4) their level of agreement with such statements as the relevance of the course to their work, the consonance between what they had been led to expect about the course and what occurred, and the sufficiency of conceptual information (beyond practical information) about supervision.

Summaries based on participants' responses indicated that participants were in almost complete positive agreement regarding the relevance, utility, and immediate applicability of course information. Differences of opinion emerged over the ideal number of training sessions.

This article describes one tested model found to be effective for the training of new supervisors (and even some seasoned ones) in various social service settings (public, private, large, small, broadly focused, and narrowly focused). The model has been presented in multisession workshops on 10 occasions in various settings to more than 250 supervisors.

Rationale

Being promoted to the role of supervisor in a social service agency is often akin to being a newly elected public official: one is amazed at the number of debts, trade-offs, and masters to be served as well as the relentlessness of expectations from others. These surprises are complicated by the role evolution from clinician to supervisor or manager.

An effective supervisor needs refined and consciously utilized interpersonal skills and an awareness of effective ways to handle management tasks. Most clinicians rightfully assume that they have some talent in managing interpersonal relationships and that this talent will serve them well in their supervisory duties. The rub comes when they discover that although clinical skills help in a managerial role, they are different from supervisory skills and new theories, precepts, and behaviors are needed.

The managerial dimension of supervision requires the supervisor to enable others to accomplish organizational goals. The supervisor's job, then, is to participate in determining, formulating, and effecting organizational policies (Steiner, 1977). Few people are able to perform management functions (usually described as planning, organizing, motivating, and controlling) in a comprehensive sense. Work, and life in general, are simply too complicated and unpredictable for such absolute demarcations of tasks (Mintzberg, 1975). Nonetheless, the management activities incumbent upon supervisors can be described and taught and, even if complicated by competing tasks and roles, are important to learn if effective management is to be more than a matter of good will and blind luck.

Historical Note

In social service agencies, the role of supervisor has an interesting history. In the days of the charity organizations, supervisors were actually volunteer staff who supervised paid staff. Often supervisors were wealthy women who gave not only money but also time and advice in order to foster the goals of the charity organization. With the advent of academic degrees in social service work and the advent of clinical services that required academic preparation, formal training of supervisors and coming up through the ranks from "doer" to "teacher" became the norm. In recent years, many graduate schools have devoted courses, even degree programs, to the art and science of management, often, however, without emphasizing prior experience in the practice field, which can be very helpful to effective human service management.

Debate over the responsibility of graduate schools to prepare social service supervisors has been carried on for almost two decades (Sarri, 1971; Kazmerski & Macarov, 1976). Less attention has been focused on the most effective timing and format of such training. I believe that on-the-job training and continuing education courses for persons with several years of practice experience are the most effective ways to prepare supervisors for their management role (Patti, 1977; Mintzberg, 1975).

In many social service agencies, people who have never been clinicians hold important supervisory and management roles. Lawyers, administrators, business managers, social policy advocates, researchers, and the like perform management duties unfettered and unaided by a clinical perspective. Conversely, clinicians who assume supervisory and management duties must struggle to decide when to use a clinical model and when to use an organizational model in responding to issues. The training ingredients discussed in the following section are designed as a topical guide for sorting through training needs.

Essential Training Ingredients

Supervisory training, like most training efforts, seems to work best when the training plan is purposeful and clear. Training should be reserved for persons who currently supervise regular agency staff. The advantage of this guideline is that such persons bear the title, role, and status of a supervisor and must perform in situations in which ideas discussed in training may be tested and from which examples of supervisory issues may be drawn.

Generally, restricting the training group to staff from a single agency is beneficial. Such persons are governed by the same personnel regulations, agency history and mission, and upper management. Also, restricting participants to staff from one agency means that the diverse responsibilities of staff can be discussed, thus creating another dimension of learning in the workshop.

When supervisors from more than one agency are brought together, it is advantageous to require that the agencies from which they come are as similar as possible. Similarity of tasks creates a bond among supervisors during training. Too much diversity (different tasks and different agencies) makes for too little common ground. In other words, when participants do not share comparable job tasks or at least the experience of working in the same type of agency, it is difficult for them to identify with one another. Too much disparity among participants can inhibit their training and motivation.

Another technique used to facilitate group cohesion is development of an operational contract. Components of the contract should include confidentiality, participation by all members, establishing personal learning goals, and agreement to provide feedback about the usefulness of the course. Some aspects of this contract can be explicit and others implicit. To illustrate, each member of the training groups may be asked to provide the instructor with a brief vignette of a real-life supervisory issue with which that person has struggled. These vignettes can be compiled and given to all group members, then discussed during the portion of the course most relevant to the vignette. In this way, the course will be relevant to some degree for each participant. Confidentiality about these vignettes should be ensured. Although trainers may promise confidentiality with regard to participants' superiors, such trust must be earned. Participants in prior training groups can help reassure participants that this aspect of the contract will not be abridged.

Essential to establishing this contract is the agreement of higher administrators to honor confidentiality. They must understand that confidentiality and personal learning goals of participants will not run counter to the values and mission of the agency.

In the training model described here, each workshop series lasted for 15 hours over a six-week period. Time was allowed for discussion of special interests of group members, but because good supervision has many essential components, standardized topics were also developed and covered. Effort was made to emphasize the knowledge and skills derived from participants' preexisting clinical experience and to connect these experiences and skills with meaningful supervisory attributes. The following subjects were covered in the sessions:

- Describing and analyzing essential knowledge and skills for supervisors
- The role of authority and structure in supervision
- Motivation as a supervisory task
- Dealing with different levels of staff
- Discipline and evaluation of staff
- Responding to staff frustration and burnout

■ Values and ethics in supervision
■ Life after supervision (i.e., supervision as a career and/or as an interim duty)

Instructional Emphasis

The course included formal presentations on each topic covered in addition to one or two assigned readings on the topic. However, group discussion of each topic was emphasized. Videotapes, role playing, and small group discussions were also used. Each participant was asked to prepare a written vignette on a supervisory concern to be discussed with the group. Discussion of these concerns focused on practical ways to deal with the problem as well as the principles that guide such responses. The vignettes served a core objective of the course, that is, they provided real-life examples with which to illustrate and apply concepts and precepts of day-to-day management. Such discussions also provided an ideal forum for blending clinical experiences with organizational management principles and needs. Under the rubric of essential knowledge and skills, the traditional *tasks* of supervision (administration, teaching, helping) were portrayed in conjunction with specific *forms* of supervision (subject-focused, person-focused, integrative) (Johnson, Haas, & Loomis, 1981). Comparisons were made between supervision and other practice roles (teacher, consultant, psychotherapist). Processes by which people commonly become effective supervisors were also explored, including role adoption, emulation or modeling, reframing current skills, formal education, exhortation and prescription, and selection (Akin & Weil, 1981).

The variables that determine the manner or emphasis of supervision were discussed, for example, the particular agency, setting, program, objective, task, history of the task, availability of other resources, and the culture and subculture in which each of these factors might occur. Not the least important of these variables, of course, are the supervisor's theoretical and intellectual orientations and his or her perspective on the most effective use of personal knowledge and skills.

Defining Supervision

Supervision is a component of management, with the functions of management being those of planning, organizing, motivating, and controlling professional activities for the benefit of the clients, the agency, and the agency employees (in that order). Effective management depends on good leadership—the final item of discussion addressed under the introductory topic.

Informal Theories

Addressing the ideas of authority and structure in supervision raised important topics about "homemade" theories concerning effective supervision, sources of and methods for expressing authority, learning styles of supervisees, and limi-

tations of the supervisor's responsibility (e.g., must the boss always be the boss?) in the training sessions. General ways that supervisees learn were identified as intellectual, intuitive, or experiential (Urbanowski & Dwyer, 1988). The occasional nonlearner was also discussed.

Discussion of theories about supervision focused on the pet notions of participants regarding the behaviors and attitudes they felt affected supervision. The underlying premise was that most people (even supervisors) want to have a distinctive manner and style of supervision. To generate illustrations of homemade principles, participants were asked to reflect (outside of the course) on what elements in their supervision or the supervision they had received might never be part of supervision theory but worked well for them. Responses included ideas such as find ways to have fun with your staff as a group, discover and promote areas of professional development for staff, use bulletin boards wisely and well, and follow up swiftly in responding to inquiries and requests from supervisees.

Forms of Supervisory Authority

Sources of authority for the supervisor, for example, role, status, expertise, accolade, alliance, or folklore, were explored in an effort to bring together various aspects of supervision. The workshop emphasized that it was not necessary or beneficial to hold onto all vestiges of authority. Pitfalls of supervision (incorrect priorities, poor delegation, too much or too little leadership, and problems with exercising authority vs. being a nice person) were discussed. Limitations in the responsibilities of supervisors invariably generated lively discussion, ranging from work role and nonprofessional behavior to behaviors away from work that might cast a shadow on one's professional role. Although drawing boundaries to authority and responsibility is ultimately a personal decision, helpful precepts for doing so invariably emerged after the group reflected on the topic.

Motivation

Motivation is a topic fraught with complexities, beginning with the question of whether employees can be motivated by others or whether motivation must come from within. Adopting the notion that motivation comes from within, the participants were introduced to the provocative theories of Herzberg (1968), who differentiates between hygiene (cleaning up the dissatisfactions of the work environment) and motivation, wherein people are challenged through activities that allow them to expand their current skills and interests into new and broader skills and interests. In order to ground this theory, comparisons were made to Maslow's (1954) hierarchy of needs, in which motivation is ranked high in importance. The hierarchy of needs is a motivational model familiar to most clinically trained persons. Through the use of data from prior research (United Way of Chicago, 1980), it was possible to poll participants on factors that motivate them, then compare the responses of group participants with findings from managers in business settings. Three factors identified by workshop participants (feeling my job is important, being able to explore new areas, and opportunity to use initiative) of the top five motivating factors were invariably the same as those found in business groups.

Levels of Staff

For a frontline supervisor, dealing with various levels of staff is a delicate process that is not often explicitly discussed in training programs. However, many clinical supervisors must be concerned about the performance of clerical or maintenance staff although lacking direct authority over them. On the other hand, responding to requests from upper management staff, who may be several levels above the supervisor, forces participants to consider how priorities are established, when to follow communication chains, when—if ever—to "leapfrog" management levels to deal with specific issues, and how to put appropriate limits on the readiness of frontline supervisors to respond to all requests emanating from a higher organizational authority. Such scenarios also generate discussion of responses that prove useful when upper management staff members bypass the supervisor and delegate tasks to people whom the supervisor manages.

Discipline and Evaluation

Discipline and evaluation in supervisory and management duties are related issues. The original understanding of the term *discipline* is that it involves *teaching* a person the preferred behaviors so that problems in performance are minimized. Conventionally, discipline has become simply a less incendiary word for punishment; "disciplinary hearing" is kinder to the ear and ego than is "punishment planning session." In the workshop sessions, discipline was defined as corrective supervisory/administrative action.

In presenting the topic of discipline, it was useful to focus on what makes some supervisors reluctant to confront infractions by subordinates. Often supervisors are in a quandary regarding the importance of the infraction and are concerned about demoralizing staff by being too fussy. Many supervisors, moreover, find it difficult to be firm—sometimes because they do not agree with a policy that they are required to enforce.

Failure to document employee infractions, however, is probably the most recurrent and complicating problem supervisors face with regard to discipline (Halloway & Broger, 1989). Due process begins with factual documentation followed by systematic and regulated disciplinary procedures. These steps, in sequential order, commonly include simple correction; counseling interview; verbal warning; written reprimand; demotion, probation, or suspension; and termination. Immediate response to concerns, clarity about what must change, and brevity with regard to simple corrections are useful guidelines for disciplinary interventions. All supervisors, however, need agency-specific guidelines regarding appropriate disciplinary actions as well as knowledge of how to compile supporting documentation that leads along the continuum from simple correction to demotion or termination.

Evaluation processes are related to disciplinary processes, in part because discipline of a subordinate influences the process of evaluating that person. These processes are also connected by the fact that many supervisors find both tasks onerous. Furthermore, supervisors generally receive little training in evaluation.

Supervisors often find that senior administrators are fastidious about evaluation procedures. Evaluation includes protocols about when and how frequently to evaluate employees; documentation; deciding among similar evaluative terms such as "excellent," "outstanding," and "superior" (hardly self-evident terms); and establishing annual performance goals for experienced and proficient supervisees. Besides offering some ideas on procedures for evaluation, the workshop training focused on developing a philosophy of evaluation. Issues such as the significance of tone or emphasis in a written document were considered, as well as the notion that a supervisee's use of the evaluation process is itself a component of the evaluation process. Because no comprehensively useful and precise evaluation form exists, supervisors must assume responsibility for contributing ideas to the refinement and improvement of evaluation forms and processes.

Stress and Burnout

Stress and burnout of staff are perennial concerns for supervisors in social service agencies, where many staff mistakenly believe that human service organizations should be above and beyond bureaucratic influences and where the social problems that the agency confronts are enormous and intractable. Recognizing and addressing stressors need not be viewed as indulgent, but rather as a way of defusing shared frustrations and inviting a collaborative problem-solving process. It is useful to distinguish among organizational, interpersonal, and personal sources of stress, while reflecting upon where remedial efforts might best be focused.

Values and Ethics

Values and ethics in supervision are determined, in part, by formal professional standards.

For supervisors, the question of whose interests should be first served in a conflict (client, agency, or employee) is sometimes easy to answer but difficult to implement. Ethical supervision needs to be guided by principles that are articulated and shared by the supervisor, understood by the supervisee, and not formulated at the expense of any of the parties served. Ethical supervision also should aim to enhance employees' professional growth. Making training, education, and assigned tasks consonant with the supervisee's aspirations and aptitudes (to the degree possible within the realm of the agency's mission) is beneficial to the supervisory process. The interpersonal lessons of clinical practice are relevant to the supervisory relationship and other staff relationships. These concerns are most aptly applied, however, to the *structure* of the relationship (e.g., meeting a person at his or her own level, treating a person with respect and dignity). In other words, supervisors should not provide therapy under the guise of supervision (Cohen, 1987).

Life after Supervision

A broad subject area in the supervisory training program dealt with professional life after supervision. For some participants, supervision was perceived as a steppingstone to other professional activities. Others perceived supervision as a temporary role that would be left to return to clinical practice or other involvements. Invariably, many supervisors found that their role made them feel isolated and that it significantly altered their relationship with co-workers. Training emphasized that peer resources are essential for supervisors and may need to be formally organized. A major frustration for supervisors was the lack of a peer group for discussing the pressures they faced.

The Agency

A final—but by no means minor—ingredient for effective supervisory/management training is discussion of the goodness-of-fit between the agency and trainer. Retaining an outside trainer/consultant who is not immersed in the daily pressures of an agency has advantages. However, the trainer needs to be aware of the agency's mission, history, needs, formal structure, and informal processes. Much of this information can be absorbed over time if a trusting relationship is established between the agency administrators and the trainer. Trusting relationships cushion hostilities and negative suspicions when mistakes or problems occur.

Frank discussions in training sessions may, at times, create tension throughout the agency ranks. Such discussions can best be survived if the trainer acts as the buffer and absorber of factional concerns. The astute choice of a trainer goes a great distance in parlaying a well-planned training program into a professional growth experience for the agency as well as for its emerging supervisors.

REFERENCES

Akin, G., & Weis, M. (1981). The prior question: How do supervisors learn to supervise? *Social Casework, 62,* 472–479.

Cohen, B. Z. (1987). The ethics of social work supervision revisited. *Social Work, 32,* 194–198.

Herzberg, E. (1968). One more time: How do you motivate employees? *Harvard Business Review, 46,* 53–62.

Holloway, S., & Broger, G. (1989). *Supervising in the human services.* New York: Free Press.

Johnson, J., Haas, M., & Loomis, L. (1981). *Consultation or supervision.* Jane Addams School of Social Work, University of Illinois, Chicago.

Kazmerski, K., & Macarov, D. (1976). *Administration in the social work curriculum.* New York: Council on Social Work Education.

Maslow, A. H. (1954). *Motivation and personality.* New York: Harper and Brothers.

Mintzberg, H. (1975). The manager's job: Folklore and fact. *Harvard Business Review, 53* (July–August), 49–62.

Patti, R. (1977). Patterns of management activity in social welfare organization. *Administration in Social Work, 1,* 5–18.

Sarri, R. (1973). Effective social work intervention in administration and planning roles: Implications for education. In *Facing the challenge.* New York: Council on Social Work Education.

Steiner, R. (1977). *Managing the human service organization.* Beverly Hills, CA: Sage Publications.

United Way of Chicago. (1980). *Handbook on Supervision.* Chicago: Author.

Urbanowski, M., & Dwyer, M. (1988). *Learning through field instruction: A guide for teachers and students.* Milwaukee: Family Service America.

TO DO OR NOT TO DO: SOCIAL WORK EDUCATION FOR PRIVATE PRACTICE

CAROLYN A. WALTER, GEOFFREY L. GRIEF

Should we educate students for private practice? The purpose of this paper is to address this issue for social work education and practice and to provide a framework for teaching that bridges many of the differences inherent in the social work agency/private practice debate.

In its very early years (1955-61) NASW showed little interest in clinical issues or the question of private practice. NASW, in 1964, officially legitimized private practice as an area of social work for meeting human needs. However, at the same time NASW affirmed that "practice within socially sponsored organization structures must remain the primary avenue for the implementation of the goals of the profession" (Kurzman, 1976: 366).

The continuing rise in the number of masters' and doctoral level social work students planning to enter private practice (Wallace, 1982; Rubin and Johnson, 1984) has caused heated debate within schools of social work. What is this debate about?

One of the critical issues being debated is: Are we losing our mission as social workers if graduates do not work in social work agencies? Many social work educators view social workers as alienating themselves from the social work profession when they become private practitioners. With the increasing number of graduates entering private practice there is great concern that the "social" aspect of the profession is being neglected. Behind this debate is concern that the private practitioners will elect not to work with poor clients or "less desirable" clients—those who are difficult to engage or who may exhibit disruptive, acting-out behavior (Kurzman, 1976).

This action is in direct conflict with the professional social worker's responsibility

> to serve not only those who can afford to pay, but those who cannot; to help not only those who seek services but those who need protective care and are in a relatively poor position either to request or to pay for such services. (Kurzman, 1976: 367).

Although there is widespread acceptance of the person in environment interface in graduate social work curricula, the growing interest of social work students in private practice raises doubt about the impact of the dual focus orientation in professional education (Rubin and Johnson, 1984).

Concern also exists that because private practice tends to focus on the direct-service role of professional practice, private practitioners will relegate social action and policy concerns to others or "see (those) responsibilities as a separate part of the professional function" (Kurzman, 1976: 365). Although most private practitioners do stay involved in both community and professional activities (Levin, 1974: 27) this action does not foster the social work professional goal of facilitating systemic social change based on practice with clients (Kurzman, 1976). Among social work educators there is a deep-seated concern that private practitioners will lose their identity as social workers when they cut themselves off from their social function.

Other issues being debated among educators are: Should students who want to do "therapy" be encouraged to attend a different professional school? What differentiates the education that social work practitioners receive from the training received by other mental health practitioners? What is the practice-education-research partnership when the practice is private practice instead of agency practice? And finally, should we discuss private practice with our students as a viable option for practice?

Why are professional social workers turning to private practice? Social workers may be increasingly choosing private practice as a viable option for full-time and part-time employment as the opportunities diminish for social workers to practice clinical social work within agencies in the way that they would like. Private practice may afford greater autonomy for both the worker and the client. Many social workers "see private practice as an opportunity to pursue to the fullest extent with their clients the goals determined by clients" (Levin, 1976: 356). Social workers may feel constrained by agency policy regarding goal setting while private practice provides an opportunity to help clients exercise a greater degree of self-determination—an important social work value.

Moreover, private practice is accountable to the client or consumer first, and to the profession and the public, second and third respectively (Levin, 1976). Many social workers have entered the profession out of a desire to serve clients; although the agency context is important it is often not their first concern. In a study by Fitzdale (Levin, 1976), she found that experience with clients revealed that their expectations included continuity of service from the same practitioner, immediate service and assignment of a specific counselor when requested. Private practitioners are more able to be accountable to their clients in these areas.

Private practice provides an alternative career choice for social workers who are interested in direct practice and want to make it the main focus of their careers. The social work profession has been unable to devise an appropriate career ladder for direct practitioners, other than upward movement into administration. Many social workers would like to continue "honing" their skills as practitioners but cannot find ways to do this while moving upward professionally or financially. Private practice affords them this opportunity.

It is the authors' opinion that the primary goal of social work education is to train for agency-based practice. At the same time private practice is here to stay and provides an attractive alternative for many graduate social work students. The issues of private practice versus agency practice cannot be ignored but must be debated in classroom discussions so that attempts can be made to link social work values and ethics with the private practice sector. As educators, we can help students place private practice in the larger context of the social work profession and to realize that private practice is one of a range of social work services — it is not a separate entity with different values and ethics. It is the "very uniqueness of the social work mandate that has drawn many students to the profession." For many students this mandate to serve those in need represents the reason that they have chosen social work over other helping professions (Kurzman, 1976: 367).

The following points deal with integrating private practice into the social work curriculum:

1. *Most important is that issues concerning private practice be discussed in the classroom.* Just as work in public agencies is discussed, so should work in private practice. Social work educators seem to believe that by not discussing private practice two things will happen: they are going to "rescue" the profession by maintaining its focus on social work's historic mission or that private practice will go away. Neither necessarily would be the case. Social work does not have to lose its mission if we continue to teach it in an exciting way and a way that capitalizes on the reasons many students come into the field of social work in the first place. Being good teachers will help that mission a great deal more than creating a Chinese Wall where students talk about private practice outside of class but are careful not to discuss it in front of professors who they know disapprove of it. We agree with Kurzman that social workers should not be educated to become psychotherapists but "professional(s) . . . who will be able to make skillful use of several social work methods in a variety of settings and deploy a range of practice modalities" (1976: 367).

Private practice is not going to go away by educators avoiding it. It has been around for over 60 years (Golton, 1971; Pleck and Plotkin, 1951). Not only is it older than most of us who teach, it has staunch proponents among our ranks. And, in fact, many educators are in private practice and may sometimes make for more exciting teachers as they are able to bring to class real life examples that they are struggling with. Educators who are involved part-time in agency-based practice have the same excitement to bring. Contrast classes taught by an active practitioner of any stripe with those of professors who have not met with a client for 15 years. The ivory tower existence of professors is a problem in all professional fields and needs to be addressed, though not in this forum.

Thus it must be accepted and openly acknowledged that private practice will go on regardless of what schools of social work do about it. As educators we cannot be bad role models by avoiding open discussion of something that some wish would go away. If we do not talk about it, we teach students to hide their identity as social workers which will eventually lead to their not identifying themselves with the profession if they become private practitioners.

2. *Once the discussion about private practice is open, we recommend that it be coupled with education for social responsibility.* We grant that many students see themselves as "mini-shrinks" when they first enter school which contributes to a negative elitist view of private practitioners. We must begin to differentiate for students what a social worker does in private practice that is different than what other mental health professionals do in private practice. We do this now with these roles in agency-based practice. The piece that makes social workers both in and out of agencies different from others can be exemplified by cases where the private practitioner focuses on referrals, hooking up with resources, making home visits, and intervening in the environment on behalf of the client. The lack of reimbursement for some of these services and the financial impact on the private practitioner also need to be addressed as does the issue of "pro bono" service. The social worker's knowledge of the social welfare system is also a key element of private practice and should be covered. As these foci are covered in classes where agency-based social work is discussed, it would be easy to include a few private practice examples. Naturally, schools already educate for social responsibility but the link to it in private practice may need to be articulated clearly for students.

3. *As we recommend that private practice be treated as a viable form of social work practice* (see also Barker, 1984; Levenstein, 1964), *we believe that issues around confidentiality, ethics, client self-determination, and advocacy be addressed in relation to the private practitioner.* Addressing these issues, however, should not detract from discussions about social work practice in agencies. Rather, as the educator provides examples of confidentiality or ethical dilemmas, cases should include those faced by the private practitioner. Thus issues around private practice would still be raised without any time being taken away from the course content and the teaching of the values and ethics of our profession.

4. *We recommend that social work students and graduates who decide to do private practice be encouraged to provide their services to social welfare agencies on either a voluntary or paid part-time basis.* In this way, the mission of our profession would continue to be served. This would also represent a commitment to the field of social work that would benefit both the agency being served and the practitioner. The agency would benefit from the voluntary time given or from the paid experience of a clinician entering the agency with an "out of agency" perspective. The practitioner would benefit from having another forum within which to evaluate the effectiveness of his or her practice and also from the continued contact with other practicing social workers. Service on boards of agencies could also be a helpful method of interaction for all involved.

We are aware, as Kelley and Alexander (1985) point out, that many social workers are in private practice part-time and in agency practice part- or full-time. Their commitment to social work is not an issue. In fact, what private practice offers them is extremely important as it enables them to supplement their income to a level that many find sufficient to stay in the profession. Without private practice, we might lose many of our agency workers who might have to choose a more lucrative profession.

Private practice can be advantageous for the client, too. According to Levin (1976), it offers clients either the illusion or the actuality of choice in treatment that is often not available in agencies. Since autonomy is so important for clients, the option of working privately with a social worker can have helpful treatment impact if autonomy is fostered.

5. Some of the possible benefits that accrue to the social worker and to the profession from private practice need to be considered:

a. Many lay people do not realize that social workers do private practice. Inquiries into what social work practice is can help educate the population about other aspects of social work.

b. Private practitioners often have higher status in the community. The more social work is associated with private practice the more a trickle-down effect may help other social workers.

c. Private practitioners, especially in states where social workers receive third party payments, can earn an attractive income. This opportunity may attract more people into the profession. This is happening already among the students who enter the field wanting to be therapists. Schools that are hard-pressed for higher enrollment are loath to turn down these students. Especially with this group of students, the melding of private practice with social responsibility and the values, ethics, and other underpinnings of social work is crucial. If the field stays open to these students, they may turn out to be a new breed of less dedicated social work professionals UNLESS we can educate them properly. Denying the existence of private practice is not the way to do that.

d. Research opportunities are plentiful in private practice. Unbound by agency red tape, the greater autonomy of private practice helps practitioners to feel freer in exploring research-related avenues. This, too, benefits the profession and the client.

e. Private practice offers a viable career choice particularly for the seasoned social worker (Maturin et al., 1987). In the 1970s, the number of social work graduates hit an all time high (Tolson, 1986). Most of these social workers are now entering the second decade of practice. It is incumbent upon educators to be attentive to the needs of this growing population. Whether they are working in an agency full-time and maintaining a practice on the side or doing full-time private practice, we should not make them feel guilty about what they are doing. Schools of social work can "develop continuing education courses to help social workers meet the ongoing needs of skill development and requirements for recertification" (Grosser and Block, 1983; 260). Better they be educated by us, than by institutes not connected to the social work profession. And, better they stay in our field and feel comfortable, than we lose our most experienced.

For example, one "seasoned" professional social worker who has been practicing in various social work agencies for over twenty years (and for the past twelve years serving primarily in an administrative position) is considering either leaving the profession or becoming a full-time private practitioner. One of his reasons for this major career change is his discontent with his agency's concern for survival as an agency instead of focusing both agency resources and energy on client needs. Another reason he is considering full-time private practice is his desire—working directly with client concerns and needs. His work as a full-time administrator, while providing him with a good salary, does not meet his deep-seated needs for intrinsic pleasure in his work.

CONCLUSIONS

Private practice is here to stay. Schools of social work and the profession benefit from its existence as a career option. Denying or refusing to discuss private practice in class is going to hurt the field for many of the reasons outlined. The authors suggest the beginning of a dialogue about private practice in social work curricula as a method of enhancing social work education, our profession, and service to the client.

REFERENCES

Barker, R.L. 1984. *Social Work in Private Practice: Principles, Issues, and Dilemmas*. Silver Spring, MD: National Association of Social Workers.

Golton, M.A. 1971. "Private practice in social work," *Encyclopedia of Social Work* (16th issue). Washington, DC: National Association of Social Workers, 949-955.

Grosser, R., and Block, S. Fall 1983. "Clinical social work practice in the private sector: A survey," *Clinical Social Work Journal* 11(3): 245-262.

Kelley, P., and Alexander, P. 1985. "Part-time private practice: Practical and ethical considerations," *Social Work* 30(3): 254-258.

Kurzman, P.A. 1976. "Private practice as a social work function," *Social Work*, 21(5): 363-368.

Levenstein, S. 1964. *Private Practice in Social Casework*, New York: Columbia University Press.

Levin, A.M. 1976. "Private practice is alive and well," *Social Work*, 21(5): 356-362.

Levin, A.M. 1974. *Handbook on the Private Practice of Social Work*. Washington, DC: National Association of Social Workers.

Maturin, S.; Rosenberg, B.; Levitt, M.; and Rosenblum, S. 1987. "Private practice in social work: Readiness and opportunity," *Social Casework*, 68(1): 31-37.

Peek, J., and Plotkin, C. June 1951. "Social casework in private practice," *Smith College Studies in Social Work*, 21.

Rubin, A., and Johnson, P. Spring 1984. "Direct practice interests of entering MSW students," *Journal of Education for Social Work*, 20(2): 5-16.

Tolson, E.R. 1986. "Changes in enrollment and applications to graduate school of social work: 1972-1982," *Journal of Social Work Education* 22(2): 82-97.

Wallace, M.E. May 1982. "Private practice: A nationwide study," *Social Work* 27(3): 262-267.

EXPANDING THE ROLE REPERTOIRE OF CLINICIANS

HAROLD H. WEISSMAN, IRWIN E. EPSTEIN, ANDREA SAVAGE

THE DISCONTINUITIES BETWEEN clinical practice and administration have been amply noted in the literature.[1] However, the fact that these discontinuities are of two different orders has not been sufficiently noted. The first order of discontinuity refers to those real differences in perspective, responsibilities, and skills that exist between administrative and clinical practice; the second order refers to discontinuities that result from an inadequate role definition of clinical practice.

Considerably less discontinuity would occur if the profession recognized that clinical social workers utilize a variety of skills in their daily work, many of which are administrative. In many agencies the mode of practice has changed in the past two decades from one in which the primary source of help was focused on the relationship between worker and client to one in which many helping relationships exist between and among workers from a variety of professions, agencies, and clients or targets of intervention.

Thus the context of practice exerts an increasingly important influence on the delivery of service. The agency determines for clinicians not only who their clients will be, but also to a significant extent what and how long services will be provided and under what conditions they may be continued or terminated. In order to practice their profession, clinicians must be able to make their own agency and other agencies work for their clients.

Clinical practice is best viewed in the context of agency-based practice. To function in this context clinicians need an expanded role repertoire. The present article briefly outlines ten supplementary and supportive roles to the traditional treatment role. These supplementary roles include organizational diagnostician, expediter, case manager, colleague, advocate, program developer, organizational reformer, supervisor, practice researcher, and employee. A framework for role analysis is presented: (1) What skills are required for the role? (2) What new demands are made of clinicians and to what extent are traditional skills useful in assuming the role? (3) What attitudes, values, or beliefs on the part of clinicians enhance or inhibit their ability to carry out the role?

The article also presents a training guide that describes the requisites for particular roles; notes the differences, where they exist, between role demands and the clinician's role conceptions; and suggests how clinicians may deal with these discrepancies. Thus the guide rests on the assumption that without the ability to handle these various demands and discrepancies, clinical workers will not be able to perform their roles adequately.[2]

Although it is assumed that many variables other than a worker's counseling skill have a crucial impact on what happens to clients, the article does not intend to suggest that the traditional therapeutic skills are in some way obsolete or unnecessary. All that is proposed is that other skills, primarily administrative in nature, are important for clinicians to master if they are to help people in an agency context.

Organizational Diagnostician

The most effective clinical social workers are those who combine clinical skills with the ability to locate and diagnose organizational-structure problems that affect service delivery to clients. The diagnostician must be able to (1) master the uses of formal and informal organization; (2) understand the factors that affect goal attainment and goal displacement; (3) understand the structure, use, and misuse of authority; and (4) know the overall effect of internal and external organizational constraints.

Clinicians must understand organizational constraints and be able to conceptualize the sources of, if not the solutions to, problems in service delivery caused by these constraints.[3] The ability to diagnose organizational problems also helps maintain worker morale when organizations are unable to confront and solve problems. Thus staff training should focus attention on the following concepts: (1) Organizational conflict is not inherently dysfunctional and may, in fact, contribute to organizational effectiveness. (2) Crises in organizational functioning may present opportunities for organizational change. (3) The social and physical environment of an agency can affect the outcome of service.

Organizational diagnosis is, in many ways, analogous to clinical diagnosis. It uses logical frameworks based on values, assumptions, and theories to understand and solve a problem. Both clinical and organizational diagnoses are affected by the theories of causality that the individual brings to his or her practice.

To effectively perform the role of organizational diagnostician, clinicians must shed the common belief that structure is inevitably an impediment to service delivery. Instead, the diagnostician must see the ways in which structure can contribute to positive organizational outcomes. Finally, workers must understand that the agency is not a family and that it functions on the basis of very different expectations. Understanding these differences is necessary for a productive and satisfying work experience.

Expediter

Expediting is the art of getting things done. Clinicians must be able to expedite: make referrals, secure services for clients, activate social networks to support clients, work to change clients' physical and social environments.

Expediting in an agency setting would be a simple task if workers possessed all the information, authority, resources, and skills that are required to get things done for and with their clients. However, in many situations, clinicians do not possess the needed requisites. Even when they do, expediting may require the clinician to overcome passive lack of cooperation or open resistance, as well as myriad other reactions of agency superiors, subordinates, peers, clients, staff, and other agencies.

Expediting is a three-phase process: (1) securing the cooperation of significant others,[4] (2) carrying out the tasks, and (3) following up to ensure that the task is accomplished well. Many traditional skills can be used to carry out the expediter role. However, the most important skills include listening skills to determine and deal with resistance to requests or suggestions and the crisis-intervention skills that help workers deal with bottlenecks in service.

Workers must also be able to deal with the interruptions and crises involved with clinical work. Neither clinical practice nor administrative practice is exempt from these concerns. In the same vein, the worker must be able to stick with a particular task and not avoid or pass the task to others.

Case Manager

The case manager is responsible for identifying, securing, and coordinating services to clients from his or her own and other agencies and for providing direct therapeutic assistance to clients. The case-manager role usually embodies both therapeutic and managerial functions. Case management is a three-step process that includes assessment and planning, coordinating delivery of basic services, and monitoring and reviewing client progress.

A grounding in systems theory provides the case manager with tools for analyzing opportunities and barriers to interagency coordination. Natural helping networks and self-help groups can be significant resources for case managers and their clients. Both case managers and workers must find ways to develop sufficient authority to ensure that cooperating agencies and individuals provide services to clients.[5]

Many clinical-practice skills can be used in case management. The stages of clinical practice, with its beginning, middle, and ending phases, closely mirror the three stages of the case-management process — assessment and planning, coordinating delivery of services, and monitoring and reviewing progress. Although case planning is often viewed as a purely rational process, the negative attitudes of other professions and departments may act as barriers to smooth interprofessional coordination. An awareness of these attitudes and stereotypes helps a clinical case manager develop strategies to maximize effective service among organizations and agencies.

Colleague

In the role of colleague, clinicians are constantly called upon to engage in inter- and intraprofessional collaboration and problem solving on behalf of clients. The effective colleague must appreciate the varying personal, professional, departmental, and organizational goals, values, and frames of reference of their coworkers. Employing a basic principle from social-exchange theory, the colleague seeks to maximize both the psychic and material rewards of co-professionals with whom they work while minimizing the psychic and material costs of collaboration.

Collegiality plays an important role in the handling of uncertainty, a constant issue in clinical practice. Colleagues provide support and enable one another to acknowledge areas of uncertainty. Both clinicians and administrators need to develop this skill.

Clinicians must also be effective listeners and communicators. The ability to hear and respond appropriately to the latent messages of inter-professional communications is crucial. The view that only clinicians care or know about clients and that the administrative staff is the enemy is an unfortunate barrier to collegiality. Effective colleagues avoid falling into this perspective; they are skeptical of an "only way" method for achieving clinical goals.[6]

Advocate

To advocate is to plead another's cause. Working on behalf of individual clients or groups of clients, clinicians often act as advocates in obtaining changes in the interpretation of rules, for securing services to which clients are entitled, for seeking redress from arbitrary decisions, and for obtaining reforms in laws and program structures.

Clinicians should understand the differences between case and group or class advocacy, and the ways in which each serves the other. Clinicians must also be able to assess realistically the risks of advocacy — both for the client and for themselves as agency representatives. In addition, they must be able to employ conflict strategies on behalf of the client or client group comfortably and strategically.

Finally, workers must learn to view advocacy as an exchange relationship between the advocate and the target of change. This administrative concept provides an understanding of the dynamics of effective advocacy and services generates creative strategies of advocacy.[7]

Advocacy and clinical social work practice are analogous in that both begin with an understanding of the problem as viewed by the client. Both roles carry the responsibility of pointing out alternative ways of viewing and resolving the problem, and both roles are ultimately responsible for letting the client decide which strategy among various problem-solving strategies will be chosen. Finally, both strategically employ conflict and conciliation as a way of achieving socially desired ends, although the targets and tactics may differ significantly.

To effectively practice advocacy, clinicians must believe that personal problems can have material and environmental causes. The clinician who is an effective advocate must be attuned to and comfortable with engaging in conflict strategies when a client's situation requires such action. An advocate cannot wear a cloak of professional neutrality and must understand organizational dynamics.

Program Developer

Clinical social workers have opportunities to develop new programs based on their assessment of unmet client needs, gaps in service, bureaucratic obstacles, and so forth. For example, they may develop groups that teach advocacy skills to clients, discharge planning groups, or groups for women who are returning to work. Workers generally fail in their attempts to design programs if they focus solely on what clients need and do not consider system needs such as departmental rivalries, professional status, cost and financial constraints, or ideological differences. The design process can be conceptualized in three stages: program initiation, program implementation, and program institutionalization. Effective program development depends on careful analysis of the resources and skills that are needed at each stage.

To design a program, the worker must obtain feedback from clients and other members of the agency. Although feedback is a term that elicits positive feelings, it is not easy to obtain and is sometimes difficult to utilize. Clinicians who wish to design programs must become knowledgeable about the problems and pitfalls of obtaining feedback about programs. Can the agency tolerate negative feedback? How will it respond to negative feedback? Can challenges to the existing hierarchy and the conflict that might be engendered by feedback be handled by the agency? How? To be effective program developers, clinicians must rid themselves of the attitude that program design must focus exclusively on meeting client needs.

For new programs to be successfully implemented, they must be designed to meet agency, system, and staff needs as well as client needs.[8] Similarly, since clinicians who wish to develop new programs do not generally have a job description that mandates such a role, they must develop a network of like-minded staff for ideas and support.

Organizational Reformer

All clinicians experience situations at one time or another wherein agency policy, procedures, personnel, or goals seem to inhibit the effective delivery of service. In such situations, identifying what needs to be changed and how to effect change becomes an important professional issue.

Organizations are structured so that those at the bottom of the structure have the least opportunity, at least in the short term, to effect changes in policies and procedures. Staff should be trained in legitimate ways by which lower-level staff can increase their influence in the organizations in which they work. Such training should include the process, strategies, and tactics of initiating and implementing reforms.

Many traditional clinical skills can be used in

the role of organizational reformer. Partializing problems and understanding the nature of resistance are the most obvious skills.[9] However, changing clients and changing organizations are considerably different tasks. Issues such as the reformer's lack of accessibility to those in authority, the reformer's difficulty in getting an agency to seriously explore options for change, and the reformer's potential difficulty in countering organizational "group think" should be included in training programs.

It is difficult to be a reformer in one's own agency. Many an agency reactionary began as an agency reformer. This warning is intended to preserve reformers, not dissuade reform.

Supervisor

Social workers are likely to be involved in supervision at each stage of their agency careers. As line workers, they supervise paraprofessionals and volunteers; as they move up in the agency hierarchy, they supervise other line workers and students. It is difficult for clinicians who are trained to focus on individual clients to shift their focus to agency concerns.[10] Therefore, staff should be trained in the skills, attitudes, and knowledge required of supervisors, especially as this training relates to the transition from worker to supervisor. Training should include information about the psychodynamics of the decision-making process. Supervisors should understand the importance of developing sufficient influence in the agency to perform multifaceted managerial tasks as well as educational tasks: for example, evaluation of subordinates, assignment of work loads, obtaining resources for workers, and interpretation of policies. Certain skills are common to the clinical and supervisory roles. For example, the ability to deal with resistance is a skill that is common to both roles: the clinician must be able to deal with client resistance to treatment and the supervisor must deal with worker resistance in the form of tardiness, lack of productivity, and so forth. Clinicians should be made aware of the strains inherent in the supervisory role.

Workers who cannot deal with tension will not be able to function well as supervisors. A supervisor must meet the demands of those beneath and those above him or her in the agency hierarchy. The tension and disagreement that result from different points of view and different interests can promote creative solutions to problems with clients and within the organization. Thus tension and conflict are not necessarily dysfunctional.

Practice Researcher

Although social work education attempts to inculcate the value of actively participating in and remaining current with research, most agency practice situations do not reinforce this value. However, clinicians have many opportunities to engage in research when the term is broadened to include knowledge development, as well as the more traditional research activities of experimentation and verification of facts. Knowledge-development activities can range from systematic diagnostic assessment to single-case studies of treatment to problem-oriented recording.

The major skills involved in performing a practice research role include the ability to conceptualize one's own practice and to clearly define one's purposes. Practice researchers must understand descriptive and quasi-experimental research designs, which can enable them to collect and interpret valid and reliable information. This ability enables clinical social workers to learn systematically from their successes and failures and to add to practice knowledge by formulating hypotheses that can later be tested by more empirical methods.

Although many clinical social workers view research and clinical practice as antithetical, they have much in common; both are problem-solving efforts that emanate from knowledge development. To assume the role of a practice researcher, clinicians must discard many false, yet pervasive assumptions. These assumptions include the belief that research is necessarily cold and antihumanistic; that clinical social work is an art that cannot and should not be subject to systematic inquiry; that scientific inquiry will destroy the creative, intuitive aspects of clinical social work practice; and that research requires statistical techniques and procedures that are too complex to be useful to practitioners.[11]

Employee

While clinicians assume many roles in an agency, they are certainly also employees. What is good for the agency is not necessarily good for its workers. Although some clinicians believe that strain does not exist between what clients want and what workers are willing or able to do for clients, considerable strain, in fact, exists.

Clinicians are interested in salaries, working hours, working conditions, job security, and promotion. To suggest that conflict does not exist between these interests and what might be best for clients is to obscure reality. Working with difficult, unpleasant, or very needy clients may create stress for workers. Organizational arrangements, including aspects of the formal and informal structure, may themselves be sources of stress. Employees are frequently caught between agency demands for productivity, documentation, and control and their own inclinations to exercise professional discretion on behalf of clients.

Clinicians must be able to manage these tensions realistically. They must develop a variety of coping techniques, understand the potential and limitations of unions for dealing with job-related stresses and strains, and develop an operational approach to participative management and accountability in terms of their effects on workers and worker interactions with agency systems and clients. The hopeless/helpless attitudes of some clients and the potentially hopeless/helpless attitudes of some workers in dealing with the stresses they feel on the job are similar.

Workers who chronically complain are similar to clients who have lost the capacity to confront their problems.[12] Workers can learn, as can their clients, to be more assertive and independent while understanding the constraints of agency practice. Workers must not only understand their personal and professional goals, but must be able to evaluate an agency in terms of whether it is a fit place for professionals to work.

Conclusion

Sharply dividing clinical practice from administrative practice is a serious conceptual error, both for clinicians and administrators. To bridge this gap, staff training must broaden the knowledge, skills, and competencies required to deliver quality social services. When service is provided through a social agency, clinicians must be able to draw upon a repertoire of roles if they are to help people. A narrow focus on the client and his or her relationship to the worker is seldom adequate and only perpetuates the dichotomy between administration and clinical practice.

1. Rino Patti and Michael Austin, "Socializing the Direct Service Practitioner in the Ways of Supervisory Management," *Administration in Social Work* 1 (Fall 1977): 273–80.

2. Harold Weissman, Irwin Epstein, and Andrea Savage, *Agency-Based Social Work: Neglected Aspects of Clinical Practice* (Philadelphia: Temple University Press, 1983).

3. See Neil Clapps, "Diagnosing an Informal System," in *Organizational Diagnosis*, ed. Marvin Weisbord (Reading, Mass.: Addison-Wesley, 1978), pp. 86–89.

4. Alvan Zander, "Resistance to Change," in *Social Work Administration: A Resource Book*, ed. Harry Schatz (New York: Council on Social Work Education, 1970), pp. 253–57.

5. A conceptual basis for achieving these ends is provided by Sol Levine and Paul E. White, "Exchange as a Conceptual Framework for the Study of Interorganizational Relationships," *Administrative Science Quarterly* 5 (March 1961): 583–601.

6. Alfred J. Kahn, "Institutional Constraints to Interprofessional Practice," in *Medicine and Social Work*, ed. Helen Rehr (New York: Prodist, 1974), p. 19. This article provides a broad discussion of these issues.

7. For a discussion of strategies and tactics, see Warren Schmidt and Robert Tannenbaum, "Management of Differences," in *Organizational Diagnosis*, pp. 124–35.

8. Julie Abramson, "A Non-Client-Centered Approach to Program Development in a Medical Setting," in *Agency-Based Social Work*, pp. 178–86.

9. For examples, see Stephen Holloway and George Brager, "Some Considerations in Planning Organizational Change," *Administration in Social Work* 4 (Winter 1977): 349–58.

10. See Lois Abramczyk, "The New M.S.W. Supervisor: Problems of Role Transition," *Social Casework* 61 (February 1980): 83–90.

11. Harold H. Weissman, "Clients, Staff and Researchers: Their Role in Management Information Systems," *Administration in Social Work* 1 (Spring 1977): 43–52.

12. Christina Maslach, "Burned Out," *Human Behavior* 5 (September 1976): 16–18.

MANAGEMENT APPLICATIONS OF BEHAVIORAL SCIENCE KNOWLEDGE
JOHN S. WODARSKI, ANGELA PALMER

IT HAS BECOME POPULAR to refer to the present era of social services as the "age of accountability." This phrase denotes a noticeable trend toward evaluation of human service organizations and their employees in terms of effective and efficient service delivery. In recent years especially, increasing attempts have been made to render such assessments more empirically sound through the use of evaluative criteria.

Within human service agencies, accountability is a term that carries with it many negative connotations. Staff and management alike may have ambivalent or even hostile feelings regarding its usefulness. Workers who deal in human relationships and other affective components may view attempts to quantify practice results as inaccurate or inappropriate. They usually resent potential client time being spent in evaluation or the implication that their own skills are being questioned. In addition, staff members may fear that results could be used to punish them or relieve them of their jobs. On the other hand, management may feel that poor employee ratings will reflect unfavorably on their own supervisory skills. Administrators may fear that, in the interest of measurable objectives, quantity will undermine quality of service or that the program's very existence could be threatened.[1]

Despite the tendency to underrate or criticize the notion of accountability, it was born of a number of legitimate considerations. Are clients getting what they need and expect? Are agencies and staff performing professionally and effectively? Are monies being spent on useful and genuine services? Are the funds expended reasonable for the objectives that are attained? As Alfred Kadushin has pointed out, "...taxpayers, state legislators, the federal government, local community and client groups are demanding precise answers to questions about agency operations."[2] The demonstration of accountability to such interested parties for their own reasons may yield the additional benefit of enhanced credibility for human service organizations and their employees.

Certainly the responsibility of and capacity for administration to influence employee output are crucial aspects of accountability. L. J. Ganser identified the "real task of administration" as that of converting the individual's potential for responsible performance into that kind of performance within a large organization.[3] This suggests that in order to achieve agency goals, the needs and expectations of its employees must be addressed. This article will examine a number of behavioral science research findings aimed at achieving effective management of human service agencies and will present the implications for human service practitioners.

Work Characteristics

Among the most obvious and verbalized concerns of workers in all fields are those of salary, workload, and work schedule. Nevertheless, there has been considerable disagreement regarding the nature and extent of the effect that these factors really have on employee performance within human service organizations.

Salary

Low pay has indeed been identified by some as a major cause of discontent and eventual burnout among human service staffs. Curt Tausky pointed out the potential of remuneration for keeping workers in even unfulfilling occupations. William H. Franklin, Jr. proposed that increased efforts and performance could be a significant result of monetarily rewarding outstanding work contributions. Salary has been substantiated as an effective impetus for increasing appropriate therapeutic behaviors among psychiatric aides and for reducing tardiness among industrial workers and absences by medical center employees. Research conducted by James L. Farr as well as Dale A. Pommer and Darlene Streedbeck also indicated that worker productivity may be increased by making it contingent upon pay. William Harris and associates studied the effects of a number of management strategies upon certain teacher behaviors; in that instance, pay was found to be the sole incentive that was effective with all participants. Furthermore, Ovid Pomerleau and associates noted that, once provided, removal of cash rewards resulted in blatant verbal criticisms, complaints, and threats among the affected employees.[4]

A lack of prestige, perceived as being associated with low pay levels, has also been recognized as related to dissatisfaction among social service employees. Jerald Greenberg and Suzyn Ornstein demonstrated that, under certain circumstances, elevated status may be a feasible substitute for augmented earnings when job responsibilities are increased. Level of education has been established as a variable directly related to satisfaction with pay; that is, increased education requires like supplements in wages in order to be acceptable to the employee. Other scholars, however, have suggested that empirical research has yet to verify unequivocally salary itself as a primary factor in worker satisfaction and motivation.[5]

Workload and Work Schedule

There is more concurrence regarding the influence of caseloads and work schedules on employee satisfaction. Howard Aldrich observed that "most social service agencies face demands that are far greater than they can possibly meet with their limited resources."[6] With this in mind, Harold H. Weissman criticized schools of social work for underemphasizing the realities of large caseloads. Worker deterioration is viewed as an inevitable result of the emotional and cognitive overload experienced with heavy caseload responsibilities and multiplicity of "jobs" inherent in many social work occupations. Lloyd Baird noted four likely reactions of dissatisfied employees as (1) subtle or overt sabotage of the organization, (2) apathetic work effort, (3) departure from the organization, and (4) increased work effort as an attempt to gain desired objectives, the latter being the least likely to occur.[7]

The concept of "triage," or prioritizing, has been suggested as one means of effective caseload management. Following this prescription, cases would be handled in the order of their relative importance or severity. This strategy is aimed at diminishing the perceived pressure on human service workers to fulfill every client's needs all the time. Job sharing or worker rotation are additional ways of affording agency employees opportunities to recoup their cognitive and emotional resources. Jerry Edelwich and Archie Brodsky stressed the importance of staff commitment to this concept so as to effectively overcome the potential drawbacks of decreased service continuity, abbreviated contact with worksite, and split pay. Building in "breathers" is also recognized as an appropriate antidote for draining work schedules.[8] According to Rex Skidmore, "it is...important for each staff member to have some time to meditate, evaluate, justify, plan and create to the advantage of the agency."[9] Victor Savicki and Eric J. Cooley acknowledged the importance of having those breaks "covered," so that employees do not return to further exaggerated case responsibilities. James J. Borland recommended a number of alternatives for providing time away from stressful tasks; some of these include recording, attending nonclient meetings, teaching, developing pet projects, or simply taking time off.[10]

Diversity of cases or tasks has also been identified as influential in worker satisfaction. "Routinization and job monotony have been characterized as major problems for...social workers."[11] Thus, in addition to size, modification of the types and difficulties of cases according to employee needs or preferences is suggested for alleviating worker stress.[12]

Whatever methods for caseload assignment and management are employed, it is important that inherent responsibilities are clearly defined for the workers who are expected to handle them. Workers necessarily must understand precisely what constitutes "good performance" if they are to achieve it.[13] Donald K. Granvold and Kadushin suggested that clarification of responsibilities and objectives is even more effective when jointly established by staff and supervisors. This is analogous to the concept of structure; that is, an individual should know what is expected, in what time frame, and how attainment of goals will be evaluated. Each referred to this system as "Supervision by Objectives," based largely on the same philosophy as the popular "management by objectives." From research with employees of a mental health clinic, Lee W. Frederiksen discovered that, in order to maximize desired treatment behaviors, a self-reinforcing, employee-designed scheduling program provided a successful means of case management. This largely entailed a clearly designated standard for intensive treatment over a brief, specified time period, useful in limiting build-up of stagnant cases.[14]

Staff Development

Many organizations have included staff development techniques in their efforts to improve management and staff operation. "Staff development refers to all the procedures an agency might employ to enhance the job-related knowledge, skills and attitudes of its total staff...."[15] Skidmore reiterated that definition, adding: "Staff development is usually made possible by an administration that is sensitive to change and wants to keep abreast of the new knowledge explosion and skills that are reported on regularly in the literature or by professional associates."[16] He went on to point out the importance of making these kinds of opportunities available to the veterans as well as the neophytes within an agency. James Bolt and Geary A. Rummler asserted that employees need a climate of continual renewal. A key element in enhancing worker productivity via organizational response has been identified as insuring that individuals have the skills, knowledge, and capacity to perform as desired.[17]

There are a number of ways in which staff development may take place. Kadushin described supervision as the individualized education of a worker regarding specific cases or situations. This process typically requires one-to-one interaction between supervisor and supervisee and may occur in formal or informal conferences between the two. Structured educational supervision of this sort may be impractical, in terms of lost work time and related costs, for many human service facilities.

In-service training is provided to a group of employees with similar job classifications or responsibilities and contains somewhat more generalized content. It is a task-centered practice aimed at facilitating change or improvement of service operations. This can occur through staff meetings or through specially designed training sessions within or outside the organization.[18]

A given staff development technique would be selected in terms of the population it is intended to benefit, including staff, administrators, and the agency itself. This necessitates preassessment of needs, interests, motivation, and knowledge and experiential bases of potential participants. Focusing and developing a strategy around specified agency or employee goals would also facilitate their fulfillment. Objective evaluation following the learning episode is critical to determine its effectiveness. Paul Abels suggested inclusion of evaluative criteria during the course of the program as well. William J. Reid and Christine Beard recommended continued consultation after an in-service experience as a means of

maintaining any changes or improvements it produced.[19]

Common methods of staff development include the use of lectures, case presentations or studies, role playing, simulation games, independent or self-developed learning programs, and group activities such as retreats or marathons. Skidmore also encouraged external opportunities, for instance, "continuing education, workshops, institutes, teaching, and exchanging positions with workers in other agencies or schools of social work."[20] Educational experiences that include active participation of staff are generally viewed as more meaningful and beneficial to the learner, with longer-lasting effects.[21]

Several researchers have maintained that various methods—including modeling, behavior rehearsal and videotape feedback; role play and feedback; discussion; social reinforcement and feedback; study guides; situational examples; and instructions and feedback—have been substantiated as to their effective influence on worker performance.[22] Comparing "instructions-oriented" with "active learning" training techniques, Charles A. Maher found the latter, entailing extensive participant involvement, to be significantly more effective. Terry J. Page and associates advocated the use of pyramidal training (teaching a small group of persons who then teach others) as an effective, cost-efficient, and applicable means of improving employee service delivery. Still others have suggested that multifaceted staff development programs or training "packages" yield the greatest success.[23]

Communication

Within most work settings, formal and informal boundaries exist between lines of status or power. According to Edelwich and Brodsky, "staff polarization is [an] aspect of organizational life that creates resentment and reduces effectiveness of personnel."[24] In 1983, Skidmore also stressed the importance of communication as it relates to efficiency, effectiveness, and morale within human service agencies. Communication, then, serves the organization by improving productivity and the employee by promoting satisfaction with the job. Kadushin acknowledged that active representation of worker interests and viewpoints is requisite to effective administrative supervision.[25] Describing communication as a fundamental and primary interactive process, Skidmore, citing Carlisle, noted that "interaction is to the organization what the cell is to the human body."[26] For communication to have genuine impact on employee morale, however, it must occur in an atmosphere of mutual trust and respect, conducive to building confidence in the belief that input will have an effect. Robert J. Benford noted that employees need to have access to information about ways that their individual job performance contributes to organizational goals.[27]

Enhancing lines of communication among and between staff members and administration may occur both informally and in more structured circumstances. Ideally, the process will allow for management to receive as well as furnish information. Methods may range from intraoffice "grapevines" to suggestion or complaint boxes to formalized conferences. In all instances, communication must be clear.[28]

Ombudsman

Utilization of an ombudsman has been suggested as one feasible and cost-efficient means of facilitating information flow within an organization. They are neutral advocates whose main concern is protection against bureaucratic abuse in all its forms and promotion of responsive service delivery...[by]...(1) investigating complaints, (2) initiating general inquiries, (3) recommending ways of strengthening service delivery, and (4) intervening to see that change is effected."[29] However, virtually no evaluations of such procedures have occurred.

Feedback

Accumulated data indicate feedback is a form of intraorganizational communication that deserves significant attention. Simply defined, feedback is the provision of information regarding past performance; it may occur between any combination of participants, including management, staff, and consumers. As a communicative process, feedback has the potential to be either significantly constructive or destructive.

Extensive research on feedback and its effects has resulted in the need to clarify its differential elements. Among the resulting classifications are included (1) individual versus group; (2) private versus public; (3) personal versus mechanical; (4) immediate versus delayed; and (5) schedule, that is, the frequency with which it occurs. Donald M. Prue and John A. Fairbank have added issues of content and source, while Lee W. Frederiksen and his associates have gone even further to include the use or omission of a goal or standard against which to measure achievements. The numerous dimensions of feedback and its interrelatedness with other management interventions have made it somewhat difficult to verify empirically that feedback alone actually causes the improvements often credited to it. In certain cases, researchers have acknowledged that desired changes may actually be a by-product of instructional or other related components of feedback.[30]

Feedback has been identified as an element critical to fostering motivation on the job. In at least one study, it was linked to individuals' perceptions of their own competence.[31] Kadushin suggested that workers both anticipate and welcome such postinstruction from their supervisors, but there are indications that workers often do not receive the desired feedback. "We can learn from our mistakes only if we can find out what they are and have the opportunity of analyzing them."[32] Franklin noted that an effective feedback system is a two-way process affording employees opportunities to share perceptions and suggestions. Others have proposed that the technique is more productive when it consistently includes approving statements, with these being further enhanced by modeling and constructive criticism. Supervisory or organizational feedback is deemed especially important to work populations who are unable to generate their own, for example, those working with infants.[33]

In addition to individualized supervisory conferences, Ayala Pines and Ditsy Kafry as well as Virginia Glicken acknowledged the importance of obtaining feedback from colleagues. Jadwiga Judd, Regina E. Kohn, and G. L. Schulman recommended utilization of group supervision as a medium for acquiring an increased body of knowledge and experience from co-workers. Such feedback would be "case-focused" and should also enhance each worker's self-reliance and respect for his or her own knowledge and competency. Edward W. Davis and Marjie C. Barrett pointed out the "supportive" benefit of peer feedback in addition to the functional exploration of alternative problem solutions.[34]

Andre Delbecq and Dennis Ladbrook viewed feedback as promoting employee and agency growth via teaching, sharing, clarifying, and creating teamwork. They suggested a nonjudgmental, information-sharing form of feedback within the context of stable, trusting relationships between participants as most beneficial. Donald K. Granvold also pointed out the importance of feedback "quality" as related to its effectiveness. One study demonstrated the specificity of feedback effects (the tendency to influence only those behaviors for which it was provided), implying a need to select target behaviors carefully for the intervention.[35]

Maher stated that his research "demonstrated that performance feedback can be incorporated into the management of human service organizations with a focus on performance of human service·professionals." Cost-efficiency and effectiveness have been lauded as primary selling points for this strategy. Emphasizing these advantages and others, Maher observed that "...characteristics such as cost-effectiveness, programmatic simplicity, flexibility and an emphasis upon positive consequences have made performance feedback an attractive intervention technique for organizations."[36]

Another form of feedback is derived from the job itself. Very often this can be largely negative, such as client recidivism. In response to this and the need for clearer, more accurate information about service delivery, increasing attention is being directed to obtaining feedback from consumers. Although not extensively employed thus far, consumer feedback may someday offer significant contributions regarding client needs and perceptions as related to program design and delivery.[37]

Management Orientations

According to Skidmore, leadership within an organization can be defined both as a position and as an ability. The former refers to the individual's responsibility for "guiding and directing" in certain work situations. The latter implies a capacity to influence others to follow those directions. Certainly, the two aspects are greatly interrelated.[38] In addition to directing, supervising, and consulting, Rino Patti recognizes the role as it relates to authority: "The manager sets a pattern that cues the staff on such important matters as how much discretion will be allowed in the performance of tasks, the circumstances under which staff participation in administrative decisions will be allowed and the extent to which the manager will tolerate negative feedback."[39]

Historically, leadership within industrial and human service organizations has been based on a predominantly authoritarian stance. Responsibility and power are afforded top-level administrative positions and delegated hierarchically downward. Such were the prescriptions of Weber's bureaucratic structure, McGregor's Theory X, and others. "This classical, formal structure tends toward rigidity and minimizes the opportunity for staff participation in any area beyond their immediately circumscribed area of responsibility."[40] Even in 1983, Richard A. Weatherly pointed

out that "the political conditions under which public welfare services are provided reinforce an essentially authoritarian management posture."[41]

An essentially opposing response to such scientific management techniques of leadership is the laissez-faire method of management. The laissez-faire method allows for almost complete control of the agency by the staff. Savicki and Cooley seemed to indicate little regard for this strategy when they stated, "...workers who have confidence in the leadership and communication of their administrators and who are receiving adequate supervision are less likely to burn out."[42]

The disparity between those two very extreme types of organizational governance has been bridged somewhat through participatory forms of management and leadership styles. Participative decision making requires that individual resourcefulness and creativity are invested toward the achievement of agency goals.[43] In reference to the similarly conceived task-centered concept of administrative organization, Harry Schatz stated that "this approach maximizes the opportunity for staff members with diverse competencies and with responsibilities at all levels to work together in reaching a common objective."[44] Awarding employees with increased decision-making power and autonomy becomes somewhat self-fulfilling; that is, expectations for responsible performances beget responsible performances. The benefits of positive expectations from self and others have been emphasized by other scholars as well.[45]

Skidmore pointed out the feeling of "belonging to a team" derived from staff involvement in agency governance. Robert Blake and Jane Mouton strongly advocated the interdependence that is a natural component of participatory management. Indeed, a correlation between participation and job commitment has been emphasized in recent years. Feelings of achievement and satisfaction essential to high morale "...are engendered when executives and staff members jointly plan the total operation of an agency, making it possible for each staff member to feel needed and effective."[46] In research, participation in management activities has been linked with decreased role conflict and ambiguity, reduced organizational hostility and increased exposure to diverse skills and knowledge and increasing employee acceptance of and adherence to resultant policies or practice.[47]

Having reviewed substantial literature on the topic, Robert H. Garin and John F. Cooper reiterated this point, stating: "A supervisory style that is employee-oriented—that is one that demonstrates concern for employee satisfaction without sacrificing production goals—is more conducive to good morale and productivity than is a style that is production-oriented.[48]

Maryanne Vandervelde expanded the concept of participative decision making to stress the importance of attributing genuine influence to employee input. She perceived human service organizations to be especially suited to her participative and influence-based decision-making management style because of "...their complicated environments, their problems of professionalism and their complex technologies."[49] Weatherly also maintained that participation perceived by employees to be tokenism yields no noteworthy benefits.[50]

Although not of major theoretical import to the behavioral science orientation, many of today's management strategies are related to assumptions regarding basic human needs for self-respect, autonomy, and achievement. Edelwich and Brodsky pointed out that failure of administration to respond or attend to such necessities is experienced by employees as a lack of appreciation.[51] Citing Sutermeister, Glicken states, "If individuals are to be motivated to perform their best, they must have opportunities to satisfy these needs."[52]

Moreover, new theoretical thinking is exploring learning through modeling as it relates to the exercise of leadership. In this instance, modeling is viewed as a planned effort to change behavior. Organizational leaders can utilize modeling in the development of leadership behavior in subordinates. Modeling is seen as important to organizational functioning because it is a frequent and often rewarding occurrence, although usually unsystematic and haphazard. Types of behavior-change through modeling include (1) establishing and reinforcing appropriate behaviors, (2) changing the frequency of existing behaviors, and (3) providing behavioral cues (that is, model acts as a cue to an employee to begin a previously learned behavior) or behavioral facilitation. In addition to being a behavior model, a leader should provide public reward to reinforce modeling of other employees.[53]

In their training and as a professional group, social workers have even greater emphasis placed on individual rights to fulfillment of those higher-level needs. Precluding their satisfaction is viewed by some observers as the foundation of staff burnout or low morale, the proverbial antithesis of effective work performance. Lack of appreciation demonstrated by many human service consumers can serve to diminish further workers' self-concepts as well as goals, indicating still greater needs for intragency or organizational support. Kadushin described supportive supervision as providing workers with psychological and interpersonal resources that enable them to mobilize emotional energy necessary for effective job performance.[54]

Organizational Behavior Management

Organizational behavior management involves the process of making specific job-related behaviors occur more or less often, depending on whether they enhance or hinder organizational goal attainment, through systematic manipulation of antecedent conditions that serve as cues and immediate pleasing or displeasing consequences. This definition makes a distinction between behavioral science techniques and those founded upon human relations theory regarding higher-level needs. While Robert Kreitner has emphasized that difference, Brethower has nonetheless suggested that the two management orientations need not be antagonistic.[55]

Use of Evaluation Data to Improve Practice

Adequate baseline data on practice competencies will provide the information necessary to facilitate the development of a competency-based practice. Supervision should be provided in such a manner that it will help the worker alter dysfunctional practice behavior. Such a process should include:

1. Pinpointing the worker's behaviors that need to be altered,
2. Measuring the frequency of such behaviors,
3. Developing a program to alter the worker's behavior, and
4. Providing the worker with feedback on targeted behaviors.

Videotaping client and worker interactions should facilitate isolation of behaviors that need to be altered and likewise provide the opportunity for supervisors to reinforce the worker's favorable practice behavior. For example, a macrolevel competency that should be used in the assessment of a residential treatment program for children would be data on the agency's implementation of a training program for new staff to introduce the theoretical practice model being employed. Criteria to evaluate this competency would include a number of staff development activities, money allocated to such activities, and initial orientation procedures. Data for the assessment of the competency would include budget, training manuals, the number of training sessions, and record of staff participation in such activities.

Worker Performance

Two problems certain to be encountered by employers in the future are absenteeism and decreased worker productivity. Ed Pedalino and Victor N. Gamboa executed an interesting study in which they utilized monetary reinforcement contingencies in order to decrease employee absenteeism at an industrial plant. Similarly, James Hermann and associates utilized monetary reinforcement contingencies with industrial workers to increase punctuality on the job.[56] Much research is beginning to accumulate from behavioral analysis to indicate that monetary reinforcers should be made contingent upon specific job performances. Research indicates that this can improve such activities as job finding, accurate change-making in a family-style restaurant, job performance of workers in neighborhood youth corps, professional and nonprofessional workers' performance in an institution for the mentally retarded and on psychiatric wards, and teachers' behaviors with students.[57] Moreover, research seems to indicate that incentives are necessary for good therapeutic practice; that is, in order for professionals to change their behaviors, feedback must occur and incentives be provided for changes.[58] Other research seems to indicate that the workers are more highly productive when they are satisfied with what they are doing; when administrators or executives show consideration for their concerns, and model appropriate behavior; when channels of communication are open; when workers have autonomy in accomplishing tasks and are reinforced for good work; when administrators set an example in terms of working productively; and when they have a chance to complete a whole task. Such work environments are characterized as being very reinforcing.[59] Early applications of behavioral science knowledge at a human service agency were carried out by Roger M. Lind, who linked individuals' malperformance to other committee members' behavior during committee meetings. Some of the committee behaviors chosen for modification were: interruption rate, inattentiveness, cross talk, and comments inappropriate for the topic under discussion.[60] Reinforcement contingencies were implemented to end cross talking and interruptions, to link hand raising and request for recognition, and to limit the length of discussion. Positive reinforcers—smiles, recognition through not talking, and turning on tape recorders—and negative reinforcers—looking away, turning off the tape recorder and temporary termination of note taking—were utilized by the change agent to either decrease or increase appropriate committee behaviors. Moreover, the change agent raised his or her hand to obtain recognition to speak and spoke only when called upon, thereby modelling appropriate behavior and facilitating such behavior by committee members.

Another strategy involved reducing tardiness in workers at a human service agency. The primary response to tardiness was punishment; an employee who was late was called to the office and made to wait five to ten minutes in the waiting room before being confronted about his or her behavior. Punishment was chosen because other positive reinforcers such as monetary incentives, promotion, and bonuses were out of the question because of administrative constraints.[61]

R. C. Rinn and J. C. Vernon reported the use of monetary incentives in a community mental health center. The purposes were to facilitate workers' acquisition of knowledge and treatment skills and workers' implementation of skills in terms of record-keeping competencies such as specifying a written contract between the worker and client concerning therapy goals, collecting and graphing data, keeping current dictation on behavior to be modified and techniques to be employed, and entering process and termination notes. Worker salary increments were based on how well they executed these functions. The use of concrete standards reduced subjective biases involved in delivering increments and facilitated progress in attainment of treatment objectives.[62]

Aspects to Consider

As mentioned at the outset, accountability demands objectives and measurable criteria. Managements of human service organizations are encouraged to employ precise, empirically established methods toward achievement of that end. Behavioral science strategies are compatible with this trend; used conscientiously and ethically, they may serve the humanitarian interests within professional work settings as well. Certainly, the most effective behavioral science techniques stress positive measures—provision of monetary bonuses, restructuring of job design or work schedule, assuring opportunities for skills and knowledge enhancement, and affording constructive or supportive feedback.[63] For all its negative connotations for human service employees and administrators, the increased focus on accountability is steadily progressing toward assurance of circumstances amenable to both populations.

Substantial research is now available that will facilitate the management of human service agencies. Any manager of other workers should consider the following aspects of supervision:

1. Provide clear communications as to what is expected in terms of job performance. Establish realistic time-limited goals. Indicate to workers how these goals will be evaluated.

2. Develop a data system that will enable the measurement and the reporting of progress toward goals.

3. Have frequent feedback sessions which are constructive and are executed in a professional manner and which enable determination of the progress toward goals.

4. Deliver consequences on the attainment of subgoals and subsequent larger goals.

5. Make rewards, both material and social, contingent upon the execution of specific duties.

6. Model appropriate behavior expected of workers.

1. John S. Wodarski, *Role of Research in Clinical Practice* (Baltimore: University Park Press, 1981).

2. Alfred Kadushin, *Supervision in Social Work* (New York: Columbia University Press, 1976), p. 52.

3. L. J. Ganser, "The Human Aspects of Administration," in *Social Work Administration: A Resource Book*, ed. Harry Schatz (New York: Council on Social Work Education, 1970).

4. James L. Farr, "Incentive Schedules, Productivity and Satisfaction in Work Groups: A Laboratory Study," *Organizational Behavior and Human Performance* 17 (October 1976): 159–70; William H. Franklin, Jr., "Six Critical Issues for the Eighties," *Administrative Management* XLIII (January 1982): 24–27, 54; V. William Harris et al., "Instructions, Feedback, Praise, Bonus Payments and Teacher Behavior," *Journal of Applied Behavior Analysis* 8 (Winter 1975): 462; Ovid Pomerleau, Philip H. Bobrove, and Rita H. Smith, "Rewarding Psychiatric Aides for the Behavioral Improvement of Assigned Patients," *Journal of Applied Behavior Analysis* 6 (Fall 1973): 383–90; Dale A. Pommer and Darlene Streedback, "Motivating Staff Performance in an Operant Learning Program for Children," *Journal of Applied Behavior Analysis* 7 (Summer 1974): 217–21; Curt Tausky, *Work Organizations: Major Theoretical Perspectives*, 2nd ed. (Itasca, IL: F. E. Peacock, 1978).

5. Jerry Edelwich and Archie Brodsky, *Burn-Out: Stages of Disillusionment in the Helping Professions* (New York: Human Sciences Press, 1980); Jerald Greenberg and Suzyn Ornstein, "High Status Job Title as Compensation for Underpayment: A Test of Equity Theory," *Journal of Applied Psychology* 68 (May 1983): 285–97.

6. Howard Aldrich, "Centralization Versus Decentralization in the Design of Human Service Delivery Systems: A Response to Gouldner's Lament," in *The Management of Human Services*, ed. Rosemary C. Sarri and Yeheskel Hasenfeld (New York: Columbia University Press, 1978), p. 57.

7. Lloyd Baird, "Managing Dissatisfaction," *Personnel* 58 (May/June 1981): 12–21; Dalton S. Lee, "Staying Alive in Child Protective Services: Survival Skills for Worker and Supervisor, Part I—A Preliminary Examination of Worker Trauma," *Arete* 5 (Spring 1979): 195–208; Harold H. Weissman, *Overcoming Mismanagement in Human*

Service Professions (San Francisco: Jossey-Bass Publishers, 1973).

8. Edelwich and Brodsky, *Burn-Out*.

9. Rex Skidmore, *Social Work Administration: Dynamic Management and Human Relationships* (Englewood Cliffs, NJ: Prentice-Hall, 1983), p. 168.

10. James J. Borland, "Burnout Among Workers and Administrators," *Health and Social Work* 6 (February 1981): 73–78; Victor Savicki and Eric J. Cooley, "Implications of Burnout Research and Theory for Counselor Educators," *The Personnel and Guidance Journal* 60 (March 1982): 415–19.

11. Howard J. Karger, "Burnout as Alienation," *Social Service Review* 55 (June 1981): 279.

12. Edward W. Davis and Marjie C. Barrett, "Supervision for Management of Worker Stress," *Administration in Social Work* 5 (Spring 1981): 55–64.

13. Baird, "Managing Dissatisfaction"; James Bolt and Geary A. Rummler, "How to Close the Gap in Human Performance," *Management Review* 71 (January 1982): 38–44.

14. Lee W. Frederiksen, "Behavioral Reorganization of a Professional Service System," *Journal of Organizational Behavior Management* 2 (Fall 1978): 1–9; Donald K. Granvold, "Supervision by Objectives," *Administration in Social Work* 2 (Summer 1978): 199–211; Kadushin, *Supervision in Social Work*.

15. Kadushin, *Supervision in Social Work*, p. 125.

16. Skidmore, "Social Work Administration," p. 235.

17. Bolt and Rummler, "How to Close the Gap in Human Performance."

18. Kadushin, *Supervision in Social Work*; William J. Reid and Christine Beard, "An Evaluation of In-Service Training in a Public Welfare Setting," *Administration in Social Work* 4 (Spring 1980): 71–85.

19. Paul Abels, *The New Practice of Supervision and Staff Development: A Synergistic Approach* (New York: Association Press, 1977).

20. Skidmore, *Social Work Administration*, p. 243.

21. Craig W. LeCroy, "Practitioner Competence in Social Work: Training and Evaluation," *Journal of Social Service Research* 5 (1982): 71–82.

22. Gary Adams, Robert Tallon, and Patrick Rimell, "A Comparison of Lecture Versus Role-Playing in the Training of the Use of Positive Reinforcement," *Journal of Organizational Behavior Management* 2 (Summer 1980): 205–11; LeCroy, "Practitioner Competence in Social Work"; Charles A. Maher, "Improving the Delivery of Special Education and Related Services in Public Schools," *Journal of Organizational Behavior Management* 3 (Spring 1981): 29–44; Charles A. Maher, "Performance Feedback to Improve the Planning and Evaluation of Instructional Programs," *Journal of Organizational Behavior Management* 3 (Winter 1981/82): 33–40.

23. Charles A. Maher, "Training of Managers in Program Planning and Evaluation: Comparison of Two Approaches," *Journal of Organizational Behavior Management* 3 (Spring 1981): 45–56; Terry J. Page, Brian A. Iwata, and Dennis H. Reid, "Pyramidal Training: A Large Scale Application with Institutional Staff," *Journal of Applied Behavior Analysis* 15 (Fall 1982): 335–51.

24. Edelwich and Brodsky, *Burn-Out*, p. 120.

25. Kadushin, *Supervision in Social Work*; Skidmore, *Social Work Administration*.

26. Skidmore, *Social Work Administration*, p. 173.

27. Robert J. Benford, "Found: The Key to Excellence," *Personnel* 58 (May/June 1981): 68–77; Kadushin, *Supervision in Social Work*.

28. Charles E. Redfield, "The Theory of Communication: Its Application to Public Administration," in *Social Work Administration: A Resource Book*, ed. Harry Schatz (New York: Council on Social Work Administration, 1970).

29. Raymond Fox, "The Ombudsman: A Process for Humanizing Accountability," *Administration in Social Work* 5 (Summer 1981): 47–48.

30. Lee W. Frederiksen et al., "Specificity of Performance Feedback in a Professional Service Delivery Setting," *Journal of Organizational Behavior Management* 3 (Winter 1981/82): 42; Donald M. Prue and John A. Fairbank, "Performance Feedback in Organizational Behavior Management: A Review," *Journal of Organizational Behavior Management* 3 (Spring 1981): 1–16.

31. Judith L. Komaki, Robert L. Collins, and Pat Penn, "The Role of Performance Antecedents and Consequences in Work Motivation," *Journal of Applied Psychology* 67 (June 1982): 334–40.

32. Kadushin, *Supervision in Social Work*, p. 175.

33. Franklin, "Six Critical Issues for the Eighties"; George R. Kunz et al., "Evaluating Strategies to Improve Careprovider Performance on Health and Developmental Tasks in an Infant Care Facility," *Journal of Applied Behavior Analysis* 15 (Winter 1982): 521–31.

34. Davis and Barrett, "Supervision for Management of Worker Stress"; Virginia Glicken, "Enhancing Work for Professional Social Workers," *Administration in Social Work* 4 (Fall 1980): 61–74; Jadwiga Judd, Regina E. Kohn, and G. L. Schulman, "Group Supervision: A Vehicle for Professional Development," *Social Work* 7 (January 1962): 96–102; Ayala Pines and Ditsy Kafry, "Occupational Tedium in the Social Services," *Social Work* 23 (November 1978): 499–507.

35. Andre Delbecq and Dennis Ladbrook, "Administrative Feedback on the Behavior of Subordinates," *Administration in Social Work* 3 (1979): 153–66; Granvold, "Supervision by Objectives."

36. Maher, "Performance Feedback to Improve the Planning and Evaluation of Instructional Programs," p. 39.

37. Lee, "Staying Alive in Child Protective Services"; David J. Warfel, Dennis M. Maloney, and Karen Blase, "Consumer Feedback in Human Service Programs," *Social Work* 26 (March 1981): 151–58.

38. Skidmore, *Social Work Administration*.

39. Rino Patti, "Toward a Paradigm of Middle-Management Practice in Social Welfare Programs," in *The Management of Human Services*, ed. Rosemary C. Sarri and Yeheskel Hasenfeld (New York: Columbia University Press, 1978), p. 279.

40. Harry Schatz, "Staff Involvement in Agency Administration," in *Social Work Administration: A Resource Book*, ed. Harry Schatz (New York: Council on Social Work Education, 1970), p. 282.

41. Richard A. Weatherly, "Participatory Management in Public Welfare: What are the Prospects?" *Administration in Social Work* 7 (Spring 1983): 48.

42. Savicki and Cooley, "Implications of Burnout Research," p. 416.

43. Maryanne Vandervelde, "The Semantics of Participation," *Administration in Social Work* 3 (Spring 1979): 65–77.

44. Schatz, "Staff Involvement in Agency Administration," p. 282.

45. Dov Eden and Gad Ravid, "Pygmalion Versus Self-Expectancy: Effects of Instructor and Self-Expectancy on Trainee Performance," *Organizational Behavior and Human Performance* 39 (December 1982): 351–64.

46. Robert Blake and Jane Mouton, "Increasing Productivity Through Behavioral Science," *Personnel* 58 (May/June 1981): 59–67; Skidmore, *Social Work Administration*.

47. Susan E. Jackson, "Participation in Decision-Making as a Strategy for Reducing Job Related Strain," *Journal of Applied Psychology* 68 (February 1983): 3–19.

48. Robert H. Garin and John F. Cooper, "The Morale-Productivity Relationship: How Close?" *Personnel* 58 (January/February 1981): 57–62.

49. Vandervelde, "The Semantics of Participation," p. 74.

50. Weatherly, "Participatory Management in Public Welfare."

51. Edelwich and Brodsky, *Burn-Out*.

52. Glicken, "Enhancing Work for Professional Social Workers," p. 61.

53. Henry P. Sims, Jr., and Charles C. Manz, "Social Learning Theory: The Role of Modeling in the Exercise of Leadership," *Journal of Organizational Behavior Management* 3 (Winter 1981/82): 55–63.

54. Davis and Barrett, "Supervision for Management of Worker Stress"; Edelwich and Brodsky, *Burn-Out*; Glicken, "Enhancing Work for Professional Social Workers"; Kadushin, *Supervision in Social Work*.

55. Robert Kreitner, "The Feedforward and Feedback Control of Job Performance Through Organizational Behavior Management," *Journal of Organizational Behavior Management* 3 (Summer 1981): 3–20.

56. James Hermann, et al., "Effects of Bonuses for Punctuality on the Tardiness of Industrial Workers," *Journal of Applied Behavior Analysis* 6 (Winter 1973): 563–70; Ed Pedalino and Victor N. Gamboa, "Behavior Modification and Absenteeism: Intervention in One Industrial Setting," *Journal of Applied Psychology* 59 (December 1974): 694–98.

57. Duane L. Bacon, Barbara J. Fulton, and Richard W. Malott, "Improving Staff Performance Through the Use of Task Checklists," *Journal of Organizational Behavior Management* 4 (Fall/Winter 1982): 17–25; Katrina M. Brown, B. S. Willis, and Dennis H. Reid, "Differential Effects of Supervisor Feedback and Feedback Plus Approval on Institutional Staff Performance," *Journal of Organizational Behavior Management* 3 (Spring 1981): 57–68; James Conrin, "A Comparison of Two Types of Antecedent Control Over Supervisory Behavior," *Journal of Organizational Behavior Management* 4 (Fall/Winter 1982): 37–48; Earl T. Patterson, James C. Griffin, and Marlon C. Panyan, "Incentive Maintenance of Self-Help Skill Training Programs for Nonprofessional Personnel," *Journal of Behavior Therapy and Experimental Psychiatry* 7 (October 1976): 249–53.

58. Frederiksen et al., "Specificity of Performance Feedback"; John Krapfl, "Behavior Management in State Mental Health Systems," *Journal of Organizational Behavior Management* 3 (Fall 1981): 91–105.

59. Fred Luthans and Mark J. Martinko, "Organizational Behavior Modification: A Way to Bridge the Gap Between Academic Research and Real World Application," *Journal of Organizational Behavior Management* 3 (Fall 1981): 33–50.

60. Roger M. Lind, "Applications of Socio-Behavioral Therapy to Administrative Practice," in *The Socio-Behavioral Approach and Application to Social Work*, ed. E. Thomas (New York: Council on Social Work Education, 1967).

61. Judi Komaki, "Why We Don't Reinforce: The Issues," *Journal of Organizational Behavior Management* 4 (Fall/Winter 1982): 97–100; Lind, "Applications of Socio-Behavioral Therapy."

62. David C. Bolin and Laurence Kivens, "Evaluation in a Community Mental Health Center: Huntsville, Alabama," *Evaluation* 2 (1974): 26–34; R. C. Rinn and J. C. Vernon, "Process Evaluation of Outpatient Treatment in a Community Mental Health Center," *Journal of Behavior Therapy and Experimental Psychiatry* 6 (April 1975): 5–11.

63. Roger Bourdon, "Measuring and Tracking Management Performance for Accountability," *Journal of Organizational Behavior Management* 4 (Fall/Winter 1982): 101–12; Gerald L. Mayhew, Patience Ehyart, and John D. Cone, "Approaches to Employee Management: Policies and Preferences," *Journal of Organizational Behavior Management* 2 (Winter 1979): 103–11.